Nurturing Our Humanity

Nurturing Our Humanity

How Domination and Partnership Shape Our Brains, Lives, and Future

RIANE EISLER, JD, PHD (HON)

President, Center for Partnership Studies

DOUGLAS P. FRY, PHD

Professor & Chair
Department of Peace and Conflict Studies
University of North Carolina at Greensboro

OXFORD
UNIVERSITY PRESS

OXFORD
UNIVERSITY PRESS

Oxford University Press is a department of the University of Oxford. It furthers
the University's objective of excellence in research, scholarship, and education
by publishing worldwide. Oxford is a registered trade mark of Oxford University
Press in the UK and certain other countries.

Published in the United States of America by Oxford University Press
198 Madison Avenue, New York, NY 10016, United States of America.

Library of Congress Cataloging-in-Publication Data
Names: Eisler, Riane, author. | Fry, Douglas P., 1953– author.
Title: Nurturing our humanity : how domination and partnership shape our
brains, lives, and future / Riane Eisler and Douglas P. Fry.
Description: New York : Oxford University Press, [2019] |
Includes bibliographical references and index.
Identifiers: LCCN 2018061070 | ISBN 9780190935726
Subjects: LCSH: Interpersonal relations. | Dominance (Psychology) |
Partnership—Psychological aspects. | Human evolution.
Classification: LCC HM1111.E37 2019 | DDC 302—dc23
LC record available at https://lccn.loc.gov/2018061070

3 5 7 9 8 6 4 2

Printed by Sheridan Books, Inc., United States of America

Contents

1

Our Story

For millennia, humans have imagined a peaceful and just world. Sometimes we only imagined this world in an afterlife. But over the last centuries, many of us have imagined it right here on Earth. Not a utopia, not a perfect world. But a world where peace is more than just an interval between wars, where dire poverty, brutal oppression, insensitivity, cruelty, and despair are no longer "just the way things are."

Now there is a new urgency to our wish for a more humane world. Every day we are bombarded by news of barbaric human rights abuses, terrorist attacks, proliferation of nuclear weapons, and a drift back to strongman rule. The destruction of our natural environment continues at an accelerating pace, endangering our global life-support systems. New technologies, from artificial intelligence to biological engineering, could have catastrophic results if guided by cultural values of greed, megalomania, and disregard for human rights.

From all sectors—religious and secular, philosophical and scientific, and thousands of small groups worldwide—come calls for cultural transformation: for building a truly humane culture. The pivotal question is whether such a culture—one that supports rather than inhibits human well-being and our capacities to love, create, and prosper—is possible.

Nurturing Our Humanity offers extensive evidence that we *can* construct this humane culture. Based on findings from both biology and social sciences, we today know that the cultural environments we create affect nothing less than how our brains develop and hence how we think, feel, and act. But *Nurturing Our Humanity* takes bioculturalism further. It examines our cultural environments through a powerful new analytical tool: the Biocultural Partnership-Domination Lens.

Rather than viewing societies through the lenses of familiar social categories such as religious versus secular, Eastern versus Western, rightist versus leftist, or capitalist versus socialist, which only describe a particular aspect of society, the Biocultural Partnership-Domination Lens uses two larger cultural configurations at opposite ends of a continuum: the *partnership system* and the *domination system*. This broader frame makes it possible to identify the conditions that support the expression of our human capacities for caring, creativity, and consciousness or, alternately, for insensitivity, cruelty, and destructiveness. It upends age-old assumptions about human nature and the supposed impossibility of improving the human condition, showing how we can bring about fundamental change. The new interdisciplinary perspective of the Biocultural Partnership-Domination Lens reveals how cultural beliefs and social institutions such as politics, economics, and education affect, and are in turn affected by, childhood and gender relations; highlights the impact of these early experiences and observations on how our brains develop; and shows how we can use our knowledge of human development to construct equitable and sustainable cultures that maximize human well-being.

Nurturing Our Humanity re-examines vital matters ranging from sex, love, intimacy, parenting, and romance to human rights, social justice, politics, economics, violence, and values from this integrative perspective. It sheds new light on critical current issues, all the way from climate change, scapegoating, authoritarianism, racism, and other forms of in-group versus out-group thinking to contemporary disputes about biological and cultural evolution, economics, national and international politics, religious fundamentalism, and the uses and potential abuses of technological breakthroughs.

We explore how our capacities for caring, creativity, and consciousness go way back in evolutionary time and are integral to human nature, and we show that there have been, and continue to be, cultures that orient to the partnership side of the continuum. We look at how domination systems produce high levels of stress—from stressful early family experiences to the artificial creation of economic scarcity—and how this plays out in the neurochemistry of the brain, tending to keep people at a less advanced level of overall human development that interferes with the full flourishing of those very qualities that make people happiest: security, empathy, consciousness, creativity, and love. On the other hand, partnership-oriented environments—as illustrated by conditions in contemporary societies ranging from the Minangkabau in Southeast Asia to European Nordic nations—enhance the expression of our human capacities for health, happiness, well-being, consciousness, and creativity.

We draw from recent studies showing that the difficulty some people have in dealing with change (with its implications for denial of climate change and other present threats) and the tendency of such people to support punitive political agendas (such as capital punishment, heavy investment in prisons and the military, and scapegoating of minorities, women, and gays) are associated with a particular kind of brain development in people who are taught early on that dominating or being dominated are our only alternatives. We explore how patterns of touch, intimacy, and sexuality differ at opposite ends of the domination-partnership continuum and how the confluence of caring with coercion and pain is one of the most effective mechanisms for socializing people to suppress empathy and submit to domination as adults. We examine how the erotization of domination and violence lies behind mass shootings of women in the United States and Canada by some men who call themselves incel (involuntarily celibate) and behind the enslavement of women by fundamentalist groups like ISIS (the Islamic State of Iraq and Syria). We then contrast these unhealthy interactions with healthy ones supported by partnership-oriented cultures and look at how we receive neurochemical rewards of pleasure when we give or receive empathic love.

Covering a wide swath of prehistory and history, we take a fresh look at many conventional assumptions about religion and science. We see, for example, how Western science came out of a hierarchical, conformist, misogynist, all-male medieval clerical culture (a world without women and children) and how it took more than 700 years for women's, men's, and gender studies to emerge in universities; how Freud's secular theories replicated the earlier religious ideology of original sin and male supremacy; and how in all spheres (from the family, politics, and the academy to mainstream and popular culture worldwide), the underlying tension between movement toward partnership and the resistance/regressions to domination has played out over millennia.

But our focus is primarily on our present and future, on how we can draw on our enormous evolutionary gifts—our extraordinary capacities for empathy, creativity, caring, cooperation, and conscious choice—to build the missing cornerstones that support a more equitable, caring, and sustainable partnership future.[1] In this introductory chapter, we share some aspects of our personal histories, orientations, and goals and also place the central message of this book within the context of our past work. Then we discuss the key concepts of *partnership systems* and *domination systems* and introduce the ways they are integral to the Biocultural Partnership-Domination Lens. We close the chapter by highlighting the need to exchange a domination-oriented narrative for a completely different story, one based on life-enhancing partnership principles such as equality, care, compassion, and sustainability.

Early Influences and Insights

When Riane was six, the German and Austrian Nazis took over her native Vienna. Riane's father was dragged off by the Gestapo. Her mother miraculously obtained his release, and the family fled to Cuba. They were on one of the last ships before the *MS St. Louis*, carrying 930 Jewish refugees from Europe, was turned back by Cuban authorities. Because neither Cuba nor the United States nor any other country in the Western hemisphere let the *St. Louis* dock, it was forced to return to Europe, where many on board eventually died in Nazi death camps.

Riane remembers standing at the Havana waterfront watching how, after long days of waiting and hoping they would be permitted to disembark, the doomed families on the *St. Louis* disappeared over the horizon. As she looked out at sea and listened to her parents' anguished conversation, she could not understand how people could be so cruel, so indifferent to the suffering of others.

There were other formative experiences for Riane: fleeing Vienna at night with only what they could carry, the plunge from affluence to dire poverty in cockroach-infested Havana tenements, radical changes in languages, equally radical changes in beliefs and customs.

That is how Riane learned that what people consider givens are not universal. It is also how she learned about the power of cultural narratives, including popular myths and scientific theories, to shape what people consider normal and right. The foundations of a small girl's existence were demolished overnight by the resurgence of myths and theories about Jews as subhuman and dangerous. From one day to the next, Riane was transformed by the Nazi's anti-Semitic cultural narratives from a cute little girl whom people smiled at into a hunted and despised "other."

With her move to the United States in 1946 came further formative experiences. As she and her parents arrived at last to the promised land of American liberty and equality, they found in Miami, their port of entry, yet another disempowered out-group, or "other." In the rigidly segregated US South of that time, they discovered one more variation of the all-too-familiar use of cultural narratives to justify the persecution and subordination of "inferior" beings.

The accumulation of these kinds of experiences brought recurrent questions: Are patterns of prejudice, cruelty, and violence inevitable? Are they human nature? Or is something else at work?

As time went on, these questions came up again and again. They came with shattering force after World War II when the world saw the newsreels of the Nazi death camps, the mountains of piled-up bodies, the hollow-eyed skeletal survivors. These questions became more insistent when Riane later read *Treblinka*, the harrowing account of life and death in one of the "better" Nazi camps. They erupted when she looked at the photo of a happy-looking crowd of men in *Life* magazine and discovered they were not at a football rally but at a lynching party, smiling into the camera after sadistically murdering a black man. When Riane studied sociology at the University of California, these questions were at the back of her mind. They were there as she became involved first in the civil rights movement and then in the feminist movement.

At that point, Riane became aware of yet another devalued "other." This "other" had been there all the time, center stage. But because she had been taught to take it for granted, its inferior status had been invisible. Her awakened consciousness—that she was part of a female "other," split off from and at the same time subsumed by the in-group of "mankind"—again shook the foundations of Riane's existence. She realized that this prototypical in-group/out-group division had profoundly influenced her entire life. It had shaped her sense of self, relations, thoughts, feelings, everything.

This consciousness came to Riane relatively late, after much of her formal and informal education in history, archaeology, and the study of myth; after law school; after employment as a social scientist and attorney; after activism in the civil rights and anti–Vietnam war movements; after marriage, motherhood, and divorce. It came to Riane suddenly in the late 1960s when, like thousands of other women, she awoke as if from a lifelong trance.

It was only then that Riane fully understood that our consciousness, or lack thereof, is largely a function of our cultural contexts, and particularly of cultural myths and theories about "human nature." What until then had been abstract—the influence of myths and theories on how we relate to ourselves and others—became of intense personal significance.

Riane then understood that theories are not abstract, academic playthings irrelevant to our day-to-day lives. On the contrary, theories have enormous power in shaping how we think, feel, and live—just ask any African American who came of age during an era when theory held that whites are innately superior intellectually, morally, and every other way. Riane also understood that the myths and theories about femininity and masculinity, which we all internalized without much consideration, shaped how she saw herself and how others saw her. Gradually she began to suspect that the widespread internalized sex roles and myths about femininity and masculinity were responsible for much that ails our lives and our world.

In the process of making all this conscious, Riane felt a need for new ways of thinking and feeling that could help her make better sense of, and find better guidance for, her own life and that of her two daughters. Riane was also impelled in her search by the urgency of humanity's situation.

As an inhabitant of a planet whose life-support systems are being systematically undermined by human activities such as carbon emissions, excessive population growth, irresponsible resource exploitation, and other threats to our environment, Riane saw the critical need for new ways of thinking and living. And the magnitude and rapidity of cultural, social, and technological change made it clear that transformative shifts—such as what she herself had been experiencing—are realistic possibilities. In short, both Riane's personal experiences and our common human experiences at this critical time in history led to the research that defined her work over decades.

Like Riane, Doug's early life experiences shaped his perceptions and concerns as well as his choice to become an anthropologist focusing on peace and human nature. Although a boy at the time of the Cuban missile crisis in October 1962, the near destruction of the world made a huge impression on his young mind. He recalls how his parents, like many people in the early 1960s, considered digging a fallout shelter. Their anxious discussions sparked Doug to contemplate what a world filled with poisonous radiation would be like, as his family huddled in a cement pit underground, eating canned tamales, sardines, and spam for months, maybe years. Doug questioned his parents about radiation and was not happy with the answers they gave about the poisonous, invisible fallout that would cause cancers, sickness, then death, not only of people but also of all the birds and animals. To a child's mind, having a nuclear war was the scariest and stupidest idea imaginable.

About a decade later when Doug discovered anthropology at the university, he began looking at humanity from a macroscopic perspective that makes comparisons across cultures and millennia. He fell in love with anthropology and how it widens our view beyond our own culture and beyond current-day events. This broader perspective, Doug thought early on, could be useful for understanding warfare and also our human capacity for peace.

In fact, as key lessons, anthropology shows that while humans have the capacity to be violent, we also possess a powerful potential for peace.[2] In theory, any human might commit murder, but in reality, most of us never do. Anthropology holds some true treasures relevant to human survival, including documentation that nonwarring peace systems can be created, descriptions of how peaceful societies successfully keep the peace and promote cooperation and well-being, and the solid evidence from prehistory and the comparison of social systems showing that war is not inextricably bound up with human nature.[3] Yet, beginning with debates with members of his own family, Doug realized that a substantial number of people assume war to be just part and parcel of human nature. This erroneous view in and of itself is an obstacle to achieving peace.[4]

Doug has lived in Mexico conducting anthropological fieldwork among Zapotec speakers of Oaxaca (1981–1983), has lived and taught in Finland (1995–2014), and has conducted cross-cultural research on numerous cultures. Living outside his native US culture has taught Doug firsthand lessons about cultural differences in values, beliefs, and institutions. His work also has taught him about the myriad ways that people keep the peace or, in those cases where the peace has been broken, about the paths that people take to mend damaged relationships and restore social harmony. For example, across diverse cultural settings, third parties intervene, sometimes in dramatic ways, to restore the peace. In their fields near the Nile, two Nubian brothers regularly argued about how to share the irrigation water.[5] Their uncle overheard the shouting. He found a flat stone and placed it in the middle of the irrigation ditch, where offshoots of water went to each man's land, thus dividing the irrigation flow equally. "Putting a stone in the middle" was a structural solution to this conflict, grasped by someone who was not involved in the dispute, and humans practice this type of conflict resolution all the time. It is so normal that it rarely makes the news.

In recent research, Doug has focused on archaeological and nomadic forager studies showing that war is a rather recent social invention, arising under particular circumstances that correspond with the rise of domination systems. Later in this book, we will examine the evidence in more detail. The archaeological sequences show transitions from originating nomadic foraging conditions of warlessness to war at different locations at different times, as well as how war became more common and destructive a mere 4,000 to 6,000 years ago.[6] Furthermore, a careful examination of nomadic forager societies suggests the evolutionary deep roots of partnership systems, rife with sharing, caring, cooperation, reciprocity, and equity, suggesting that humans may be primed for developing social relationships of this nature.[7]

Doug's motivations for teaming up with Riane in the writing of this book stem ultimately from a deep concern for the future of humanity, coupled with a great appreciation for Riane's work.

Doug first heard of Riane in the late 1980s from his father, psychiatrist C. Brooks Fry, who praised Riane's work. He had just attended one of her lectures and had exchanged a few words with her afterward. At the lecture, the elder Fry had purchased *The Chalice and the Blade*, which he later gifted to Doug.[8] This particular copy has Riane's telephone number written inside the front cover, along with Brooks' pronunciation pneumonic for her name, and printed on the front cover is a laudatory quotation from luminary Ashley Montagu that reads, "The most important book since Darwin's *Origin of Species*." As Brooks realized decades ago, Doug would appreciate this innovative book. Perhaps he also realized that Riane and Doug were kindred spirits in key ways.

First, Riane and Doug both have a tendency to step back from an issue to gain a macroscopic view. Riane talks of systems and cultural configurations, and Doug writes about patterns and social models. Whereas both authors recognize the crucial importance of data and details, they share an aim of seeing the forest *and* the trees as they draw on research findings from multiple fields to paint their interpretations across a wide canvas.

Second, both Riane and Doug are motivated to do everything possible for the improvement of the human condition. We have already told how Riane's early experiences shaped her work for peace, human rights, and social justice. When Doug was growing up, his grandmother, psychologist Ruth Thacker Fry, would sometimes remark that the family consists of caregivers and humanitarians. Doug took on the humanitarian charge, engaging in peace education and activism over the course of his life.

Third, Riane and Doug could be called *realistic optimists* in that they recognize the magnitude of the challenges faced by humanity and yet believe that even huge problems can be solved. As President Kennedy said in 1963,

"Our problems are manmade. . . . No problem of human destiny is beyond human beings."[9]

The Importance of Systemic and Macroscopic Views

Riane's research addresses the *big picture* questions. It uses a new method of analysis: the study of Relational Dynamics. These dynamics are, *first*, what kinds of relations—from intimate to international—a particular culture encourages or discourages; and, *second*, how key elements of a culture interactively relate to shape and maintaining its basic character.

Riane notes that this method owes a great deal to one of her early professional experiences. Although she holds a degree in sociology, she realized that her courses did not concern themselves with interactive dynamics. What opened her eyes was working at the Systems Development Corporation, an offshoot of the Rand Corporation, at a time when scientists were just beginning to talk about "systems analysis." Riane did not like the work because her employers were only interested in military systems, but she learned a basic principle of systems thinking: that looking at how different parts of a system interact makes it possible to see more than just the sum of the system's parts.

Systems thinking is at the core of this book. The study of Relational Dynamics draws from a much larger database than customary studies of how humans behave individually and in groups. Much of Doug's research also focuses on systems. For instance, he studies *peace systems*, clusters of neighboring societies that do not make war with each other, and sometimes not at all.[10] The key questions are: How do people create peace systems? How are they maintained? Peace systems exist in various parts of the world from Malaysia and Australia to Brazil and Canada. The European Union also is a peace system because it was formed out of the ashes of war with the explicit goal of preventing future conflagration on the continent. A mere 70 years after the end of World War II, war within the EU system has become virtually unthinkable. This success story demonstrates that constructing other peace systems, including ultimately a Global Peace System, is conceivably possible.[11]

Riane's approach has always included the whole of humanity, both its female and male components. Her analytical lens also captures the whole of our lives, not only the so-called public sectors such as politics and economics but also the more intimate spheres of family and close relations. In addition, her perspective takes into account the whole of our history, including the thousands of years we call prehistory.

Sources for the multidisciplinary study of Relational Dynamics have included cross-cultural anthropological surveys[12]; anthropological and sociological studies of individual societies[13]; writings by historians, analyses of laws, moral codes, art, literature (including fiction, biographies, and autobiographies), scholarship from psychology, economics, education, political science, philosophy, religious studies (including the study of "mystery cults" around the Mediterranean from before the rise of Christianity), archeological studies (primarily of Western prehistory because of greater availability of materials, but also some of Indian, Latin American, and Chinese prehistory), and the study of both Western and Eastern myths and legends; and data from more recently developed fields, such as primatology, neuroscience, chaos theory, systems self-organizing theory, nonlinear dynamics, gender studies, women's studies, and men's studies.[14]

Looking at this larger picture made it possible to see patterns: interactions among key elements of social systems that keep repeating themselves cross-culturally and historically. Riane identified two contrasting configurations: the domination system and the partnership system.

In contrast to conventional social categories such as religious versus secular, Eastern versus Western, rightist versus leftist, or industrial versus preindustrial or postindustrial, the categories of the partnership system and the domination system show that the social construction of the roles and relations of the two basic forms of humanity—males and females—is of central significance for a society's beliefs and institutions, all the way from the family, education, and religion to politics and economics. These categories also show the crucial importance of the early years of life: that what people in a society consider normal or abnormal, moral or immoral, and even possible or impossible is profoundly affected by the kinds of relationships children experience and observe.

In other words, unlike most studies of human societies, as well as the social categories we have been taught, the social categories of domination and partnership systems do not split off matters relating to the majority of humanity as "just" women's or children's issues. They show interconnections between these critical matters and politics, economics, religion, and other areas that are the focus of conventional approaches.

We believe that within the next decades these interconnections will be generally recognized as key to understanding human societies. We also believe that at this point in human history, such an integrated analysis is essential.

Fortunately, we are now at the point where, for the first time, the data for such an integrated systemic approach are beginning to be available. If we, for example, view gender historically, we see that it only began to gain attention during the 1700s and 1800s, and then only in treatises dealing with feminism. It was not until the late 1960s that the subject of gender began to break into research and education, but again it was segregated into the academic ghetto of women's studies. Even the more recent men's studies, gender studies, and queer studies are marginalized in our siloed universities.

It was also not until recent times that gender entered popular discourse. So in the media we now find topics such as discrimination against girls and women, sexual assault and harassment, male anger against loss of what sociologist Michael Kimmel calls "aggrieved entitlement," and so forth.[15] And not until recently have the neurochemical effects of childhood experiences and observations received both scholarly and media attention.

The Biocultural Partnership-Domination Lens

Riane first presented the partnership-domination continuum in *The Chalice and the Blade: Our History, Our Future*.[16] The title uses the symbols of the chalice and the blade as metaphors for power: one appropriate for partnership systems and the other for domination systems. This book introduced cultural transformation theory, a new reading of both history and prehistory. Cultural transformation theory takes into account matters omitted in earlier narratives. It probes otherwise invisible connections, for example, whether a society is more warlike or peaceful and whether or not violence is part of childrearing, whether the female and male forms of humanity are considered equal or unequal and whether a society is more generally equitable or inequitable. In subsequent books, Riane used the partnership-domination frame to examine different ways of structuring families and education, sexuality and spirituality, healthcare and environmental sustainability, technology and economics.

This book starts where these earlier volumes left off, by exploring fully a host of synergetic biocultural interactions among evolutionary-neuroscientific-developmental and social-cultural-institutional variables, always with an eye turned toward their application for human betterment and survival on our troubled planet.

For those readers unacquainted with the partnership-domination perspective, we want to quickly provide some familiar examples. We have seen the domination system historically in the rule by terror of Genghis Khan and the autocratic family patriarch of earlier times. Nowadays, we see it in despotic rulers, such as the religious heads of ISIS or a secular Kim Jong-un, and at the familial level in abusive parental behavior. Whether within a family or more generally within a society, social systems that orient closely to the domination side of the continuum are ultimately held together by fear and force, as illustrated by customs of child and wife beating, persecution of minorities, threats or displays of torture and death, and wars of conquest. In this system, beliefs and social structures support rigid top-down rankings, and the closer a culture or subculture orients to it, the more stressful it is. In contrast, the partnership configuration is more peaceful, egalitarian, gender-balanced, and environmentally sustainable. As in the strivings of countless families, businesses, and communities today, the partnership system consists of beliefs and structures that support relations based on mutual benefit, respect, and accountability. Fear and force are *not* woven into the cultural tapestry of the partnership system because they are not needed to maintain rigid top-down rankings, whether it is man over man, man over woman, race over race, religion over religion, or nation over nation. Instead of hierarchies of domination, some partnership societies have what Riane calls hierarchies of actualization, where parents, teachers, and leaders use power to empower rather than disempower. So love, care, nurturance, and creativity can flourish.

As noted, we adopt a *biocultural perspective* to examine human possibilities, especially the enormous capacities made possible by our human brain. Biological and social sciences have now amply documented that the polarized nature versus nurture divide is a nonissue, an unrealistic model that befuddles rather than enlightens.[17] As neuroscientist Cordelia Fine writes, "The new neuroconstructivist perspective on brain development emphasizes the sheer exhilarating tangle of a continuous interaction among genes, brain, and environment."[18]

The Biocultural Partnership-Domination Lens provides an integrative perspective that reveals critical connections between parts of social systems that have generally been studied in segregation from one another.[19] While many studies show the enormous impact of what children experience and observe on the rest of their lives, the focus of these studies has been on the role of families, without taking into account that families do not spring up in isolation from the larger cultures in which they are embedded. Moreover, how a society constructs the roles and relations of the two basic forms of humanity is in most social analyses still only a sidebar.

By contrast, the social categories of the partnership system and the domination system show that the different ways human societies socialize the male and female halves of humanity for "masculine" and "feminine" roles is how people learn to view themselves and others. These new social categories also factor in extensive evidence from psychology and neuroscience that children's early experiences and observations powerfully affect brain development—and with this, how people think, feel, and act, including the kinds of cultures they construct. They further take into account the impact of stories, especially stories about human possibilities.

Even now, there are many global good news stories that do not get as much attention as coverage of war and terrorism. For instance, nuclear testing has been halted by the holders of the major nuclear arsenals, Russia, the United States, Britain, France, and China; smallpox has been eliminated from the globe; after the nations of the world took action under the Montreal Protocol in 1987, the gaps in the Earth's ozone layer have begun to recover; through concerted cooperative action among all the countries with Mediterranean shorelines, the Mediterranean Sea has not become a dead sea as was predicted in the 1970s; nonviolent "people power" has over the last decades ousted dictatorial regimes in Chile, Argentina, Poland, former Czechoslovakia, Tunisia, Serbia, and elsewhere; and following centuries of bloody strife, peace is now a reality within the European Union. As we will see in this book, these kinds of stories show that humanity can form a successful partnership for human well-being and survival.

Creating a New Narrative: Beyond Dark Tales about Humanity

Because stories are major transmitters of culture, fundamental change requires new narratives—especially about human nature. In poet Matthew Arnold's depiction of a martial nightmare, the world:

... Hath really neither joy, nor love, nor light,
   Nor certitude, nor peace, nor help for pain;
   And we are here as on a darkling plain
   Swept with confused alarms of struggle and flight,
   Where ignorant armies clash by night.[20]

Indeed, wherever we turn, in magazines and newspapers, on television, or in bestselling books, the hackneyed message is the same: human nature is bad. Look at the evidence—greed, murder, rape, endless war. That is just how it is, always has been, and forever will be.

Despite all the evidence to the contrary, these kinds of stories about an innately flawed human nature persist. A familiar brand of narrative describes our species as so defective as to require supernatural redemption; for instance, through the sacrificial death and resurrection of a god or through a series of earthly reincarnations. Another brand solves human defectiveness by imposing strict social controls, as illustrated in Plato's philosopher kings or Freud's superego.

In addition to these powerful normative narratives, other storylines claim that we have only gradually, and at best partially, emerged from an original condition of savagery that still persists under a thin veneer of civilization. This evolutionary narrative holds that our savage natal condition still lurks just under the skin—and accounts for the chronic injustice and barbaric violence of recorded history. "Scratch an altruist, watch a hypocrite bleed" captures this idea that goodness is only skin-deep.[21] And while most social scientists have rejected religious dogmas of original sin and simplistic notions of killer instincts, selfish genes, reptilian brains, Id monsters, or the shadow, this brotherhood of demonic constructs continues to present domination relations as inevitable.

Another regular feature of our normative narratives is that they generally ignore the majority of humanity: women and children. Even sociology, anthropology, and history have ignored the fundamental importance for human behavior of the formative childhood years—an omission that is astonishing. Similarly amazing is the omission of one half of our species from depictions of the human adventure, such as when museum dioramas present male apes gradually transforming into human males, while females are simply left out of the picture.

In these narratives, the female half of humanity appears in a footnote, if at all, in connection with the family, sex, love, or peripheral "women's issues." Even where women are included, they have rarely been protagonists. It has been like a play with a cast of gender stereotypes, where men are active superiors and women passive inferiors in what is often accurately termed "the story of man."

For far too long, humanity has been mired in the "darkling plain" of such tales."[22] So strong is their grip that, like the internal censor Freud postulated, they have often blocked out everything that contradicts them, not only in popular but also in scientific thinking and writings.

It is encouraging that, despite all this, we are beginning to gain a deeper and more hopeful understanding of ourselves and our world. Especially encouraging are the insights emerging from paleoanthropology, primatology, forager research, and gender studies as well as chaos theory, nonlinear dynamics, and neuroscience.

In this book, we consider how evidence from these and other fields supports a new narrative about both biological and cultural evolution. Instead of a unilinear progression from savagery to civilization, this is a multilinear, open-ended narrative.[23] We look at evolution, not as the result of simple causes and effects, but in terms of interactive processes, taking into account that this is how complex living systems, including human beings and human societies, actually operate, and that living systems are capable of fundamental change or transformation.

There is strong evidence that over the millennia of human biocultural evolution, most societies were constructed along partnership lines. Yet domination systems—with their inherent exploitation of people and nature, social and economic inequities, and direct and structural violence—came to predominate on the global stage.

To borrow the words of the former head of the Worldwatch Institute, Lester Brown, "this is no way to run a planet."[24] As we will detail, the domination system has held humanity back—and through today's ever more fearful, frenzied, and greed-driven technologies of destruction and exploitation, it may lead to our species' extinction.

There is, however, nothing inevitable about the Apocalypse. We *can* change our course. It is our hope that this book will help support this change, demonstrating that a more peaceful, equitable, and fulfilling way of life—a truly advanced humane society—is biologically possible and culturally attainable.

Notes

1. Frans de Waal, *The Age of Empathy: Nature's Lessons for a Kinder Society* (New York: Broadway Books, 2009); Douglas P. Fry, "Life without War," *Science* 336 (2012): 879–884, doi: 10.1126/science.1217987; Douglas P. Fry, *The Human Potential for Peace: An Anthropological Challenge to Assumptions about War and Violence* (New York: Oxford University Press, 2006); Ashley Montagu, *Growing Young* (New York: McGraw-Hill, 1981); Riane Eisler, *The Chalice and the Blade: Our History, Our Future* (San Francisco: Harper & Row, 1987).

2. Fry, *The Human Potential for Peace*; Fry, "Life without War"; Geneviève Souillac and Douglas P. Fry, "Indigenous Lessons for Conflict Resolution," in *The Handbook of Conflict Resolution Theory and Practice*, eds. Peter T. Coleman, Morton Deutsch, and Eric C. Marcus (San Francisco: Jossey-Bass, 2014); La Donna Harris and Jacqueline Wasilewski, "Indigeneity, An Alternative Worldview: Four R's (Relationship, Responsibility, Reciprocity, Redistribution) vs. Two P's (Power and Profit). Sharing the Journey Towards Conscious Evolution," *Systems Research and Behavioral Science* 21 (2004): 489–503, doi: 10.1002/sres.631.

3. Fry, *The Human Potential for Peace*; Fry, "Life without War"; Douglas P. Fry, "Cooperation for Survival: Creating a Global Peace System," in *War, Peace, and Human Nature: Convergence of Evolutionary and Cultural Views*, ed. Douglas P. Fry (New York: Oxford University Press, 2013); Geneviève Souillac and Douglas P. Fry, "Anthropology: Implications for Peace," in *The Palgrave Handbook of Disciplinary and Regional Approaches to Peace*, eds. Oliver P. Richmond, Sandra Pogodda, and Jasmine Ramovic (London: Palgrave, 2016).

4. Fry, *The Human Potential for Peace*.

5. Robert Fernea, "Putting a Stone in the Middle: The Nubians of Northern Africa," in *Keeping the Peace: Conflict Resolution and Peaceful Societies around the World*, eds. Graham Kemp and Douglas P. Fry (New York: Routledge, 2004).

6. Fry, *The Human Potential for Peace*; Jonathan Haas and Matthew Piscitelli, "The Prehistory of Warfare: Misled by Ethnography," in *War, Peace, and Human Nature: Convergence of Evolutionary and Cultural Views*, ed. Douglas P. Fry (New York: Oxford University Press, 2013); Raymond C. Kelly, *Warless Societies and the Origin of War* (Ann Arbor: University of Michigan Press, 2000).

7. Fry, "Cooperation for Survival"; de Waal, *The Age of Empathy*.

8. Eisler, *The Chalice and the Blade*.

9. The full speech, delivered as a commencement address at American University, can be found in Jeffery Sachs, *To Move the World: JFK's Quest for Peace* (New York: Random House, 2013).

10. Douglas P. Fry, "Anthropological Insights for Creating Nonwarring Social Systems," *Journal of Aggression, Conflict and Peace Research* 1 (2009): 4–15, doi: 10.1108/17596599200900008; Fry, "Life without War"; Douglas P. Fry, Bruce D. Bonta, and Karolina Baszarkiewicz, "Learning from Extant Cultures of Peace," in *Handbook on Building Cultures of Peace*, ed. Joseph de Rivera (New York: Springer, 2008).

11. Fry, "Cooperation for Survival."

12. See e.g., George P. Murdock, *Ethnographic Atlas* (Pittsburgh: University of Pittsburgh, 1969); Robert B. Textor, *A Cross Cultural Summary* (New Haven, CT: Human Relations Area Files, 1967); Peggy R. Sanday, *Female Power and Male Dominance: On the Origins of Sexual Inequality* (New York: Cambridge University Press, 1981); Scott Coltrane, "Father-Child Relationships and the Status of Women: A Cross-Cultural Study," *American Journal of Sociology* 93 (1988): 1060–1095, doi: 10.1086/228864.

13. See e.g., Ruth Benedict, *The Chrysanthemum and the Sword: Patterns of Japanese Culture* (Boston: Houghton Mifflin, 1946); Anthony Giddens, *The Constitution of Society* (Berkeley: University of California Press, 1984); Lila Abu-Lughod, *Veiled Sentiments: Honor and Poetry in a Bedouin Society* (Berkeley: University of California Press, 1986); Jiajin Min, ed., *The Chalice and the Blade in Chinese Culture: Gender Relations and Social Models* (Beijing: China Social Sciences Publishing House, 1995).

14. Examples of references on beliefs, laws, and the importance of childhood are: William Blackstone, *Commentaries on the Laws of England* (Oxford: Clarendon Press, 1765); C. Fred Blake, "Foot-Binding in Neo-Confucian China and the Appropriation of Female Labor," *Signs* 19 (1994): 676–712, doi: 10.1086/494917; Avshalom Caspi et al., "Role of Genotype in the Cycle of Violence in Maltreated Children," *Science* 297 (2002): 851–854, doi: 10.1126/science.1072290; Bram Dijkstra, *Idols of Perversity: Fantasies of Feminine Evil in Fin-de-Siècle Culture* (Oxford: Oxford University Press, 1986); Anthony Giddens, *The Transformation of Intimacy: Sexuality, Love, and Eroticism in Modern Societies* (Stanford, CA: Stanford University Press, 1992); Darcia Narvaez et al., eds., *Ancestral Landscapes in Human Evolution: Culture, Childrearing and Social Wellbeing* (New York: Oxford University Press, 2014); Samuel Noah Kramer and John Maier, *Myths of Enki: The Crafty God* (New York: Oxford University Press, 1989); Nanno Marinatos, *Minoan Religion: Ritual, Image, and Symbol* (Columbia, SC: University of South Carolina Press, 1993). More comprehensive sources from which the study of relational dynamics draws can be found in writings such as Riane Eisler, *The Chalice and the Blade: Our History, Our Future* (San Francisco: Harper & Row, 1987); Riane Eisler, *Sacred Pleasure: Sex, Myth, and the Politics of the Body* (San Francisco: HarperCollins, 1995); Riane Eisler, *Tomorrow's Children: A Blueprint for Partnership Education in the 21st Century* (Boulder, CO: Westview Press, 2000); Riane Eisler, *The Real Wealth of Nations: Creating a Caring Economics* (San Francisco: Berrett-Koehler, 2007); Riane Eisler, "Protecting the Majority of Humanity: Toward an Integrated Approach to Crimes against Present and Future Generations," in *Sustainable Development, International Criminal Justice, and Treaty Implementation*, eds. Marie-Claire Cordonier-Segger and Sébastien Jodoin (Cambridge, UK: Cambridge University Press, 2013); Riane Eisler, "Human Possibilities: The Interaction of Biology and Culture," *Interdisciplinary Journal of Partnership Studies* 1 (2014): 3, doi: 10.24926/ijps.v1i1.88; Riane Eisler and Daniel Levine, "Nurture, Nature, and Caring: We Are Not Prisoners of Our Genes," *Brain and Mind* 3 (2002): 9–52, doi: 10.1023/A:1016553723748; Riane Eisler and Teddie M. Potter, *Transforming Interprofessional Partnerships: A New Framework for Nursing and Partnership-Based Health Care* (Indianapolis, IN: Sigma Theta Tau, 2014).

15. Michael Kimmel, *Angry White Men: American Masculinity at the End of an Era* (New York: Nation Books, 2013).

16. Eisler, *The Chalice and the Blade*.

17. David Bjorklund and Anthony Pellegrini, *The Origins of Human Nature: Evolutionary Developmental Psychology* (Washington DC: American Psychological Association, 2002); Robin Dunbar, Louise Barrett, and John Lycett, *Evolutionary Psychology* (Oxford: Oneworld Press, 2007); Ernst Mayr, "Cause and Effect in Biology," *Science* 134 (1961): 1501–1506, doi: 10.1126/science.134.3489.1501.

18. Cordelia Fine, *Delusions of Gender: How Our Minds, Society, and Neurosexism Create Difference* (New York: W. W. Norton, 2011), 176–177.

19. Riane Eisler, "Societal Contexts for Family Relations: Development, Violence and Stress," in *Contexts for Young Child Flourishing: Evolution, Family and Society,* eds. Darcia Narvaez et al. (New York: Oxford University Press, 2016). See also Alan H. Goodman and Thomas L. Leatherman, *Building a New Biocultural Synthesis: Political-Economic Perspectives on Human Biology* (Ann Arbor: University of Michigan Press, 1998); Charles M. Super and Sara Harkness, "The Developmental Niche: A Conceptualization at the Interface of Child and Culture," *International Journal of Behavioral Development* 9 (1986): 545–569, doi: 10.1177/016502548600900409; Carol M. Worthman, "The Ecology of Human Development: Evolving Models for Cultural Psychology," *Journal of Cross-Cultural Psychology* 41 (2010): 546–562, doi: 10.1177/0022022110362627; Carol Stinson, Barry Bogin, and Dennis O'Rourke, *Human Biology: An Evolutionary and Biocultural Perspective* (New York: John Wiley & Sons, 2012); Bjorklund and Pellegrini, *The Origins of Human Nature*; Barak Morgan et al., "Human Biological Development and Peace: Genes, Brains, Safety, and Justice," in *Pathways to Peace: The Transformative Power of Children and Families*, eds. James F. Leckman, Catherine Panter-Brick, and Rima Salah (Cambridge, MA: MIT Press, 2014).

20. Matthew Arnold, "Dover Beach," in *Seven Centuries of Verse: English and American*, ed. A. J. M. Smith (New York: Scribner, 1967), 476.

21. Michael T. Ghiselin, *The Economy of Nature and the Evolution of Sex* (Berkeley: University of California Press, 1974), 274.

22. Arnold, "Dover Beach."

23. See e.g., Riane Eisler, "Human Possibilities: An Integrated Systems Approach," *Journal of Global Education* 69 (2013): 269–289, doi: 10.1080/02604027.2013.803361; Riane Eisler, "Our Great Creative Challenge: Rethinking Human Nature—and Recreating Society," in *Everyday Creativity and New Views of Human Nature*, ed. Ruth Richards (Washington DC: APA Books, 2007); Riane Eisler, "Cultural Transformation Theory: A New Paradigm for History," in *Macrohistory and Macrohistorians*, eds. Johan Galtung and Sohail Inayatullah (Westport, CT: Praeger Publishers, 1997).

24. Lester Brown, personal communication, ca. 1994.

2

Evolution, Ideology, and Human Nature

Brain scans. Functional MRIs. Neuroscience. Everywhere we turn these days, these words leap out at us. The information is potentially revolutionary. But for many of us it is just another stream of factoids coming at us in disconnected bits and pieces.

So we tend to miss the most important fact revealed by neuroscience: that the neural patterns for our minds are greatly influenced by our environment, particularly in our early years. In other words, who we are is shaped through the interaction of our genes with our environments over the course of early development and into adulthood.[1]

But it is not only information overload that makes it hard for this key message from neuroscience to register. The cultural barriers are strong and deep and involve all-too-familiar tales of an unchangeable, innately selfish, violent "human nature."

These narratives appear again and again in popular books and articles; in the movies, TV, and on the Internet; and in everyday conversations and political discourse: our genes are in a no-holds-barred battle for survival. Rape, warfare, murder, and other cruelties are what allowed our ancestors to triumph in the survival-of-the-fittest contest. These "evolutionary imperatives" shaped the genes we carry, which in turn direct our behavior.

While most scientists do not take such an extreme position, there are definite battle lines about whether or not our genes keep us trapped in destructive behaviors. And this is not only an academic debate. It pits those who believe we can change human behavior through personal and cultural choices against those who believe our brains are largely hardwired to obey millennia-old genetic programming. Deterministic thinking is reflected, for example, when Michael Ghiglieri asks, "Are men born to be lethally violent? The answer is yes. Aggression is programmed by our DNA."[2]

If we believe we are governed by nasty evolutionary imperatives, we cannot solve problems such as violence and oppression. If our genes trap us in ruthlessly selfish and cruel behaviors, there is no point in trying to build more humane societies. By such reasoning, we are doomed from the moment sperm meets egg and mixes the age-old DNA into a new being, making each individual a prisoner of genes carried forward in time from the era of our ancient hominin ancestors. To counter these ideas, we have to understand the biases behind them and the scientific data that refute them.

Nurturing Our Humanity adopts a very different evolutionary perspective, a view that recognizes the human capacities for change and choice and emphasizes biocultural interaction over determinism. This emerging perspective on human origins and behavior hypothesizes, on the basis of much data, that the default tendencies in our very social species are toward prosocial helping and caring behaviors and concludes that, although we cannot create a world that is totally free of violence and cruelty, we can construct cultures with low levels of violence and oppression where our human capacities for creativity, caring, and consciousness are allowed to develop and flourish.

From Creation to Evolution

Most cultures have origin myths that explain how life and humans appeared on Earth. In an ancient Sumerian account, the Goddess Nammu births Heaven and Earth.[3] According to a Hopi story, Hard Beings Woman breathes life into male and female effigies.[4] According to a Chinese myth, a female deity called NuWa creates the world.[5] In Japanese mythology, the creators are the goddess Izanami and the god Izanagi.[6] In a Persian story, a male named Gayomart begets life by himself: when he dies, his semen falls on Earth, and the first human couple is born from two rhubarb shrubs.[7] In the Judeo-Christian Bible, a powerful male deity called Yahweh is the creator of life: land, sea, sun, moon, animals, and humans spring into existence in response to his commands; later, when humans disobey his orders, Yahweh sentences them to eternal misery and condemns woman to be subordinate to man.[8]

All these very different accounts tell us that life and then humanity were created by powerful supernatural beings. These supernatural beings are projections of particular cultures and social structures, reinforcing prevailing ideas of what is normal, right, and inevitable.

Today, scenarios of supernatural creation coexist with scientific theories of evolution. While these evolutionary theories are in part based on deductions from observations and laboratory experiments, they, too, can reflect particular cultural assumptions.[9]

The landmark book for the Western scientific approach to evolution, Charles Darwin's *Origin of Species*, was published in 1859 during a time of great cultural and intellectual ferment. Other naturalists had questioned the idea that all Earth's creatures were created in one fell swoop by an all-powerful God. In 1794, Erasmus Darwin, Charles Darwin's grandfather, and again, in 1809, Jean Baptiste Lamarck, proposed that the many life forms on our planet, including our own, gradually developed through natural processes. But Charles Darwin's work provided the controversial breakthrough that triggered the research and theorizing that continues today.[10]

Darwin proposed that when environments change, species either adapt accordingly or die out. The key process of adaptation through natural selection entails three interrelated principles.[11] First, within a breeding population, variation exists. Second, some variants in the population are more successful at survival and reproduction than are others and hence contribute relatively more offspring to the next generation. That is, they have higher reproductive fitness. Third, this fitness is inheritable, at least to some extent. Darwin provided examples of protective coloration to illustrate the process of natural selection, explaining that:

> It may metaphorically be said that natural selection is daily and hourly scrutinizing throughout the world, the slightest variations; rejecting those that are bad, preserving and adding up all that are good; silently and insensibly working, *whenever and wherever opportunity offers.* . . . When we see leaf-eating insects green, and bark-feeders mottled-gray; the alpine ptarmigan white in winter, the red-grouse the colour of heather, we must believe that these tints are of service to these birds and insects in preserving them from danger.[12]

As Darwin's theorizing predated an understanding of genetics, he necessarily left open questions about how characteristics are transmitted from earlier to later generations. Then, in 1937, Theodosius Dobzhansky, an experimental geneticist, published *Genetics and the Origin of Species*.[13] He and a number of other scholars forged what is called the neo-Darwinian synthesis, or simply neo-Darwinism, combining genetics with the study of evolutionary processes.

From Darwinism to Determinism

During the last decades of the 20th century, a new field called sociobiology gained popularity, especially through the writings of Edward O. Wilson and Richard Dawkins.[14] Gradually, sociobiology morphed into evolutionary psychology, but despite this name change, like sociobiologists, most evolutionary psychologists argue that how we behave today is largely the result of hominin/human adaptations to ancestral environments. They further argue that, regardless of how maladaptive this may be under present circumstances, the behaviors of modern humans are still driven by this millennia-old evolutionary legacy.[15]

Many sociobiologists and evolutionary psychologists are ingenious, even brilliant, theory builders. Some of their explanations for how selection operates in nonhuman species have inspired important research. When they insist that human behavior is not shaped solely by experience and learning, that we have to look at biological factors, they are, of course, right. When they point out that human biology developed over many millennia of evolution, they are correct. There is no question that genes must be considered in explaining human behavior, both individually and collectively.[16] There is also no question that in the course of evolution, living organisms developed behavioral patterns for self-preservation that we still carry today, for example, preprogrammed reactions to danger triggered by the sight of a snake or an unanticipated loud noise.

One goal of this book is to balance evolutionary psychology that favors selfishness, competition, and self-interest with a consideration also of the prosociality, cooperation, and caring that generally has been overlooked, minimized, and denied despite its obvious importance during human evolution and in human societies around the world.[17] We question the negative view of human nature that runs through some evolutionary psychological writings: a view that readily lends itself to justifying injustice and violence as "just the way things are."[18]

We also question the linear deterministic thinking that runs through some of this literature. Although they may not intend to do so, some evolutionary psychologists give the impression that human behavior is the product of a one-way genetic process, rather than synergetic interaction of genes and experience.[19]

Even when they recognize that learning affects behavior, these theorists contend that influencing human behavior through education is an uphill struggle if it runs into what they claim are evolutionary imperatives embedded in human nature. And either explicitly or implicitly, according to many evolutionary psychologists, these evolutionary imperatives boil down to one implacable, overriding motivation: selfishness.

In explaining the thesis of his famous book *The Selfish Gene*, biologist Richard Dawkins summed up this view vividly: "We, and all other animals, are machines created by our genes. Like successful Chicago gangsters, our genes have survived, in some cases for millions of years, in a highly competitive world. This entitles us to expect certain qualities in our genes. I shall argue that a predominant quality to be expected in a successful gene is ruthless selfishness."[20]

After *The Selfish Gene* came out in 1976, Dawkins was widely criticized for equating self-interest, which is certainly a major factor in human behavior, with ruthless selfishness. So in the 1989 edition of his book, Dawkins responded by adding a chapter on how, in his words, "even with selfish genes at the helm, nice guys can finish first."[21]

In this later edition, Dawkins acknowledged that cooperation can be a good evolutionary strategy. But in his scheme of things, cooperation, love, kindness, and other "soft" behaviors are still only products of selfish genes striving to replicate themselves or related genes that carry the same pattern of information.

A number of evolutionary psychologists make still a further argument.[22] They claim that because of biological imperatives that developed in the course of evolution, our behaviors are driven by specialized, inherited genetic responses to particular environmental stimuli. Jerome Barkow, Leda Cosmides, and John Tooby contend that we are like computers with complex software programs. "What is special about the human mind," they assert, "is not that it gave up 'instinct' in order to become flexible, but that it proliferated 'instincts'—that is, content-specific problem-solving specialization." These writers maintain that to understand human behaviors, we have to look not at learning but at a "superstructure of evolved functional specializations."[23] In other words, they propose that our minds do not grow through learning, but that our heads are like robots, filled with millions of cognitive cubbyholes programmed for reactions to the circumstances we happen to come across.

Other evolutionary psychologists even claim that "the increasingly sophisticated human capacity for deceiving one another is what eventually gave rise to that entirely new level of representational activity we call symbolic culture."[24] In other words, language, art, music, and so much of what we enjoy as beautiful, meaningful, and humane are the result of nastiness and deceit.

The Power of Ideology

Although in other respects evolutionary psychologists reject religious explanations, the notion of an innately flawed, ruthlessly selfish human nature is very similar to the religious dogma of original sin that for centuries justified strict top-down controls and punishments. It is also parallel to a strong strain in Western philosophical tradition. The British philosopher Thomas Hobbes saw the life of "man" (the life of women did not count) as "solitary, poor, nasty, brutish, and short."[25] In his parable of the master and the slave, the influential German philosopher Georg Wilhelm Friedrich Hegel saw only the possibility of dominating or being dominated.[26] Another celebrated German philosopher, Friedrich Nietzsche, denounced the Christian ideal of caring and compassion as slave morality.[27] Even the iconic Immanuel Kant could see nothing good in "man's" nature, claiming that only the transcendent qualities of pure reason and practical reason account for morality.[28] The point is that sociobiology and its offspring, evolutionary psychology, have arisen within the larger frame of this cultural milieu and reflect a decidedly biased view of human nature.[29]

Current theories focusing on selfishness and violence also follow the tradition of 19th-century social Darwinists. Herbert Spencer, from whom Darwin took the phrase "survival of the fittest," was a great favorite of the robber barons of unregulated capitalism. This should not surprise us. If the "fittest" are the most brutal and callous, and this results from natural selection, one can easily argue that exploitive and unprincipled economic arrangements are inevitable results of the laws of nature. This view is reflected by scholars and lay people alike, as in a letter to the editor of *Time*, which reads: "Modern psychology tells us it is the genetically determined, typical male aggression, the 'dark side of man,' that helps men climb the corporate ladder."[30]

Most evolutionary psychologists try to distance themselves from social Darwinism. Like Dawkins, they make a point of distinguishing between selfish genes and selfish behaviors, arguing that selfish genes can lead to unselfish, even altruistic, behaviors if these help genes pass themselves on to the next generation. Usually, however, this important point is merely given lip service, whereas the bulk of what evolutionary psychologists write contradicts this distinction.

For instance, Dawkins writes that we must teach our children altruism because "we cannot expect it to be part of their biological nature."[31] He does not explain why, if altruism is not part of our biological nature, we are able to learn it.

Again and again, in these writings the emphasis is on the dark and dire side of human nature.[32] Melvin Konner writes, for instance, "I will argue that there is in human nature a natural tendency to violence and, additionally to war." David Livingstone Smith also assumes that humans have a warlike nature and then proceeds to construct an imagined evolutionary scenario to explain that which he assumes: "We inherited our warlike nature from prehistoric bands that were able to kill their neighbors and acquire their resources. These groups flourished while the pacifists withered on the evolutionary vine."[33]

These writers also claim that there are what they call evolutionary payoffs for cruel and violent behaviors.[34] Michael Ghiglieri opines, "because rape is so widespread and rampant around the planet, by males both human and nonhuman, it is clearly a male biological adaptation."[35] In the same vein, Randy Thornhill and Craig Palmer argue that rape was specifically selected for, as in certain insects that have an appendage with no function other than restraining a female during forced copulation.[36]

Thornhill and Palmer hasten to add that they deplore rape. But deplorable or not, according to them, rape is simply a successful evolutionary strategy that helps men pass on their genes—an argument that ignores, among other things, that rapists sometimes kill their victims or target women who are too old or too young to conceive, which are hardly ways to pass on genes. This argument also is contradicted by the existence of numerous societies where rape is either very rare or not known to exist—refuting the knighting of human rape as an evolved adaptation.[37]

Numerous evolutionary psychologists maintain that, like rape, warfare is adaptive and originated because of evolutionary payoffs to fitness.[38] They, too, brush over the fact that caring, sharing, nurturing, and loving, as well as helping, forgiving, conflict-resolving, and acting nonviolently, predominate in the human repertory of behavior.[39]

These writers do *not* say that caring and nonviolence are part of our biological human nature, or else we would not be capable of them. Instead, they give the impression that what is really natural, indeed inevitable, are violence and cruelty—as reflected in their book titles: *The Murderer Next Door, Demonic Males, The Darker Side of Man, The Most Dangerous Animal: Human Nature and the Origins of War,* and *A Natural History of Rape: Biological Bases of Sexual Coercion.*[40]

What these authors are actually expressing is an *ideology* that serves to justify the direct and structural violence of hierarchies of domination and the rigid ranking of some people over others. Theirs is an authoritarian worldview in which no real agency is given to the individual, where humans are controlled by powerful forces, be they genes or those at the top of a domination hierarchy.

Control by Selfish Replicators

The value of theories lies in their power to explain and predict. The theory of adaptation through natural selection explains and predicts how species evolve, survive, or die out. A huge amount of data support this powerful theory, which has helped us understand the history of life on the planet.

However, the argument that our cultures and behaviors can be explained by selfish genes ruthlessly seeking to replicate themselves and that rape, murder, and warfare are reflections of this goes way beyond the concept of natural selection and is infused with ideology.[41] While writers taking this position may say that they are only using metaphors, their message is clear: we act, not out of our own will, but according to the will of invisible selfish replicators.

There is a difference between the *description* of what happens through natural selection and the *attribution of will and motive* to invisible forces. It is one thing to say that some genes get passed on and others do not because some women and men survive, reproduce, and leave more offspring compared with others. It is quite another to say that "the individual is a survival machine built by a short-lived confederation of long-lived genes,"[42] that, driven by selfish genes "selfish greed seems to characterize much of child behavior,"[43] or to compare genes to Chicago gangsters.[44] Such phrasing suggests that genes *want* to be passed on and that they ensure this by getting people to do violent and ruthless things.[45]

It is like saying that there are storms because gods of wind and water cause them. Just as people used to attribute nasty motives to spirits, deities, or demons—as in the old saying, "the devil made me do it"—such thinking attributes nasty motives to genes. Instead of being told we are possessed by devils, we are informed that we are puppets of our selfish genes.

Amazingly, Darwinism and neo-Darwinism are often invoked to support this position that genes drive us to cruelty and violence—when in reality neither Darwin nor the prime architects of the neo-Darwinian synthesis held this view. As David Loye documents, these interpretations completely ignore what Darwin actually asserted in *The Descent of Man*: that in human evolution natural selection declines in significance, with learning, mutual aid, love, and what he called the development of the moral sense becoming primary shapers of who we are and can become.[46]

Likewise, Dobzhansky, Julian Huxley, and Ernst Mayr, three of the fathers of neo-Darwinian theory, emphasized that human evolution transcends prior evolutionary dynamics.[47] As John O'Manique writes in *Origins of Justice*, for Dobzhansky the human species is a transcendental product of evolution that has powers of creativity whereby it innovates within parameters which it itself constantly pushes outward.[48] Dobzhansky especially emphasized the importance of culture in human affairs. "The most significant product, and the paramount determining factor, of human evolution is culture," he tells us, and "culture is not transmitted biologically through some special genes; it is acquired anew in every generation by learning and instruction, in large part through the medium of the symbolic language."[49]

The Mounting Challenge to Determinism

By now we hope it is clear that we are not anti-evolutionary but rather anti-deterministic and that we are pointing out how ideology can masquerade as science. When comparing what Darwin and neo-Darwinists actually say with the selfish gene script, one has to be amazed at the disconnect. And the notion that ruthless genes drive our behavior seems all the more bizarre in light of many real-world observations to the contrary.

For instance, if humans were simply driven by selfish genes, how do we account for the people who saved Jews during the Nazi occupation of Europe? The Nazis made it clear that they would summarily execute not only the people who helped the Jewish population but also their entire families. So why would anyone endanger the lives and genes of their loved ones and themselves to protect nonrelatives? The eminent Harvard design artist Krzysztof Wodiczko, born in Warsaw in 1943, once remarked, "It takes 47 people to save one Jewish family."[50] When asked what he meant by 47, Wodiczko explained that everyone in a Warsaw building, all 47 neighbors, cooperated to hide and provide food for his family during the Nazi occupation. In Denmark, through a massive cooperative effort, more than 90 percent of Danish Jews were hidden and then smuggled out of the country to Sweden before Hitler's Third Reich could round them up for deportation to concentration camps.[51]

Moreover, if humans were simply motivated by evolutionary imperatives that drive us to purely self-centered acts, why have millions of people throughout recorded history worked to change unjust and cruel customs and policies—sometimes at the cost of their lives? And if our cultures were just the product of ancient self-interested evolutionary imperatives, how could many cultures over the last centuries have succeeded in making fundamental cultural changes that we today take for granted—from abolishing slavery to ending witch-burning? If selfish genes hardwire our brains, how could people develop new ways of thinking and new social structures in so short a time?

The answer is that rather than being hardwired for ruthless selfishness and violence, a huge corpus of evidence, as we will explore in this book, indicates that humans have also evolved powerful capacities, indeed proclivities, for empathy, equity, helping, caring, and various other prosocial acts.[52] Today, some evolutionary psychologists such as Jonathan Haidt acknowledge the importance of these human capacities. Others, such as Steven Pinker, are taking note of how behaviors and social institutions can and do change in just a few hundred years.[53]

In his 2002 bestseller *The Blank Slate*, Pinker denied that the cultural environments we create make any difference, arguing that neither families nor peer groups count and that the only factor to consider, in addition to genes, is chance. He wrote that violence is "a near-inevitable outcome of the dynamics of self-interested, rational social organisms."[54] But a decade later, in his *The Better Angels of Our Nature*, Pinker takes a very different stand. Arguing that violence has actually decreased over recent centuries, Pinker now asserts that these behavioral changes are far too recent to be attributable to genetic changes, and therefore we must look at factors such as better government, the Enlightenment, greater prosperity, health, education, trade, and improvements in the status of women to explain them. In this 2011 book, Pinker proposes that a civilizing process, a humanitarian revolution, and a rights revolution—in other words, changes in culture— are key to changes in behavior.[55]

But lest we think that Pinker made a complete turnaround, it is by no means clear that he has changed his mind about the primacy of genes be- cause he has not repudiated his earlier assertions. Nor has Pinker reversed his stance that prehistoric human societies were racked with violence "in a state of nature."[56] So the path toward a more balanced perspective for explaining human behaviors and institutions will not be quick or easy.

Nonetheless, the evidence challenging deterministic assumptions of human selfishness and violence is accumulating at an ever-faster pace. This makes what the historian of science Thomas Kuhn called a scientific para- digm shift an increasing possibility.[57]

Study after study drawing from archaeology and observations of contem- porary nomadic foraging societies—analogs for life among ancestral no- madic forager groups over the course of human evolution—are demolishing popular notions of our species as inherently warlike naked apes. As Doug has realized, "the often expressed idea that members of one nomadic band regularly raid other bands to steal women, gain territory, or simply to kill as many people as possible is for the most part a misconception not substanti- ated by a visit to the facts."[58] Other scholars point to archaeological findings showing that warfare, male dominance, and rigid social stratification (the configuration of domination systems) only began to appear a few millennia ago.[59] As we will consider in more detail later, even the arrival of agriculture did not always bring warfare.

For instance, Brian Ferguson reports what appears to be a 10,000-year period of peace in the Southern Levant of the Near East.[60] From about 15,100 years ago until 5,200 years ago, there are only a handful of skeletons showing lethal violence over thousands of years, with no mass casualties, no sacked settlements, no fortifications, and no placement of settlements in naturally fortified locations—in short, none of the usual indicators of war. Ferguson opines, "The people of the Southern Levant domesticated na- ture. It is a pessimistic view indeed to presume they were not also capable of domesticating conflict."[61]

Another example of enduring peace comes from an early agrarian set- tlement called Çatalhöyük in Anatolia. Here there are no convincing signs of destruction through warfare for 1,000 years.[62] Houses and grave goods show no signs of large disparities between haves and have-nots. And verifying its more partnership-oriented social configuration, Ian Hodder, the archaeologist currently excavating Çatalhöyük, notes with some amazement, "even analyses of isotopes in bones give no indication of divergence in lifestyle translating into differences in status and power between women and men," suggesting "a society in which sex is relatively unimportant in assigning social roles, with neither burials nor space in houses suggesting gender inequality."[63]

There are similar findings from the Minoan civilization that flourished on the Mediterranean island of Crete until about 3,500 years ago, contradicting the view that centralized, complex, technologically and artistically advanced cultures require massive inequalities and control through violence.[64] Findings such as these do not bear out the notion of evolutionary imperatives that drive us to inequity and violence.

New Evidence about Human Nature

There is now a plethora of evidence from many fields, ranging from ethnography, history, and psychology to genetics, neuroscience, and ethology, that provide a shock-and-awe set of counter-arguments to the assumption that selfishness and violence are central to what it means to be human. Certainly human beings are capable of engaging in atrocities, brutality, and mayhem. That is obvious. But, as we will explore in this book, our "better angel" capacities, to borrow Pinker's phrase, for empathy, mutuality, caring, and restraint against violence, actually manifest themselves across cultures; occur far more frequently than physical violence in any society; are critical for the raising of the young; and have clear survival value.

Proposing that humans have a proclivity for prosocial behaviors such as caring for and connecting with others over raw violence and selfishness may seem like heresy in face of popular and scientific writings that focus on the darker sides of human nature. However, viewed from an evolutionary perspective, as biologist Frans de Waal documents in *The Age of Empathy*, helpfulness, mutuality, and empathy actually have a long and deep evolutionary history.[65]

Caring, sharing, tending, and befriending may have originated in relations between kin and other group members—especially between mother and child. But in the course of evolution, these prosocial proclivities not only extended to others but also left a deep mark on the human brain.[66] To illustrate, experiments show that babies cry more when they hear the taped cries of other babies than when they hear recordings of their own crying, suggesting that they are responding empathically to someone else's distress, not just to a certain pitch of sound.[67] Babies also seem to want to assuage the pain of others: once they have enough physical competence, starting at about 1 year old, they soothe others in distress by stroking and touching or by handing over a bottle or toy.[68]

Toddlers, too, have a basic impulse toward mutuality and helpfulness that has been experimentally verified. Felix Warneken of the Max Planck Institute for Evolutionary Anthropology did an experiment where 18-month-olds watched him "struggling" with ordinary tasks such as hanging towels with clothespins or stacking books. Over and over, as he "accidentally" dropped a clothespin or knocked over books, every one of the 24 toddlers participating in his experiment offered him help within seconds—but only if Warneken appeared to need help. When he threw a pin on the floor or deliberately knocked over a book, they did not respond. However, if it looked like he needed help, they quickly toddled over, grabbed the object, and eagerly handed it back to him.[69] To test the toddlers' motivations, Warneken made a point of *not* thanking them, much less rewarding them. This indicates that their motives stemmed from empathy and altruism rather than an expectation of praise or a reward. They were simply responding to a stranger's need by coming forward to help.

Theories that people are only helpful when they are related or expecting a payback ignore the evidence.[70] And this evidence not only is about human helpfulness but also is about that of other species.[71] For example, dolphins and gorillas have rescued humans: creatures they are clearly *not* related to, and from whom, as Warneken found with the toddlers he studied, they are not expecting a reward.

This leads to a very important finding from neuroscience: our impulses toward empathy, helpfulness, and mutuality are linked not to extrinsic rewards but to rewards intrinsically embedded in our brain's neurophysiology.[72] In later chapters, we will look at brain scans studies showing that when we engage in mutually beneficial behaviors, even with strangers, the "pleasure centers" of our brain light up.[73] Even more striking is that neural reward areas light up *more* when we care for others than when we only look out for ourselves.[74]

What these kinds of findings indicate is that in the course of evolution humans developed a brain primed more for living in partnership-oriented societies. However, and this is a key point, these capacities are inhibited, or at best compartmentalized, in domination systems through socialization, values, social practices, and institutions.

As we will develop in this book, looking at our history from this perspective helps us solve the puzzle of why there has been so much cruelty and destructiveness when evolution equipped our species with such an enormous genetic capacity for empathy, working together, sharing, caring, and helping.

We today know from neuroscience that stress can inhibit our capacity for empathy, mutuality, and caring by changing our brain neurochemistry.[75] And, starting with the crucial early family relations, domination-oriented societies are extremely stressful.[76]

This does not mean there is no stress in partnership-oriented cultures. There are always stresses in life. Stressful relations and conditions, however, are not inherent in the partnership system, as they are in the domination system.

When people grow up in domination cultures or subcultures, they tend to develop brains adjusted to these environments. Indeed, in settings based on strict rankings of domination and submission, this strategy may even be a survival requisite. In such environments, people do not usually survive long if they fail to obey orders. They are burned at the stake, stoned to death, shot, or imprisoned, as we see in much of Western history and still in far too many places today.

Under these conditions, harsh, stressful parenting would be a domination system's maintenance requirement because it teaches people early on to either control others or submit to those in control. So also would constant early exposure to relations where difference—beginning with the basic difference between male and female—is equated with dominating or being dominated, since domination systems require acceptance of top-down rankings as normal and inevitable.

In addition, domination systems have other effective self-maintenance mechanisms. Economically, they create artificial scarcities of resources for those on bottom (slaves, serfs, "lower classes," and out-groups) as well as insecurity for those on top. These scarcities and insecurities create enormous stress. So also does violence or the threat of violence—starting with the violence and abuse children experience or observe in their families, all the way to constant battles for control by those on top, which historically have often been violent.

Further stress, as we will also explore in later chapters, stems from the conflation of caring and coercion built into domination childrearing, leading to denial (including identification with the "strong") and deflection of fear and rage to out-groups. The socialization of males to equate masculinity with domination and violence is still another source of stress, as is the attendant devaluation of anything stereotypically associated with "inferior" women (such as caring, caregiving, and nonviolence). All this manifests itself in the development of neural structures primed for fight, flight, or freeze, which promote fear and denial, suppress empathy, and constrict consciousness of a partnership alternative.

Toward a New Biocultural Synthesis

This brings us to the need for a biocultural paradigm that combines recent and classic findings into a new framework for better understanding how our brains interact with our environments, especially with our cultural environments as mediated by families, education, politics, economics, and other social institutions. Different strands of such a framework are gradually beginning to emerge. For example, the term *biocultural* is increasingly used in a variety of disciplines such as anthropology and cultural psychology.[77]

The Biocultural Partnership-Domination Lens takes this emerging new framework further by adding to gene-environment interaction the partnership-domination social continuum. It proposes that the combination of the partnership-domination continuum with what we are learning about brain development and subsequent brain functioning can bring multiple avenues of scholarship together to reveal otherwise invisible patterns that can help us move to a more sustainable future.

While the Biocultural Partnership-Domination Lens is still under construction and awaits input and testing, by melding what we are learning from the biological sciences, especially from neuroscience, with findings from the social sciences, especially from the study of relational dynamics, anthropology, and psychology, it provides an integrative new perspective for addressing the following key questions:

1. What set of variables supports the development of a brain neuro-chemistry programmed for fight-or-flight, dissociation, insensitivity, and violence?

2. What set of variables supports the expression of our prosocial human capacities for empathy, nonviolence, creativity, caring, and conscious choice?

3. How do we decrease influences of the former set of variables as we simultaneously augment the effects of the latter set of variables?

As we will explore in depth, unlike other social-cultural categories, the partnership system and the domination system take our early experiences into full account. This difference in perspective is of crucial importance because we know today that we are not born with fully developed brains and that how our brains develop is largely a function of early life experiences.[78]

In other words, unlike other social-cultural categories, the partnership system and the domination system take into consideration the enormous impact of our early environment on brain development, both during childhood and over the course of our lifetime. As neuroscientist Bruce Perry notes, "by birth the human brain has developed to the point where environmental cues mediated by the senses play a major role in determining how neurons will differentiate, sprout dendrites, form and maintain synaptic connections and create the final neural networks that convey functionality." Moreover, he adds, by adolescence, the majority of the changes taking place in the brain are determined by experience, not genetics.[79]

Using the analytical lens of the partnership-domination continuum, as reflecting two cultural configurations at opposite poles, makes it possible to see important connections that are otherwise invisible. We can then see the link between what happens in intimate relations and other relations— including national and international ones. In other words, because the partnership-domination continuum provides a lens for looking at an *entire* society—not only its political and economic relations but also its family and other intimate relations—it makes it possible to see larger patterns.

We see, for example, that cultures where families are generally more egalitarian and women have higher status, such as Sweden, Finland, Iceland, and Norway, are more democratic, equitable, and peaceful. We also begin to understand why authoritarian and violent cultures—whether secular like Germany under the Nazis or religious like the Taliban or ISIS—favor a highly punitive, rigidly male-dominated family.

Most studies of so-called religious fundamentalism, which we would call domination fundamentalism, have focused on how its leaders—be they Eastern or Western, Muslim or Christian—want to impose authoritarian theocratic control and intolerance of other faiths. Another frequently noted aspect of fundamentalism is its association with the violence of holy wars and terrorism.[80] Most observers, however, fail to note the connection between these characteristics and the fact that a top priority for fundamentalists of all stripes is pushing women back to their traditional or subservient place in a punitive, authoritarian "traditional" family.

Over the last centuries, as massive technological changes destabilized social structures, there has been movement toward partnership, at least in some world regions. While not so long ago it was believed that kings have a divinely ordained right to rule, and fealty and obedience were the cultural ideals, today most people hold democracy and freedom as coveted ideals.

But the movement to challenge top-down control has primarily focused on dismantling the top of the domination pyramid: what is conventionally defined as politics and economics. It has paid much less attention to gender and parent-child relations—the relationships that most profoundly affect the development of the brain—and with this, how we feel, think, and act.

Once we connect these dots, we see that in a domination system, familial, educational, religious, political, and economic structures—*not* an imagined human nature wired for oppression and violence—are what gets in the way of our human capacities, indeed, propensities, for empathy, caring, and mutuality. Identifying these dynamics, in turn, makes it possible to identify interventions that can more effectively bring about positive social change. The Biocultural Partnership-Domination Lens treats biological and cultural evolution as a unified field reflecting gene-culture interactions. It reveals patterns in what otherwise seems random and disconnected, pointing to ways of achieving systemic and sustainable change.

Moreover—and this is a critical point—this lens not only examines how environments affect human behavior but also considers, in a process akin to the evolutionary concept of niche construction, how human behavior in turn affects our physical and cultural environments.[81] It shows that because our brains have evolved the flexibility to adjust to different environments, they tend to develop differently in partnership- and domination-oriented systems, and that the effects of these different environments are particularly powerful over the course of child and adolescent neural development. However, we again want to emphasize that this is not a one-way process. What we think, feel, and do also affects which of our genetic possibilities are expressed. It affects the kinds of cultures we create.

In short, we propose that there are synergistic interactive relationships between biology, culture, and human agency. But before we explore these interactions further, we will in the next chapter look at another pivotal, still generally ignored, aspect of human evolution: the emergence of love.

Notes

1. On developmental gene-environment interaction, see David F. Bjorklund and Anthony D. Pellegrini, *The Origins of Human Nature: Evolutionary Developmental Psychology* (Washington, DC: American Psychological Association, 2002); Frances A. Champagne, "Epigenetics of Mammalian Parenting," in *Ancestral Landscapes in Human Evolution: Culture, Childrearing and Social Wellbeing*, eds. Darcia Narvaez et al. (New York: Oxford University Press, 2014); Eric B. Keverne, "Epigenetics: Significance of the Gene-Environment Interface for Brain Development," in *Pathways to Peace: The Transformative Power of Children and Families*, eds. James F. Leckman, Catherine Panter-Brick, and Rima Salah (Cambridge, MA: MIT Press, 2014); Darcia Narvaez, *Neurobiology and the Development of Human Morality: Evolution, Culture, and Wisdom* (New York: Norton, 2014); and Robert M. Sapolsky, *Behave: The Biology of Humans at Our Best and Worst* (New York: Penguin, 2017).
2. Michael P. Ghiglieri, *The Dark Side of Man: Tracing the Origins of Violence* (Reading, MA: Perseus, 1999), 30.
3. Joan O'Brien, "Nammu, Mami, Eve and Pandora: 'What's in a Name?'" *Classical Journal* 79 (1983): 35–45.
4. Paula Gunn Allen, *The Sacred Hoop: Recovering the Feminine in American Indian Traditions* (Boston: Beacon Press, 1992).
5. Junsheng Cai, "Myth and Reality: The Projection of Gender Relations in Prehistoric China," in *The Chalice and the Blade in Chinese Culture: Gender Relations and Social Models*, ed. Min Jiayin (Beijing: China Social Sciences Publishing House, 1995).
6. Joyce Chapman Lebra, Joy Paulson, and Elizabeth Powers, eds., *Women in Changing Japan* (Stanford, CA: Stanford University Press, 1978).
7. Bruce Lincoln, "The Indo-European Myth of Creation," *History of Religions* 15 (1975): 121–145, doi: 10.1086/462739.
8. Genesis 1–3.
9. See Douglas P. Fry, *The Human Potential for Peace* (New York: Oxford University Press, 2006), for an exploration of the thesis that cultural beliefs greatly affect the scientific process and various examples of how a Western view of humanity as inclined toward violence and war recurs in scientific and popular writing; Marshall Sahlins, *The Western Illusion of Human Nature* (Chicago: Prickly Paradigm Press, 2008); Robert W. Sussman, "Why the Legend of the Killer Ape Never Dies: The Enduring Power of Cultural Beliefs to Distort Our View of Human Nature," in *War, Peace, and*

Human Nature: The Convergence of Evolutionary and Cultural Views, ed. Douglas P. Fry (New York: Oxford University Press, 2013).

10. The 19th-century scholar Jean Baptiste Lamarck was the first to propose evolution at the species level, though he is today primarily identified with the theory of inheritance of acquired or learned characteristics. But Charles Darwin developed this theory of evolution via natural selection, spawning what in the 20th century has become known as neo-Darwinism. While there are different strands of neo-Darwinism, its basic tenet is that, as Darwin wrote in *Origin of Species*, natural selection favors those individuals and species that successfully compete in the struggle for existence by gradually adapting to their environments, a process that, borrowing from Herbert Spencer, Darwin called the "survival of the fittest."

11. Richard C. Lewontin, "The Units of Selection," *Annual Review of Ecology and Systematics* 1 (1970), 1–18, doi: 10.1146/annurev.es.01.110170.000245; see also Douglas P. Fry, "The Evolution of Aggression and the Level of Selection Controversy," *Aggressive Behavior* 6 (1980): 69–89, doi: 10.1002/1098-2337(1980)6:1<69.

12. Charles Darwin, *Origin of Species: By Means of Natural Selection of the Preservation of Favoured Races in the Struggle for Life* (Mentor paperback edition, New York: Norton, 1958, originally published in 1859), 90, 91, italics in original.

13. Theodosius Dobzhansky, *Genetics and the Origin of Species* (New York: Columbia University Press, 1982, originally published in 1937).

14. Edward O. Wilson, *Sociobiology: The New Synthesis* (Cambridge, MA: Harvard University Press, 1975); Richard Dawkins, *The Selfish Gene* (New York: Oxford University Press, 1976).

15. See, e.g., David Buss, *Evolutionary Psychology: The New Science of the Mind* (Boston: Allyn and Bacon, 1999); Jonathan Haidt, *The Righteous Mind: Why Good People Are Divided by Politics and Religion* (New York: Pantheon, 2012); Steven Pinker, *How the Mind Works* (New York: W.W. Norton, 1997).

16. Bjorklund and Pellegrini, *The Origins of Human Nature*; Robin Dunbar, Louise Barrett, and John Lycett, *Evolutionary Psychology* (Oxford: Oneworld Publications, 2007).

17. Walter Goldschmidt, *The Bridge to Humanity: How Affect Hunger Trumps the Selfish Gene* (New York: Oxford University Press, 2005).

18. For examples of this type of thinking, see Buss, *Evolutionary Psychology*; Melvin Konner, "Human Nature, Ethnic Violence, and War," in *The Psychology of Resolving Global Conflicts: From War to Peace, Volume 1: Nature vs. Nurture*, eds. Mari Fitzduff and Chris E. Stout (Westport, CT: Praeger, 2006); Pinker, *How the Mind Works*.

19. See for example the last chapter of Wilson's *Sociobiology*, on genes for war, homosexuality, and so forth, or Konner, "Human Nature, Ethnic Violence, and War," linking war and violence to natural selection.

20. Dawkins, *The Selfish Gene*, 2.

21. Richard Dawkins, *The Selfish Gene* (New York: Oxford University Press, 1989 edition).

22. Jerome Barkow, Leda Cosmides, and John Tooby, eds., *The Adapted Mind: Evolutionary Psychology and the Generation of Culture* (New York: Oxford University Press, 1992).

23. Barkow, Cosmides, and Tooby, *The Adapted Mind*, 39, 113.

24. Robin Dunbar, Chris Knight, and Camilla Power, eds., *The Evolution of Culture: An Interdisciplinary View* (New Brunswick, NJ: Rutgers University Press, 1999), 6.

25. Thomas Hobbes, *Leviathan: Or the Matter, Forme and Power of a Commonwealth Ecclesiastical and Civil* (Oxford: Basil Blackwell, 1946, originally published in 1651), 82.

26. G. W. F. Hegel, *Phenomenology of Spirit,* trans. A. V. Miller (Oxford: Clarendon Press, 1977, originally published in 1807).

27. Friedrich Nietzsche, *On the Genealogy of Morality,* trans. Maudemarie Clark and Alan J. Swensen (New York: Vintage Books, 1967, originally published in 1887).

28. Immanuel Kant, *Foundations of the Metaphysics of Morals and What Is Enlightenment,* trans. Lewis White Beck (New York: Macmillan, 1990, originally published in 1785).

29. See Douglas P. Fry and Geneviève Souillac, "The Relevance of Nomadic Forager Studies to Moral Foundations Theory: Moral Education and Global Ethics in the Twenty-First Century," *Journal of Moral Education* 42 (2013): 346–359, doi: 10.1080/03057240.2013.817328; Geneviève Souillac and Douglas P. Fry, "Anthropology: Implications for Peace," in *Dimensions of Peace*, eds. Oliver P. Richmond, Sandra Pogodda, and Jasmine Ramovic (London: Palgrave, in press); Fry, *The Human Potential for Peace*.

30. "Letter to the Editor," *Time,* May 8, 2000, 11.

31. Dawkins, *The Selfish Gene*, 1976 edition, 139. Dawkins is right that we should teach our children altruism but not for the reasons he said, that it is not part of our biological nature. We should do this because it is a part of our biological nature that needs to be nurtured.

32. Buss, *Evolutionary Psychology*; Richard Wrangham and Dale Peterson, *Demonic Males: Apes and the Origins of Human Violence* (Boston: Houghton Mifflin, 1999); Ghiglieri, *The Dark Side of Man*; Konner, "Human Nature, Ethnic Violence, and War."

33. Konner, "Human Nature, Ethnic Violence, and War," 1; David Livingstone Smith, *The Most Dangerous Animal: Human Nature and the Origins of War* (New York: St. Martin's Griffin, 2007), 81.

34. Buss, *Evolutionary Psychology*; Bobbie Low, "An Evolutionary Perspective on War," in *Behavior, Culture, and Conflict in World Politics*, eds. W. Zimmerman and H. Jacobson (Ann Arbor: University of Michigan Press, 1993); Pinker, *How the Mind Works*; Smith, *The Most Dangerous Animal*.

35. Ghiglieri, *The Dark Side of Man*, 103.

36. Craig T. Palmer and Randy Thornhill, *A Natural History of Rape: Biological Bases of Sexual Coercion* (Cambridge, MA: MIT Press, 2000).

37. Leigh Minturn, Martin Grosse, and Santoah Haider, "Cultural Patterning of Sexual Beliefs and Behavior," *Ethnology* 8 (1969): 301–308, doi: 10.2307/3772759; see also Fry, *The Human Potential for Peace*, chapter 5.

38. For example, Buss, *Evolutionary Psychology*; Ghiglieri, *The Dark Side of Man*; Low, "An Evolutionary Perspective"; Smith, *The Most Dangerous Animal*; Wrangham and Peterson, *Demonic Males*; Richard Wrangham and Luke Glowacki, "Intergroup Aggression in Chimpanzees and War in Nomadic Hunter-Gatherers: Evaluating the Chimpanzee Model," *Human Nature* 23 (2012): 5–29, doi: 10.1007/s12110-012-9132-1. For multidimensional critiques of the idea that war is an evolved adaptation, see Fry, "The Evolution of Aggression"; Fry, *The Human Potential for Peace*; Douglas P. Fry, "The Evolution of Cooperation: What's War Got to Do with It?" *Reviews in Anthropology* 42 (2013): 102–121, doi: 10.1080/00938157.2013.788351; Douglas P. Fry, "The Evolutionary Logic of Human Peaceful Behavior," in *Peace Ethology: Behavioral Processes and Systems of Peace*, eds. Peter Verbeek and Benjamin A. Peters (New York: Wiley and Sons, 2018).

39. For instance, Thornhill and Palmer, *A Natural History of Rape*; Ghiglieri, *The Dark Side of Man*.

40. David Buss, *The Murderer Next Door: Why the Mind Is Designed to Kill* (New York: Penguin Press, 2005); Ghiglieri, *The Dark Side of Man*; Smith, *The Most Dangerous Animal*; Thornhill and Palmer, *A Natural History of Rape*; Wrangham and Peterson, *Demonic Males*.

41. See Douglas P. Fry, "Anthropology, War, and Peace: Hobbesian Beliefs within Science, Scholarship, and Society," in *Dangerous Liaisons*, eds. Laura McNamara and Robert Rubinstein (Santa Fe, NM: School for Advanced Research Press, 2011); Sahlins, *The Western Illusion*.

42. Dawkins, *The Selfish Gene*, 1989 edition, 44.

43. Dawkins, *The Selfish Gene*, 1989 edition, 128.

44. Dawkins, *The Selfish Gene*, 1989 edition, 2.

45. Especially in his revised 1989 edition of *The Selfish Gene*, Dawkins in some passages says he does not impute purpose to genes, and only writes of purpose and motivation as metaphors. But what he actually writes again and again contradicts this. For example, he states that genes "instruct" us so that we are "genetically programmed" (p. 2), that genes "cooperate" (p. 45), that parents behave in ways dictated by their genes (pp. 124–125), that "successful genes" have a "long reach" (chapter 13)—statements that impute will and agency to genes.

46. David Loye, *Darwin's Lost Theory* (Pacific Grove, CA: Benjamin Franklin Press, 2007); David Loye, *Rediscovering Darwin: The Rest of Darwin's Theory and Why We Need It Today* (Pacific Grove, CA: Romanes Press, 2018); Charles Darwin, *The Descent of Man* (Princeton, NJ: Princeton University Press, 2010, originally published in 1871), 404, see also 89–90; see also Goldschmidt, *The Bridge to Humanity*.

47. Dobzhansky used the term *transcend* to mean "to go beyond the limits of, or to surpass the ordinary, accustomed, previously utilized or well-trodden possibilities of a system," Theodosius Dobzhansky, *The Biology of Ultimate Concern* (New York: Meridian, 1969), 44.

48. John O'Manique, *The Origins of Justice: The Evolution of Morality, Human Rights, and Law* (Philadelphia: University of Pennsylvania Press, 2003).

49. Dobzhansky quoted in David L. Sills and Robert King Merton, *International Encyclopedia of the Social Sciences* (New York: Macmillan, 1968), 236.

50. Krzysztof Wodiczko, personal communication, March 2015.

51. Karen Cantor and Camilla Kjaerilff, *The Danish Solution* (Singing Wolf Documentaries, 2010), http://www.snagfilms.com/films/title/the_danish_solution.

52. Frans de Waal, *The Age of Empathy: Nature's Lessons for a Kinder Society* (New York: Broadway, 2009); Steven Pinker, *The Better Angels of Our Nature: Why Violence Has Declined* (New York: Viking, 2011); Sarah B. Hrdy, *Mothers and Others: The Evolutionary Origins of Mutual Understanding* (Cambridge, MA: Harvard University Press, 2009); James Rilling, "The Neurobiology of Cooperation and Altruism," in *Origins of Altruism and Cooperation*, eds. Robert W. Sussman and C. Robert Cloninger (New York: Springer, 2011); Barak Morgan et al. "Human Biological Development and Peace: Genes, Brains, Safety, and Justice," in *Pathways to Peace: The Transformative Power of Children and Families*, eds. James Leckman, Catherine Panter-Brick, and Rima Salah (Cambridge, MA: MIT Press, 2014); Douglas P. Fry, "Life without War," *Science* 336 (2012): 879–884, doi: 10.1126/science.1217987.

53. Haidt, *The Righteous Mind*; Pinker, *The Better Angels of Our Nature*.

54. Steven Pinker, *The Blank Slate: The Modern Denial of Human Nature* (New York: Viking, 2002), 329.

55. Pinker, *The Better Angels of Our Nature*. Pinker also claimed that violence is much greater among our early ancestors, but the data he relied on are not sound (see Douglas P. Fry, ed., *War, Peace, and Human Nature: Convergence of Evolutionary and Cultural Views* (New York: Oxford University Press, 2013).

56. Pinker, *The Better Angels of Our Nature*, xxi.

57. Thomas S. Kuhn, *The Structure of Scientific Revolutions* (Chicago: University of Chicago Press, 1970). Kuhn noted that instead of being a linear process, the evolution of knowledge tends to come in bursts of clarity, which occur in response to *anomalies*—findings that cannot be explained by the current set of assumptions and provide irreconcilable evidence that the existing paradigm no longer works; see Fry, "Life Without War"; Douglas P. Fry, "Cooperation for Survival: Creating a Global Peace System," in *War, Peace, and Human Nature: Convergence of Evolutionary and Cultural Views*, ed. Douglas P. Fry (New York: Oxford University Press, 2013) enumerates some of the evidence favoring a new perspective on human nature wherein the behavioral defaults would seem to reflect avoidance and restraint in the use of serious aggression, cooperation, helping, caring, empathy, and other types of prosocial behavior. This view differs somewhat from Pinker's *Better Angeles of Our Nature* thesis because Pinker, while recognizing "better angels" such as empathy and self-control, nonetheless views humans as inherently violent in a state of nature.

58. Douglas P. Fry, *War, Peace, and Human Nature: Convergence of Evolutionary and Cultural Views* (New York: Oxford University Press, 2013), 11.

59. R. Brian Ferguson, "The Prehistory of War and Peace in Europe and the Near East," in *War, Peace, and Human Nature: Convergence of Evolutionary and Cultural Views*, ed. Douglas P. Fry (New York: Oxford University Press, 2013); Jonathan Haas, "War,"

in *Encyclopedia of Cultural Anthropology, Volume 4*, eds. David Levinson and Melvin Ember (New York: Henry Holt and Company, 1996); Jonathan Haas, "The Origins of War and Ethnic Violence," in *Ancient Warfare: Archaeological Perspectives*, eds. J. Carman and A. Harding (Gloucestershire, UK: Sutton Publishing, 1999); Jonathan Haas, "Warfare and the Evolution of Culture," in *Archaeology at the Millennium: A Sourcebook*, eds. G. Feinman and T. D. Price (New York: Kluwer Academic/Plenum, 2001); Donald Henry, "Preagricultural Sedentism: The Natufian Example," in *Prehistoric Hunter-Gatherers: The Emergence of Cultural Complexity*, eds. T. Price and J. Brown (New York: Academic Press, 1985); Raymond Kelly, *Warless Societies and the Origin of War* (Ann Arbor: University of Michigan Press, 2000); Bruce Knauft, "Violence and Sociality in Human Evolution," *Current Anthropology* 32 (1991): 391–428, doi: 10.1086/203975.

60. Ferguson, "The Prehistory of War and Peace."

61. Ferguson, "The Prehistory of War and Peace," 229.

62. James Mellaart, *Çatal Hüyük* (New York: McGraw Hill, 1967).

63. Ian Hodder, "Women and Men at Çatalhöyük," *Scientific American* 290 (2004): 77–83, doi: 10.1038/scientificamerican0104-76.

64. See, e.g., Nikolas Platon, *Crete* (Geneva: Nagel Publishers, 1966); Marija Gimbutas, *The Goddesses and Gods of Old Europe* (Berkeley: University of California Press, 1982); Riane Eisler, *The Chalice and the Blade: Our History, Our Future* (San Francisco: Harper & Row, 1987); Nannos Marinatos, *Minoan Religion: Ritual, Image, and Symbol* (Columbia, SC: University of South Carolina Press). These findings are still sometimes disputed, despite the evidence of lack of fortifications in the island's various city states and an art that does not idealize war or warriors and, in addition to its celebration of nature, features powerful women (such as the "procession fresco" where a priestess blesses the priests bringing her gifts of fruit and wine). For example, Barry Molloy, who starts his article with the statement that warfare is inherent in humans because of "socio-biological instincts such as acquisition of a mate or status" (91), claims that Minoan Crete was a martial society, conflating the later Mycenaean period (ruled by a warrior aristocracy in Crete as well as on the Greek mainland) with the Minoan period, and ignoring all evidence of peace rather than warfare during that earlier time. (Barry P.C. Molloy, "Martial Minoans? War as a Social Process, Practice, and Event in Bronze Age Crete," *Annual of the British School at Athens*, 107 (2012): 87–142, doi: 10.1017/S0068245412000044.

65. de Waal, *The Age of Empathy*. See also Frans de Waal, *Good Natured: The Origins of Right and Wrong in Humans and Other Animals* (Cambridge, MA: Harvard University Press, 1996); Jaak Panksepp, *Affective Neuroscience: The Foundations of Human and Animal Emotions* (New York: Oxford University Press, 1998); James K. Rilling, "Neuroscientific Approaches and Applications within Anthropology," *Yearbook of Physical Anthropology* 51 (2008): 2–32, doi: 10.1002/ajpa.20947; James K. Rilling et al., "Neural Correlates of Social Cooperation and Non-Cooperation as a Function of Psychopathy," *Biological Psychiatry* 61 (2007): 1260–1271, doi: 10.1016/j.biopsych.2006.07.021; Rilling, "The Neurobiology of Cooperation and Altruism," 2011.

66. See, e.g., Hrdy, *Mothers and Others*.

67. Marco Dond, Francesca Simion, and Giovanna Caltran, "Can Newborns Discriminate between Their Own Cry and the Cry of Another Newborn Infant?" *Developmental Psychology* 35 (1999): 418–426, doi: 10.1037/0012-1649.35.2.418. These and other findings contradict the influential view of Jean Piaget, that children could not feel empathy until around age 7 or 8 when he believed they achieve cognitive abilities that allow seeing things from another person's perspective.

68. For a good summary of some of these studies, see Daniel Goleman, "Researchers Trace Empathy's Roots to Infancy," *New York Times Archives* 1989, http://www.nytimes.com/1989/03/28/science/researchers-trace-empathy-s-roots-to-infancy.html?pagewanted=all&src=pm.

69. Felix Warneken and Michael Tomasello, "Altruistic Helping in Human Infants and Young Chimpanzees," *Science* 311 (2006): 1301–1303, doi: 10.1126/science.1121448.

70. See, e.g., William T. Harbaugh, Ulrich Mayr, and Daniel Burghart, "Neural Responses to Taxation and Voluntary Giving Reveals Motives for Charitable Donations." *Science* 316 (2007): 1622–1625, doi: 10.1126/science.1140738.

71. Frans B. M. de Waal, Kristin Leimgruber, and Amanda R. Greenberg, "Giving Is Self-Rewarding for Monkeys," *Proceedings of the National Academy of Sciences (PNAS)* 105 (2008): 13685–13689, doi: 10.1073/pnas.0807060105; Marc Bekoff and Jessica Pierce, *Wild Justice: The Moral Lives of Animals* (Chicago: University of Chicago Press, 2009).

72. Rilling, "The Neurobiology of Cooperation and Altruism."

73. James K. Rilling et al., "Opposing BOLD Responses to Reciprocated and Unreciprocated Altruism in Putative Reward Pathways." *NeuroReport* 15 (2004): 1–5.

74. See, e.g., James K. Rilling et al., "A Neural Basis for Social Cooperation." *Neuron* 35 (2002): 395–405, doi: 10.1016/S0896-6273(02)00755-9; and Rilling, "The Neurobiology of Cooperation and Altruism,"

75. See, e.g., C. Sue Carter, "The Chemistry of Child Neglect: Do Oxytocin and Vasopressin Mediate the Effects of Early Experience?" *Proceedings of the National Academy of Sciences (PNAS)* 102 (2005): 18247–18248, doi: 10.1073/pnas.0509376102; Keverne, "Epigenetics"; and Kristin Valentino, Michelle Comas, and Amy K. Nuttall, "Child Maltreatment and Early Mother-Child Interactions," in *Ancestral Landscapes in Human Evolution*, eds. Darcia Narvaez et al. (New York: Oxford University Press, 2014).

76. Julie B. Kaplow and Cathy Spatz Widom, "Age of Onset of Child Maltreatment Predicts Long-Term Mental Health Outcomes." *Journal of Abnormal Psychology* 116 (2007): 176–187, doi: 10.1037/0021-843X.116.1.176.

77. A. H. Goodman and T. L. Leatherman, *Building a New Biocultural Synthesis: Political-Economic Perspectives on Human Biology* (Ann Arbor: University of Michigan Press, 1998); Charles Super and Sara Harkness, "The Developmental Niche: A Conceptualization at the Interface of Child and Culture," *International Journal of Behavioral Development* 9 (1986): 545–569, doi: 10.1177/016502548600900409; Carol M. Worthman, "The Ecology of Human Development: Evolving Models for Cultural Psychology," *Journal of Cross-Cultural Psychology* 41 (2010): 546–562,

doi: 10.1177/0022022110362627; Sara Stinson, B. Bogin, R. Huss-Ashmore, and D. O'Rourke, eds., *Human Biology: An Evolutionary and Biocultural Perspective* (New York: Wiley-Liss, 2000).

78. Rilling, "Neuroscientific Approaches and Applications within Anthropology"; Sapolsky, *Behave*; C. Sue Carter and Stephen W. Porges, "Peptide Pathways to Peace," in *Pathways to Peace: The Transformative Power of Children and Families*, eds. James F. Leckman, Catherine Panter-Brick, and Rima Salah (Cambridge, MA: MIT Press, 2014); Keverne, "Epigenetics"; Morgan et al., "Human Biological Development"; Panksepp, *Affective Neuroscience*.

79. Bruce Perry, "Childhood Experience and the Expression of Genetic Potential." *Brain and Mind* 3 (2002): 79–100, doi: 10.1023/A:1016557824657. See also Bruce Perry et al., "Childhood Trauma, The Neurobiology of Adaptation, and 'Use-Dependent' Development of the Brain: How 'States' Become 'Traits,'" *Infant Mental Health Journal* 16 (1995): 271–291, doi: 10.1002/1097-0355(199524).

80. Mark Kurlansky, *Nonviolence: The History of a Dangerous Idea* (New York: Modern Library, 2008).

81. Agustin Fuentes, "Cooperation, Conflict, and Niche Construction in the Genus *Homo*," in *War, Peace, and Human Nature: Convergence of Evolutionary and Cultural Views*, ed. Douglas P. Fry (New York: Oxford University Press, 2013). Fuentes explains that niche construction is "the building and destroying of niches by organisms *and* the synergistic interaction between organisms and environments," 80, emphasis in original.

3

Love, the Brain, and Becoming Human

Michelangelo's magnificent *Pieta* is one of our most moving works of art because it so powerfully expresses the love of a mother for her child. We are deeply affected by love stories such as *Romeo and Juliet* and by great humanitarians who dedicate their lives to caring for others. All these expressions of love touch something inside us that developed in the course of evolution: our human need and capacity for love.

Spiritual seers have long said that love is the key to fulfillment, contentment, and joy. Most of us have experienced these feelings when we love and are loved.

So it is hardly news that love makes us feel good. What *is* news is that the feelings of well-being and pleasure we associate with love are part of human biology. Love triggers neurochemical messages of well-being and pleasure. Our bodies give us these rewards when we are loved and when we love others, whether it is a child, a lover, a parent, a friend, or even a pet.

As neuroscientists Steven Quartz and Terrence Sejnowski note, brain studies support the proposition that the bonds of love, whether between parent and child, lovers, or close friends, may all have a common biological root, activating neurochemicals that make us feel good.[1] Like other human capacities, such as consciousness, learning, and creativity, love has a long and fascinating evolutionary history. Indeed, as we will explore in this chapter, the evolution of love appears to be integral to the development of our human brain.

Evolutionary Trends

Many evolutionary developments seen in humans are, to varying degrees, found in other species. Traits such as behavioral plasticity, dependence on learning, and consequently significant cultural variation, as well as capacities for cooperation, prosociality, creativity, inventiveness, self-awareness, and consciousness, have precursors in mammals and non-human primates.[2] There is evidence of reasoning and problem-solving among chimpanzees, crows, and elephants. All three species can figure out complex ways of accessing food, and elephants are noted for their great memory.[3] As for culture, monkeys and apes have rudimentary cultures that are shared by group members, learned, and transmitted across generations.[4]

These evolutionary trends toward behavioral flexibility, innovation, learning, and cultural transmission are dramatically illustrated by the classic story of Imo, a teenage Japanese macaque who, out of the blue, made innovative breakthroughs in her troop's feeding practices. Japanese scientists provisioned the macaques with yams to lure them out of the dense forest on the island of Koshima and better observe their behavior. The monkeys would come to the beach where the yams were placed, brush off the sand, and eat. One day, Imo began dipping the yams in a tide-pool to wash off the sand. When scientists put out wheat grains on the beach, Imo was inventive again. She discovered that wheat grains float and sand grains sink, and began to separate wheat grains from sand by dropping them in the water.

So the capacity for behavioral flexibility and creative innovation clearly exists in Japanese macaques and other primate species. Moreover, within a few years almost every monkey in Imo's troop had adopted the new techniques that she introduced, illustrating that behavior can be transmitted through learning. The case of Imo also demonstrates that primates can respond proactively, not merely reactively, to their environments.[5]

But the appearance of humans ushers in a new level of capacities, needs, and motivations. We create new environments, both physical and cultural. We create ideas, cultures, and technologies that to a significant extent feed back to mold human relations and human development.

These human activities constitute a form of niche construction, in the words of biologists F. John Odling-Smee and colleagues, "whereby organisms, through their activities and choices, modify their own and each other's niches."[6] Odling-Smee and his colleagues explain that an ecological niche is the position that a given species occupies in the environment, including all physical and biological interactions and factors. They further note that "by transforming natural selection pressures, niche construction generates feedback in evolution, on a scale hitherto underestimated, and in a manner that alters the evolutionary dynamic."[7]

This is not to say that members of nonhuman species do not also modify their environments and have ideas, cultures, or technologies. But humans engage in niche construction more than any other species, as they interact with and alter the biotic and abiotic elements of the environments. And our technologies are enormously more complex and powerful than the simple tools used, for example, by crows, monkeys, and apes.[8]

In addition, there are significant features of human cultures that are absolutely unique. Mozart's music, Shakespeare's plays, Hildegard von Bingen's mysticism, Elizabeth Cady Stanton's passion for women's rights, and Gandhi's crusade for freedom and peace are different from anything we see in other species. These differences do not fit into the propositions discussed in the previous chapter that emphasize evolutionary selfishness.

Of course, humans are not immune to the forces of natural selection. But there would not be an Albert Schweitzer or Mother Teresa devoting their lives to caring for total strangers if caring and love were just a tightly regulated outcome of purely selfish genes. Nor does a ruthless-gene view of the world explain Nelson Mandela's reaching out in friendship and forgiveness to the people who oppressed black South Africans. These are famous persons, but their actions are not exceptional: from societies around the globe come daily examples of kindness and assistance given to strangers as well as acts of forgiveness and reconciliation.[9] The nomadic pastoral Gabra people of East Africa have a saying, for instance, that "A poor man shames us all," through which they express the moral responsibility in their society to help those in need.[10]

Or in the words of U2's Bono, "When I came here [to Africa], and visited hospitals with thousands of people camping outside for treatment, for drugs that were not available, I wanted to do what I could to make the madness stop. Watching lives implode in front of your eyes for no reason. Children in their mother's arms go into that awful silence. And looking to the side and seeing the health workers and seeing the rage inside of them. I just thought: I'll do what I can."[11]

Reductionist propositions cannot explain why so many of us spontaneously feel concern for people living on the other side of the world. Nor do they explain why so many people display loving kindness to complete strangers. To understand these humane feelings and actions requires a fresh look at how they evolved.

The Evolution of Caring and Love

The feelings, motivations, and behaviors we call love have deep evolutionary roots. Indeed, these roots go back millions of years before our species emerged. Most reptiles lay their eggs and leave the next generation to hatch on their own. Some reptiles, such as the rainbow lizard, have been observed to eat their offspring instead of caring for them, a fate that can befall any hatchling that doesn't run off and hide.[12] But when it comes to mammals, the picture changes dramatically because immature mammals require care to survive.[13]

Mammalian mothers actively care for their offspring, sometimes risking their lives to protect them. Mother ground squirrels make alarm calls to warn their brood of an approaching hawk, and mother bears are renowned for protecting their cubs from danger.[14] North American black bears, for instance, receive maternal care and protection for 18 months as they learn a plethora of skills necessary for their survival.[15] A dramatic example of maternal protection involves an alley cat named Scarlett who suffered severe burns as she ran repeatedly into a burning building until she had retrieved her entire litter from the flames.

The evolution of mammalian nurturing represents a phylogenetic shift in the direction of care and empathy.[16] In some species, such as owl monkeys, marmosets, and tamarins, fathers also engage in empathic caring.[17] In other species, such as elephants, caring and empathy extend to other members of the herd. As Riane was privileged to observe in Africa, when danger threatens, adult elephants form a protective circle around the young.

Caring can even extend to other species, like when dogs or dolphins save human lives, occasionally at the cost of their own. A father swimming with three teenage girls encountered a great white shark. He told the press afterward that dolphins " 'started to herd us up, they pushed all four of us together by doing tight circles around us. . . . [The shark] was only about two metres away from me, the water was crystal clear, and it was as clear as the nose on my face,' he said. At that point, he realised that the dolphins 'had corralled us up to protect us.' "[18] Another dramatic example of interspecies protective behavior comes from a female gorilla who in 1996 cradled an injured little boy who had fallen into the gorilla enclosure at the Brookfield Zoo in Chicago and then brought him safely to the zookeepers.[19]

When it comes to humans, caring is integral to human survival. Human infants require much longer, sustained, and intense care than the young of other species. Consequently, the capacity for sustained nurturing evolved as a key part of the human behavioral repertoire.[20]

The origins of our care-rewarding neurochemistry—and the importance of love in human relations—can thus be explained in terms of natural selection.[21] Neuroscientist Lucy R. Brown, anthropologist Helen Fisher, and psychologist Arthur Aron have proposed that the neural circuitry supporting romantic love probably evolved to motivate couples to remain together and provide care for their young during their offspring's most vulnerable years.[22] But parental and romantic love are only two aspects of love. Once the capacity for loving appeared on the evolutionary scene, love became a feature in relationships beyond those directly connected with reproduction.[23]

As Brown put it, love seems to be a motivational drive in itself, not unlike the drive for food, sleep, and sex.[24] Humans express love not only for their children but also for unrelated persons. People who adopt children, including those of another race or nationality, typically love, protect, and nurture them as devotedly as do biological parents. And thousands of organizations all over the globe extend humanitarian assistance to people in need, even to people traditionally considered enemies.

These caring emotions and behaviors once again contradict a strictly selfish gene view of the world. Since the beneficiaries of the care are not genetically related to those providing it or in a position to reciprocate, assistance to those in need, along with the associated compassionate feelings, can be explained instead as a function of motivational dynamics that arose because natural selection favored their development.[25]

The striving for self-preservation and reproduction certainly plays an important part in human needs and motivations. However, a selfish gene perspective can explain neither humanitarian acts directed at strangers nor our powerful yearning for beauty, meaning, and love. Nor can it account for faith in a loving deity or in the belief that God is love.[26] Such spiritual extensions of love transcend reductionist genetic explanations.

The fact that humans love and care for their pets also contradicts a selfish gene view of the world.[27] Identification with and concern for wildlife and a belief that all life is interconnected—an idea at the core of some indigenous belief systems as well as the contemporary ecological movement—are further extensions of the human impulses toward empathy, love, and caring.

So while the original selective pressure for love likely came from the need to care for dependent young and to provide them with the protection and nurturance they need to survive, over the course of human evolution love became a motivation in its own right. It became a *new* dynamic that must be taken into account in the study of human possibilities. Indeed, we go further: love is a dynamic that helps *explain* the emergence of humanity in both meanings of the word.

Love and the Emergence of Humanity

Could the evolution of caring, culminating in the deep emotion we call love, have been a prerequisite for our species' capacities for well-developed intelligence, symbolic thinking, learning, communication, consciousness, caring, planning, creativity, and choice? We hypothesize that this is the case and propose that once love arrived on the evolutionary stage, it developed its own dynamics, bringing new needs, capacities, and motivations.

The development of the capacities that make us uniquely human required a much larger, more complex brain.[28] This larger brain required a larger cranium, which in turn necessitated the evolution of a larger birth canal. But the human brain continues to develop after birth, particularly during the first years, and then extending into a person's early 20s.[29] Especially during the earliest years of life, children require love, not just rote caring, if they are to adequately develop.[30] We agree with neuropsychologist Ruth Feldman, who places emphasis on "the primary role of love as a central motivating force of developmental progress as a critical ingredient in the survival, safety, and well-being of the young." Adults must be motivated to respond to the needs of the young, and hence a neurochemical reward system evolved to provide pleasure for engaging in loving care.[31]

Thus, the emergence of our species would not have been possible without the emergence of caring and love.[32] This does not mean that love was the *cause* of the appearance of humanity. But it was a critical feature in human evolution. As neuroscientist Sue Carter notes, "Even the resilient and highly flexible human infant needs some social predictability and support to prosper."[33] They need love.

Moreover, love goes along with and reflects new human capacities, needs, motivations, and possibilities. One such development was greater intelligence, and with it, our species' enormous capacity for learning. Still another was our capacity for language and other types of symbolic communication that play key roles in cooperation for mutual benefit. Also crucial were our capacities for consciousness, creativity, planning, and choice. All these developments relate to the evolution of our larger and more complex brain and were facilitated by the evolution of extended caring, and from there, love.[34]

As neuroscientist Paul MacLean points out, the large and complex human brain developed over a long evolutionary process.[35] The most ancient parts of our central nervous system are the spinal cord, hindbrain, and midbrain and their surroundings. This ancient brain system is present in fish and amphibians and contains the basic mechanisms for physical survival and reproduction, including regulation of breathing and blood circulation. With the evolutionary appearance of reptiles, the forebrain and the lower layer of what is called the limbic system, the seat of emotions, evolved. With mammals, we find an expansion of the limbic system and a well-developed neocortex, the seat of more advanced cognition.[36]

The neocortex, literally the "new bark" since it covers much of the brain, includes the occipital, parietal, temporal, and frontal lobes. The neocortex began to emerge tens of millions of years ago. But its development accelerated only a few million years ago, when the human evolutionary lineage separated from other apes.[37]

The prefrontal cortex, evolutionarily speaking, is the youngest brain structure. It sits directly behind the forehead and through its intricate network of connections to other parts of the brain and body is pivotal for planned action, moral reasoning, and social development.[38]

Along with each of these evolutionary changes in the brain came a new range of capacities. In turn, selection pressures favoring capacities for learning, language and symbolic communication, social intelligence, creativity, and so forth may have spurred further changes in brain size and functioning.

Larger brains resulted in neotenous, dependent young in need of greater care. And in this process, love became a central feature in what it means to be human.

Love and the Human Brain

Since many of the qualities that distinguish us as humans were made possible by our larger, more complex brains, we are proposing that the evolution of this larger, more complex brain may not have been possible were it not for the evolutionary movement toward nurturing love in a synergetic evolutionary movement toward a brain capable of other well-developed human characteristics. Indeed, we know that the prefrontal cortex facilitates empathic caring because empathy and moral judgment are severely impaired when it is injured.[39]

A related evolutionary development is that humans are readily able to reflect on their feelings, beliefs, motivations, and actions, aspects of what neuroscientist Antonio Damasio calls expanded consciousness.[40] Although expanded consciousness is found in some nonhuman primates and other mammals in rudimentary form, it is most developed in humans.

Expanded consciousness is a necessary precursor for language, art, and other forms of symbolic expression and communication.[41] It makes possible a sense of past, present, and future, and thus the capacity to make long-range plans.[42] It is fundamental to developing a sense of morality and internalizing right and wrong. And it can facilitate the expansion of love to people who are not close relatives.

Expanded consciousness is also a major factor in conscious choices. Humans, more than any other species, have the capacity for reflecting on options and deciding what course to take. And in humans, choices are largely a function of learning.

Certainly, many animals, from elephants and dolphins to monkeys and apes, are adept learners, as illustrated by Imo's macaque troop emulating her food-cleaning discoveries. But in human evolution, learning became the primary mechanism both for acquiring novel behaviors and for changing existing ones. Humans learn across the life span, particularly when we are young, from parents, peers, and other people; at home, in school, within the community, and at ceremonial events; from oral tradition, the mass media, study, and imitation.

The complexity of the human brain also makes possible our great capacities for innovation and creativity, which in turn have led to an enormous range of material technologies and diverse cultural beliefs and practices. However, as the human urge to explore and create demonstrates, we do not just innovate and create in response to new environmental stimuli. We actively search for and initiate change. We do this almost from the moment we are born, as anyone who has watched a baby actively try to change its environment can attest.

Humans also imagine the future, make plans, and act on their plans. Neuroscientist Karl Pribram experimentally confirmed that this "future sense orientation" also can be found in monkeys, so it is probably connected to Imo having been able to imagine more effective ways of cleaning sand off her food. Pribram found that when monkeys were trained to press different bars depending on whether they saw circles or stripes, their brain waves indicated *intention* to act, not just action.[43]

Pribram further found that our well-developed and complex human cortex connects to evolutionarily older neural structures to guide behavior through what he called feed-forward loops, affecting both cognition and emotion.[44] Other scientists have found that when this feed-forward connection is severed in lobotomized individuals, their capacity for self-regulation and long-range planning is impaired. Additionally, these individuals lose their capacity for empathy and caring.

Not only that—and this is extremely significant for how the cultural environments we create shape our brains—empathy, the capacity to care, self-regulation, and long-range planning can also be compromised in individuals who were abused in childhood. In other words, empathy, caring, self-regulation, and planning are dramatically affected by a *lack of love*.[45]

Human Development and Love

Joan L. Luby and her colleagues showed that a child provided with good parental nurturing, even under otherwise stressful conditions, can develop a brain with a larger hippocampus—a key brain structure for learning, memory, and response to stress.[46] So the quality of nurturance directly affects the structure of the brain.[47]

Rats also develop better if they are given loving care. Rat pups of attentive mothers, those who spent more time licking and grooming their offspring, performed much better on tests for spatial learning and memory and were less fearful than pups whose mothers were less attentive. The benefits, which not only were obvious at a young age but also endured throughout life, were clearly linked to attentive maternal care: when pups born to *non*-nurturing mothers were raised by highly attentive mothers, they were indistinguishable from offspring born to highly attentive mothers.[48]

As Michael Meaney, founder of this McGill University rat research project, observed, that loving care sets off a chain of biochemical reactions that stimulate brain and memory development. A lot of early loving stimulates brain development. So also does high-quality rat daycare. Meany notes that these results for rats parallel findings that children from emotionally and intellectually deprived homes benefit greatly from high-quality infant care programs.[49]

Like seedlings hungry for sunshine, children will reach out across amazing distances and barriers to bring love into their lives. They can be amazingly resilient in harsh environments as long as the hope and promise of love exists. But without this hope, children face an uphill struggle and all too often face lifelong cognitive and emotional problems. Even if they do not have difficulty in forming or maintaining relationships, their relationships often replicate the damaging patterns of their childhood: they tend to experience greater difficulties in expressing and addressing their emotional needs than people who had more opportunity in early life to learn productive emotional skills. They also often have great difficulty in impulse regulation, including regulation of violent impulses. In sum, lack of love in childhood tends to limit a person's options for cognitive skill and emotional expression later in life.

The serious effects of lack of love in infancy and childhood have been extensively documented.[50] For instance, during the 1980s, the Romanian dictator Nicolas Ceausescu prohibited family planning. He actually required women to undergo monthly gynecological examinations to prove that they were not using birth control. Even under these circumstances, most parents took care of their children. But thousands of unwanted children were abandoned by parents who could not, or would not, raise them. Many of these children ended up in orphanages staffed by overworked, underpaid attendants who had little time or inclination to give them emotional comfort and caring.

Frequently these children died, but many of the survivors, including those later adopted by compassionate families, suffered lifelong developmental damage. Indeed, measures of frontal-occipital circumference, a reasonable estimate of brain size, were abnormally low in many of these orphans.[51]

There are also heartbreaking stories from Chinese orphanages, where girls abandoned by parents because males were considered more valuable withered away and died from a lack of caring attention. Again, even when these children were adopted by loving parents, they often suffered lasting developmental damage from their early lack of loving care.[52]

As Bruce Perry writes, "when early life neglect is characterized by decreased sensory input (e.g., relative poverty of words, touch and social interactions) there will be a similar effect on human brain growth as in other mammalian species."[53] Perry found that the regions of the cortex and limbic system responsible for emotions, including love, are 20 to 30 percent smaller in the brains of severely abused or neglected children.[54] In other words, brain sections responsible for emotions, including love, may be notably smaller in children who do not receive love and other stimuli needed for full human development.

There are hopeful indications that with intensive professional help, at least in some cases, part of this damage can be reversed. But it takes years of skilled intervention and care and massive investment of public resources, which are not often allocated to these ends. Significantly, as Dave Ziegler, a pioneering psychologist who developed such a residential care program, emphasizes, the key to these efforts is love.[55]

In light of these kinds of findings, the evolutionary function of love assumes an even larger meaning that takes us beyond *survival* to the critical matter of human *development*. Children need *loving environments* in order to fully develop their human capacities for love, consciousness, creativity, planning, and choice.

Love, Cultural Biases, and Scientific Findings

We have been looking at severe cases of love deprivation. But to varying degrees, domination cultures and subcultures distort and inhibit our human capacity to express love in healthy and caring ways. Parents in such cultures or subcultures often learn to say, "I am hitting you because I love you," and men socialized for a "masculinity" of domination are said to hit women "out of love."

Women, too, are socialized to accept all this in domination systems. For instance, a South American Yanomamö woman, upon comparing with another wife the injuries inflicted on them by their husbands, concluded that her companion's husband must truly care for her "since he has beaten her on the head so frequently!"[56]

These distortions of our human need and capacity for love perpetuate cycles of brutality and violence that, as we have seen, are sometimes blamed on evolutionary imperatives or other supposedly inevitable aspects of human nature in keeping with the cultural belief that humans are innately flawed. Indeed, in contrast to the evolutionary view of love we have been proposing, a number of sociobiologists claim that the motivation for loving behaviors is actually selfishness.[57]

Robert Trivers, who introduced the concept of reciprocal altruism, defines selfishness as "an act benefitting the actor at a cost to someone else," and altruism as "an act that benefits another organism at a cost to the actor."[58] This evolutionary perspective tars any behaviors truly motivated by empathy and concern for others as evolutionary losses. It makes genuine altruism appear unnatural at the same time that selfishness is crowned as the logical outcome of natural selection. While this may not be Trivers' intent, as evolutionary theorist David Loye notes, this view conveys as the supposedly harsh reality that evolution justifies unscrupulous, even ruthless behavior.[59]

The fact that the sociobiological and evolutionary psychological vocabulary borrows heavily from the language of neo-liberal or trickle-down capitalist economists also is revealing. Everything is just a matter of gains or losses. Catch phrases such as parental investment semantically convey that love is no more than a self-interested investment made for the evolutionary payoff of reproductive success.

The beliefs underlying these views of human nature and motivation also reflect the ranking of traditional masculine traits and behaviors over stereotypically feminine traits and behaviors. In these assertions, the love and empathy associated traditionally with women are of little intrinsic worth. What really matters is "masculine" strength and prowess. This gender-biased narrative is also reflected in heroic epics wherein a masculine protagonist trounces his opponents and thereby wins a mate.

The related claim that primate females prefer the most aggressive males is another sociobiological motif that deserves to be questioned. As primatologists such as Barbara Smuts have observed, females often chose to mate with males with whom they feel safe and who help them care for their offspring, *not* with the dominant male.[60]

Turning to humans, here, too, the evidence is too contradictory to support the proposition that women prefer aggressive men. Anthropologist Patricia Draper, for example, explains how the Ju/'hoansi of the African Kalahari are uncomfortable around men with violent tempers, and the much reported assertion that Yanomamö killers have more wives and offspring than nonkillers has been thoroughly debunked and thus cannot lend support to the notion that women prefer killers.[61]

Nonetheless, the claim that male aggressiveness is natural for primates, and hence humans, is hard to dislodge—even though the degree of dominance reflected in nonhuman primate species ranges from nonexistent to unmistakable. On the low end of the aggressiveness scale, muriqui monkeys of South America are known for their "exceptionally low rates of agonistic interactions" and stumptail macaques are relatively good-natured.[62] At the other extreme, chimpanzees sometimes gang up on lone individuals from other groups and viciously kill them.[63]

Yet even here we must be cautious in our conclusions about chimpanzees. As Jane Goodall points out, "It is easy to get the impression that chimpanzees are more aggressive than they really are. In actuality, peaceful interactions are far more frequent that aggressive ones; mild threatening gestures are more common than vigorous ones; threats per se occur much more often than fights; and serious wounding fights are very rare compared to brief, relatively mild ones."[64]

Sex, Caring, and Bonobos

This takes us to an important primate species that, unlike chimpanzees, rarely figures in the scientific literature: the bonobos. Indigenous to the tropical forests of the Democratic Republic of the Congo, bonobos are as closely related to humans as are chimpanzees. But unlike chimpanzees, bonobos do *not* have a male-dominated social structure and their social relations are much more geared toward sharing and caring. And while the chimpanzee is often invoked in explaining human behavior, including sexual behavior, actually bonobo sexuality is much closer to human sexuality than that of the chimpanzee.

Unlike other primates, female bonobos are sexually active most of the year. Their genitals, like those of human females, rotate forward, making it possible for them to copulate face-to-face. As primatologist Frans de Waal notes, penis lengths in bonobo males, in contrast to other apes, even "surpass those of the human male." And, as is the case with humans, bonobo sexuality is often focused on pleasure, not just reproduction.

A notable feature of bonobos is that sharing sexual pleasure is, in the words of de Waal, often a bonding and even peacemaking ritual. As Takayoshi Kano, a primatologist who studied bonobos in the wild for decades, writes, "most other animals copulate only as an act of reproduction," but for bonobos nonreproductive copulations "diminish hostility and help to estab-lish and maintain intimacy between females and males."[65]

Bonobos are not an aggression-free species. But unlike chimpanzees, bonobos have never been observed engaging in lethal aggression. And whereas chimpanzee males sometimes kill infants, there are no reported instances of infanticide among the bonobos. Primatologist Suehisa Kuroda sums it up for bonobos: "their aggressive behavior is mild."[66]

Even violence between different bonobo groups is extremely rare. "Male bonobos do not form the tight bands that are associated with the male co-operative killing behavior of chimpanzees," explain primatologists Frances White, Michel Waller, and Klaree Boose.[67] "Disputes and social tensions among bonobos are often diffused through sexual behavior."[68] Kano reports observing how when two different bonobo groups met at a feeding site, the tension of the encounter was broken first by sex between a female and male from each group and then when a female engaged in genital rubbing with several females of the other group.[69]

Use of nonreproductive sex by bonobos in what de Waal calls a "peace-making ritual" raises interesting questions about primate—including hominin and human—evolution. It suggests an important evolutionary de-velopment: the use of sex as a means of reinforcing social relations based on the give-and-take of shared pleasure rather than on coercion and fear.

When it comes to caring, bonobos are also, as de Waal writes, "highly empathic." For example, he notes that "As soon as one bonobo has even the smallest injury, he or she will be surrounded by others who come to inspect, lick, or groom."[70]

Moreover, de Waal and Frans Lanting note that there is no evidence that ensuring paternity is an issue for bonobo males.[71] And, as Kano observes, among bonobos "elements of dominance do not enter into sexual activity."[72]

All this directly contradicts the dogma that a male-dominated, chroni-cally violent social organization is inherent in primates as part of our evolu-tionary heritage. But despite this—or probably because of it—until recently bonobos have been generally ignored in the scientific literature.

Most revealing is that the evolutionary psychological literature generally fails to mention the absence of concern about paternity and the absence of male sexual coercion of females among bonobos because these observations contradict their assertions that as a cross-species principle, evolution favors violent competition, including rape, and that male dominance and violence against females are evolutionary adaptations.[73]

Bonobo society is not male-dominated. Females, particularly mothers, play key social roles. Bonobo males do not use sexual coercion against females, and female bonobos form strong social bonds and effectively cooperate to keep male aggression down.

It is also worth pointing out, as primatologists de Waal, Sue Savage-Rumbaugh, and others who have worked closely with bonobos note, that bonobos are in significant respects smarter than chimpanzees, as demonstrated by their superior capacity to learn. The work of primatologist Sue Savage-Rumbaugh teaching bonobos language skills is particularly fascinating. Bonobos such as Kanzi, Panbanisha, and her son Nyota have learned to use a keyboard with English words to communicate in ways that were once thought impossible for primates other than humans.[74]

This leads to the important question of whether the greater mental capacity and greater empathy of bonobos compared to chimpanzees are related to the less stressful, less aggressive, and more partnership-oriented nature of bonobo groups wherein sharing and caring rather than controlling and hurting are socially supported.

Indeed, recent findings show that the brains of bonobos and chimpanzees have developed differently. James Rilling and his colleagues found that brain areas involved in the perception of another's distress, such as the amygdala and anterior insula, are larger in bonobos than in chimpanzees.

Bonobo brains also contain better-developed pathways to control aggressive impulses. Rilling and his colleagues write that, "We suggest that this neural system not only supports increased empathic sensitivity in bonobos, but also behaviors like sex and play that serve to dissipate tension, thereby limiting distress and anxiety to levels conducive with prosocial behavior."[75]

The facts that bonobos in so many ways resemble humans more than chimpanzees and other primates and that their behaviors are based more on bonds of sharing care and pleasure than on domination and violence should be considered in evaluating other aspects of current evolutionary thinking, including prevailing ideas about early human social organization.

As de Waal reflects, "I sometimes try to imagine what would have happened if we'd known the bonobo first and the chimpanzee only later or not at all. The discussion about human evolution might not revolve as much around violence, warfare, and male dominance, but rather around sexuality, empathy, caring, and cooperation."[76]

An Emerging View on Human Evolution

Gradually, an alternative evolutionary perspective has been emerging that provides building blocks for a new view of our species that takes into account the importance of motivations such as caring, curiosity, and creativity, rather than reducing us to puppets of selfish genes. Noting that earlier evolutionary narratives focused on the bonding of men to more effectively hunt and kill, Adrienne Zihlman, Nancy Tanner, and Sally Linton Slocum propose that the first social bonds were actually between mothers and infants and that they were based on sharing and caring, providing the foundation for social bonds later in life.[77] Zihlman, Tanner, and Slocum also shift the focus from strictly "man the hunter" to recognize the important role of "woman the gatherer" in human evolution, a view supported by studies of extant nomadic forager societies showing that most daily calories are derived from the gathering activities primarily performed by women, with protein being supplied largely by the hunting activities of men.[78]

Further challenging the idea that not only bonding but also language first developed from men's need to communicate during hunts, Zihlman, Tanner, and Slocum suggest that this human capacity, which makes possible our complex social networks, also arose out of the caring bonds between mothers and children.[79] Biologist Humberto Maturana also argues that the origins of language are rooted in loving behaviors and introduces the phrase "the biology of love."[80] Similarly, MacLean proposes that language arose in the loving relationship between mother and child.[81]

De Waal identifies empathy, caring, and the drive for peaceful relations as important evolutionary developments that are observable in nonhuman species as well as humans. He locates the evolutionary roots of morality not only in other primates but also in social species more generally, such as elephants and dolphins. "If exploitation of others were all that matters," de Waal observes, "evolution should never have gotten into the empathy business."[82]

Darwin himself wrote of the softer, more stereotypically feminine aspects of evolution, suggesting that mutual aid and love are part of the biological basis for morality in our species. As Loye points out, Darwin referred to love 95 times, to moral sensitivity 92 times, and to selfishness only 12 times (and then in negative terms) in *The Descent of Man*.[83]

John O'Manique also emphasizes that morality has evolutionary roots. He proposes that love and altruism are not dependent on selfish motivations and that the emergence of the human capacity for self-conscious reflection, which includes consciousness of others, is basic to empathy and cooperation.[84]

Like Zihlman and her colleagues, O'Manique views the caring bonds between mothers and children as the evolutionary foundation for morality, and ultimately justice. He, too, recognizes the need for a more gender-balanced evolutionary narrative.

Evidence for this new, more balanced evolutionary story has been accumulating in recent years. For example, archeological finds point to the importance of women in the Paleolithic or Old Stone Age. The majority of stone carvings of this era are of female figurines. And a recent analysis of the handprints sometimes found on the walls of famous cave sanctuaries shows that the majority were female hands.[85]

Dean Snow, the archeologist who made this discovery using analyses of the differing finger formations on female and male hands, notes in an interview that Paleolithic artists may have "signed" their work using stenciled depictions of their own hands. Female and male hands differ, and a study of the handprints indicates that if they are in fact "signatures," then contrary to sex-biased assumptions, most of the artists were women rather than men.[86]

In the early Neolithic, too, female figurines are ubiquitous—until they rather abruptly disappear. Yet even after this cultural shift, female deities were still prominent. For example, the Egyptian Goddess Isis was revered as a dispenser of wisdom, counsel, and justice, and in ancient Sumer the most widely worshipped deity was Inanna, the Goddess of Love.[87]

Going back even further, if we use the recurring patterns visible across ethnographies of nomadic foragers as a frame of reference for gender relations in most of prehistory, then the theme that emerges is one of egalitarianism. In assessing nomadic forager gender relations, Karen Endicott concludes that "rather than assigning all authority in economics, political, or religious matters to one gender or the other, hunter-gatherers tend to leave decision-making about men's work and areas of expertise to men, and about women's work and expertise to women, either as groups or individuals."[88]

The work of psychiatrists and psychologists such as Roberto Assagioli, Kasimierz Dabrowski, Abraham Maslow, and other humanist scholars adds another dimension to this expanded account of human evolution. They make a distinction between what Maslow calls defense or survival motivations and growth or self-actualizing motivations, such as the desire for fairness, the striving for a higher goal, and the need to be loved and to love. Dabrowski considers that the human drive to become attuned to our higher nature constitutes human authenticity. Assagioli focuses on what he calls the superconscious as the source of our higher aspirations and moral drives.[89]

Indeed, a host of clinical psychologists have demonstrated that humans have a whole range of motivations beyond survival and reproductive fitness—from satisfying an intrinsic curiosity to the striving for excellence, and from searching for meaning to yearning for love.[90] Some of these motivations may be helpful for surviving and passing on genes, but with the evolution of a large neocortex and the corresponding expanded behavioral plasticity, the human possibilities multiply. The daring of explorers driven by curiosity, for example, has led both to new discoveries and to their untimely demise. The motivation to excel can be so stressful that it adversely affects health and survival. High achievers often have high blood pressure, heart attacks, and strokes.

Creativity, too, seems to be an intrinsic human motivation, closely tied to self-actualization.[91] Many people report that in the throes of creativity—of writing, painting, composing music, or thinking in innovative ways—they experience a high, a feeling of excitement and well-being that spurs them on.[92]

In addition, and this is one of the central messages of this chapter, love is an intrinsic motivation in its own right. While the origin of the human capacity and need for love can be explained in terms of the longer maturation period required for our survival and development, particularly the development of our brain, once this capacity and need appeared, love became a motivation in many relations beyond those connected with reproduction.[93]

Without love—given and received—our lives would feel diminished in meaning. This deep human need for meaning is another motivation that cannot be explained in terms of the replication of genes, or even by our survival drive.

However, when it comes to the crucial question of whether our needs for meaning and love are met and whether our capacities for creativity and love are expressed or inhibited, as we will see in later chapters, we need to consider whether a society orients to the partnership or domination end of the continuum. But first, as a further backdrop to understanding what is possible for us as humans, the next chapter outlines additional evidence from neuroscience demonstrating the enormous role of experience in gene expression.

Notes

1. Steven R. Quartz and Terrence J. Sejnowski, *Liars, Lovers, and Heroes: What the New Brain Science Reveals about How We Become Who We Are* (New York: William Morrow, 2002). See also C. Sue Carter, "Neuroendocrine Perspectives on Social Attachment and Love," *Psychoneuroendocrinology* 23 (1998): 779–818, doi: 10.1016/S0306-4530(98)00055-9; Ruth Feldman, "Oxytocin and Social Affiliation in Humans," *Hormones and Behavior* 61 (2012): 380–391, doi: 10.1016/j.yhbeh.2012.01.008. The exact neurochemistry and neural pathways involved in these sensations of pleasure are only beginning to be investigated. For example, some studies suggest that the neurochemical reward circuitry for caring behaviors and for addictions that deliver pleasure through endogenous opiates may be the same. See, e.g., Eric B. Keverne, Nicholas D. Martensz, and Bernadette Tuite, "Beta-endorphin Concentrations in Cerebrospinal Fluid of Monkeys Are Influenced by Grooming Relationships," *Psychoneuroendocrinology* 14 (1989): 155–161, doi: 10.1016/0306-4530(89)90065-6; Jaak Panksepp, Eric Nelson, and Marni Bekkedal, "Brain Systems for the Mediation of Social Separation-Distress and Social-Reward Evolutionary Antecedents and Neuropeptide Intermediaries," *Annals of the New York Academy of Sciences* 807 (1997): 78–100, doi: 10.1111/j.1749-6632.1997.tb51914.x; Larry J. Young et al., "Cellular Mechanisms of Social Attachment," *Hormones and Behavior* 40 (2001): 133–138, doi: 10.1006/hbeh.2001.1691.

2. Human brain size increase, development of the neocortex, and certainly also structural changes within the brain are seen by physical anthropologists to be a major trend across the last 6 million years of hominin evolution. Associated with increased brain size and reorganization are a host of traits from increased capacity for speech and symbolic communication to social skills and great behavioral plasticity. See, e.g., Darcia Narvaez, *Neurobiology and the Development of Human Morality: Evolution, Culture, and Wisdom* (New York: Norton, 2014); Mark Dyble et al., "Sex Equality Can Explain the Unique Social Structure of Hunter-Gatherer Bands," *Science* 348 (2015): 796–798, doi: 10.1126/science.aaa5139; Agustin Fuentes, "Cooperation, Conflict, and Niche Construction in the Genus *Homo*," in *War, Peace, and Human Nature: The Convergence of Evolutionary and Cultural Views*, ed. Douglas P. Fry (New York: Oxford University Press, 2013); Ashley Montagu, *Growing Young* (New York: McGraw-Hill, 1981).

3. Joshua M. Plotnik et al., "Elephants Know When They Need a Helping Trunk in a Cooperative Task," *Proceedings of the National Academy of Sciences (PNAS)* 108 (2011): 5116–5121, doi: 10.1073/pnas.1101765108. Available online: http://www.pnas.org/content/108/12/5116.

4. See, e.g., regarding apes, Frans de Waal, *The Age of Empathy* (New York: Harmony Books, 2009) and for an example of cultural tradition involving baboons, Robert M. Sapolsky, "Rousseau with a Tail: Maintaining a Tradition of Peace among Baboons," in *War, Peace, and Human Nature: Convergence of Evolutionary and Cultural Views*, ed. Douglas P. Fry (New York: Oxford University Press, 2013). Regarding tool use, see, e.g., C. Schrauf et al., "Do Chimpanzees Use Weight to Select Hammer Tools?" *PLoS ONE* 7, e41044, doi:10.1371/journal.pone.0041044.

5. Masao Kawai, "Newly-Acquired Pre-cultural Behavior of the Natural Troop of Japanese Monkeys on Koshima Island," *Primates* 6 (1965): 1–30, https://doi.org/10.1007/BF01794457. The story of Imo can also be found in a number of popular works, including William H. Calvin, *The Throwing Madonna: Essays on the Brain* (New York: McGraw-Hill, 1983). For a recent work on the cultural transmission of learned behaviors by nonhuman species, see Frans de Waal, *The Ape and the Sushi Master* (New York: Basic Books, 2001).

6. Quotation is available online: http://lalandlab.st-andrews.ac.uk/niche/.

7. Quotation is available online: http://lalandlab.st-andrews.ac.uk/niche/. See also R. L. Day, Kevin N. Laland, and F. John Odling-Smee, "Rethinking Adaptation: The Niche-Construction Perspective," *Perspectives in Biology and Medicine* 46 (2003): 80–95, doi: 10.1353/pbm.2003.0003; and F. John Odling-Smee, Kevin N. Laland, and Marcus F. Feldman, *Niche Construction: The Neglected Process in Evolution* (Princeton, NJ: Monographs in Population Biology, Volume 37, 2003).

8. Fuentes, "Cooperation, Conflict, and Niche Construction in the Genus *Homo*."

9. Michael E. McCullough, *Beyond Revenge: The Evolution of the Forgiveness Instinct* (San Francisco: Jossey-Bass, 2008); Douglas P. Fry, "Conflict Management in Cross-Cultural Perspective," in *Natural Conflict Resolution*, eds. Filippo Aureli and Frans de Waal (Berkeley: University of California Press, 2000).

10. David Maybury-Lewis, *Millennium: Tribal Wisdom and the Modern World* (New York: Viking, 1992).

11. "Bono: 'There's A Difference Between Cosying Up to Power and Being Close to Power,'" *Guardian*, September 21, 2013. Available online: http://www.theguardian.com/music/2013/sep/22/bono-campaigner-u2-global-poverty.

12. Paul D. MacLean, *The Triune Brain in Evolution: Role in Paleocerebral Functions* (New York: Springer, 1990), 115–116. Not all reptiles cannibalize their young. Crocodiles, for example, protect the eggs they lay and also care for the baby crocodiles that emerge from them. But most reptiles do not.

13. Jaak Panksepp, *Affective Neuroscience: The Foundations of Human and Animal Emotions* (New York: Oxford University Press, 1998).

14. Paul W. Sherman, "Nepotism and the Evolution of Alarm Calls," *Science* 197 (1977): 1246–1253, doi: 10.1126/science.197.4310.1246.

15. Alyssa A. Vitale, *Reproductive Ecology of Black Bears in Maine: Maternal Effect, Philopatry, and Primiparity*. Ph.D. Dissertation, University of Maine (2015), available online at: Alyssa A. Vitale, "Reproductive Ecology of Black Bears in Maine: Maternal Effect, Philopatry, and Primiparity," *Electronic Theses and Dissertations* 2305 (2012), https://digitalcommons.library.umaine.edu/etd/2305.

16. Paul J. Zak, Angela A. Stanton, and Sheila Ahmadi, "Oxytocin Increases Generosity in Humans," *PLoS ONE* 11 (2007): e1128, doi: 10.1371/journal.pone.0001128.
17. See, e.g., Carsten Schradin et al., "Prolactin and Paternal Care: Comparison of Three Species of Monogamous New World Monkeys," *Journal of Comparative Psychology* 117 (2003): 166–175, doi: 10.1037/0735-7036.117.2.166; Charles Snowden and T. Zeigler, "Growing Up Cooperatively: Family Processes and Infant Development in Marmosets and Tamarins," *Journal of Developmental Processes* 2 (2007): 40–66. Available online: http://citeseerx.ist.psu.edu/viewdoc/download?doi=10.1.1.325.8840&rep=rep1&type=pdf. Another example of paternal care further down the phylogenetic scale is sea horses: the female lays eggs, but the male carries them in his pouch for most of the time between fertilization and birth, and the little seahorses are born out of his pouch, as described in Edward O. Wilson, *Sociobiology: The New Synthesis* (Cambridge, MA: Harvard University Press, 1975), 326.
18. "Dolphins Save Swimmers from Shark Attack," *Guardian*, November 23, 2004. Available online: https://www.theguardian.com/world/2004/nov/23/1.
19. "20 Years Ago Today: Brookfield Zoo Gorilla Helps Boy Who Fell into Habitat," *Chicago Tribune*, August 15, 2016, Available online: http://www.chicagotribune.com/news/ct-gorilla-saves-boy-brookfield-zoo-anniversary-20160815-story.html. Sadly, a related incident in 2016 at the Cincinnati zoo resulted in shooting of a gorilla, as reported in the news, "Cincinnati Zoo Gorilla Shooting: Mum of Rescued Boy Questioned by Police in Child Neglect Investigation," *Mirror*, June 2, 2016. Available online: https://www.mirror.co.uk/news/world-news/cincinnati-zoo-gorilla-shooting-mum-8106015. It seems that the gorilla may have been needlessly killed and in fact was protecting the boy, as in the previous case in Chicago.
20. Another highly intelligent species, elephants also require many years to grow up, and elephants have an extremely long period of pregnancy: 22 months. See, e.g., *Live Science*, "What Animal Has the Longest Pregnancy?" March 2, 2011. Available online: https://www.livescience.com/33086-what-animal-has-the-longest-pregnancy.html.
21. Sarah Blaffer Hrdy, *Mothers and Others: The Evolutionary Origins of Mutual Understanding* (Cambridge, MA: Harvard University Press, 2009); Carter, "Neuroendocrine Perspectives on Social Attachment and Love"; C. Sue Carter, "The Chemistry of Child Neglect: Do Oxytocin and Vasopressin Mediate the Effects of Early Experience?" *Proceedings of the National Academy of Sciences (PNAS)* 102 (2005): 18247–18248, doi: 10.1073/pnas.0509376102; Feldman, "Oxytocin and Social Affiliation in Humans."
22. Helen E. Fisher, Arthur Aron, and Lucy R. Brown, "Romantic Love: An fMRI Study of a Neural Mechanism for Mate Choice," *Journal of Comparative Neurology* 493 (2005): 58–62.
23. Similarly, John O'Manique proposes that kin selection and reciprocity are factors in the evolution of altruism but that they must be distinguished from altruism itself; see John O'Manique, *The Origins of Justice: The Evolution of Morality, Human Rights, and Law* (Philadelphia: University of Pennsylvania Press, 2003).

24. Brown quoted in "Romantic Love Is Long-Term Focused Attention," *Toronto Star*, February 14, 2003; see also personal communication with Brown, March 4, 2003.

25. Frans de Waal, *Age of Empathy*; Walter Goldschmidt, *The Bridge to Humanity: How Affect Hunger Trumps the Selfish Gene* (New York: Oxford University Press, 2005); Robert M. Sapolsky, *Behave: The Biology of Humans at Our Best and Worst* (New York: Penguin, 2017).

26. See Riane Eisler, *Sacred Pleasure: Sex, Myth, and the Politics of the Body* (San Francisco: Harper Collins, 1995) as well as Riane Eisler, *The Chalice and the Blade: Our History, Our Future* (San Francisco: Harper Collins, 1987) for an analysis of how the equation of love with the powers that govern the universe has ancient cultural roots in more partnership-oriented societies as well as how the view of God as angry and punitive is integral to domination rather than partnership forms of spirituality.

27. Of course, loving is beneficial to us. People who love their pets may live longer. For example, it's been shown they are more likely to live longer after a heart attack (Mwenya Mubanga et al., "Dog Ownership and the Risk of Cardiovascular Disease and Death—A Nationwide Cohort Study," *Scientific Reports* 7, 15821 (2017), doi: 10.1038/s41598-017-16118-6.). Nonetheless, it's an illogical stretch to therefore claim that love for pets is driven by genes seeking to replicate themselves.

28. T. A. Chaplin et al., "A Conserved Pattern of Differential Expansion of Cortical Areas in Simian Primates," *Journal of Neuroscience* 33, 38 (2013): 15120–15125, doi: 10.1523/JNEUROSCI.2909-13.2013.

29. Montagu, *Growing Young*.

30. John Bowlby, *The Roots of Parenthood* (London: National Children's Home, 1953); John Bowlby, "The Nature of the Child's Tie to His Mother," *International Journal of Psychoanalysis* 39 (1958): 350–373; Harry Harlow, "The Nature of Love," *American Psychologist* 13 (1958): 673–685, doi: 10.1037/h0047884; Eric B. Keverne, "Epigenetics: Significance of the Gene-Environment Interface for Brain Development," in *Pathways to Peace: The Transformative Power of Children and Families*, eds. James F. Leckman, Catherine Panter-Brick, and Rima Salah (Cambridge, MA: MIT Press, 2014); Narvaez, *Neurobiology and the Development of Human Morality*.

31. Keverne, "Epigenetics"; Ruth Feldman, A. Vengrober, and R. P. Ebstein, "Affiliation Buffers Stress: Cumulative Genetic Risk in Oxytocin-Vasopressin Genes Combines with Early Caregiving to Predict PTSD in War-Exposed Young Children," *Translational Psychiatry* 4 (2014): e370, doi: 10.1038/tp.2014.6.

32. Hrdy, *Mothers and Others*; C. Sue Carter, "The Chemistry of Child Neglect: Do Oxytocin and Vasopressin Mediate the Effects of Early Experience?" *Proceedings of the National Academy of Sciences (PNAS)* 102 (2005): 18247–18248, doi: 10.1073/pnas.0509376102.

33. Carter, "The Chemistry of Child Neglect: Do Oxytocin and Vasopressin Mediate the Effects of Early Experience?" 18247.

34. The capacities for learning, consciousness, symbolic communication, creativity, choice, planning, and love are so much more advanced in humans that the difference

between us and other species is not just quantitative but qualitative. This does not mean that we should think of ourselves as the apex of evolution, much less as rulers of the world entitled to dominion over other life forms. Nor does it mean that the brain alone is responsible for the characteristics that make us uniquely human. But looking at the evolution of the brain makes it possible to see how the emergence of our species initiated a new chapter in evolution, which in turn brought a new level of motivational dynamics.

35. MacLean, *The Triune Brain in Evolution*.
36. MacLean, *The Triune Brain in Evolution*.
37. Dolphins and whales also have advanced neocortices.
38. Antonio R. Damasio, *Descartes' Error* (New York: Grosset/Putnam, 1994); David Loye, "The Moral Brain," *Brain and Mind* 3 (2002): 133–150, doi: 10.1023/A:1016561925565; Daniel S. Levine, Samuel J. Leven, and Paul S. Prueitt, "Integration, Disintegration, and the Frontal Lobes," in *Motivation, Emotion, and Goal Direction in Neural Networks*, eds. Daniel S. Levine and Samuel Leven (Mahwah, NJ: Erlbaum, 1992); J. H. Walle Nauta, "The Problem of the Frontal Lobe: A Reinterpretation," *Journal of Psychiatric Research*, 8 (1971): 167–187, doi: 10.1016/0022-3956(71)90017-3; Karl H. Pribram, "The Primate Frontal Cortex—Executive of the Brain," in *Psychophysiology of the Frontal Lobes*, eds. Karl H. Pribram and Aleksandr R. Luria (New York: Academic Press, 1973).
39. See, e.g., Steven W. Anderson et al., "Impairment of Social and Moral Behavior Related to Early Damage in Human Prefrontal Cortex," *Nature Neuroscience* 2 (1999): 1032–1037, doi: 10.1038/14833.
40. Antonio Damasio, *The Feeling of What Happens* (New York: Harcourt, 1999), 311.
41. Despite his use of the term "extended consciousness," Antonio Damasio indicates that this is a new level of consciousness. John O'Manique uses the term "self-consciousness" and makes it clear that he means also consciousness of other, though the term does not seem to include this (O'Manique, *The Origins of Justice*).
42. Terrence W. Deacon, *The Symbolic Species: The Co-evolution of Language and the Brain* (New York: Norton, 1998); O'Manique, *The Origins of Justice*.
43. George Miller, Eugene Galanter, and Karl Pribram, *Plans and the Structure of Behavior* (New York: Adams Bannister Cox, 1986).
44. Miller, Galanter, and Pribram, *Plans and the Structure of Behavior*. This use of the term "feedforward" is in the sense of "top-down feedforward" (going from plans to actions) proposed by Karl Pribram, rather than in the sense of the older "bottom-up feedforward," such as the passage of a visual image from the retina to the cortex.
45. Keverne, "Epigenetics"; Feldman et al., "Affiliation Buffers Stress."
46. Joan L. Luby et al., "Maternal Support in Early Childhood Predicts Larger Hippocampal Volumes at School Age," *Proceedings of the National Academy of Sciences (PNAS)*, 109 (2012): 2854–2859, doi: 10.1073/pnas.1118003109.
47. Carter, "The Chemistry of Child Neglect"; Feldman et al., "Affiliation Buffers Stress"; Keverne, "Epigenetics."
48. Darlene Francis et al., "Nongenomic Transmission Across Generations of Maternal Behavior and Stress Responses in the Rat," *Science* 286 (1999): 1155–1158,

doi: 10.1126/science.286.5442.1155. Rachel Ehrenberg, "Motherly Love Coddles the Brain," *Science*, August 2, 2004. Available online: http://www.sciencemag.org/news/2004/08/motherly-love-coddles-brain.

49. See, e.g., Liz Warwick, "More Cuddles, Less Stress," *Bulletin of the Centre of Excellence for Early Childhood* 4 (October 2005), 2. Available at: http://excellence-jeunesenfants.ca/documents/BulletinVol4No2Oct05ANG.pdf.

50. See, e.g., Dorota Iwaniec, *The Emotionally Abused and Neglected Child* (Chichester, UK: Wiley and Sons, 2006); Sue Gerhardt, *Why Love Matters: How Affection Shapes a Baby's Brain* (New York: Routledge, 2015); Robert F Anda et al., "The Enduring Effects of Abuse and Related Adverse Experiences in Childhood," *European Archives of Psychiatry and Clinical Neuroscience* 256 (2016): 174–186, doi: 10.1007/s00406-005-0624-4. An early work in this area was Dorothy Burlingham and Anna Freud, *Infants without Families* (Oxford, UK: Allen and Unwin, 1944).

51. Bruce D. Perry, "Childhood Experience and the Expression of Genetic Potential: What Childhood Neglect Tells Us about Nature and Nurture," *Brain and Mind* 3 (2002): 79–100, doi: 10.1023/A:1016557824657. Strangely, autistic children seem to have accelerated brain growth in the early years.

52. Studies of "deprivation dwarfism" also show how critical love is for babies and children. This condition has been found in children living with parents unable to give them loving care. In six children affected by this condition, Robert Patton and Lytt Gardner found that even though these children had adequate nutrition, they suffered from emotional disturbances that adversely affected their endocrine systems, stunting their growth. Hospitalization allowed their growth to catch up. But when they were returned to their original home environments, their normal growth stopped (Lytt Gardner, "Deprivation Dwarfism," *Scientific American* 227 (1972): 76–82, doi: 10.1038/scientificamerican0772-6; Robert Patton and Lytt Gardner, *Growth Failure in Maternal Deprivation* (Springfield, IL: Charles Thomas, 1963).

53. Perry, "Childhood Experience and the Expression of Genetic Potential: What Childhood Neglect Tells Us about Nature and Nurture," 92–93.

54. Perry, "Childhood Experience and the Expression of Genetic Potential: What Childhood Neglect Tells Us about Nature and Nurture."

55. Dave Ziegler, *Raising Children Who Refuse to Be Raised* (Jaspar Mountain, OR: Jaspar Mountain Press, 2002). Ziegler's book describes the highly successful SCAR/Jaspar Mountain program, which has helped traumatized children whom no one else could help.

56. Napoleon Chagnon, *Yanomamö* (Fort Worth, TX: Harcourt Brace Jovanovich, 1992, 4th edition), 125.

57. An example of this view is provided by Michael Ghiselin, who writes, "What passes for cooperation turns out to be a mixture of opportunism and exploitation." Michael Ghiselin, *The Economy of Nature and the Evolution of Sex* (Berkeley: University of California Press, 1974), 247.

58. Robert Trivers, *Social Evolution* (San Francisco: Benjamin-Cummings, 1985), 456–457.

59. David Loye, *Darwin's Lost Theory* (Carmel, CA: Benjamin Franklin Press, 2007).

60. Barbara Smuts, *Sex and Friendship in Baboons* (New York: Aldine du Gruyter, 1985).

61. Patricia Draper, "The Learning Environment for Aggression and Anti-Social Behavior among the !Kung (Kalahari Desert, Botswana, Africa)," in *Learning Non-Aggression: The Experience of Non-Literate Societies*, ed. Ashley Montagu (New York: Oxford University Press, 1978); see also Christopher Boehm, *Hierarchy in the Forest* (Cambridge, MA: Harvard University Press, 1999), 80; Napoleon Chagnon, "Life Histories, Blood Revenge, and Warfare in a Tribal Population," *Science* 239 (1988): 985–992, doi: 10.1126/science.239.4843.985; Stephen Beckerman et al., "Life Histories, Blood Revenge, and Reproductive Success among the Waorani of Ecuador," *Proceedings of the National Academy of Sciences (PNAS)* 106 (2009): 8134–8139, doi: 10.1073/pnas.0901431106; R. Brian Ferguson, *Yanomami Warfare: A Political History* (Santa Fe, NM: School of American Research Press, 1995); Douglas P. Fry, *The Human Potential for Peace: An Anthropological Challenge to Assumptions about War and Violence* (New York: Oxford University Press, 2006); Jacques Lizot, "On Warfare: An Answer to N. A. Chagnon," trans. Sarah Dart, *American Ethnologist* 21 (1994): 845–862, doi: 10.1525/ae.1994.21.4.02a00100; Marta Miklikowska and Douglas P. Fry, "Natural Born Nonkillers: A Critique of the Killers-Have-More-Kids Idea," in *Nonkilling Psychology*, eds. Daniel J. Christie and Joám Evans Pim (Honolulu: Center for Global Nonkilling, 2012); John H. Moore, "The Reproductive Success of Cheyenne War Chiefs: A Contrary Case to Chagnon's Yanomamö," *Current Anthropology* 31 (1990): 322–330, doi: 10.1086/203846.

62. Karen Strier, "Social Plasticity and Demographic Variation in Primates," in *Origins of Altruism and Cooperation*, eds. Robert W. Sussman and C. Robert Cloninger (New York: Springer, 2011), 182; see also Frans de Waal, *Peacemaking among Primates* (Cambridge, MA: Harvard University Press, 1989).

63. Richard Wrangham and Dale Peterson, *Demonic Males: Apes and the Origins of Human Violence* (Boston: Houghton Mifflin, 1996); Richard Wrangham and Luke Glowacki, "Intergroup Aggression in Chimpanzees and War in Nomadic Hunter-Gatherers: Evaluating the Chimpanzee Model," *Human Nature* 23 (2012): 5–29, doi: 10.1007/s12110-012-9132-1; Michael L. Wilson, "Chimpanzees, Warfare, and the Invention of Peace," in *War, Peace, and Human Nature: Convergence of Evolutionary and Cultural Views*, ed. Douglas P. Fry (New York: Oxford University Press, 2013).

64. Jane Goodall is quoted in Marc Bekoff and Jessica Pierce, *Wild Justice: The Moral Lives of Animals* (Chicago: University of Chicago Press, 2009), 4.

65. Takayoshi Kano, "The Bonobos' Peaceable Kingdom," *Natural History* 99 (1990): 62–70, 67.

66. Suehisa Kuroda, "Social Behavior of the Pygmy Chimpanzees," *Primates* 21 (1980): 181–197, 181, doi: 10.1007/BF02374032. See also de Waal, *The Age of Empathy*; de Waal, *Peacemaking among Primates*; Frances White, Michel Waller, and Klaree J. Boose, "Evolution of Primate Peace," in *War, Peace, and Human Nature: Convergence of Evolutionary and Cultural Views*, ed. Douglas P. Fry (New York: Oxford University Press, 2013).

67. White, Waller, and Boose, "Evolution of Primate Peace," 392.

68. White, Waller, and Boose, "Evolution of Primate Peace," 392.

69. Kano, "The Bonobos' Peaceable Kingdom," 70.

70. Frans de Waal, *The Bonobo and the Atheist: In search of Humanism among the Primates* (New York: Norton, 2013), 80.

71. Frans de Waal and Frans Lanting, *Bonobo: The Forgotten Ape* (Berkeley: University of California Press, 1997).

72. Kano, "The Bonobos' Peaceable Kingdom," 70.

73. Wrangham and Peterson, *Demonic Males*; Randy Thornhill and Craig T. Palmer, *A Natural History of Rape: Biological Bases of Sexual Coercion* (Cambridge, MA: MIT Press, 2000).

74. See, e.g., Sue Savage-Rumbaugh and R. Lewin, *Kanzi: The Ape on the Brink of the Human Mind* (New York: Wiley, 1994); Pär Segardahl, William Fields, and Sue Savage-Rumbaugh, *Kanzi's Primal Language: The Cultural Initiation of Primates into Language* (New York: Palgrave Macmillan, 2005).

75. James Rilling et al. "Differences between Chimpanzees and Bonobos in Neural Systems Supporting Social Cognition," *Social Cognitive and Affective Neuroscience* 7 (2011): 369–379, 369, doi: 10.1093/scan/nsr017.

76. Frans de Waal, *Our Inner Ape* (New York: Riverhead Press, 2005), 30.

77. Nancy Tanner and Adrienne Zihlman, "Women in Evolution. Part I: Innovation and Selection in Human Origins," *Signs: Journal of Women in Culture and Society* 1 (1976): 585–608, doi: 10.1086/493245; Adrienne L. Zihlman, "Women in Evolution, Part II: Subsistence and Social Organization among Early Hominids," *Signs: Journal of Women in Culture and Society* 4 (1978): 4–20, doi: 10.1086/493566. See also Carter, "Neuroendocrine Perspectives on Social Attachment and Love"; Carter, "The Chemistry of Child Neglect."

78. Frank Marlowe, *The Hadza Hunter-Gatherers of Tanzania* (Berkeley: University of California Press, 2010).

79. Adrienne Zihlman, "Women's Bodies, Women's Lives: An Evolutionary Perspective" in, *The Evolving Female: A Life-History Perspective,* eds. Mary Ellen Morbeck, Alison Galloway, and Adrienne L. Zihlman (Princeton, NJ: Princeton University Press, 1997), 187. See also Adrienne Zihlman, "The Paleolithic Glass Ceiling: Women in Human Evolution," in *Women in Human Evolution,* ed. Lori Hager (New York: Routledge, 1997), 97. Other scholars such as Nancy Tanner [Nancy Tanner, *On Becoming Human* (Cambridge, MA: Cambridge University Press, 1981)] and Sally Linton Slocum [Sally Slocum, "Woman the Gatherer: Male Bias in Anthropology," in *Toward an Anthropology of Women,* ed. Reina Reciter (New York: Monthly Review Press, 1975)] have taken similar positions. But their writings are not part of the academic canon.

80. Humberto Maturana and Francisco Varela, *The Tree of Knowledge: The Biological Roots of Human Understanding* (Boston: Shambhala, 1992). In Maturana's preface to the Spanish edition of my book *The Chalice and the Blade* (*El Caliz y la Espada,* Santiago, Chile: Editorial Cuatro Vientos, 1990), he introduces the concept of "the biology of love," which he has since developed further in his book *The Origins of Humanness in the Biology of Love,* written with the psychologist Gerda Verden-Zoller

[Humberto R. Maturana and Gerda Verden-Zoller, *Origins of Humanness in the Biology of Love* (Durham, NC: Duke University Press, 1998)].

81. MacLean, *The Triune Brain in Evolution*. See also Paul D. MacLean, "Women: A More Balanced Brain?" *Zygon* 31 (September, 1996): 421–439, where MacLean develops this theme further, proposing that evolutionary factors have contributed to a greater balance of function in women's brains—an evolutionary development he believes contributes to less dualistic and hierarchical thinking.

82. Frans de Waal, *The Age of Empathy*, 43; see also Frans de Waal, *Good Natured: The Origins of Right and Wrong in Humans and Other Animals* (Cambridge, MA: Harvard University Press, 1996).

83. David Loye, *Darwin's Lost Theory*, 2007.

84. O'Manique, *The Origins of Justice*.

85. Dean R. Snow, "Sexual Dimorphism in European Upper Paleolithic Cave Art," *American Antiquity* 78 (2013): 746, doi: 10.7183/0002-7316.78.4.746. Snow's study began more than a decade ago when he came across the work of John Manning, a British biologist who had found that men and women differ in the relative lengths of their fingers: women tend to have ring and index fingers of about the same length, whereas men's ring fingers tend to be longer than their index fingers. He then examined the stencils of hand prints in several Upper Paleolithic caves and found that three fourths were the prints of women's hands.

86. In his interview with *National Geographic*, when asked why these prints were made, Snow commented that in a preliterate society, this was most probably the artists' way of signing their work ["Were the First Artists Mostly Women?" (*National Geographic*, October 8, 2013. Available online: http://news.nationalgeographic.com/news/2013/10/131008-women-handprints-oldest-neolithic-cave-art/.)] These art and the paintings of animals are usually of pairs (female and male), which the French archeologist Andre Leroi Gourhan attributes to these ancient people's interest in the regeneration of life through the union of female and male. Andre Leroi Gourhan, *Prehistoire de l'Art Occidental* (Paris: Edition D'Art Lucien Mazenod, 1971). See also Eisler, *The Chalice and the Blade*; Eisler, *Sacred Pleasure*.

87. Eisler, *The Chalice and the Blade*; Eisler, *Sacred Pleasure*.

88. Karen Endicott, "Gender Relations in Hunter-Gatherer Societies," in *The Cambridge Encyclopedia of Hunters and Gatherers*, eds. Richard B. Lee and Richard Daly (Cambridge, MA: Cambridge University Press, 1999), 411–418, 415.

89. See Abraham Maslow, *Toward a Psychology of Being* (Princeton, NJ: Van Nostrand, 1968); Roberto Assagioli, *Psychosynthesis: A Manual of Principles and Techniques* (New York: Viking Press, 1965); and Kazimierz Dabrowski, *Positive Disintegration* (Boston: Little, Brown, 1964). See also Elizabeth Maxwell, "Self as Phoenix: A Comparison of Assagioli's and Dabrowski's Developmental Theories," *Advanced Development* 4 (January 1992): 31–48. Another source is David Loye, *The Glacier and the Flame*, unpublished manuscript.

90. See, e.g., Edward L. Deci and Richard M. Ryan, *Intrinsic Motivation and Self-Determination in Human Behavior* (New York: Plenum Press, 1985); Robert W. White, "Motivation Reconsidered: The Concept of Competence," *Psychological*

Review 66 (1959): 297–333, doi: 10.1037/h0040934; Abraham Maslow, *The Farther Reaches of Human Nature* (New York: Viking, 1971).

91. The most explicit statement that self-actualization is a biological motive is found in the work of Abraham Maslow, e.g., Abraham Maslow, *Toward a Psychology of Being* (New York: Van Nostrand, 1968) and Abraham Maslow, *The Farther Reaches of Human Nature* (New York: Viking Press, 1971).

92. Mihaly Csikszentmihalyi, *Flow: The Psychology of Optimal Experience* (New York: Harper Collins, 1990); Deci and Ryan, *Intrinsic Motivation*.

93. Goldschmidt, *Bridge to Humanity*.

4

The Biology of Experience

This may seem astonishing, but a 13th-century experiment already proved that, rather than following invariant genetic instructions, our brain circuitry is strongly shaped by experience. The experiment was ordered by the Holy Roman Emperor Frederick II of Hohenstaufen, who decided he would discover the natural language of God by having children brought up in total silence. So he decreed that a group of infants be taken from their mothers and raised by caretakers who provided them food and shelter in total silence.[1] But instead of revealing the language of God, the children spoke no language whatsoever.[2]

These unfortunates, all of whom died in childhood, had the genetic potential to speak a language. However, without the experience of hearing spoken words, they did not develop the neural circuitry to express this human potential.

This cruel experiment showed that our brain circuits, and therefore our abilities and behavior, are strongly shaped by our environment, which for humans is primarily our surrounding culture. Specifically, it showed that while humans have evolved a genetic predisposition for learning language, to realize this potential we have to be exposed to language. Frederick's experiment also illustrates the role of culture in molding experience, since a ruler could only exercise such autocratic powers at a time when Western culture oriented far more closely to the domination system.

Examples of how cultural environments affect the expression of genetic potentials abound. For instance, a few centuries ago only a tiny percentage of the population of Western Europe could read. They had the genetic potential to do so, but for most people this capacity remained untapped. The potential to read became widely expressed in the population only with greater access to education, which in turn was brought forth by cultural movement in a partnership direction.[3]

In succeeding chapters, we will look in some detail at how human abilities, behaviors, and beliefs, including what is considered normal and abnormal, desirable or undesirable, and moral or immoral, are directly influenced by where a society is situated on the partnership-domination continuum—and how this plays out in the neural development of our brains. But to better understand how experience can influence whether genetic capacities are expressed or inhibited, we will first look at a number of fascinating studies, including findings from the emerging field of epigenetics.

Epigenetics

Even highly heritable traits are affected by environmental conditions. Height, for example, has heritability of at least 90 percent, which means that 90 percent of the height difference between any two people is caused by their different DNA.[4] As a result, you would expect very little effect from environmental factors. Nonetheless, Japanese children born and reared in the United States, on average, were considerably taller than their grandparents who grew up in Japan with very different diets and other life experiences. After World War II, as the Japanese became more prosperous and this prosperity was more widely shared, heights also increased in Japan, with the average height of Japanese 11-year-olds increasing by more than 5½ inches in just 50 years.[5]

This is just one example of experiential effects that span generations. For instance, studies show that what a woman experiences during pregnancy can affect her children and in some cases her grandchildren.[6] One of the earliest, and probably most famous, studies that show these transgenerational environmental effects was based on birth records collected during the so-called Dutch Hunger Winter. This calamity was caused by a German-imposed food embargo in western Holland toward the end of World War II that led to death by starvation of some 30,000 people. As Tessa Roseboom and her colleagues report: "Throughout the winter of 1944–1945 the population had to live without light, without gas, without heat, laundries ceased operating, soap for personal use was unobtainable, and adequate clothing and shoes were lacking in most families. In hospitals, there was serious overcrowding as well as lack of medicines. Above all, hunger dominated all misery."[7] But the consequences of these experiences were much farther reaching. What scientists later found is that children who had been in gestation at any point during the famine had a markedly higher incidence of diabetes, and if their mothers had experienced the famine during the period of early gestation, they also had higher rates of obesity and coronary heart disease. Additionally, adult women who had been conceived right before, during, or after the famine had about five times the rate of breast cancer compared with nonexposed women.[8]

Developmental neuroscientist Eric B. Keverne points out the general implications of such findings. As he writes, the environment circumstances to which children are exposed "in the mother's womb, and even in the grandmother's womb, can change their metabolic profile, brain development profile, and a propensity for psychiatric dysfunctions."[9]

Other studies confirm these long-term experiential effects. For example, a 2013 study shows that mouse pups—and even the offspring's offspring— can inherit a fearful association of a certain smell with pain, even if they have not experienced the pain themselves, and without the need for genetic mutations.[10] Kerry Ressler and Brian Dias designed a simple experiment in which laboratory mice were trained to associate the smell of acetophenone (a scent like that of cherries and almonds) with electric shocks. Not only did the animals shudder in the presence of acetophenone without a shock, but so also did their pups, even though they had never encountered acetophenone in their lives.[11]

The most striking findings from this study were the accompanying changes to the brain structures that process odors. The mice sensitized to acetophenone, as well as their descendants, had changes in their brain, such as in those areas involved in processing fear, and produced more neurons to detect the odor compared with control mice and their progeny.[12]

Such changes in brain structures and behaviors that do *not* entail gene mutations are increasingly being confirmed. For example, mice fed a high-fat diet throughout their pregnancies and lactation periods produced offspring that were larger than normal—a trait that was also passed on to their offspring's offspring.[13] Other studies indicate that a father's experiences and behaviors can also influence his offspring's health. For example, a 2013 study in which male mice were fed a folate-deficient diet found that the offspring they sired had increased rates of birth defects.[14]

Another experiment exposed fruit flies to a drug called geldanamycin and found unusual growths on their eyes that lasted through 13 generations. Though in humans most epigenetic effects do not last so very long, still another study found that roundworms fed with a certain bacteria exhibit changes that are transmitted to at least 40 generations.[15]

These kinds of groundbreaking experiments showing that structural cell changes can occur *without* genetic changes led to the new field of epigenetics, and with it, a partial revival of Lamarck's theories about the transmission of acquired traits from one generation to another. Biomedical researcher Yan Jiang and colleagues succinctly define epigenetics as "a type of molecular and cellular 'memory' that results in stable changes in the gene expression without alternations to the DNA sequence itself."[16]

While epigenetics is today successfully demolishing dogmas of genetic determinism, it was actually prefigured by earlier studies of human and nonhuman species showing that both prenatal and postnatal experiences affect traits and behaviors. A notable example is an experiment performed in the 1960s by neuropsychologist Gilbert Gottlieb focusing on ducks. Ducks seem to be genetically preprogrammed to respond to species-specific maternal calls. However, Gottlieb found that when wood duck embryos were exposed to mallard duck maternal calls, once hatched the wood duck chicks showed a strong preference for the mallard call over the call of their own species.[17] Gottlieb also found that when mallard ducks were raised in social groups rather than in isolation, they could be induced to prefer chicken calls to those of their own species. "Social rearing with peers establishes such a highly malleable state in the embryos and hatchlings," Gottlieb wrote, "that a species-atypical preference could be induced, one that overrides the usual canalizing influence of exposure to their own contact calls."[18]

That early experience influences which genetic possibilities are expressed or suppressed—even affecting so-called instincts—has also been documented by experiments with mammals. Among the most famous are Harry and Margaret Harlow's pioneering studies on the early experiences of infant rhesus monkeys.[19] Their experiments found that monkeys raised in isolation developed the extreme pathologies often seen in severely neglected and abused children. The monkeys would stare fixedly into space and hug or rock themselves interminably. They would react to the approach of people by biting or scratching bleeding holes in their own skin. When housed with other monkeys, they were not able to have sex.[20] Instead, they would indiscriminately hit and bite, in apparent terror. When females from this group were artificially inseminated, they were not able to give their offspring attention, much less affection. They carelessly stepped on their progeny, shoved them away, and sometimes deliberately injured them.[21]

It has now also been demonstrated that one mechanism through which parenting style in rhesus monkey mothers affects their offspring's behaviors involves the serotonin system.[22] A multidisciplinary research team made up of developmental psychologists, primatologists, and other scientists investigated the effects of variable parenting styles early in life on the monkeys' neurochemical profiles in the second year of life. The researchers found that high rates of maternal rejection led to increased rates of anxiety and fearfulness, as mediated by serotonergic mechanisms. These findings suggest that different types of maternal care result in developmental differences in the brains, notably involving the serotonin system of the young monkeys. In short, at least if you are a rhesus monkey, rejection by mom affects both your brain development and your anxiety levels.[23]

For one more example of the epigenetic effects of the environment on brain development, we turn to controlled studies on laboratory rats by William Greenough and his colleagues, who found that the growth of neural synapses is directly affected by experience in rats.[24] The typical lab rat, even if treated well, lives in a cage that lacks stimulation. Greenough and his collaborators instead put rats in a large wire-mesh cage filled with a daily-changing set of toys and other objects, and let them out once a day in an open field where there were other toys and objects. The rats reared in this enriched environment not only performed better than rats raised in less stimulating conditions but also developed more synapses in their brains.[25] Recall also the McGill University study by Meany and his colleagues, mentioned in Chapter 3, where rats whose mothers were more attentive—as well as rats born from less caring mothers who were placed in a caring rat "daycare" program—developed more brain neural connections than those who were short-changed on care and attention.[26]

Primate Brains, Behaviors, and Cultural Change

Even species with far less genetic flexibility than ours can radically change their behaviors—and their brain neurochemistry—when social circumstances change. For example, male savanna baboons are known to be rather aggressive primates. Males harass and attack females, who are only half their size and have much smaller canine teeth. They also can terrorize lower-ranking males with threats and physical attacks. But primatologists Robert Sapolsky and Lisa Share discovered that even baboons can shift to a much less violent, more affiliative way of life.[27]

One troop that Sapolsky and Share studied, which they called the Garbage Dump Troop, slept near the trash heap at a tourist lodge in Kenya. Another troop, which they called the Forest Troop, slept in trees about one kilometer from the dump. They, too, wanted access to the dump goodies, but only the most bellicose Forest Troop males got dump food, since they had to compete with the Garbage Dump Troop for this resource. The less aggressive males in Forest Troop simply stayed away.

Then, the dump became contaminated with bovine tuberculosis (TB), and over the course of two years almost all the Garbage Dump Troop died out. However, among Forest Troop members, only the most aggressive males succumbed, since they had been the regular patrons of the contaminated site. This left alive the females, juveniles, and only the more socially affiliated and unaggressive males of Forest Troop, who had not eaten the TB-tainted food.

At this point, the Forest Troop's culture underwent a radical shift, becoming a much more congenial community. There were still fights and struggles for dominance. As Sapolsky remarked, "We're talking about baboons here."[28] But both females and males of all ranks spent more time grooming, being groomed, and huddling close to troop mates than is typical of savanna baboons.

One of Sapolsky and Share's most striking findings was that the neurochemistry of the Forest Troop monkeys changed when this cultural shift occurred. Hormone samples showed far less evidence of stress, as reflected in lower levels of cortisol and neurochemical markers of anxiety in even the lowest-ranking individuals, compared with baboons living in other troops.[29]

Just as striking—and significant—is that, more than two decades later, the troop retained its more peaceful character. And this occurred despite the fact that all the original males had died off or left, and new ones had replaced them in accordance with the baboon pattern of submales migrating to another troop after puberty.

At first, the investigators had thought the reason that the troop's relations became less tense and violent was the changed ratio of females to males, which was now two-to-one. But other troops with a similar preponderance of females were as truculent as ever. Clearly, what was happening was a cultural and, with it, a behavioral shift. Not only was the troop's new culture being transmitted to the next generation, but it also was being adopted by new males coming into the troop.

Sapolsky and Share concluded that one reason might be the treatment of these new males by resident females. When they studied interactions between females and new transfer males, they found that females treated new transfer males in the same affiliative manner that they treated resident males. There were other factors, such as the lower rates of male aggression by resident males and the more relaxed social structure, as well as new males observing how resident males interacted with females and each other. Sapolsky calls this process a self-perpetuating cascade with "more affiliative males resulting in less-stressed females who are more likely to act prosocially toward new males, resulting in new males becoming more affiliative."[30]

Whatever the mechanism of cultural transmission, the persistence of a more peaceful mode of relations offers proof that new ways of relating can be socially transmitted to newcomers arriving from more aggressive baboon cultures. Moreover, the shift to a less violent culture also offers proof that the typical aggressiveness of savanna baboons is not decreed by their genes: baboon culture can shift in the space of a generation to become less aggressive and more affiliative, and these changes can become the new cultural norm that is adopted by arriving outsiders.

Commenting on the Forest Troop shift toward peace, Frans de Waal writes, "The good news for humans is that it looks like peaceful conditions, once established, can be maintained. And if baboons can do it, why not us?"[31] De Waal also notes that studies of other primates confirm the social impact of learning from others among nonhuman primates. For example, if normally combative rhesus monkeys are reared with more conciliatory stump-tailed monkeys, the rhesus monkeys also learn tolerance, peacemaking, and hugging.[32]

Families, Cultures, and Human Brain Development

Unlike Sapolsky and Share, who examined the relationship between culture and neurochemistry, most neuroscientists studying humans have a much narrower focus. They, too, examine the connection between neurochemistry and environments. But the environmental contexts they look at are usually much smaller. They have focused on how the brain develops differently in different family circumstances, and especially on how people who grow up in harsh families seem to have disrupted patterns of both serotonin and dopamine activity, leading to depression, irritability, and other mood problems.[33]

For example, studies show that the brains of people with a family background of abuse and violence tend to have lower levels of serotonin, a calming neurotransmitter, and higher levels of cortisol, the major stress hormone. One of the first studies to show this came in 1984, when researchers correlated lower levels of serotonin with lack of good caregiving.[34] Low levels of dopamine, a neurotransmitter associated with positive moods, also seem to be caused by the stress of being deprived of nurturing care early in life. Developmental neuroscientist Eric Keverne points out how "evidence is thus rapidly accumulating that demonstrates how adverse environments can bring about epigenetic changes to brain and other tissues. The human brain is especially vulnerable because of its long postnatal development, involving widespread frontal and temporal neocortical reorganization at puberty."[35]

Focusing even more narrowly are works proposing that the determining factor in how people feel and act, and thus in the development of their brain neurochemistry, is whether or not they had a secure bond with their mother. These works draw heavily from the attachment theory of psychiatrist and psychoanalyst John Bowlby, who proposed that babies have an innate need for attachment to their mothers, and that when this need is not satisfied the result will be long-term cognitive, social, and emotional difficulties. Bowlby further proposed that this is rooted in our ancient evolutionary heritage in nomadic foraging societies when presumably children who stayed closer to their mothers had a better chance of surviving—and thus that daycare and other modern ways of childcare go against our nature and are harmful to children.[36]

However, many scholars have questioned Bowlby's theories.[37] They point out that while mothers are certainly important, they are not the only adults with whom children bond, and that, despite Bowlby's assertion that mother-child attachment was much stronger among our nomadic forager evolutionary ancestors than in modern times, in most of today's nomadic forager societies, infants and toddlers are frequently held by relatives, including older siblings, as well as other group members.[38] They also cite studies showing that children today can fare better when their mothers have other interests or jobs.[39]

The idea that mothering has severely deteriorated in modern Western times is also hard to support. Actually, a few centuries ago in most farming families, mothers spent a huge amount of time on various subsistence tasks as well as cooking, cleaning, and washing clothes, so that children, especially girls, took over much of the care of their younger siblings. Indeed, for much of human history a variety of people, not just mothers, have taken care of babies and infants.[40]

This does not mean that secure attachments are not important. But whether a child bonds with a mother or other adults is only one factor in the kinds of people children become. The culture or subculture into which the child is born makes a huge difference.

What both sides of the argument about attachment theory fail to address is that families do not arise in isolation. Families are formed by people who have learned what kinds of relations are considered normal and moral in their particular culture or subculture. This does not mean that all families conform to a culture's family ideal. For example, studies indicate that highly authoritarian and punitive families were the norm in Nazi Germany. Yet, as Pearl and Samuel Oliner found in their famous study of German helpers of Jews, the Germans who saved Jews from the Holocaust generally came from democratic and caring families—families that did not conform to what was then the German cultural norm.[41]

Families in domination systems typically are authoritarian and male-dominated, with stressful and punitive childrearing.[42] Pediatricians and other child experts have begun to document that the "traditional" highly punitive and often violent childrearing typical of domination systems is damaging to people's mental and even physical health.[43] But the damage done by this kind of childrearing goes further because children are taught that rankings of domination are normal and that they must submit to those in control. This stressful childrearing is a way that domination systems perpetuate themselves from generation to generation.

The Neurochemistry of Stress

In studying the effects of stress, scientists have identified three basic responses: fight-or-flight; dissociation, sometimes called *fight, flight, or freeze*; and what neuropsychologist Shelley Taylor and her associates call "tend-and-befriend."[44] Each of these responses activates different neurochemical patterns and behaviors.

Most studies of the effects of stress have focused on fight-or-flight or disassociation. But Taylor and her associates observed that women also frequently deal with stress by joining together to care for one another and for their own and others' children.[45] So they began to study the neurochemistry of this previously ignored "feminine" response to stress. And what they found is that the tend-or-befriend response involves oxytocin, vasopressin, and other substances connected with bonding, caring, and caregiving.

Actually, oxytocin is not only present in women. It is present in both sexes and seems to provide the same anxiety-reducing benefits to both.[46] For instance, administering oxytocin to rats counteracts many of the typical physiological and behavioral effects of stress in both males and females, decreasing the amount of cortisol and reducing activity in the sympathetic part of the autonomic nervous system, which is activated in the fight-or-flight response.[47] In addition, when scientists bred male mice that lack a gene for producing oxytocin, they found that this interfered with social memory and hence long-range social bonding. Unlike normal mice, these animals could not remember the smell of another mouse they had groomed or played with, even though their memory for other kinds of smells was intact.[48]

Vasopressin is another substance that seems to promote caring and caregiving in males as well as females. Vasopressin has a molecular structure very similar to oxytocin, and both men and women release vasopressin in response to stress. But whereas oxytocin may be blocked by male hormones, the effect of vasopressin may be enhanced by them.[49] This is suggested by studies of the prairie vole, where males play an important parenting role and have high levels of vasopressin.[50] Since human males can also engage in caregiving, vasopressin may be particularly important for these behaviors in men, as well as in counteracting the negative effects of stress.[51]

However, persistent stress decreases the activity of these stress-reducing and bonding-inducing systems and therefore the ability to bond.[52] As James Henry and Sheila Wang write, when stress is severe or chronic, these neurochemical processes become less active. Instead, "there is a long-lasting activation of the sympathetic system evidenced by sustained elevations in urinary norepinephrine and epinephrine. . . . The victims are vigilant, readily angered and display a dysphoria with a lack of interest in daily activities."[53]

In other words, persistent or traumatic stress decreases the amounts of oxytocin and vasopressin and the turnover of neurotransmitters such as serotonin, which has a calming effect, and dopamine, which produces positive feelings.[54] Instead, chronic or intense stress brings into play hormones such as cortisol, norepinephrine, and epinephrine that are often associated with fight-or-flight responses, including aggressive and other negative behaviors.[55]

The fight-or-flight response to stress developed in the course of evolution as an adaptation to dangerous situations, such as when quick action to escape or defend against a predator was needed for survival. The adaptation of freezing so as not to attract attention when a predator approaches occurs in some species and possibly was a precursor to the dissociative response of withdrawing from painful experiences in humans, including through drugs.

Some of these responses can still have survival value today. We may not have to watch for a saber-toothed tiger jumping out from behind a rock, but we still have to respond fast if a truck jumps a highway divider and comes at us head-on.

The problem is that in rigid domination environments where stressful experiences are extreme and/or chronic, the neurochemical processes associated with fight-or-flight and dissociation become habitual. They can then become dangerous, both personally and socially.[56] For instance, the high cortisol levels in individuals suffering from extreme and/or chronic stress have been associated with impulsive violence, which poses a danger to both the individual and others.[57] Robert Sapolsky illustrates this phenomenon when he notes, "economic downturns increase rates of spousal and child abuse."[58] The neurochemical profiles associated with depression or the use of drugs or alcohol for psychological escape also aggravate rather than solve problems. And both these responses can be dangerous and ineffective for dealing with complex social challenges, such as conflict between groups and nations or environmental and economic problems.

Genes and Experiences

There are of course genetic differences in individual predispositions to depression or aggression and violence, so none of this means that genes make no difference. However—and this is a critical point—whether these genetic predispositions are expressed, and how much this expression becomes habitual, heavily depend on how many positive or stressful life events an individual experiences.

This was dramatically demonstrated in a study of men with a low-activity version of a gene called monoamine oxidase A, or MAOA, which has been implicated in a higher propensity for violence. What the study showed is that this gene does *not* predict who will become violent: only those men who were mistreated as children, defined as having been rejected by their mothers, physically or sexually abused, or subjected to frequent changes in their primary caregivers, were more likely as adults to engage in antisocial behavior, including violent crime.[59] Men who carried the so-called violence gene but had loving, healthy childhoods did not grow up to become violent. Again, in this case we see that the biocultural interaction of genes and experience accounts for human behavior.

Studies of adopted children also show that even where there may be strong genetic predispositions, these are not necessarily expressed. In a study of Danish children of criminal and noncriminal parents who were adopted, Sarnoff Medick and Barry Hutchings found that although 24 percent of them exhibited criminal behavior when both the biological and the adopting parents were criminal, 20 percent did so when only the biological father was criminal, 15 percent did so when only the adopting parent was criminal, and 13 percent did so when neither set of parents was criminal.[60]

Clearly, genes made a difference, but the fact that highest probability of criminality was when both biological and adopting parents were criminals illustrates the interaction between genes and environment. Even more important is that fully 80 percent of those with a criminal biological father did *not* exhibit criminal behaviors.

Nonetheless, adoption studies showing a correlation between genes and behavior are still frequently cited to support the position that what really matters are genes. This not only ignores studies showing the importance of experience in affecting the expression of genes but also ignores studies showing that the adoptive parents' background is not the only, or even the most important, factor. Their *behavior* also matters.

A series of adoption studies by Remi Cadoret and colleagues from 1983 to 1995 point to the key role of modeling in shaping behavior. They found that antisocial behavior in children, adolescents, and adults is significantly higher in adoptees placed in home environments where the adopting parents display antisocial behavior or alcoholism. In addition, antisocial behaviors increase if the adopting parents have marital problems, legal problems, or suffer from depression or anxiety disorders.[61]

Socioeconomic factors also play a role. Adopted children whose biological parents are delinquent or criminal and who are placed in a home with lower socioeconomic status are more likely to develop problems with substance abuse than those placed in homes with a higher socioeconomic status. [62] In 1996, Michael Bohman reported similar findings from studies of adopted children whose biological parents had a history of petty crime. If adopted into well-functioning homes, 12 percent of these children committed petty crimes as adults. However, if adopted into environmentally risky homes, their rate of petty criminality in adulthood rose to 40 percent.[63]

Our Flexible Brain

What we have been looking at comes down to an often ignored overriding fact: the human brain is enormously flexible. For a large-brained species like ours, there is a vast spectrum of behavioral capacities. We are genetically equipped for destructiveness and creativity, cruelty and caring, rote conformity and independence, and suppression of awareness as well as development of consciousness about ourselves, others, and nature.

As we have seen, our human brain continues to develop for a long time after we are born. In fact, the prefrontal cortex, which plays such a critical role in human behavior, does not fully develop until *after* puberty.[64] Electroencephalographic studies have even shown that the frontal lobes undergo a second growth spurt as the teens give way to young adulthood, between the ages of 19 and 21 or so. This helps explain why experiences during these years of college, work, or military life can powerfully affect both behavior and values.[65]

Behavior and values can also change radically in adulthood. Even though the effects of emotional damage in childhood can usually not be completely erased, they can be reduced by therapeutic interventions. We are then able to reflect on our behavior and change it.

We can also modify destructive thought patterns and behaviors in supportive environments that show us that we have alternatives. Take the dramatic case of Larry Trapp, a Grand Dragon of the Ku Klux Klan in Nebraska who became a speaker for religious and racial tolerance and respect for human rights. What radically changed him was experiencing a caring relationship. When Michael and Julie Weisser, a Jewish cantor and his wife, moved into Trapp's neighborhood, they returned his hate phone calls with loving kindness and offers to help him get groceries, medicines, and other necessities he could not get himself because he was going blind. In response, Trapp not only renounced this racism and anti-Semitism but also strongly denounced these and eventually even converted to Judaism.[66]

This great flexibility of the human brain means that positive experiences should also selectively strengthen neural circuits that represent positive emotions and caring social bonding in adults as well as children. A striking example is that when fathers spend time with their children, their levels of testosterone drop. This effect of behavior on neurochemical states has been shown repeatedly, including by a large study that found that those fathers who reported three hours or more of daily childcare had lower testosterone compared with fathers not involved in care.[67] Cross-culturally, another study found that fathers in a Tanzanian group where fathers are involved in parenting had low testosterone, while those from a neighboring culture without active fathering did not—a subject we will return to when we look at the lack of a clear relationship between testosterone and violence.[68]

Evidence that experience affects the strength of brain synapses accounts in some measure for the capacity of adults to change behavior through learning. But there is much more: over the past decades scientists have found evidence of new neural development in our brains as adults. While it was long thought that only synaptic connections change in the course of life, now studies dramatically show neural development as well.

For instance, an experiment by neuroscientist Fred Gage and his colleagues found not only that new neurons are born in adult brains but also that the survival of these neurons is affected by environmental factors.[69] Brain cells are so flexible that they can even change functions. In blind people who have become Braille readers, for instance, the region of the brain that usually processes vision—and which is not being used in non-Braille-reading blind people—changes function. Norihiro Sadato and his colleagues discovered through functional magnetic resonance imaging (fMRI) that the "visual" region was instead processing tactile sensations, receiving signals from the fingers rather than the eyes.[70]

Many other studies show that behavior affects neurons. For example, a study by scientists at Wayne State University showed that behaviors can change the shape of neurons in ways that affect susceptibility to heart attacks. While a number of earlier studies already showed that exercise can remodel the brain by prompting the creation of new brain cells and inducing other changes, this study found that inactivity, too, can remodel the brain. Being sedentary changes the shape of certain neurons in ways that significantly affect not just the brain but also the heart—helping explain, in part, why a sedentary lifestyle is so bad for us.[71]

Based on such findings, neuroscientists now recognize that profound neural changes can, and do, take place throughout life. This is the crux of constructive learning theory developed by Quartz and Sejnowski, which proposes that brain development is *not* merely the pruning of neural connections but a progressive increase in representational complexity. This increase in complexity culminates in the cortex, which is key to constructive learning.[72] That is, learning does not merely fill our heads with information. Learning affects nothing less than the construction of our brains.

Quartz and Sejnowski emphasize that the theory of constructive learning is not a return to the *tabula rasa* or blank slate theory of the brain. Rather, our genes give us a unique capacity to learn and change behavior as needed in different circumstances, including, as they note, through both cultural and technological innovations.[73] They observe that learning is a dynamic biocultural interaction between genes and experience in which culture, as well as our human capacity for creativity, must be taken into account.

In short, we humans are neurologically flexible *not* despite of our genes but *because* of them.[74] And this flexibility makes it possible for us to change not only our behaviors but also our cultures.

Cultures and Choices

Just as we can develop new ways of thinking and change our emotional reactions, we can change the systems of beliefs and social institutions that compose cultures. The malleable nature of cultural beliefs and institutions is mirrored in the great variation that exists among human societies.

For instance, in Victorian England, the mark of a truly feminine woman was pallid weakness. Among some tribes in Kenya, by contrast, women were perceived as strong enough to carry enormous loads of wood and water over long distances. The Samurai of medieval Japan, like many societies today, equated masculinity with being a fierce warrior. But among the Hopi Indians of North America, a man was supposed to be peaceful and nonaggressive, an ideal regaining currency as we move more in a partnership direction and men embrace "feminine" parenting at the same time that women move into management and other so-called "masculine" roles.[75]

Similarly, the games children play differ from culture to culture. Children of the cattle-herding Banyoro of the East Africa culture "played at going out to war, fighting battles and capturing prisoners and cattle and bringing the spoils to the king; they married and built their kraals, observing taboos as their elders did; they bought, sold, and exchanged cattle and tended them, healing them of various diseases."[76] By contrast, Batek children of Malaysia, who come from a nomadic foraging society that neither herds cattle nor engages in war, play at hunting or moving camp. "They chopped down trees. They built fires and cooked food. They pretended to smoke porcupines out of holes. . . . When one child held his hands up like claws, growled, and ran after the others, everyone begin playing the game of tiger, with much spontaneous role switching between tigers and people—and who was chasing whom."[77]

Childcare, too, is greatly influenced by culture, varying enormously, from habitual violence and strict controls, such as the swaddling that immobilizes infants found in a number of cultures, which was still practiced in Prussia as late as the 19th century, to the free, gentle, and responsive methods recommended by child development studies as Western culture has moved more to the partnership side of the continuum. Yet traditions of domination in childcare are still very much with us. Hitting children to discipline them is widely accepted, even though such assaults on adults are considered crimes. The sexual mutilation of girls practiced in large parts of Africa, Asia, and the Middle East is only now being recognized as a brutal human rights violation. Female infanticide and giving girls less food and healthcare than boys is still practiced in parts of Asia—a cruel discrimination often perpetrated by mothers on their own daughters in accord with cultural beliefs that sons are more valuable. Similarly, so-called honor murders of girls by their own families in many parts of the Middle East and South Asia are still generally culturally accepted and thus rarely punished.

It is difficult to fathom how parents could be so cruel to their own children. Yet these traditional practices—stemming from cultures where control by men over women, parents over children, and rulers over subjects was the unquestioned moral norm—continue to be transmitted from generation to generation. Even in cultures where these top-down rankings are no longer so rigid, parental love is often expressed in coercive and punitive ways because this mind-binding tangle of caring and coercion has been transmitted from generation to generation in domination systems.

Of course, children must also listen to parents in partnership-oriented cultures so that they do not run into traffic, play with poisonous snakes, or otherwise hurt themselves. But the object of these constraints in partnership cultures is not to teach children that the will of their parents is the law, as it is in strict domination cultures where children must be reared in ways that ensure they will accept rigid top-down social and economic controls.

These more partnership-oriented norms were thought up by people who did not operate under rigid rankings of domination or else who saw the possibilities of other childrearing methods even when rigid control was still promoted on traditional or religious grounds. This was possible because of the human capacity to be *proactive* rather than merely reactive: to learn, to create, and to choose.

This ability to choose also applies to changing our cultures. For instance, the Waorani of Ecuador reduced a very high rate of killings by more than 90 percent in just a few years by adopting new, less violent ways of dealing with conflict. As anthropologists Clay and Carole Robarchek observed, "the killing stopped because the Waorani themselves made a conscious decision to end it."[78] Anthropologist Kirk Endicott provides another case from the Chatham Islands in the Pacific involving the Moriori people.[79] They shifted from cycles of blood feuding to dealing with their grievances in nonlethal ways, for instance, fighting with sticks no thicker than a thumb and stopping immediately at the first sight of blood. These new rules prevented bloodshed and halted interpersonal conflicts before they could escalate to the group level. In rural Mexico, a village plagued by violence redistributed land and implemented a total ban on alcohol consumption and the carrying of weapons, with a resulting marked reduction in violence.[80] The members of all these cultures chose to move from the violence inherent in domination systems, in which dominating or being dominated is the only perceived choice, to less violent, more partnership-oriented cultural norms.

But, unfortunately, traditions of domination and violence are still deeply entrenched in many cultures worldwide. Indeed, for much of history, human choices have been severely limited by cultural constraints. Kings and nobles were ranked over craftspeople and merchants, feudal lords were ranked over peasants, men were ranked over women. Not only were these rankings maintained through force or its threat, but people were also taught that no one should try to change his or her station because an individual's place in society was considered part of a fixed, divinely ordained order that must never be questioned. The few who challenged this order faced torture and often death.

Still today, for many people, inequitable economic arrangements, despotic regimes, authoritarian families, rigid male dominance, violence, hunger, disease, malnutrition, poverty, lack of education, and the persistence of religious and secular teachings about the inevitability of all this prevent meaningful choices. But over the last centuries, a growing fraction of humanity has realized that the circumstances of our lives are not inevitable, that there are alternatives, and that we can make choices.

The growing consciousness that we have choices has been largely about *individual choices*. This has been very important. But perhaps even more important is that progressive social and political movements over the last 300 years have also been animated by the consciousness that we have *cultural choices*—which directly affect our individual choices, with the two obviously intertwined.

The rest of this book looks at our cultural choices from the integrated perspective of the Biocultural Partnership-Domination Lens introduced in Chapters 1 and 2. It exposes harmful domination cultural patterns that continue to influence our beliefs, behaviors, and brains, even threatening our survival. It describes partnership cultural alternatives. And it proposes key interventions that can help us build a more secure, just, equitable, and peaceful world for individuals, families, communities, and all humanity.

Notes

1. Thomas Curtis Van Cleve, *The Emperor of Frederick II if Hohenstaufen: Immutator Mundi* (Oxford: Oxford University Press, 1972).
2. Van Cleve, *The Emperor of Frederick II if Hohenstaufen: Immutator Mundi*, 314. In the words of the Chronicle of Salimbene written by a 13th-century Italian Franciscan monk, Frederick "made linguistic experiments on the vile bodies of hapless infants, bidding foster-mothers and nurses to suckle and bathe and wash the children, but in no wise to prattle or speak with them; for he would have learnt whether they would speak the Hebrew language (which had been the first), or Greek, or Latin, or Arabic, or perchance the tongue of their parents of whom they had been born. But he laboured in vain, for the children could not live without clappings of the hands, and gestures, and gladness of countenance, and blandishments." Salimbene quoted in the *Cambridge Encyclopedia of Language*. Available online: http://www.kabalarians. com/forum/forum_posts.asp?TID=723.
3. One thousand years ago, only a small percentage of the population of Western Europe could read—even though humans have the genetic potential to learn to read. In the United States, as late as the 1820s, only 20 percent of the general population could read, and the illiteracy rate for African Americans was 80 percent, reflecting the fact that they were systematically denied the opportunity to learn to read. So this genetic potential remained untapped until the advent of universal public education. (National Center for Educational Statistics. *National Assessment of Adult Literacy [NAAL]*. Available online: https://nces.ed.gov/naal/lit_history.asp).

4. Height is coded for by hundreds of genes, with none describing even 1 percent of the variability.

5. William H. Angoff, "The Nature-Nurture Debate, Aptitudes, and Group Differences," *American Psychologist* 43, 9 (1988): 713–720, doi: 10.1037/0003-066X.43.9.713; Howard W. French, "Tokyo Journal: The Japanese, It Seems, Are Outgrowing Japan," *New York Times*, February 1, 2001. Available online: http://www.nytimes.com/2001/02/01/world/tokyo-journal-the-japanese-it-seems-are-outgrowing-japan.html.

6. Eric B. Keverne, "Epigenetics: Significance of the Gene-Environment Interface for Brain Development," in *Pathways to Peace: The Transformative Power of Children and Families*, eds. James F. Leckman, Catherine Panter-Brick, and Rima Salah (Cambridge, MA: MIT Press, 2014).

7. Tessa Roseboom, Susanne de Rooij, and Rebecca Painter, "The Dutch Famine and Its Long-Term Consequences to Adult Health," *Early Human Development* 82 (2006): 485–491, 487, doi: 10.1016/j.earlhumdev.2006.07.001.

8. Roseboom, Rooij, and Painter, "The Dutch Famine"; Keverne, "Epigenetics"; see also L. H. Lumey, "Decreased Birthweights in Infants after Maternal in utero Exposure to the Dutch Famine of 1944-1945," *Paediatrics and Perinatal Epidemiology* 6 (1992): 240–253, doi: 10.1111/j.1365-3016.1992.tb00764.x; Robert Sapolsky, personal communication, April 2018.

9. Keverne, "Epigenetics," 68.

10. Brian G. Dias and Kerry J. Ressler, "Parental Olfactory Experience Influences Behavior and Neural Structure in Subsequent Generations," *Nature Neuroscience* 17 (2014): 89–96, doi: 10.1038/nn.3594.

11. Ressler quoted in Ewen Callaway, "Fearful Memories Haunt Mouse Descendants: Genetic Imprint from Traumatic Experiences Carries through at Least Two Generations," *Nature* (December 1, 2013), doi:10.1038/nature.2013.14272. Available online: http://www.nature.com/news/fearful-memories-haunt-mouse-descendants-1.14272.

12. Dias and Ressler, "Parental Olfactory Experience," 89–96.

13. Alison Abbott, "Obesity Linked to Grandparental Diet: Mice Eating High-Fat Foods Confer Changes on at Least Two Subsequent Generations," *Nature* (November 20, 2008): doi: 10.1038/news.2008.1240.

14. Romain Lambrot et al., "Low Paternal Dietary Folate Alters the Mouse Sperm Epigenome and Is Associated with Negative Pregnancy Outcomes," *Nature Communications* 4, 2889 (2013): article 2889, doi: 10.1038/ncomms3889.

15. Eva Jablonka and Gal Raz, "Transgenerational Epigenetic Inheritance: Prevalence, Mechanisms, and Implications for the Study of Heredity and Evolution," *Quarterly Review of Biology* 84 (2009): 131–176, doi: 10.1086/598822. This paper catalogs some 100 forms of epigenetic inheritance. Such studies have led some scientists to ponder again the view of Lamarck we glanced at in Chapter 2 that characteristics acquired by parents can be passed on to their offspring—the theory of inheritance of acquired characteristics. See, e.g., R. Jaenisch and A. Bird, "Epigenetic: How the Genome Integrates Intrinsic and Environmental Signals," *Nature Genetics* 33 (2003): 245–254, doi: 10.1038/ng1089; John Cloud, "Epigenetics: Why Your DNA Isn't Your Destiny,"

Time, January 6, 2010. Available online: http://www.time.com/time/health/article/0,8599,1951968,00.html.

16. Yan Jiang et al., "Epigenetics in the Nervous System," *Journal of Neuroscience* 28 (2008): 11753–11759, doi: 10.1523/JNEUROSCI.3797-08.2008.

17. Gilbert Gottlieb, *Synthesizing Nature-Nurture* (Mahwah, NJ: Erlbaum, 1997), 102–103.

18. Gottlieb, *Synthesizing Nature-Nurture,* 105. Gottlieb concluded that "external sensory and internal neural events excite or inhibit gene expression" and that theories explaining behavior must take into account what happens in the course of development (134).

19. Harry F. Harlow, "The Nature of Love," *American Psychologist* 13 (1958): 673–685, doi: 10.1037/h0047884.

20. Sometimes these monkeys would attempt to have sex with "inappropriate" targets for their ardor (e.g., water bottles) (Robert Sapolsky, personal communication, April 2018).

21. Harry Harlow and Margaret Harlow, "Social Deprivation in Monkeys," *Scientific American* 207 (1962): 136–150. Available online: http://www.jstor.org/stable/24936357.

22. Dario Maestripieri et al., "Influence of Parenting Style on the Offspring's Behaviour and CSF Monoamine Metabolite Levels in Crossfostered and Noncrossfostered Female Rhesus Macaques," *Behavioural Brain Research* 175 (2006): 90–95, doi: 10.1016/j.bbr.2006.08.002.

23. Maestripieri et al., "Influence."

24. Teresa Jones and Robert Greenough, "Ultrastructural Evidence for Increased Contact between Astrocytes and Synapses in Rats Reared in a Complex Environment," *Neurobiology of Learning and Memory* 65 (1996): 48–56.

25. Jeffrey A. Klein et al., "Selective Synaptic Plasticity within the Cerebellar Cortex following Complex Motor Skill Learning," *Neurobiology of Learning and Memory* 69 (1998): 274–289.

26. Darlene Francis et al., "Nongenomic Transmission Across Generations of Maternal Behavior and Stress Responses in the Rat," *Science* 286 (1999): 1155–1158, doi: 10.1126/science.286.5442.1155.

27. Robert M. Sapolsky and Lisa J. Share, "A Pacific Culture among Wild Baboons: Its Emergence and Transmission," *Public Library of Science Biology* 2 (2004): e106, doi: 10.1371/journal.pbio.0020106; Robert M. Sapolsky, "Rousseau with a Tail: Maintaining a Tradition of Peace among Baboons," in *War, Peace, and Human Nature: The Convergence of Evolutionary and Cultural Views,* ed. Douglas P. Fry (New York: Oxford University Press, 2013).

28. Robert Sapolsky quoted in Natalie Angier, "No Time for Bullies: Baboons Retool Their Culture," *New York Times,* April 13, 2004. Available online: http://www.nytimes.com/2004/04/13/science/no-time-for-bullies-baboons-retool-their-culture.html.

29. Robert Sapolsky, "Rousseau with a Tail"; Sapolsky and Share, "A Pacific Culture among Wild Baboons."

30. Sapolsky, "Rousseau with a Tail," 434.

31. De Waal quoted in Natalie Angier, "No Time for Bullies: Baboons Retool Their Culture," *New York Times*, April 13, 2004.

32. Frans de Waal, *Peacemaking among Primates* (Cambridge, MA: Harvard University Press, 1989).

33. Shelley E. Taylor, *The Tending Instinct: How Nurturing Is Essential to Who We Are and How We Live* (New York: Henry Holt, 2002), 64; see also Julie B. Kaplow and Cathy Spatz Widom, "Age of Onset of Child Maltreatment Predicts Long-Term Mental Health Outcomes," *Journal of Abnormal Psychology* 116 (2007): 176–187, doi: 10.1037/0021-843X.116.1.176; C. Sue Carter, "The Chemistry of Child Neglect: Do Oxytocin and Vasopressin Mediate the Effects of Early Experience?" *Proceedings of the National Academy of Sciences (PNAS)* 102 (2005): 18247–18248, doi: 10.1073/pnas.0509376102; "Low Levels of Neurotransmitter Serotonin May Perpetuate Child Abuse Across Generations," *ScienceDaily*, November 2, 2006. Available online: https://www.sciencedaily.com/releases/2006/11/061102092229.htm.

34. L. Rosenblum and G. Paully, "The Effects of Varying Environmental Demands on Maternal and Infant Behavior," *Child Development* 55 (1984): 305–314, doi: 10.2307/1129854.

35. Keverne, "Epigenetics," 73.

36. John Bowlby, *Attachment: Attachment and Loss, Volume 1* (New York: Basic Books, 1969). Bowlby's ideas had a great influence on the way researchers thought about attachment, and much of the discussion of his theory has focused on his belief in monotropy—that is, instinctive need for attachment to one person: the mother.

37. H. Rudolph Schaffer and Peggy Emerson, *The Development of Social Attachments in Infancy* (Lafayette, IN: Purdue University Press, 1964); Michael Rutter, "Maternal Deprivation, 1972-1978: New Findings, New Concepts, New Approaches," *Child Development* 50, 2 (1979): 283–305, doi: 10.2307/1129404; Saul McLeod, "Bowlby's Attachment Theory," *Simply Psychology*, 2007. Available online: https://www.simplypsychology.org/bowlby.html.

38. For example, Schaffer and Emerson, *The Development of Social Attachments in Infancy*, in their studies found that specific attachments started at about 8 months and, very shortly thereafter, the infants became attached to other people. By 18 months very few (13%) were attached to only one person; some had five or more attachments. Similarly, Rutter, "Maternal Deprivation 1972-1978," pointed out that there are several indicators of attachment, and that studies of children of mothers who have outside jobs can fare well, and in some cases better than, children whose mother stays at home. Among other critics of this theory are scientists showing that mothers are the exclusive caregivers in only a very small percentage of human societies; often there are a number of people involved in the care of children, such as relations and friends [Thomas Weisner et al., "My Brother's Keeper: Child and Sibling Caretaking," *Current Anthropology* 18 (1977): 169–190, https://doi.org/10.1086/201883]; and protest or distress when attached person leaves has been shown for a variety of attachment figures—fathers, siblings, peers, and even inanimate objects.

Critics such as Rutter have also accused Bowlby of not distinguishing between deprivation and privation—the complete lack of an attachment bond, rather than its loss. Rutter stresses that the *quality* of the attachment bond is the most important factor, rather than just deprivation. For a summary of criticisms of Bowlby, see Saul McLeod, "Bowlby's Attachment Theory"; on care of infants by multiple caretakers in nomadic band societies, see Sarah B. Hrdy, *Mothers and Others* (Cambridge, MA: Harvard University Press, 2009); Kirk M. Endicott and Karen L. Endicott, *The Headman Was a Woman: The Gender Egalitarian Batek of Malaysia* (Long Grove, IL: Waveland, 2008); and Carter, "The Chemistry of Child Neglect."

39. McLeod, "Bowlby's Attachment Theory"; Rutter, "Maternal Deprivation"; Nancy Folbre and Julie A. Nelson, "For Love or Money—Or Both?" *Journal of Economic Perspectives* 14 (2000): 123–140, doi: 10.1257/jep.14.4.123.

40. Darcia Narvaez, *Neurobiology and the Development of Human Morality: Evolution, Culture, and Wisdom* (New York: Norton, 2014); Darcia Narvaez, "The 99 Percent—Development and Socialization within an Evolutionary Context: Growing Up to Become 'A Good and Useful Human Being'" in *War, Peace, and Human Nature: The Convergence of Evolutionary and Cultural Views*, ed. Douglas P. Fry (New York: Oxford University Press, 2013); Hrdy, *Mothers and Others.*

41. Samuel Oliner and Pearl Oliner, *The Altruistic Personality: Rescuers of Jews in Nazi Europe* (New York: The Free Press, 1988).

42. See, e.g., Christopher Ellison and John Bartkowski, "Religion and the Legitimization of Violence: Conservative Protestantism and Corporal Punishment," in *The Web of Violence: From Interpersonal to Global*, eds. Jennifer Turpin and Lester Kurtz (Urbana: University of Illinois Press, 1997).

43. Kristin Valentino, Michelle Comas, and Amy Nuttall, "Child Maltreatment and Early Mother-Child Interactions," in *Ancestral Landscapes in Human Evolution*, eds. Darcia Narvaez et al. (New York: Oxford University Press, 2014); Kaplow and Widom, "Age of Onset of Child Maltreatment"; Carter, "The Chemistry of Child Neglect."

44. Taylor, *The Tending Instinct*; see also Robert M. Sapolsky, *Behave: The Biology of Humans at Our Best and Worst* (New York: Penguin, 2017).

45. Taylor, *The Tending Instinct*, 25.

46. Mary Cho, Courtney DeVries, Jessie Williams, and C. Sue Carter, "The Effects of Oxytocin and Vasopressin on Partner Preferences in Male and Female Prairie Voles (*Microtus Ochrogaster*)," *Behavioral Neuroscience,* 113 (1999): 1071–1079, http://dx.doi.org/10.1037/0735-7044.113.5.1071; Kerstin Uvnäs-Moberg, "Oxytocin May Mediate the Benefits of Positive Social Interactions and Emotions." *Psychoneuroendocrinology* 23 (1998): 819–835, doi: https://doi.org/10.1016/S0306-4530(98)00056-0; C. Sue Carter and Stephen Porges, "Peptide Pathways to Peace," in *Pathways to Peace: The Transformative Power of Children and Families*, eds. James Leckman, Catherine Panter-Brick, and Rima Salah (Cambridge, MA: MIT Press, 2014).

47. Uvnäs-Moberg, "Oxytocin May Mediate the Benefits of Positive Social Interaction and Emotion."

48. Jennifer Ferguson, Larry Young, Elizabeth Hearn, Martin Matzuk, Thomas Insel, and James Winslow, "Social Amnesia in Mice Lacking the Oxytocin Gene," *Nature Genetics* 25 (2000): 284–288, doi:10.1038/77040.

49. Taylor, *The Tending Instinct*, 31; Sapolsky, *Behave*; Carter, "The Chemistry of Child Neglect"; Carter and Porges, "Peptide Pathways to Peace."

50. Thomas Insel, James Winslow, and their colleagues also discovered that oxytocin has broader importance for bonding [Thomas Insel, "Oxytocin—A Neuropeptide for Affiliation: Evidence from Behavioral, Receptor Autoradiographic, and Comparative Studies," *Psychoneuroendocrinology* 17 (1992): 3–35, doi: https://doi.org/10.1016/0306-4530(92)90073-G; Thomas Insel et al., "Oxytocin, Vasopressin, and the Neuroendocrine Basis of Pair Bond Formation," in *Vasopressin and Oxytocin: Advances in Experimental Medicine and Biology*, eds. Hans H. Zingg, Charles Bourque, and Daniel G. Bichet. Boston: Springer, 1998; see also Carter and Porges, "Peptide Pathways to Peace"]. Insel and colleagues looked at two species of North American rodents that are closely related but have radically different social organization: the *prairie vole*, which is monogamous with strong male-female pair bonding and both parents involved in care of young, and the *montane vole*, which is promiscuous with fathers uninvolved with young. See also Carter, "The Chemistry of Child Neglect"; and Sapolsky, *Behave*.

51. While in most mammalian species females have taken the major caregiving role, this does not mean that human males cannot be caregivers. Females may in the course of evolution have developed biochemical patterns that favor caregiving behaviors. But whether or not human females are more genetically predisposed than males to learn caregiving, as well as to "tending and befriending" rather than fighting or fleeing, we still have the role of experience in gene expression to deal with. And this is where environmental cues—and particularly the cultural environment—again come in.

52. James Henry and Sheila Wang, "Effects of Early Stress on Adult Affiliative Behavior," *Psychoneuroendocrinology* 23 (1998): 863–875, doi: 10.1016/S0306-4530(98)00058-4.

53. Henry and Wang, "Effects of Early Stress," 867.

54. Carter and Porges, "Peptide Pathways to Peace"; Ruth Feldman, "Oxytocin and Social Affiliation in Humans," *Hormones and Behavior* 61 (2012): 380–391, doi: 10.1016/j.yhbeh.2012.01.008. Low levels of serotonin have been associated with impulsive violence, as well as with suicide, which can be viewed as the ultimate flight response to stress. (William Bligh-Glover et al., "The Serotonin Transporter in the Midbrain of Suicide Victims with Major Depression," *Biological Psychiatry* 47 (2000): 1015–1024, doi: https://doi.org/10.1016/S0006-3223(99)00313-3.

55. Sapolsky, *Behave*. As Sapolsky notes, this does not mean that cortisol and norepinephrine are "bad" chemicals. Cortisol also inhibits pain receptors, while norepinephrine and epinephrine enable alertness. So these hormones are not in themselves negative, nor are all the behaviors they influence. If you are walking on a narrow ledge, chopping wood, or engaged in other activities that require extreme alertness, norepinephrine and epinephrine are useful.

56. Like all neurochemical processes, the neurochemical profiles of fight-or-flight and dissociation involve complex interactions. To illustrate, dopamine is a neurochemical

involved in a wide range of positive feelings. But dopamine is also implicated in the dissociative response of withdrawing from reality. Many addictive drugs operate by causing massive releases of dopamine in the area around the nucleus accumbens—a primary area for both natural and drug-related dopamine rewards. This dopamine "high" can then lead to the downward-cycling of drug addiction, making replenishment of dopamine dependent on further drug use. Serotonin, a neurochemical associated with stabilizing and calming emotions, is also implicated in depression—which is why antidepressants such as Prozac are designed to free more of it to flow to reduce stress. Patterns of high serotonin turnover and corresponding low levels of circulating serotonin are also associated with aggression, risk-taking, and even premature death in both humans and monkeys.

57. Taylor, *The Tending Instinct*, 66.
58. Sapolsky, *Behave*, 132.
59. Avshalom Caspi et al., "Role of Genotype in the Cycle of Violence in Maltreated Children," *Science* 297, (2002): 851–854, doi: 10.1126/science.1072290. This study was of a large sample of male children from birth to adulthood to determine why some children who are maltreated grow up to develop antisocial behavior, whereas others do not. While maltreated boys with the low variant of the neurotransmitter-metabolizing enzyme monoamine oxidase A (MAOA) were prone to violence, maltreated children with a genotype conferring high levels of MAOA expression were less likely to develop antisocial problems. These findings may partly explain why not all victims of maltreatment grow up to victimize others. See also Emily Singer, "Mistreatment during Childhood and Low Enzyme Activity May Make Men More Violent," *Los Angeles Times*, August 2, 2002. Available online: http://www.latimes.com/news/nationworld/nation/la-sci-abuse2aug02.stor.
60. Sarnoff A. Medick and Barry Hutchings, "Registered Criminality in Adoptive and Biological Parents of Registered Male Criminal Adoptees," *Proceedings of the Annual Meeting of the American Psychopathological Association* 63 (1975): 105–116.
61. Remi Cadoret et al., "Alcoholism and Antisocial Personality: Interrelationships, Genetic and Environmental Factors," *Archives of General Psychiatry* 42 (1985): 161–167, doi: org/10.1001/archpsyc.1985.01790250055007; Remi Cadoret et al., "Genetic and Environmental Factors in Adoptee Antisocial Personality," *European Archives of Psychiatry and Clinical Neuroscience* 239 (1990): 231–240, doi: 10.1007/BF01738577; Remi Cadoret et al., "Genetic-Environmental Interaction in the Genesis of Aggressivity and Conduct Disorders," *Archives of General Psychiatry* 52 (1995): 916–924, doi: 10.1001/archpsyc.1995.03950230030006.
62. Cadoret et al., "Alcoholism and Antisocial Personality: Interrelationships, Genetic and Environmental Factors"; Cadoret et al., "Genetic-Environmental Interaction in the Genesis of Aggressivity and Conduct Disorders."
63. Michael Bohman, "Predispositions to Criminality: Swedish Adoption Studies in Retrospect," in *Genetics of Criminal and Anti-social Behavior*, eds. Gregory Bock and Jamie Goode (Chichester, UK: Wiley, 1996). Also showing that a genetic predisposition can either manifest itself or not, depending largely on environmental conditions, is a Finnish adoption study by Pekka Tienari, Layman Wynne, Juha

Moring, Ilpo Lahti, M. Naarala, A. Sorri, K. Wahlberg, O. Saarento, M. Seitamaa, and M. Kaleva, "The Finnish Adoptive Family Study of Schizophrenia: Implications for Family Research." *British Journal of Psychiatry* 164 (Supplement 23, 1994): 20–26. The researchers found that adoptees who had a schizophrenic biological parent were much more likely to develop a range of psychiatric disorders (including schizophrenia) if they were adopted into dysfunctional families.

64. Keverne, "Epigenetics."

65. William Hudspeth and Karl Pribram, "Psychophysiological Indices of Cerebral Maturation," *International Journal of Psychophysiology* 12 (1992): 19–29, doi: 10.1016/0167-8760(92)90039-E; Paul Thompson et al., "Growth Patterns in the Developing Brain Detected by Using Continuum Mechanical Tensor Maps," *Nature* 404 (2002): 190–193, doi: 10.1038/35004593. Hudspeth and Pribram interpreted these changes in brain-wave patterns as representing maturation of neural structures in the frontal lobes. The nature of the maturation might be myelination, that is, formation of part of the insulating "sheath" around brain cells that improves the efficiency of electrical transmission. Or it might be formation of new synapses or connections between brain cells. Either way, Hudspeth and Pribram's findings indicate that the life changes of late adolescence and early adulthood are extremely significant for human development.

66. Karen Schneider, "Living with the Enemy," *People*, June 1, 1992. Available online: http://people.com/archive/living-with-the-enemy-vol-37-no-21/.

67. Lee Gettler et al., "Longitudinal Evidence that Fatherhood Decreases Testosterone in Human Males," *Proceedings of the National Academy of Sciences (PNAS)* 108 (2011): 16194–16199, doi: 10.1073/pnas.1105403108.

68. Sapolsky, *Behave*; Martin Muller et al., "Testosterone and Paternal Care in East African Foragers and Pastoralists," *Proceedings of the Royal Society B: Biological Sciences* 276 (2009): 347–354, doi: 10.1098/rspb.2008.1028.

69. J. Tiago Goncalves and Simon Schafer, "Adult Neurogenesis in the Hippocampus: From Stem Cells to Behavior," *Cell* 167 (2016): 897–914. doi: https://doi.org/10.1016/j.cell.2016.10.021; Steven Quartz and Terrence Sejnowski, *Liars, Lovers, and Heroes: What the New Brain Science Reveals about How We Become Who We Are* (New York: William Morrow, 2002), 7.

70. Quartz and Sejnowski, *Liars, Lovers, and Heroes*, 39–40. The flexibility of brain cells in nonhuman species was also shown when Fred Gage and his colleagues at the Salk Institute transplanted fetal pig cells into adult rat brains and found that the pig cells acted like rat cells.

71. Nicholas Mischel, Ida Llewellyn-Smith, and Patrick Mueller, "Physical (In)activity-Dependent Structural Plasticity in Bulbospinal Catecholaminergic Neurons of Rat Rostral Ventrolateral Medulla," *Journal of Comparative Neurology* 522 (2014): 499–513. doi: 10.1002/cne.23464.

72. Quartz and Sejnowski, *Liars, Lovers, and Heroes*.

73. Quartz and Sejnowski, *Liars, Lovers, and Heroes*.

74. Quartz and Sejnowski, *Liars, Lovers, and Heroes*, 27.

75. Riane Eisler, "A Time for Partnership," in *SAGA: Best New Writings on Mythology, Volume 2,* ed. Jonathan Young (Ashland, OR: White Cloud Press, 2001); Alice Schlegel, "Contentious but Not Violent: The Hopi of Northern Arizona," in *Keeping the Peace: Peaceful Societies and Conflict Resolution around the World,* eds. Graham Kemp and Douglas P. Fry (New York: Routledge, 2004).

76. John Roscoe, *The Bakitara or Bunyoro* (Cambridge, UK: Cambridge University Press, 1923), 259–260.

77. Kirk M. Endicott and Karen L. Endicott, *The Headman Was a Woman: The Gender Egalitarian Batek of Malaysia* (Long Grove, IL: Waveland Press, 2008), 117, 118.

78. Clayton Robarchek and Carole Robarchek, "Waging Peace: The Psychological and Sociocultural Dynamics of Positive Peace," in *Anthropological Contributions to Conflict Resolution,* eds. Alvin Wolfe and Honggang Yang (Athens: University of Georgia Press, 1996), 72–73.

79. Kirk M. Endicott, "Peaceful Foragers: The Significance of the Batek and Moriori for the Question of Innate Human Violence," in *War, Peace, and Human Nature: The Convergence of Evolutionary and Cultural Views,* ed. Douglas P. Fry (New York: Oxford University Press, 2013).

80. James B. Greenberg, *Blood Ties: Life and Violence in Rural Mexico* (Tucson: University of Arizona Press, 1989).

5

The Benefits of Partnership and the Costs of Domination

Not long ago, many people thought communism would cure the world's ills. But the communist revolutions in Russia and China brought further violence and repression. Today, many people think capitalism and democratic elections are the answer. They forget that Adolf Hitler was elected in Germany, Donald Trump was elected in the United States, Egyptians elected an authoritarian fundamentalist regime after the Arab Spring, and capitalism brought neither peace nor equity. Others believe that returning to prescientific Western times or replacing Western secularism, science, and technology with Eastern religions will cure our world's ills. They ignore that the religious Middle Ages were brutal and repressive, that Eastern religions have helped perpetuate inequality and oppression, and that today's fundamentalist religious cultures, both Eastern and Western, are creating, rather than solving, some of our planet's most serious problems.

If capitalist, communist, rightist, leftist, religious, secular, Eastern, and Western cultures all had patterns of violence and inequity, it should not surprise us that many people think the trouble must lie in human nature. But this view stems from the fragmented perspective of old social categories, which only describe particular aspects of cultures. A systems approach opens up wider vistas, revealing relational dynamics: interactive patterns or connections that are otherwise invisible.

Just as we need a systemic framework that describes the interaction of biology and culture in affecting behavior, we need a systemic framework that describes the mutually supporting interaction of the major components of cultures—including what is considered normal or abnormal in our foundational parent-child and gender relations.

This chapter focuses on the tension between domination systems and partnership systems as two ends of a continuum along which human societies can be organized. We look at the core components of each system, how these interact, and how growing up in societies that orient to one or the other differentially affects neurological development and hence our perceptions, cognitions, emotions, and behaviors—which in turn affect human health, happiness, well-being, and the types of societies we create.

Domination Systems and Partnership Systems

Domination systems have four mutually supporting core components.[1]

First, rigid top-down rankings, hierarchies of domination, are maintained through physical, psychological, and economic control in familial, religious, political, economic, and other social institutions.

The second component of domination systems is the ranking of one form of humanity over the other. Theoretically, this could be the female half over the male half, but historically it has been the ranking of males over females, and with this, the idealization of traits that are in domination systems equated with masculinity, such as "manly" conquest and "heroic" violence.

The cultural acceptance of abuse and violence, from child-and-wife-beating to slavery and warfare, constitutes the third component of domination systems. Violence can be direct, as in flogging, torture, and genocide, as well as structural, as noted by Johan Galtung, playing out as exploitation, repression, injustice, and social inequities enshrined within the society's norms, values, practices, and institutions.[2] Abuse and violence are built into domination systems to maintain rankings of domination.

The fourth core component consists of beliefs that rankings of domination are inevitable, even moral. In cultures and subcultures that orient closely to the domination system, we find teachings and stories telling that it is honorable to kill and enslave members of other societies, stone women to death or maim them with acid, stand by while supposedly "inferior" people are put in ovens and gassed, or beat children to impose adult control through physical force.

By stark contrast, the four interconnected core components of partnership systems support equity, caring, and well-being not only for some individuals but also for all members of the society.[3]

The first component is a democratic and egalitarian structure manifested in social practices, values, and institutions. This democratic and egalitarian focus provides the template for all social institutions, from the family to the society or state.

The second component is equal partnership between women and men. With this equality comes the high valuing, in both women and men, of qualities and behaviors such as nonviolence and caregiving that are denigrated as "feminine" in domination systems.

The third core component of partnership systems is the cultural rejection of abuse and violence. This does not mean that partnership systems are totally free of violence, but rather that abuse and violence are not systemically built into a society's values, traditions, and social institutions.

The fourth component consists of beliefs about human nature that support empathic and mutually respectful relations. Although cruelty and violence are recognized as human possibilities, they are not considered inevitable, let alone moral. Instead, typical human relations are seen as based on precepts of equality, mutual respect, compassion, caring, and cooperation geared toward the social good.

We want to again emphasize that the partnership-domination distinction transcends conventional categories such as ancient-modern, religious-secular, Eastern-Western, or preindustrial-industrial-postindustrial. For example, as we will see in later chapters, societies that orient closely to the domination end of the continuum can be Western, such as secular Nazi Germany, or Eastern, such as religious Iran and the so-called Islamic Caliphate of ISIS. Examples of partnership systems, as we will also see, include cultures from various quarters of the world, indigenous societies as well as technologically advanced nations.

We also want to quickly note two major historical shifts in the domination-partnership continuum. As we will detail in later chapters, on the grand scale that stretches back across the Pleistocene since the origin of genus *Homo*, archeological and ethnographic evidence suggests that a durable legacy of cultural orientation to partnership lasted for at least two million years.[4] Then, a domination social organization began to enter the social mainstream approximately 5,000 to 10,000 years ago, punctuated by intermittent attempts to move again toward partnership.[5] The second shift is much more recent and is ongoing: over the last several centuries, we have seen strong movement toward the partnership side of the continuum.

One progressive social movement after another has challenged entrenched traditions of domination—from the "divinely ordained" right of kings to rule to the "divinely ordained" right of men to rule over the women and children in their families and of some races or religions to dominate others. Recent history has seen the formal abolition of slavery and the outlawing of torture.[6] The Geneva Conventions have sought to reduce atrocities of war.[7] We have seen the birth of human rights and important strides for women's rights.[8] Colonialism has dwindled, and nonviolent regime changes now outnumber violent revolutions by a ratio of two-to-one.[9]

However, these challenges to top-down control have focused primarily on domination in politics and economics. The majority of progressive social movements have paid scant attention to the relations that most profoundly affect brain development: parent-child and gender relations. As a result, the domination pyramid has continued to rebuild itself on the same foundations—whether through totalitarianism, religious fundamentalism, or other domination isms.

This new understanding of what has been missing for sustainable change offers grounded hope for our future. We see that the movement toward a more partnership-oriented world has not failed—rather, it is incomplete.

The Partnership-Domination Continuum

No society orients completely toward either the domination or partnership configuration. But the degree to which a society orients to either end of the partnership-domination continuum profoundly affects which beliefs, institutions, and practices are culturally reinforced.

To illustrate, during the European Middle Ages the idea of human rights would have been beyond the pale. This does not mean there were no partnership elements in medieval culture. There was a period when the veneration of Mary as the compassionate mother of God became prominent, elevating the stereotypically "feminine" in a culture that otherwise held women in such contempt that theologians actually debated whether women, like men, have souls. For a while, communities inspired by St. Francis and St. Claire tried to practice partnership with both humans and other species, and there were even the self-supporting, self-governing, service-oriented Beguine communities, who believed women were directly empowered by God.[10] But with its Inquisition, Crusades, chronic wars, witch-burnings, and strict male control of women and children, the European Middle Ages leaned closely to the authoritarian, male-dominated, violent domination system.

These were extremely stressful times. In addition to regular exhibitions of public torture for any questioning of the divinely ordained top-down social order or for doubting that the Church taught the word of God, constant battles between nobles whose favorite sport it seemed was sacking each other's castles and decimating the surrounding farmlands, religious dogmas that condoned the abuse of women and children, and the chronic fear and suffering that all this engendered, there was also the stress and pain of poverty for the vast majority of people.

The medieval Church taught that women must obey their husbands just as common men must obey nobles, kings, popes, and bishops. Any attempt to throw off such "divinely ordained" authority was a sin against the authority of the supreme male ruler: God. A husband's use of violence against a wife who disobeyed orders or was suspected of sexual independence was considered natural and right.[11]

Parenting was, as it still is today in domination-oriented cultures and subcultures, based on harsh punishments for disobedience, which teach children to equate respect with fear, shame, and blame. As reams of psychological writings document, this harsh kind of upbringing is extremely stressful. But fear of pain is a basic motivator in domination systems.[12]

By contrast, partnership parenting is based more on praise, caring touch, modeling mutual respect, and helping children learn to care for themselves and others.[13] This is not laissez-faire parenting where anything goes. There are expectations, rules, and consequences for destructive behavior, whether to others or oneself. But parenting is authoritative rather than authoritarian and responsive rather than repressive. Family relations, including those between parents, are far less stressful and model a morality of caring rather than coercion.[14]

In these and a myriad other ways, partnership- and domination-oriented societies are fundamentally different. However, before going further, we want to clear up some possible misperceptions about these differences.

First, what distinguishes partnership systems from domination systems is *not* cooperation per se, but the ends to which it is applied. Cooperation in partnership systems is not aimed at having harmful effects on anyone; it is a prosocial endeavor. By contrast, while people also cooperate in domination systems, much of the time toward positive ends, all too often cooperation is co-opted to serve the needs of a few, exploit the many, and inflict harm. Terrorists work together to maim and kill; businesses collaborate to build monopolies that fix prices and crush competitors; secret police cooperate to execute citizens; invading armies cooperate to annihilate and destroy. Thus, a critical difference in partnership cooperation and domination cooperation is the purpose to which the teamwork is applied. In partnership systems the outcome tends to promote human well-being and can be seen as reciprocally positive or generally prosocial, whereas in domination systems cooperation can also be harnessed to exploit, subjugate, and abuse—or in other words, to dominate—other human beings.

Second, the difference between these two systems is *not* that the domination system is hierarchical and the partnership system is hierarchy-free. Some partnership-oriented systems do not have completely flat structures: parents are still responsible for children, teachers for students, and managers for workers, and there may be leaders and followers in partnership systems.[15] But the ideal norm for parents, teachers, managers, and leaders, as in some Western partnership structures, is to empower rather than disempower through what Riane calls hierarchies of actualization.[16] By contrast, hierarchies of domination are imposed and maintained by fear and force. They are held in place by the power that is idealized, even sanctified, in cultures that orient primarily to the domination system: the power to control others, inflict pain, destroy, and kill.[17] Of course, we are talking about conceptual differences; in real life there will necessarily be shades of gray, which is why we speak in terms of a partnership-domination continuum.

Third, the difference between domination and partnership systems is *not* that there is competition in the former but not in the latter, but rather that domination systems promote cut-throat, "dog-eat-dog" competition, whereas competition in partnership systems tends to be less overt and may be directed more to excellence: the achievements of others are a spur to greater accomplishments.[18] Many partnership-oriented societies across the ethnographic spectrum actively socialize children to avoid overt competition as socially undesirable, as among the Paliyan of India, the Semai and the Batek of Malaysia, and the Hopi of North America. Moreover, the competition that does exist in such cultures often takes very formalized and limited routes of expression, for instance, through contests or rituals.[19]

In domination systems, whether Western or non-Western, competition can rage out of control as individuals seek to satisfy their affect hunger by besting others rather than forming bonds with them. So it is not that partnership systems lack all competition or that domination systems are only competitive, but as the flip side of cooperation, competition in domination-oriented societies is more common, more severe, and often harmful.

Fourth, there is conflict in both systems because there will always be disagreements among people. But in partnership systems, conflict can be used to facilitate creative solutions through mediation and other techniques for finding nonviolent ways of resolving conflicts. In domination systems, conflict either is suppressed by those in power or explodes into violence— which is one of the reasons domination systems are so dangerous in this time of nuclear and biological weaponry.

Finally, biological differences between males and females are recognized in both systems. But in domination-oriented cultures, boys are socialized to be "less emotional"—which actually means they are taught that anger and contempt are permissible "masculine" emotions, but that they must re- press feelings considered feminine such as caring and empathy, lest they be despised as sissies or weak sisters. Women, too, are taught to repress part of their human repertoire. They are taught that anger and other supposedly masculine emotions are reserved for those who dominate, in other words, for men.

With movement toward the partnership side of the continuum, rigid gender stereotypes have begun to melt away—as shown by the many men today adopting "feminine" roles, such as feeding, diapering, and tending to their children's needs, and the many women entering professions once considered strictly male preserves. Exemplifying this trend, former Prime Minister of Finland, Paavo Lipponen, took paternity leave upon the birth of his daughter in 1998, and in so doing sent a subtle message to Finnish men across all professions that no job is so important that it should take prece- dence over family life and the joys and duties of fatherhood. Somehow the government continued to function in the Prime Minister's absence.

So in more partnership-oriented cultures such as Finland, gender roles are flexible. By contrast, in domination systems they are rigid, with the de- valuation of women and the "feminine."

The Human Brain, Stress, Partnership, and Domination

Differences between partnership and domination systems play out in the neurochemistry of our brains. As we saw earlier, the human brain is re- markably flexible—so much so that it can be called a work in progress. This great brain flexibility has enormous benefits. It enables us to learn, be innovative, and survive in many kinds of environments, both natural and human-made. But as we already glimpsed, this brain plasticity has drawbacks as well as benefits.

Since our brain's biological design gives it an exceptional capacity to adapt to different environments, humans are especially open to environmental influences. So if people grow up in domination cultures or subcultures, they tend to develop a certain kind of brain neurochemistry in response to these highly stressful environments.

As detailed in Chapter 4, neuroscience shows that traumatic or chronic stress leads to high levels of the hormone cortisol and the neurotransmitter norepinephrine—chemicals associated with problems of impulse regulation and propensity to violence. Conversely, free circulation of the neurotransmitters dopamine and serotonin, as well as the neuropeptide hormones oxytocin and vasopressin and other substances involved in bonding and empathy, is associated with the less violent, more caring behaviors characteristic of the partnership system.[20]

How people respond to stress is modulated through an interaction of genetic factors, environmental conditions over the course of development, and behavioral choices, so there are individual variations in the resulting patterns of brain neurochemistry. But the point is that there are central tendencies in different social environments.

This is why, again and again, people growing up with the stress of relations of domination and submission tend to develop neural and biochemical patterns that trigger fight, flight, or freeze responses. Rather than facing and dealing with a situation effectively, such individuals may blank out, automatically want to flee, or go into a physical or psychological attack mode. Some people who have experienced horrendous traumas do not seem to exhibit such responses. However, when these patterns develop, they constrict an individual's capacity for independent thought and action and lead to more abuse and suffering—which in turn maintain family, economic, social, and political institutions that chronically inhibit the expression of the human capacity for consciousness and caring.[21]

For instance, domination cultures create self-perpetuating patterns of economic scarcity due to misdistribution of resources to those on top, lack of funding for healthcare and education, diversion of resources into weaponry, and destruction of resources through war and other forms of violence.[22] These features of domination systems create stress, and with this, a general sense of anxiety, insecurity, and fear, which affects brain function.

Domination systems also fail to invest in the work of caregiving, which is still primarily performed by women, creating even further stress. This fact, in and of itself, perpetuates cycles of poverty, as evidenced by global statistics showing that the majority of the world's poor are female and that a major reason for this is that, in domination systems, women are supposed to do this caregiving work either for very low wages in the market economy or for free within households, with no pensions or social security benefits.[23] This pattern of gender inequality can occur even in wealthy nations such as the United States, where US Census Bureau statistics show that women older than 65 years are almost twice as likely to live in poverty as men of the same age.[24]

Children also suffer from such gender disparities. In the many regions of our world where cultures or subcultures are still more male-dominated, mothers, compared with fathers, tend to invest a much larger proportion of their more limited resources in feeding, clothing, and educating children.[25]

These are some of the economic reasons that domination-oriented cultures are so stressful. Of course, for those at the bottom of domination hierarchies, there is even further stress, starting in childhood. Children living in extreme poverty are often hungry, even in rich nations. Poor children often live in unsafe, vermin-infected housing or are homeless and face many dangers on the streets. Children living in less extreme poverty also tend to live in dangerous neighborhoods, with poor schools and parents stressed by economic hardships.[26]

Such stressors and hardship affect the brain. As we saw in Chapter 3, children raised in extremely deprived environments, such as Romanian orphanages, failed to develop normal neuronal connectivity, were cognitively impaired, and lacked normal motor control and language development.[27] Negative experiences in childhood, such as physical and verbal abuse, witnessing violence in the home, sexual abuse, and severe corporal punishment, are linked to health problems and early death.[28] The earlier the exposure to child maltreatment, the greater the likelihood of depression and anxiety in adulthood.[29] Stress and maltreatment affect brain development. Psychologist Darcia Narvaez reports that, among other problems, "infant maltreatment (abuse, neglect, and trauma) leads to massive physiological deficits: an overactive stress response, compromised immunity, a misdeveloped endocrine system, underdeveloped neurotransmitters (in terms of numbers and function), mistuned emotions and emotion systems, and poor integration of emotions with prefrontal controls."[30]

As K. Luan Phan, professor of psychiatry at the University of Illinois, notes, the stress-burden of growing up poor may help account for the relationship between poverty as a child and emotional and cognitive problems in adults. Phan and his colleagues found that children who had lower family incomes at age nine exhibited, as adults, greater activity in the amygdala, an area in the brain known for its role in emotions, including fear. They also showed less activity in areas of the prefrontal cortex, a part of the brain related to regulating negative emotion.[31]

Poverty is particularly stressful for many parents because in domination systems caregiving is not socially supported. To this day, despite rhetoric about the importance of mothering, in most world regions caregiving is not given government-supported training or financial assistance.[32] All this adds to children's stress.

A study conducted in Brazil suggests that living in the proximity of homicides during pregnancy stresses expectant mothers and accounts for lower birthweights of their children compared with mothers unstressed by the proximate occurrence of homicides.[33] In addition, studies show that mothers who are stressed, whether from their own early experiences or from unsafe relations with a husband or live-in male, are more likely to be abusive and/or neglectful of their children.[34] Where domination norms prevail, mothers also get little help from males because caregiving is not considered appropriate for "real men," further contributing to maternal stress.[35]

As noted earlier, neuroscientists have found a strong relationship between nurturing and the size of children's hippocampus, a brain region important to learning, memory, and response to stress. Brain scans show that children whose mothers nurtured them early in life have brains with a larger hippocampus and were less stressed—a finding congruent with the studies we looked at showing that rat pups whose caregivers were more nurturing by frequently licking them were also less prone to stress.[36] A parallel in humans has been reported by Ruth Feldman and her colleagues for children growing up in a war zone; the youngsters had an increased risk of developing post-traumatic stress disorder (PTSD), but maternal sensitive support reduced the chance of war-exposed children developing PTSD-related symptoms.[37]

Furthermore, where domination norms prevail, parents tend to teach children to conform to top-down control through stressful childrearing that heavily relies on fear or force. So, as we will later examine in more detail, empathic love is distorted and even suppressed, which directly affects how the brain develops.

The level of stress in schools is also different depending on the degree to which a culture or subculture orients to the domination or partnership side of the continuum. For example, not so long ago in the West, physical punishment was routine in schools, as is still the case today in many world regions. Fear was a major motivator routinely used by teachers, causing children enormous stress. Sadly, this is still the practice in many regions, as Riane found when researching "traditional" practices that violate the human rights of children.[38]

Working conditions also tend to be stressful in cultures and subcultures orienting closely to the domination system. Workplaces are frequently unsanitary and unsafe, as in the sweatshops still commonplace in some world regions, exemplified in news stories about the collapse of buildings in Pakistan and Bangladesh causing the death of thousands of workers.[39]

Even when conditions are better, hierarchies of domination in themselves generate stress. This was first shown by studies in the 1970s by the British physician Sir Michael Marmot and his colleagues.[40] Named the Whitehall studies for the street where much of the British civil service is housed, they showed that physical health, mental health, and even life spans correlated significantly with an individual's position in the civil service hierarchy. Those higher up in the hierarchy were healthier and lived longer than those further down.

These civil servants were not poor. Yet these relatively well-off people suffered disproportionately from stress-related problems—problems that the Whitehall study found derived from the domination hierarchy itself. Like many other bureaucracies, whether governmental or corporate, the structure of the British civil service was one of top-down commands. There was little if any discretion for variance for those on the lower rungs, as evidenced by the familiar bureaucratic refrain, "I wish I could help, but these are the rules." In such situations, violating rules is grounds for dismissal. So the further down people are in these hierarchies of domination, whether in government agencies or businesses, the more they must suppress initiative, creativity, caring, and even consciousness—otherwise, it would be too painful to enforce rules that are often very uncaring.

This suppression also is stressful. So is the fear that maintains hierarchies of domination—whether in families, workplaces, or society at large. And, as the Whitehall studies show, along with its correlates in brain neurochemistry, this stress can lead to heart attacks, diabetes, depression, alcoholism, respiratory illness, or cancer.

By contrast, workers in companies where they have some autonomy and power to make decisions report less stress and more job satisfaction.[41] Overall, these companies have a more caring ethos, which manifests itself in supportive employee benefits—from good healthcare plans and parental leave to profit-sharing and time off to engage in community service. These improvements in quality of life for workers, their families, and other members of the community contribute to good health and longevity—and more highly motivated workers.[42]

The neurochemical patterns supported by these settings facilitate greater flexibility, creativity, ability to work in teams, and other capacities that make for greater productivity. This offers advantages for both employees and employers, particularly in the postindustrial service-knowledge workplace—a subject Riane addresses in detail in *The Real Wealth of Nations*.

The large gap between haves and have-nots that characterizes domination systems is itself highly stressful. While one might think this gap only adversely affects the people on the bottom economic rungs, studies show that it adversely affects those on top as well. Until recently, researchers on inequality have focused on the plight of the poor and the shrinking middle class, documenting how inequality hurts their mental and physical health. But new studies show that status and wealth gaps make everyone—including the rich and powerful—more anxious and insecure.

Richard Wilkinson, a British epidemiologist, spent years researching these effects, which he documents in his book, coauthored with Kate Pickett, called *The Spirit Level: Why Equality Is Better for Everyone*. Wilkinson and Pickett write: "There are powerful psycho-social effects of inequality. As status differences grow, we worry more about status insecurity, we get widespread anxiety about self-esteem, and that brings rising rates of mental illness and depression."[43]

Still another adverse effect of hierarchies of domination seems to be that the people on top tend to be psychologically disconnected from those around them—not only from those below them, but from others like them. For instance, a 2010 study published in *Psychological Science* found that people of higher socioeconomic status were worse at reading other peoples' emotions, were more self-absorbed, and exhibited less empathy for others.[44] In this study, psychologists Michael Kraus, Stephane Cote, and

Dacher Keltner found that rich college students not only reported feeling less compassion than nonrich students when they watched a video about children suffering from cancer, but also that these feelings were reflected in their heart rates. The heart rate of students who were not rich slowed down as they watched the video—a physiological sign of compassion—whereas on average the rich students' hearts did not.[45]

The foregoing research shows that the effects of economic hierarchies of domination are not just bad news for people who encounter indifference and apathy from the rich. They are bad news for everyone—including the rich themselves. As the Beatles famously sang, "Can't Buy Me Love."

Partnership Leads to Happiness and Health

Empathy and caring are strongly linked to long-term happiness. Psychologist Paul Piff explains that, "Being compassionate, having empathic accuracy, being trusting and cooperative—these are keys to social connection and, in turn, happiness."[46] So the stories of unhappy rich people have a basis in psychological dynamics, in their tendency found by research to exhibit less empathy for others, not only for those who are poorer, but also for everyone. Charles Dickens drove home this point in his classic, *A Christmas Carol*, about the personal transformation of Ebenezer Scrooge from a miserably unhappy miser to a joyful benefactor.

That being on the top of domination hierarchies can lead to disconnection from others also helps explain why, once a certain level of economic security is reached, more money and status do not translate into more happiness—and can actually lead to less. However, as researchers such as Piff note, the problem is not wealth but inequality.[47]

International surveys further reflect the link between social equality and satisfaction with life: among the happiest nations are those with the least inequality, such as Sweden, Norway, Iceland, Finland, the Netherlands, and Denmark.[48] Not surprisingly, these nations orient more closely to the partnership side of the partnership-domination continuum.

While even these more partnership-oriented nations have statistical differences in health between higher and lower socioeconomic levels, their populations' average life span is 80 years. One could argue that there may be genetic factors involved. But this is not the case. The fact is that in the mid-19th century, both adult and child death rates in nations such as Sweden,

Norway, Finland, and Iceland were extremely high—which changed as these nations moved more to the partnership side of the continuum. These nations' long life spans are all the more remarkable because of their location in cold northern areas where winter days have long hours of darkness, known to lead to depression, health problems, and suicide.

The story of Finland is particularly striking. This country that straddles the Arctic Circle suffered from famines and had huge infant and adult mortality rates in the 19th century. As late as the 1940s, only 10 percent of Finns had a secondary education. But because of a determined nationwide effort that began with universal education for girls and boys and a strong women's movement, Finland gradually instituted high-quality healthcare, universal childbirth preparation for mothers and fathers, and public support for families with children in the form of child daycare and home help services. Finland has the sixth lowest infant mortality rate in the world—by comparison, the United States ranks 55th—and a premier healthcare system available to all citizens.[49] Finland makes the top ranks of United Nations measures of quality of life, including longevity, as well as the World Economic Forum's measures of global competitiveness.[50] In fact, in 2006, Finland was in first place of the World Competitiveness index, ahead of the much wealthier United States.[51]

As an anthropologist from the United States, Doug experienced a series of minor culture shocks when he lived in partnership-oriented Finland. Upon his arrival in 1995, Doug asked a Finnish immigration official about how and where he should purchase health insurance. At first, she did not even understand this US-type question. "Of course all your medical care is provided to you. It would be inhumane not to do so." Some years later, Doug needed emergency surgery and spent four days in the hospital. Doug's hospital bill totaled about $150 US dollars. When it comes to Finnish jail cells, again the idea is to be humane; they are warm and clean and have televisions and sometimes windows, although in this case Doug did not have the opportunity to try one out personally.

The Finns have a very strong sense of equality, as reflected institutionally in universal healthcare coverage. Finnish sociologist Risto Heiskala illustrates equality as a Finnish value when he writes, "all persons are seen to be equal."[52]

Finland has a government bureau of gender equality. When Doug used the phrase "the battle of the sexes," Finns said they did not understand what he meant. Doug was repeatedly told that the sexes respect each other. A sociologist friend said that the ideal was for a wife and husband, or girlfriend and boyfriend, to be "best friends." There are conflicts within relationships, of course, but there also is a feeling of partnership and mutual respect in many relationships. The members of both sexes are independent, and perhaps the women even more so than the men. There is a cultural stereotype of the "strong Finnish woman" who is self-reliant and independent, will stand up for her rights, but is not cruel or uncaring. As in any culture, most—but not all—people fulfill the expected gender roles and cultural ideals.

Finland was the first country in Europe, and the second in the world, to pass universal suffrage laws back in 1906. Women gained not only the right to vote but also the right to run for political office. Finnish women are active in Parliament and regularly serve as cabinet Ministers, and Tarja Halonen, Finland's first woman President, was elected for two six-year terms with a substantial number of men voting for her.

Doug was told that decades of Finnish women working with their male counterparts in Parliament has assured that resources were spent for education, eldercare, paid maternity and paternity leaves, daycare facilities, free school lunches for all school children in the country (here we see the ethos of equality put into practice once again), innovation in science and medicine, and the arts and culture—in other words, in ways that provide care, assistance, security, services, and happiness for the people. When Finns see a social problem, they try to fix it, often successfully. A partnership focus on human needs, the core value of equality, parity between the sexes, and prevention of abuse and violence are characteristics of Finnish society.

All this shows—on the kind of scale that should make even the most skeptical take notice—that orientation to the partnership system leads to more happiness and a better life for all. The countries with the highest happiness ratings, including Finland, have low levels of poverty and crime. They rate better than richer nations with greater inequality, such as the United States, in student achievement test scores. In these countries, there is greater gender equality, and with this, a higher valuing of stereotypically feminine values and activities such as nonviolence and caregiving by both women and men—leading to more caring policies that make life better for families and children. Not only these nations' international happiness ratings but also their compassion ratings are higher—as illustrated by the fact that they invest a larger percentage of their GDP in altruistic aid to people in the developing world.

Of course, these nations are not flawless utopias. We are simply looking at empirical evidence showing that our human capacities for empathy, compassion, and caring are more likely to be expressed in more partnership-oriented environments—and, as the studies we just considered show, that this positively correlates with higher levels of happiness. These examples also show that it is possible to create humane social practices and institutions that adequately and equitably address the needs of the citizens of a country—and that such countries exist, so we are not just talking about pie-in-the-sky fantasies. By adopting a partnership orientation, social change that shifts society away from domination hierarchies, violence, and structural violence toward greater social and gender equality, the satisfaction of needs, and the expression of human potential is possible.

Having lived in Finland and experienced a country that provides caring services to its citizens, Doug would sometimes talk, while visiting the United States, with people about the inexpensive access to high-quality healthcare available to all citizens of Finland. He found that a rote response from US citizens was, "but they have high taxes." Actually, income tax in Finland is on a graduated scale just like in the United States, and not much higher, with one difference being that extremely wealthy Finns are heavily taxed, while the average Finn is not. This taxation system again promotes equality.

The big difference between Finland and the United States is how the income tax is spent. In Finland, services for citizens are funded—universal healthcare, education, parks and recreation, childcare, assistance to the elderly, viable public transportation, and so forth—with only about three percent of the budget going to the Finnish Defense Forces. In the United States, nearly half of the income tax revenue each year—close to 50 percent—is spent on defense contractors, weapons development, the armed forces, and other military uses—or feeding the goliath that President Eisenhower dubbed "the military industrial complex." Were the United States to spend only 10 percent of each tax dollar on military pursuits instead of nearly 50 percent, this would almost double the financial resources available for everything else that currently goes underfunded.

Health, Happiness, and Social Choices

Nordic nations provide support for the expression of our human capacities for consciousness, caring, and creativity, not because they are small and relatively homogeneous (other such nations still orient closely to the domination side of the continuum), but because they chose to shift toward the partnership side of the social continuum.

This shift in large part accounts for their higher health and longevity rates not only because of their good healthcare system but also because in societies on the partnership side of the continuum, there is far less stress, starting in early childhood. As we have seen, childrearing in domination systems relies heavily on fear, abuse, and violence. A growing number of studies show that abusive childhood experiences lie behind many public health problems.

In the United States, the relationship between negative childhood experiences and severe health problems in adulthood has been extensively documented through the Adverse Childhood Experiences (ACE) study. Conducted by pediatricians and experts on childhood development and public health, the ACE research is ongoing, but it has already yielded a consensus that health and longevity are directly affected by what children experience and observe. It also has found that the frequency of adverse childhood experiences is much greater than previously thought.[53]

The ACE findings are based on long-term, in-depth analyses of more than 17,000 adults in the United States to date. Various categories of adverse childhood experiences were studied, including psychological, physical, or sexual abuse; violence against mother; and living with household members who were substance abusers, mentally ill or suicidal, or at some point imprisoned. The number of categories of these adverse childhood experiences was then compared to measures of adult risk behavior, health status, and disease, revealing how these experiences led to many illnesses as well as high mortality in adult life, with a graded relationship between the number of categories of childhood exposure and each of the adult health risk behaviors and diseases that were studied. Persons who had experienced four or more categories of childhood exposure, compared with those who had experienced none, had four to 12 times greater risks for alcoholism, drug abuse, depression, and suicide attempt; two to four times greater chances of smoking, poor self-rated health, and sexually transmitted disease; and higher rates of physical inactivity and severe obesity.[54]

Dr. Vincent Felitti concludes:

Adverse childhood experiences are surprisingly common even in the earliest years, are generally unrecognized, can be identified during childhood
by history from children and caretakers, and can start to manifest their
damage as ill health and somatization during childhood itself. As was
demonstrated in the ACE Study, what happens in childhood—like a child's
footprints in wet cement—commonly lasts throughout life. Time does not
heal; time conceals. Many of our most intractable public health problems
are the result of compensatory behaviors like smoking, overeating, and
alcohol and drug use, which provide immediate partial relief from the
emotional problems caused by traumatic childhood experiences. Those
experiences are generally unrecognized and become lost in time, where
they are protected by shame, by secrecy, and by social taboos against
exploring certain areas of human experience.[55]

These findings indicate that the childhood experiences characteristic of
our domination heritage not only lead to behaviors that cause illness and
premature death but also lead to traumas and chronic unhappiness that
people suffer from all their lives.[56] And the extent of child maltreatment
worldwide, including severe forms of violence, is staggering, as illustrated
in Box 5.1. It is also staggering how little attention is given to this pandemic
of violence against children, or its social and economic costs, and the horrendous suffering and unhappiness it causes to those who survive it.

By contrast, in partnership-oriented cultures, greater happiness prevails.
This is illustrated by the Nordic nations. There are many reasons for these
nations' high happiness ratings. One factor, as we have already glimpsed, is
a partnership orientation that promotes helpfulness, well-being, and care.

Indeed, recent studies show that, contrary to popular belief, people are
happier when they help others rather than when they just look out for themselves. For example, psychologists Lara Aknin and Elizabeth Dunn showed
that spending money on others makes a person happier than spending on
one's self.[57] And research headed by George Moll of the National Institutes
of Health has demonstrated that when altruistic choices prevail over selfish
material interests, brain regions associated with psychological rewards of
pleasure are activated.[58]

When in earlier chapters we looked at studies of the brains of the
more partnership-oriented bonobos and the dramatic changes in brain

Box 5.1 The Global Pandemic of Violence against Children

Over the last decades, for the first time in history, numerous national and international reports have documented the magnitude, severity, and systemic nature of violence against children worldwide, and that most of these crimes are never prosecuted.

Child Sexual Abuse

Fifty-five studies from 24 countries document that the incidence of sexual abuse ranges from eight to 31 percent for girls and from three to 17 percent for boys, with nine girls and three boys out of every 100 being the victims of forced intercourse or rape.[61] United Nations reports indicate an even greater percentage, based on data showing that between seven and 36 percent of adult women and between three and 29 percent of adult men reported sexual victimization in the home during their childhood.[62]

Child Marriage

The practice of childhood marriage is common in sub-Saharan Africa and Southern Asia and is also found in the Middle East, North Africa, and Latin America. In Ethiopia and parts of West Africa, girls have been married as early as age seven.[63] Yet child marriage is still justified as a religious or moral tradition in many parts of the world—even though these children are robbed of their childhood, condemned to a life of servitude, and often subject to beatings and other violence by their husbands and family (e.g., India has the highest levels of domestic violence among women married before the age of 18).[64] Many of these children die from becoming pregnant too young, and those who survive often suffer from lifelong health problems such as fistulas (in Nigeria alone, the numbers of fistula sufferers are astronomical, up to 800,000 women according to one report, many thrown out by their husbands and families to die on the streets).[65]

The Child Sex Trade and Sexual Slavery

Child marriage is a form of sexual slavery that, as in recent cases in Yemen, may result in the child bride's death from intercourse with a man more than twice her age. However, these sexually abused children are not counted in the statistics on two other closely related crimes against children: the sex trade and sexual slavery, which victimize millions of girls and a large number of boys every year. The traumatic effects of these crimes have only now begun to be examined, as is the fact that these children are sometimes sold into the sex trade by members of their own families.[66] According to UNICEF, at least 30 million children have been sexually exploited over the past 30 years.[67] In the United States alone, where human trafficking is a $9.8 billion domestic industry, at least 100,000 children are used as prostitutes each year according to Shared Hope International,[68] and a US State Department report indicates that two million children are subjected to prostitution in the global commercial sex trade every year.[69] Government complicity in these crimes is also being documented; for example, in *Child Exploitation and Trafficking*, judge Virginia Kendall and law professor T. Marcus Funk write that "public corruption in the creation, facilitation, and continuation of international child trafficking and other forms of child sexual exploitation cannot be underestimated," urging that more attention be paid to the role of public corruption in child pornography, sex trafficking, and sexual slavery.[70]

Female Genital Mutilation/Cutting

Another form of sexual violence that affects millions of girls is female genital mutilation/cutting (FGM/C). This practice is a horrendous form of torture that ranges from cutting out the clitoris to also cutting out the labia and sewing the vagina together so that it must be cut open for intercourse and again for childbirth. FGM/C is still justified on the grounds of religion and/or tradition; is often performed with rusty knives; and leaves the girls who survive with lifelong health problems, not to speak of trauma. According to the World Health Organization, 92 million girls 10 years and older have been subjected to it in Africa alone,[71] and in Egypt more than 90 percent of women are genitally mutilated.[72] In addition, FGM/C is widespread in other countries in the Middle East and Asia and is being exported by immigrants to North America, Europe, and Australia.[73]

Crimes that Target Specific Kinds of Children

FGM/C is one cruel "traditional" practice that specifically targets girls. Other crimes based on gender include female infanticide and the denial of healthcare and food to girls. The murder of female babies is still often culturally accepted in parts of Asia, the Middle East, and Africa. The Chinese government condemned these murders, particularly after its one-child policy led to an epidemic of female infanticide. Yet female babies are still murdered with impunity in rural areas in China, as described in a report in *The Economist* of how a baby was dumped to die in a garbage can while a police officer remarked he could do nothing since it was only a girl.[74] The Indian government also has taken a stand against female infanticide; but again, particularly on the local level, this crime is not generally prosecuted. The cruel practice of parents denying girls food and healthcare is also culturally condoned in parts of Asia as well as other world regions, including Latin America. For instance, in her autobiography, Rigoberta Menchu wrote (with no condemnation) that in her indigenous community, it is customary to nurse little boys longer than little girls.[75]

These discriminatory practices affect millions of girls every year, resulting in the death of many girls and the fact that many more girls are malnourished than boys—which means not only that they fail to develop their full physical and mental capacities but also that their children, both sons and daughters, do so because children of malnourished women are often born with poor health and below-par brain development.[76]

In addition to crimes that target girls are crimes that target other classes of children. An example is albino children, who in parts of Africa such as Malawi are murdered for their body parts, which are supposed to have magical qualities that bring wealth, power, and good fortune when used in rituals.[77] Also killed in countries such as Nigeria, Cameroon, Angola, and the Congo are children accused of being witches by pastors who, through a blend of Evangelical Christianity and native religions that also believe in witchcraft, charge huge sums for supposedly casting out witch spirits. Usually these children are killed by their own parents when they cannot or do not want to pay these pastors, like a little boy whose father chopped his son's head off with an ax—yet was never punished by the authorities.[78]

Another especially vulnerable group are homeless children. According to the US Department of Housing and Urban Development, in 2013, approximately eight percent of homeless people in the United States were children, and of these, 66 percent were unaccompanied children and youth, half of whom were unsheltered.[79] In addition to chronic hunger, cold, and physical and mental health problems, these children are often coerced into prostitution, pornography, and other sexual exploitation. The sex trafficking of these children reached a level of "epidemic proportion" in the United States by 2010, according to the US Federal Bureau of Investigation (FBI).[80] In other parts of the world, homeless children are also extremely vulnerable and are even being killed. For example, the news agency *teleSUR* reported that the United Nations accused Brazilian police of killing homeless children to "clean the streets" ahead of the Olympic Games 2016 in Rio de Janeiro, with these murders authorized by the government.[81]

Violence against Children in Schools

Violence against children in schools receives almost no press coverage but affects millions of children worldwide. Generally described as "corporal punishment," this practice is still legal in 90 countries, and 350 million students around the world face violence in their schools each year.[82] According to the report "Learn without Fear," this includes 33 types of violence, from beatings to hitting children on the head and "penciling" (putting a pencil between two fingers and tightly squeezing the fingers). In the United States, paddling—that is, hitting a child's buttocks with a wooden instrument—is still legal in 19 states, most of them in the South, and is sometimes very severe.[83]

Violence against Children in Homes

In most cultures, violence against children is still considered an acceptable, even moral, form of discipline. Some of this violence is extremely severe: physical blows (on many areas of the body, not only on the buttocks), kicking, shaking, throwing, scratching, pinching, biting, burning, whipping, scalding, suffocating, and beatings with belts, bats, sticks, metal rods, and other instruments. In other words, children are subjected to acts that, especially because these children are dependent on the adults who commit them, are traumatic. Yet 84% of adults in a 2005 study agreed that it is sometimes necessary to discipline a child with a good hard spanking.[84] And to this day in most world regions, using force to punish children in families is not defined as an act of violence—even though it would be criminal if used against an adult.[85]

Indentured and Forced Child Labor and Child Conscription

Children in many world regions are still forced to work in dangerous and inhuman conditions. [86] In Afghanistan, children as young as four are subject to forced labor and in-debt bondage. In Bangladesh, young children often work in exchange for advanced payments that have been made to their parents.[87] Children are also placed in combat-related roles or trained as suicide bombers. For example, the Ugandan Lord's Resistance Army (LRA) has abducted about 25,000 children since the 1980s, according to the 2008 Global Report on Child Soldiers by the Coalition to Stop the Use of Child Soldiers,[88] and according to a 2017 *Al Jazeera* report, the use of child suicide bombers, including girls, in Nigeria, Niger, Cameroon, and Chad by Boko Haram is on the rise.[89]

neurochemistry of baboons when their culture shifted away from rigid rankings of domination, we saw how partnership and domination-oriented cultural environments support very different neurochemical profiles in other primates, not only humans. In addition, we saw that family and socio-economic environments characteristic of the domination system perpetuate the highly stress-and-fear-driven neurochemistry that helps perpetuate this system.

It bears repeating that partnership-oriented cultures are not stress-free. But these cultures do not cause the unnecessary stress and suffering that so devastatingly afflict people in domination environments.

Thankfully, our built-in human yearning for caring connections protects us to some degree from the effects of these environments. Even in the strictest domination cultural environments, some people will relate in partnership ways. But to the extent that a significant part of the population is affected by life experiences characteristic of domination cultures or subcultures, negative patterns will be perpetuated from generation to generation.

This does not mean that experience is the only thing that counts. Genes matter. For instance, animal experiments and observations of humans show that genetic factors can mitigate the neurochemical effects of stress. Some people can develop a brain neurochemistry not so prone to fight, flight, or freeze responses even in the most brutal environments. So even in harsh environments, some people will be compassionate and caring, which probably reflects an evolved human propensity to be humane.[59]

Indeed, it is a testimony to the powerful human need and capacity for caring that even in rigid domination systems, there are always people who do not treat children in abusive and violent ways, and that even among children who are so treated, there are those who grow up to reject cruelty and injustice. However, based on what we are learning from neuroscience, we can predict that many people living in domination environments will develop habitual neurochemical patterns of fight, flight, or freeze to adapt to the stress inherent in rigid rankings backed up by fear and force.

We can also predict that most people who become accustomed to human rights violations in their day-to-day relations, including abuse in their families, are unlikely to champion human rights more generally. Nor, we predict, are they likely to actively promote a "culture of peace" envisioned by the United Nations, where children will be safe, loved, and supported in the full development of their human potentials.[60] This is because domination cultural environments not only harm health but also tend to keep people in an arrested state of development focused on what psychologists call "defense" or survival needs rather than "growth" or actualization needs.

In this sense, domination environments keep humanity at a less advanced level of overall human development. They interfere with the full flourishing of those very qualities that make us happiest: empathy, consciousness, creativity, and love. But it does not have to be this way. We have choices.

Notes

1. See, e.g., Riane Eisler, *The Chalice and the Blade: Our History, Our Future* (San Francisco: Harper & Row, 1987); Riane Eisler, "Cultural Transformation Theory: A New Paradigm for History," in *Macrohistory and Macrohistorians*, eds. Johan Galtung and Sohail Inayatullah (Westport, CT: Praeger Publishers, 1997); Riane Eisler, "Human Possibilities: The Interaction of Biology and Culture," *Interdisciplinary Journal of Partnership Studies*, 1 (2014): doi: 10.24926/ijps.v1i1.88.

2. Johan Galtung and Tord Höivik, "Structural and Direct Violence: A Note on Operationalization," *Journal of Peace Research* 8 (1971): 73–76, doi: 10.1177/002234337100800108; Johan Galtung, "Cultural Violence," *Journal of Peace Research* 27 (1990): 291–305, doi: 10.1177/0022343390027003005.
3. See, e.g., Eisler, *The Chalice and the Blade*; Eisler, "Cultural Transformation Theory"; Eisler, "Human Possibilities."
4. Douglas P. Fry, ed., *War, Peace, and Human Nature: The Convergence of Evolutionary and Cultural Views* (New York: Oxford University Press, 2013); Eisler, *The Chalice and the Blade*; Marija Gimbutas, *The Goddesses and Gods of Old Europe* (Berkeley: University of California Press, 1982); Marija Gimbutas, *The Civilization of the Goddess* (San Francisco: Harper, 1991); Nikolas Platon, *Crete* (Geneva: Nagel Publishers, 1966).
5. Douglas Price and James Brown, *Prehistoric Hunter-Gatherers: The Emergence of Cultural Complexity* (New York: Academic Press, 1985); Eisler, *The Chalice and the Blade*; Gimbutas, *The Goddesses and Gods of Old Europe*; Platon, *Crete*.
6. Steven Pinker, *The Better Angels of Our Nature: Why Violence Has Declined* (New York: Viking, 2011).
7. International Committee of the Red Cross, "Geneva Conventions and Commentaries." Available online: https://www.icrc.org/en/war-and-law/treaties-customary-law/geneva-conventions.
8. United Nations, General Assembly, *Universal Declaration of Human Rights* (1948). Available online: http://www.un.org/en/universal-declaration-human-rights/; Pinker, *The Better Angels of Our Nature*.
9. Erica Chenoweth and Maria Stephan, *Why Civil Resistance Works: The Strategic Logic of Nonviolent Conflict* (New York: Columbia University Press, 2011).
10. No culture, no matter how rigid its rankings of domination, can survive without at least some partnership elements. But, as historian Mary Elizabeth Perry notes, in cultures that orient primarily to the domination system, these elements are co-opted. They are exploited as well as distorted and suppressed, with caring and non-violent behaviors relegated to "inferior" groups such as women and "effeminate" men—in other words, to those who are dominated, rather than those who domi-nate. Mary Elizabeth Perry, "Deviant Women and Cultural Transformation," paper presented at the panel "Dominator and Partnership Models as Analytical Tools, 20th Anniversary Conference of the Western Association of Women Historians" (Pacific Grove, CA: Asilomar, 1989); Mary Elizabeth Perry, "The Black Madonna of Montserrat," in *Views of Women's Lives in Western Tradition*, ed. Frances Richardson Keller (Lewiston, NY: The Edwin Mellen Press, 1990).
11. Uta Ranke-Heinemann, *Eunuchs for the Kingdom of Heaven: Women, Sexuality, and the Catholic Church*, trans. Peter Heinegg (New York: Doubleday, 1990); Riane Eisler, *Sacred Pleasure: Sex, Myth, and the Politics of the Body* (San Francisco: Harper Collins, 1995).
12. See, e.g., John Read et al., "The Traumagenic Neurodevelopmental Model of Psychosis Revisited," *Neuropsychiatry* 4 (2014): 1–15, doi: 10.2217/npy.13.89. See also Riane Eisler, "Societal Context for Family Relations," in *Contexts for Young Child*

Flourishing, eds. Darcia Narvaez et al. (New York: Oxford University Press, 2016); and "How to Find Help Treating a Trauma-Related Problem," PsychGuides.com. Available online: http://www.psychguides.com/guides/trauma-symptoms-causes-and-effects/.

13. See, e.g., Licia Rando, "The Caring and Connected Parenting Guide." Available online: www.centerforpartnership or www.saiv.org.

14. Partnership parenting enables children to learn emotional self-regulation largely out of intrinsic rather than extrinsic motivations. See the section on self-regulation in Riane Eisler, *Tomorrow's Children: A Blueprint for Partnership Education in the 21st Century* (Boulder, CO: Westview Press, 2000). See also William Damon, *Moral Child: Nurturing Children's Natural Moral Growth* (New York: Free Press, 1990), which argues against both laissez-faire and authoritarian parenting in favor of what he calls authoritative parenting, and Dennis Embry, "Nurturing the Genius of Genes: The New Frontier of Education, Therapy, and Understanding the Brain," *Brain and Mind* 3 (2002): 101–132, doi: 10.1023/A:1016509908727.

15. Kurt Lewin, widely considered a father of social psychology, conducted early experiments showing that laissez-faire structures not only are inefficient but also lead to scapegoating and top-down control. Kurt Lewin, *Field Theory in Social Science* (New York: Harper & Row, 1951). Many indigenous societies are egalitarian in ethos and practice, as we will consider in Chapter 7.

16. See, e.g., Riane Eisler, *The Power of Partnership* (Novato, CA: New World Library, 2002).

17. This topic is discussed in detail in Eisler, *Sacred Pleasure*.

18. For example, in partnership-oriented schools, young people are responsible for some school rules and for seeing they are honored. This promotes habits needed to function optimally in the postindustrial information economy, where taking responsibility, flexibility, and creativity are essential. More immediately, it contributes to a mutually respectful, undisrupted, and nonviolent school environment. Despite assumptions that adolescents naturally rebel, we may find that when students feel they are heard and cared for and have a stake in their school functioning, they are less likely to reject cultural norms (Eisler, *Tomorrow's Children*).

19. Robert K. Dentan, "Notes on Childhood in a Nonviolent Context: The Semai Case (Malaysia)," in *Learning Non-Aggression: The Experience of Non-Literate Societies*, ed. Ashley Montagu (New York: Oxford University Press, 1978); Kirk M. Endicott and Karen L. Endicott, *The Headman Was a Woman: The Gender Egalitarian Batek of Malaysia* (Long Grove, IL: Waveland, 2008); Peter Gardner, "Respect for All: The Paliyans of South India," in *Keeping the Peace: Conflict Resolution and Peaceful Societies around the World*, eds. Graham Kemp and Douglas P. Fry (New York: Routledge, 2004); Alice Schlegel, "Contentious but Not Violent: The Hopi of Northern Arizona," in *Keeping the Peace: Conflict Resolution and Peaceful Societies around the World*, eds. Graham Kemp and Douglas P. Fry (New York: Routledge, 2004); see also the ethnographic examples in Alfie Kohn, *No Contest: The Case against Competition* (New York: Houghton Mifflin, 1986).

20. C. Sue Carter, "Neuroendocrine Perspectives on Social Attachment and Love," *Psychoneuroendocrinology* 23 (1998): 779–818, doi: 10.1016/S0306-4530(98)00055-9; C. Sue Carter and Stephen W. Porges, "Peptide Pathways to Peace," in *Pathways to Peace: The Transformative Power of Children and Families*, eds. James F. Leckman, Catherine Panter-Brick, and Rima Salah (Cambridge, MA: MIT Press, 2014); Ruth Feldman, "Oxytocin and Social Affiliation in Humans," *Hormones and Behavior* 61 (2012): 380–391, doi: 10.1016/j.yhbeh.2012.01.008; Michael Kosfeld et al. "Oxytocin Increases Trust in Humans," *Nature* 435 (2005): 673–676, doi: 10.1038/nature03701; Paul J. Zak, Angela A. Stanton, and Sheila Ahmadi, "Oxytocin Increases Generosity in Humans," *PLoS ONE* 11 (2007): e1128, doi: 10.1371/journal.pone.0001128.

21. C. Sue Carter, "The Chemistry of Child Neglect: Do Oxytocin and Vasopressin Mediate the Effects of Early Experience?" *Proceedings of the National Academy of Sciences (PNAS)* 102 (2005): 18247–18248, doi: 10.1073/pnas.0509376102; Eric B. Keverne, "Epigenetics: Significance of the Gene-Environment Interface for Brain Development," in *Pathways to Peace: The Transformative Power of Children and Families*, eds. James F. Leckman, Catherine Panter-Brick, and Rima Salah (Cambridge, MA: MIT Press, 2014).

22. Riane Eisler, *The Real Wealth of Nations: Creating a Caring Economics*. (San Francisco: Berrett-Koehler, 2007).

23. Eisler, *The Real Wealth of Nations*.

24. Federal Interagency Forum on Aging-Related Statistics, *Older Americans 2016 Key Indicators of Well-Being* (Washington, DC: US Government Printing Office, 2016). Available online: http://www.agingstats.gov/docs/LatestReport/OA2016.pdf; US Census Bureau figures for 2013 reported in Administration on Aging, Administration for Community Living, US Department of Health and Human Services, *A Profile of Older Americans: 2014*. Available online: https://www.acl.gov/sites/default/files/Aging%20and%20Disability%20in%20America/2014-Profile.pdf.

25. See, e.g., Judith Bruce and Cynthia Lloyd, "Finding the Ties that Bind: Beyond Headship and Household," in *Intrahousehold Resources Allocation in Developing Countries: Methods, Models, and Policy*, eds. Lawrence Haddad, John Hoddinott, and Harold Alderman (Baltimore: International Food Policy Research Institute and Johns Hopkins University Press, 1997).

26. Not only emotional but also cognitive development is affected by the stresses inherent in chronic poverty. For example, a French study of 20 children who had been abandoned in infancy by their low-socioeconomic-status parents and adopted by upper-middle-class parents showed that the adopted children's biological siblings or half-siblings who remained with the biological mother and were reared by her in impoverished circumstances were four times more likely to exhibit failures in their school performance. The adopted children's IQs also averaged 14 points higher than those of their natural siblings (Michel Schiff et al., "How Much Could We Boost Scholastic Achievement and IQ Scores? A Direct Answer from a French Adoption Study," *Cognition* 12 (1982): 165–196, doi: 10.1016/0010-0277(82)90011-7.

27. Barry Keverne, "Significance of Epigenetics for Understanding Brain Development, Brain Evolution and Behaviour," *Neuroscience* 264 (2014): 207–217, doi: 10.1016/j.neuroscience.2012.11.030.

28. Darcia Narvaez, *Neurobiology and the Development of Human Morality: Evolution, Culture, and Wisdom* (New York: Norton, 2014); Vincent J. Felitti et al., "Relationship of Childhood Abuse and Household Dysfunction to Many of the Leading Causes of Death in Adults: The Adverse Childhood Experiences (ACE) Study," *American Journal of Preventive Medicine* 14 (1998): 245–258, doi: 10.1016/S0749-3797(98)00017-8.

29. Julie Kaplow and Cathy Spatz Widom, "Age of Onset of Child Maltreatment Predicts Long-Term Mental Health Outcomes," *Journal of Abnormal Psychology* 116 (2007): 176–187, doi: 10.1037/0021-843X.116.1.176; see also Kristin Valentino, Michelle Comas, and Amy K. Nuttall, "Child Maltreatment and Early Mother-Child Interactions," in *Ancestral Landscapes in Human Evolution*, eds. Darcia Narvaez et al. (New York: Oxford University Press, 2014).

30. Narvaez, *Neurobiology and the Development of Human Morality*, 132.

31. Pilyoung Kim et al., "Effects of Childhood Poverty and Chronic Stress on Emotion Regulatory Brain Function in Adulthood," *Proceedings of the National Academy of Sciences (PNAS)* 110 (2013): 18442–18447, doi: 10.1073/pnas.1308240110.

32. For movement to change this, see www.centerforpartnership.org or www.caringeconomy.org.

33. Martin Foureaux Koppensteiner and Marco Manacorda, "Violence and Birth Outcomes: Evidence from Homicides in Brazil," *Journal of Development Economics* 119 (2016): 16–33. A summary by Aleszu Bajak, "The Prenatal Impacts of Violence," *Undark* (2016), is also available online: http://undark.org/2016/05/26/pregnancy-violence-homicide-brazil/.

34. Shelley E. Taylor, *The Tending Instinct: How Nurturing Is Essential to Who We Are and How We Live* (New York: Henry Holt, 2002); Rena L Repetti and Jenifer Wood, "Families Accommodating to Chronic Stress," in *Coping with Chronic Stress,* ed. Benjamin H. Gottlieb (Springer US, 1997). When poverty is accompanied by the danger and distress of living in neighborhoods with gangs or other street violence, there is still more stress. Parents will also be more likely to harshly control their children, if only because of fear for their safety. In the United States, both domestic violence and street crimes are more frequent in poor neighborhoods, particularly urban ones with high population density, high population turnover, and high levels of family disintegration. For a study of effects of these factors, including abuse and neglect of children, on crime rates, see, Cathy Widom and Michael Maxfield, "An Update on the 'Cycle of Violence,' " US Department of Justice, last modified February 2001. Available online: https://www.ncjrs.gov/pdffiles1/nij/184894.pdf.

35. On top of their caregiving work, mothers are expected to do all the cooking, cleaning, shopping, washing, and other chores that maintain life. If they work outside the home, they are still expected to do all this after hours. Women worldwide work significantly more hours than men and often suffer from stress due to overwork. Particularly when lack of money, living in decaying housing and run-down neighborhoods, and other

hardships are added, life for mothers is extremely stressful—with adverse effects not only for them but also for their children. And when women are physically abused by the men in their lives, stress is aggravated even more. This often leads to parenting behaviors that are extremely stressful to children.

36. Joan L. Luby et al., "Maternal Support in Early Childhood Predicts Larger Hippocampal Volumes at School Age," *Proceedings of the National Academy of Sciences (PNAS)* 109 (2012): 2854–2859, doi: 10.1073/pnas.1118003109. Interestingly, as with rat pups, the caregivers did not have to be the biological mother—a finding, as noted by the lead researchers of the study on children, Joan L. Luby, a professor of child psychiatry at the Washington University School of Medicine in St. Louis, has important implications for public policy on both childcare and parenting education.

37. Ruth Feldman, A. Vengrober, and R. P. Ebstein, "Affiliation Buffers Stress: Cumulative Genetic Risk in Oxytocin-Vasopressin Genes Combines with Early Caregiving to Predict PTSD in War-Exposed Young Children," *Translational Psychiatry* 4 (2014): e370, doi: 10.1038/tp.2014.6.

38. Riane Eisler, "Protecting the Majority of Humanity: Toward an Integrated Approach to Crimes against Present and Future Generations," in *Sustainable Development, International Criminal Justice, and Treaty Implementation,* eds. Marie-Claire Cordonier and Sebastien Jodoin (Cambridge, UK: Cambridge University Press, 2013); Riane Eisler, "Protecting Children: From Rhetoric to Global Action," *Interdisciplinary Journal of Partnership Studies* 5 (2018): Article 7, doi: 10.24926/ijps.v5i1.1125.

39. Nicholas D. Kristof and Sheryl WuDunn, *Half the Sky: Turning Oppression into Opportunity for Women Worldwide* (New York: Vintage, 2010).

40. Michael G. Marmot et al., "Health Inequalities among British Civil Servants: The Whitehall II Study," *Lancet* 337 (1991): 1387–1393.

41. Eisler, *The Real Wealth of Nations.*

42. Eisler, *The Real Wealth of Nations.*

43. Richard Wilkinson and Kate Pickett, *The Spirit Level: Why Equality Is Better for Everyone* (London: Penguin, 2009). See also Jeffrey Sachs, *The Price of Civilization* (New York: Random House, 2012).

44. Michael W. Kraus, Stephane Cote, and Dacher Keltner, "Social Class, Contextualism, and Empathic Accuracy," *Psychological Science* 21 (2010): 1716–1723, doi: 10.1177/0956797610387613.

45. Jennifer E. Stellar et al., "Class and Compassion: Socioeconomic Factors Predict Responses to Suffering," *Emotion* 12 (2012): 449–459, doi: 10.1037/a0026508.

46. Paul Piff, quoted in Jason Marsh, "Why Inequality Is Bad for the One Percent," *Greater Good,* last modified September 25, 2012. Available online: http://greatergood.berkeley.edu/article/item/why_inequality_is_bad_for_the_one_percent.

47. Paul K. Piff, "Wealth and the Inflated Self: Class, Entitlement, and Narcissism," *Personality and Social Psychology Bulletin* 40 (2014): 34–43, doi: 10.1177/0146167213501699; Dacher Keltner et al. "The Sociocultural Appraisals, Values, and Emotions (SAVE) Framework of Prosociality: Core Processes from Gene to Meme," *Annual Review of Psychology* 65 (2014): 425–460, doi: 10.1146/

annurev-psych-010213-115054; Stéphane Côté, Paul K. Piff, and Robb Willer, "For Whom Do the Ends Justify the Means? Social Class and Utilitarian Moral Judgment," *Journal of Personality and Social Psychology* 104 (2013): 490–503, doi: 10.1037/ a0030931.

48. John F. Helliwell, Richard Layard, and Jeffrey D. Sachs, eds., *World Happiness Report 2018* (New York: Sustainable Development Solutions Network. 2018). Available online: https://s3.amazonaws.com/happiness-report/2018/WHR_web.pdf.

49. "World Factbook," Central Intelligence Agency. Available online: https://www.cia. gov/library/publications/the-world-factbook/rankorder/2091rank.html.

50. Hilkka Pietila, "Eradicating Poverty by Building a Welfare Society: Finland as a Case Study," *Cooperation South* 2 (2001): 79–96.

51. See "Interesting Facts about Finland: Finland Guide," *Eupedia*. Available online: http://www.eupedia.com/finland/trivia.shtml.

52. Risto Heiskala, "How to Be a Virtuous Male/Female: The Politics of Gender in Advertisements in Some Finnish Magazines in 1955 and 1985," *Semiotica* 87 (1991): 381–409, 382.

53. Vincent J. Felitti et al., "Relationship of Childhood Abuse and Household Dysfunction to Many of the Leading Causes of Death in Adults: The Adverse Childhood Experiences (ACE) Study," *American Journal of Preventive Medicine* 14 (1998): 245–258, doi: 10.1016/S0749-3797(98)00017-8.

54. Felitti et al., "Relationship of Childhood Abuse and Household Dysfunction to Many of the Leading Causes of Death in Adults."

55. Vincent J. Felitti, "Adverse Childhood Experiences and Adult Health," *Academic Pediatrics* 9 (2009): 131–132, 131, doi: 10.1016/j.acap.2009.03.001. Available online: http://static1.squarespace.com/static/500ee7f0c4aa5f5d4c9fee39/t/ 53ecfab7e4b03cc699a85f97/1408039607750/Adverse+Childhood+Experiences+an d+Adult+Health.pdf.

56. For more research and resources, see Bessel van der Kolk, *The Body Keeps the Score: Brain, Mind, and Body in the Healing of Trauma* (New York: Penguin, 2015); and The National Child Traumatic Stress Network, available online: https://www.nctsn. org/.

57. Elizabeth Dunn, Lara Aknin, and Michael Norton, "Spending Money on Others Promotes Happiness," *Science* 319 (2008): 1687–1688, doi: 10.1126/science.1150952.

58. Jorge Moll et al., "Human Fronto–Mesolimbic Networks Guide Decisions about Charitable Donation," *Proceedings of the National Academy of Sciences (PNAS)* 103 (2006): 15623–15628, doi: 10.1073/pnas.0604475103; see also Paul J. Zak, Angela A. Stanton, and Sheila Ahmadi, "Oxytocin Increases Generosity in Humans," *PLoS ONE* 2 (2007): e1128, doi: 10.1371/journal.pone.0001128.

59. Frans de Waal, *The Age of Empathy* (New York: Harmony, 2009); Douglas P. Fry, "Life without War," *Science* 336 (2012): 879–884, doi: 10.1126/science.1217987; Douglas P. Fry, "Cooperation for Survival: Creating a Global Peace System," in *War, Peace, and Human Nature: The Convergence of Evolutionary and Cultural Views*, ed. Douglas P. Fry (New York: Oxford University Press, 2013); Keltner et al., "The Sociocultural Appraisals, Values, and Emotions (SAVE) Framework of Prosociality."

60. See Douglas P. Fry and Marta Miklikowska, "Culture of Peace," in *Psychological Components of Sustainable Peace*, eds. Morton Deutsch and Peter Coleman (New York: Springer, 2012).

61. Jurgen Barth et al., "The Current Prevalence of Child Sexual Abuse Worldwide: A Systematic Review and Meta-analysis," *International Journal of Public Health* 58 (2013): 469–83, doi: 10.1007/s00038-012-0426-1.

62. United Nations, *Promotion and Protections of the Rights of Children*, Report to the Secretary-General (New York: United Nations General Assembly A/61/150, 2006), 13.

63. United Nations, Population Fund (NFPA), *State of the World Population, 2005: Report, Child Marriage Fact Sheet*. Available online: http://www.unfpa.org/swp/2005/presskit/factsheets/facts_child_marriage.htm.

64. United Nations, Population Fund, *State of the World Population 2005*.

65. Ramita Navai, "Broken Lives: Nigeria's Child Brides Who End Up on the Streets," *Times*, November 28, 2008. Available online: http://www.timesonline.co.uk/tol/news/world/africa/article5248224.ece.

66. See, e.g., Ark of Hope for Children, "Child Trafficking Statistics," last updated July 31, 2017. Available online: https://arkofhopeforchildren.org/child-trafficking/child-trafficking-statistics.

67. United Nations Children's Fund (UNICIF), *We the Children* (New York: UNICEF, 2001). Available online: http://www.un.org/en/events/pastevents/pdfs/we_the_children.pdf.

68. Emily Stanton, "Study: At Least 100,000 Children Being Used in U.S. Sex Trade," *U.S. News*, last modified July 8, 2013. Available online: https://www.usnews.com/news/blogs/washington-whispers/2013/07/08/study-at-least-100000-children-being-used-in-us-sex-trade.

69. US Department of State, *Major Forms of Trafficking in Persons: Trafficking in Persons, 2009*. Available online: http://www.state.gov/g/tip/rls/tiprpt/2009/123126.htm.

70. Virginia Kendall and T. Markus Funk, *Child Exploitation and Trafficking: Examining Global Enforcement and Supply Chain Challenges and U.S. Responses* (Lanham, MD: Rowman and Littlefield Publishers, 2016), 79.

71. World Health Organization, *Fact Sheet: Female Genital Mutilation* (2010). Available online: http://www.who.int/mediacentre/factsheets/fs241/en/.

72. United Nations Development Fund for Women (UNIFEM), Donors Working Group, "Platform for Action towards the Abandonment of Female Genital Mutilation/Cutting (FGM/C)." Available online: http://www.who.int/reproductivehealth/publications/fgm/platform_for_action_fgm/en/.

73. World Health Organization, "Genital Mutilation (FGM)," (no date). Available online: http://www.who.int/reproductivehealth/topics/fgm/prevalence/en/.

74. "The Worldwide War on Baby Girls," *Economist*, March 4, 2010. Available online: http://www.economist.com/research/articlesBySubject/displaystory.cfm?subjectid=348951&story_id=15636231.

75. Rigoberta Menchú, Elizabeth Burgos-Debray, and Ann Wright, *I, Rogoberta Menchu: An Indian Woman in Guatemala* (New York: Verso, 1987).

76. Riane Eisler, *The Real Wealth of Nations: Creating a Caring Economics* (San Francisco: Berrett-Koehler, 2007).

77. Robyn Dixon, "In Parts of Africa, People with Albinism Are Hunted for Their Body Parts. The Latest Victim: A 9-Year-Old Boy," *Los Angeles Times*, last modified June 15, 2017. Available online: http://www.latimes.com/world/africa/la-fg-malawi-albinos-hunted-2017-story.html.

78. Tihomir Kukolja, "Saving Witch Children in Nigeria," *HuffPost*, last modified June 17, 2014. Available online: https://www.huffingtonpost.com/tihomir-kukolja/witch-children-in-nigeria_b_5149931.html.

79. Meghan Henry, Alvaro Cortes, and Sean Morris, *The 2013 Annual Homeless Assessment Report (AHAR) to Congress: Part 1 Point-in-Time Estimates of Homelessness* (US Department of Housing and Urban Development, 2013). Available online: https://www.hudexchange.info/resources/documents/ahar-2013-part1.pdf.

80. Federal Bureau of Investigation, *FBI Law Enforcement Bulletin, Human Sex Trafficking*, March 2011. Available online: https://www.hsdl.org/?abstract&did=6872.

81. "UN Body Accuses Brazil's Military Police of Killing Kids to 'Clean Streets' for Olympics, World Cup," *teleSUR*, last modified October 13, 2015. Available online: https://www.telesurtv.net/english/news/UN-Brazils-Police-Kill-Kids-to-Clean-Streets-for-Olympics-20151013-0044.html.

82. United Nations Educational, Scientific and Cultural Organization United Nations (UNESCO), *School Violence and Bullying: Global Status Report* (Paris: UNESCO, 2017). Available online: http://unesdoc.unesco.org/images/0024/002469/246970e.pdf.

83. Alison Bath, "Despite Opposition, Paddling Students Allowed in 19 States," *USA Today*, April 23, 2012. Available online: http://usatoday30.usatoday.com/news/nation/story/2012-04-22/school-corporal-punishment/54475676/1.

84. Murray Straus and Anita Mathur, "Social Change and Trends in Approval of Corporal Punishment by Parents from 1968 to 1994," in *Family Violence against Children: A Challenge for Society*, eds. Detlev Frehsee, Wiebke Horn, and Kai-D. Bussmann (New York: De Gruyter, 1996).

85. Committee on the Rights of the Child (CRC), General Comment No. 8 (2006). *The Right of the Child to Protection from Corporal Punishment and Other Cruel or Degrading Forms of Punishment* [articles 19, 28(2) and 37, interalia], CRC/C/GC/8, para 11.

86. International Programme on the Elimination of Child Labour (IPEC), "What Is Child Labour?" Available online: http://www.ilo.org/ipec/facts/lang--en/index.htm.

87. US Department of Labor, "List of Products Produced by Forced or Indentured Child Labor. Available online: https://www.dol.gov/ilab/reports/child-labor/list-of-products/.

88. Anne-Lynn Dudenhoefer, "Understanding the Recruitment of Child Soldiers in Africa," ACCORD, August 16, 2016. Available online: http://www.accord.org.za/conflict-trends/understanding-recruitment-child-soldiers-africa/.

89. "'Alarming' Rise in Boko Haram Child Suicide Bombers," *Al Jazeera*, last modified April 12, 2017. Available online: http://www.aljazeera.com/news/2017/04/rise-boko-haram-child-suicide-bombers-170412041301650.html.

6

Two Alternate Social Possibilities

Every society has biocultural constraints.[1] Children require care until they are old enough to fend for themselves. People are socialized to think and act in ways congruent with the beliefs and institutions of the culture. Commonly agreed-on symbols, in language and art, are created and replicated. The culture's accumulated knowledge and technologies are passed on from generation to generation.

However, the ways these requirements are met differ depending on the degree to which a society orients toward partnership or domination. This orientation affects the nature of childcare and socialization, gender roles and marital relations, sexuality, personal autonomy, attitudes and beliefs, egalitarian or top-down social structures, and the types of institutions that are created. These, in turn, affect life experiences, which then influence whether people are generally fearful or trusting, cruel or caring, and violent or peaceful.

Partnership and domination orientations can be found across various cultural settings, ancient and modern. For instance, neither secular totalitarianism nor religious fundamentalism is new. Both are simply recent iterations of rigid domination systems.

In this chapter, we will look at diverse societies through the analytical lens of the partnership-domination continuum and how the divergent patterns associated with orientation to the either side of their continuum play out in real life.

Partnership and Domination: Indigenous Examples

In 1987, shortly after *The Chalice and the Blade* was published, Riane received a phone call from a retired University of California anthropology professor, Stuart Schlegel. He explained that he had done fieldwork with a tribal society in the Philippines. "I did not know what to call them," he said. "I used to call them 'radically egalitarian.' But when I read your book

I realized that they are a partnership society. They have the configuration you describe: they are generally egalitarian, women and men have equal status, and they are peaceful."[2]

The people Schlegel described represent the kind of culture that was widespread in the Philippines before the arrival of strong Islamic and later also Spanish influences. In the 1960s, when Schlegel lived with the Tiruray (or as they call themselves, Teduray), they were already under strong pressure from encroaching Muslim neighbors. But they still lived in relative isolation in the dense tropical forest of the mountains of southwestern Mindanao, with an economy based on gathering wild foods, fishing, hunting, and subsistence farming.

The greatest part of Schlegel's study of traditional Tiruray life was done in Figel, a neighborhood of families who assisted one another in their horticultural and ritual activities. What first struck Schlegel is that the fundamental moral obligation for the Tiruray is respect for other persons, and respect is "the essence of tribal custom and the guiding intention of behavior felt to be most distinctively Tiruray."[3]

This culture's egalitarianism also impressed Schlegel: "all human beings, whether men or women, whether adults or children, whether the finest shaman or the most ordinary basket weaver, were considered of equal worth and of equal standing in society."[4] Not only were men *not* ranked over women, but even the spirits were not ranked over one another.

"Women and men were clearly different—and the Teduray delighted in the difference," Schlegel writes. "But they were not ranked . . . among forest Teduray *neither gender was thought superior to the other in any way*. Men and women related with empathy and an ethos of interdependence, with a mutual sharing of life's problems and joys."[5]

Among the Teduray, there was no battle of the sexes. To the contrary, Schlegel explains that "an abiding spirit of harmony existed between the sexes, and both men and women saw each other as equal participants in the great dance of life."[6] Men and women cooperated to nurture and raise children. Gender egalitarianism was obvious in working life, although the genders engaged in different tasks. Women's work tended to be less strenuous than men's chores: for instance, weeding the gardens as opposed to chopping down trees or weaving baskets compared to hunting wild pigs. However, greater male strength provided no rationale for oppression or exploitation of females by males. "All were really just different but equal specialties," explains Schlegel.[7]

Their language had no gendered pronoun system—no "he, his, him," no "she, hers, her." There were no different words for "husband" and "wife" (just spouse) and no separate words for "sister" or "brother" (just sibling). Nor did they view gender as affecting a person's disposition, potential, or personality, as is common in more male-dominated societies. As Schlegel notes, "when it came to positive and negative values of human behavior, the same criteria applied to men and women alike."[8]

The Teduray did not always behave in positive, caring ways. As Schlegel writes, "they occasionally turned to violence to settle their problems, even though their beliefs and institutions all said that violence was never right. . . . They ran off with each other's spouses, even though doing so violated their most fundamental moral norm, and they knew it. . . . They were certainly not goody-goody moral automatons in a never-never land of perfect harmony."[9]

When violence erupted, however, they had elaborate mechanisms to prevent feuding between different kinship groups seeking vengeance. To avoid cycles of violence, "legal sages" from both sides focused on working out a settlement, and both men and women played this role. In fact, one of the most respected of these legal sages was a woman called Ideng-Amig, who could be trusted to remain calm and to listen, and who, as Schlegel observed, knew how to speak with grace in the roundabout rhetoric of sessions. The dispute settlement proceedings described by Schlegel were cooperative, as the legal specialists involved strove to find just outcomes.[10] These elders sometimes lectured the disputants that self-redress was not the right way to deal with a conflict: "You must be patient and hold anger in your gall bladder."[11]

In his 1998 book, Schlegel sums up as follows: "The forest Teduray were a 'partnership society'" where "softer, stereotypically 'feminine' virtues were valued," where "community well-being was the principal motivation for work and other activities," and where "the emphasis on technology was on enhancing and sustaining life."[12]

Another indigenous society that orients to partnership is the Moso (also spelled Muoso) culture in China. These people are a subgroup of the Naxi in northwest Yunnan province about 100 miles east of the Myanmar border, speak a Tibeto-Burman language, and have drawn international interest as a growing number of cultural and ecological tourists feed the local hosting business.

Moso households operate as one big economic unit like many Chinese families. However, the traditional Moso family unit is headed by an elder woman, and she and her brothers, her daughters, and their children, with the intermittent help of the women's lovers or husbands, work together to till the land and carry on other economic activities. In the Moso matri-lineal family system, the lands and assets of a family are not subdivided on marriages and deaths. They pass through the mother's line to a new female family elder. There are no orphans or abandoned seniors, and (at least until recent decades) no illegitimate children.[13]

Women and men are equal among the Moso, so this society is not a matriarchy, although it is often referred to as one, the term defined as not being the mirror image of patriarchy but rather a society where the guiding values are nurturance and caring.[14] In his analysis, Professor Junsheng Cai describes the Moso as a society based primarily on linking rather than ranking. He writes that relations, whether inside the families or among them, are "practical lively partnerships."[15]

Since the Moso have a love marriage system, there is no fighting over sexual honor, as can occur in in societies where female sexuality is controlled by men. After their initiation to womanhood at about age 13, girls have their own rooms. Their lovers, glossed as "special friends," may visit them between midnight and dawn. A girl may invite a boy for a nocturnal visit and tell him a password. Upon arrival, he knocks on her door and says the secret word. The girl then decides whether or not to let him in. The whole matter remains a secret between them. Consequently, there is no economic or social pres-sure on the lovers, and no public shame over possible rejection.

A minority of Moso villages now have male-headed families. This mi-nority is descended from later immigrant groups, the Pumi, or Xifan, who allied themselves with the conquering imperial armies of Mongol and Manchu times and were appointed headmen over the district. The Manchu (or Qing) imperial court required that chieftainship pass to the eldest son of each appointee's legitimate wife, so patriarchal marriage became a state-imposed requirement for holding power.

During the "Great Leap Forward" in the late 1950s, the Communist cadres split the matrilineal, matrilocal households into production bri-gades with communal kitchens. As in much of China, the result was famine within two years. But the Moso had a higher than average death rate be-cause of the extra trauma of losing their whole family system. After that period, the vast majority of ethnic Moso returned to the traditional form of "non-contractual, non-obligatory, and non-exclusive" marriage.[16]

Interestingly, there has been no overpopulation problem among the Moso. Since in their system there is sexual freedom for young people from age 13, it is surprising that the average age of a woman at first childbirth is 23 years.[17] This is partly due to the absence of pressure. There is no duty to prove marriageability or fertility. And "masculinity" is not equated with control over female sexuality or maternity.[18]

All this is radically different in another indigenous society: the Maasai. Although some members of this semi-settled East African herding society are today moving away from a domination heritage, and there are now concerted efforts to empower women, traditional Maasai culture has held women and "feminine" traits and activities such as nonviolence and care-giving in low regard.[19] Men rule, and in accordance with tradition, young Maasai men identify themselves as warriors and protectors. Anthropologist Aud Talle explains that "from an early age boys are taught to be courageous and fear nothing in order to defend property and people."[20]

In precolonial times, the Maasai and other neighboring pastoralists raided for cattle and sometimes killed people from other tribes.[21] The 19th-century colonial "pax Britannica" was imposed on the Maasai and their neighbors to stop intertribal raids. However, as late as the 1970s, when the anthropologist Melissa Llewelyn-Davies made a documentary called "Masai Women," Maasai male initiations still prepared men for the role of warriors.[22]

The traditional source of wealth and status among the Maasai was cattle. Male duties involved herding and the protection of the cattle. The men grazed and watered the herds, castrated bulls, butchered animals, dug wells, and constructed cattle enclosures.[23] The women tended to the herd animals when corralled, milked the cows, prepared and served the food, cared for the children and the sick, and built houses to shelter themselves and their children.[24]

But although Maasai women participated in caring for cattle and worked from dawn to dusk, traditionally they were not allowed to own anything except the beads around their necks. In this polygamous society, women were essentially male property, first of their fathers and then of their husbands. Talle explains that "With the control of livestock [vested in the elder male Maasai] goes the control of women and children. . . . This does not mean that women are totally subdued to men, but they have few means of overruling the latter's authority. This applies to daughters toward their fathers as well as wives toward their husbands."[25] "If he so wishes, a husband may beat an obstinate wife into submission," Talle notes.[26]

Maasai rituals make the different roles, and status, of women and men clear, starting in childhood. After the imposition of the Pax Brittanica, Maasai males were forced to fulfill their warrior roles through symbolic rituals rather than warfare. The 1970 Llewelyn-Davies's film shows Maasai boys leaving their village homes to play at war. When they returned a few years later, it was after having proven themselves "real men." At that point, even though they were still young, they were ritually welcomed back, took over their inherited portion of the herds, married their first wife, and began to administer their property.[27] Girls, on the other hand, underwent very different rituals.

At puberty, Maasai girls traditionally were subjected to the brutal cutting anthropologists call female circumcision that, in a variety of forms, is still performed on millions of girls in much of Africa and the Muslim world. What this cutting actually entails is very different from the circumcision of boys, which does not maim male sexuality. Female circumcision means that young girls are de-sexed: the clitoris is mutilated or cut off, and the vagina sometimes is sewn almost completely shut. This is designed to ensure, first, their sexual abstinence and, second, their sexual docility and fidelity to their husbands.

Among Maasai, this ritual cutting in which the clitoris and labia minora are removed has to be endured by girls without anesthetic or antiseptic. The operation is usually performed by an elderly woman in the community. Twigs are used to secure the vaginal closure and cow dung applied to "help healing," with the consequence that serious infections are routine. Female circumcision initiates a new role for the 13- to 14-year-old girl, marking her formal entry into the marriage market.[28] Nowadays some Maasai are opposing the practice, although a traditional Maasai belief is that an uncircumcised woman will not be able to conceive or else will give birth to deformed children.[29]

After she is given in marriage to a man by her relatives, still little more than a child, a Maasai girl must endure another traditional "celebration." She is sent off on foot alone to her husband's village, and in this place, where she knows she will have to remain for the rest of her life since the Maasai practice patrilocality, she is received by her husband's other wives and the rest of the women of the village with threats and insults—a re-enactment of a ceremony of intimidation and degradation each woman was, in her own turn, forced to experience.[30]

As is often the case among the oppressed, in these first two rituals the immediate agents of traumatization are the girl's own kind: women. The third female Maasai ritual is administered by the men—more precisely, by the women's sons. But like the first two, it reinforces women's inferiority and subordination.

This ritual is held when the young men return to the community. For the men, it is a ceremony of coming of age and empowerment. For the women it is more degradation, humiliation, and disempowerment. On this ceremonial occasion, the sons insult and mock their mothers. The mothers then join in with their own self-deprecatory remarks. On top of this, they are by custom forced to swallow drinks containing urine.[31]

Some women undoubtedly continue to influence their sons, and in "Masai Women" we see women who seem to take pride in their sons.[32] But this rite ceremonially strips women of all authority over their own sons— who, as befits "real" men, are instead to have authority over their mothers.

Traditional Maasai culture dramatically illustrates the connection between the subjugation and exploitation of women, the maltreatment of children, and a traditionally warlike way of life.[33] We see how the suppression of authentic human perceptions and experiences leads to acceptance, even idealization, of abusive and violent relations by *both* those who are dominated and those who dominate.

The comparisons between the partnership-oriented Moso and Teduray and the domination-oriented Maasai also illustrate how in the former cases empathy can be supported by a culture's beliefs and institutions or how, like in the Maasai case, both women and men can be systematically taught to suppress empathy, even empathy for themselves. These contrasting cases further show the connection between how gender and childhood relations are culturally constructed and whether a culture is warlike or peaceful and ranked or egalitarian.

In short, if we compare the Moso and the Teduray with the Maasai, we see marked differences between these indigenous societies regarding war and peace, caring and cruelty, and equality and oppression. We also see how the extremely different beliefs and behaviors in these two tribal societies reflect the Moso's and the Teduray's close orientation to the partnership system and the Maasai's to the domination system.

Applying what we have learned from neuroscience, we can infer that such differences between domination and partnership systems are manifested not only on a social cultural level but also on a neural-psychological level within individuals.

Religious Societies at Different Ends of the Partnership-Domination Scale

The Taliban are a rigidly male-dominated, violent group. Violence is idealized, and male sexual, economic, and religious control of women is a cornerstone of a top-down social and political structure. Though the Taliban do not practice female sexual mutilation, men's honor depends on absolute control over women's sexuality.

This control of one half of the population over the other is a core element of a system based on rigid rankings—not only men over women but also "superior" groups of men over "inferior" ones. There are constant tribal feuds, "holy wars," and brutal public killings of "criminals" such as women accused of sexual transgression. For the Taliban and other Muslim fundamentalist cultures, as for the Maasai, male control over women is key to a construction of masculinity equated with domination and violence.[34]

As anthropologist Lila Abu-Lughod reports about another Muslim fundamentalist culture—a Bedouin tribe in the western desert of Egypt among whom she lived for two years—free expression of female sexuality is seen as a threat to the whole hierarchic male system. It is, in her words, an "act of insubordination and insolence."[35] She writes: "In the eyes of others, a dependent's rebellion dishonors the superior by throwing into question his moral worth, the very basis of his authority. . . . To reclaim it, he must reassert his moral superiority by declaring her actions immoral and must show his capacity to control her, best expressed in the ultimate form of violence."[36]

This "ultimate violence" is not only a man's right but also his responsibility. Murdering one's own kin—daughters, sisters, even mothers—is called an "honor killing" because "superiors" must always dominate "inferiors" such as women.[37] Terms such as honor and dishonor, moral superiority and inferiority, and responsibility and dependence are cultural justifications—and disguises—for the brutality and violence required to maintain rigid rankings of domination.

The gender apartheid that segregates women from men in most areas of life is one way of maintaining the detachment required for this brutality. Since sexual love would interfere with rigid and, if "necessary," violent male control, as Abu-Lughod documents, sexual love was a threat to the social order in this rigidly male-dominated society.

"Love matches are actively discouraged, and thwarted when discovered," Abu-Lughod writes.[38] Every attempt is made to "minimize the significance of the marital relationship and to mask its nature as a sexual bond between man and woman."[39] In other words, an important aspect of these strict domination cultures is an ideology in which love and intimacy are actively discouraged.

Men are looked down on by *both* men and women for succumbing to romantic love because it is equated with dependency, which for men is "inimical to the highest honor-linked value, independence."[40] Abu-Lughod reports that for men, any witnessed affection for or attachment to a woman, even if only in front of family members, compromises a man's right to control and receive the respect of his dependents.[41]

So the contempt for women that is part of top-down violent cultures extends to contempt for traits considered feminine and values such as empathy, nonviolence, and love, which are considered unsuitable for men. Empathy would interfere with the maintenance of rankings of domination. Nonviolence would interfere with the use of violence to maintain these rankings. Love has to be equated with possession and control. And the intimacy of love has to be prevented lest it interfere with unequal gender and family relations.

What we are examining is not a matter of being Muslim. There are Muslims who abhor violence and non-Muslims who commit atrocities. Moreover, we can find this same domination configuration in Christian cultures. Not so long ago, when Western culture still oriented more closely to the domination system than today, marriage and family relations were typically also characterized by distance, deference, and male control. In the Christian Middle Ages, violence against children and women was customary. So was brutal violence against any form of religious or political dissent, along with violent scapegoating, such as the persecution of Jews. There were incessant feuds and wars, including the medieval Church's Crusades, as well as its Inquisition and witch burnings.[42] In these Western historical examples, we also find a social organization of strict top-down physical, emotional, and economic control in both the family and the state, rigid male dominance, and socially condoned, even idealized, violence.

Whereas social stratification and violence are sometimes justified by passages from sacred scriptures, as noted earlier, domination systems are found in secular societies, too. Moreover, a partnership orientation can also be found in religious cultures.

This brings us to the Minangkabau, the fourth largest ethnic group in the West Sumatran archipelago, numbering about four million people. Like the Taliban and the Bedouin, the Minangkabau are a Muslim culture, although with strong earlier animistic and matrifocal spiritual traditions. Yet, as anthropologist Peggy Reeves Sanday writes, the Minangkabau are "the largest and most stable matrilineal society in the world today . . . well known in Indonesia for their literary flair, democratic leanings, business acumen, and 'matriarchal' ways."[43]

Because "matriarchal" is what Minangkabau people call themselves, Sanday also uses this term to describe this egalitarian and peaceful culture where women are not dominated by men. She explains, "I prefer to retain the term matriarchy out of courtesy and respect for Minangkabau usage."[44] Sanday continues: "the concept of matriarchy is relevant in societies where maternal symbols are linked to social practices influencing the lives of both sexes and where women play a central role in these practices."[45]

Nonetheless, the Minangkabau are *not* matriarchies because they are not ruled by women rather than men. What Sanday describes, based on her observations living in the Minangkabau village of Belubus on and off for 20 years, is a society that orients to the partnership system.

As among the Teduray, violence is not part of Minangkabau norms. Sanday explains that childcare is neither authoritarian nor punitive and that she never observed a child being slapped or hit. She writes, "The socialization techniques fit what one would expect from the peacefulness of Minangkabau interpersonal relations: Children aren't hit, I never heard mothers screaming at their children, children get their way frequently and no one seems to mind much."[46] The Minangkabau believe that sooner or later children will learn proper behavior. Like the Teduray, the Minangkabau also use mediation for violence prevention and nonescalation. This encourages a more peaceable way of life.

In contrast to domination-oriented ideologies, the Minangkabau view nurture as a core principle of nature. Based on her conversations with Minangkabau elders, Sanday reports:

The Minangkabau weave order out of their version of wild nature by appeal to maternal archetypes. Unlike Darwin in the 19th century, the Minangkabau subordinate male dominion and competition, which we consider basic to human social ordering and evolution, to the work of maternal nurture, which they hold to be necessary for the common good and the healthy society. . . . Social well-being is found in natural growth and fertility according to the dictum that the unfurling, blooming, and growth in nature is our teacher. . . . Like the seedlings of nature, infants must be nurtured so that they will flower and grow to their fullness and strength as adults. Generalizing this principle, nurture is the natural law that humans should follow in devising social rules. This means that culture must focus on nurturing the weak and renounce brute strength.[47]

Both men and women are expected to be nurturing in this culture, which does not regard roles we have been taught to associate only with femininity as unsuitable for men. The Minangkabau include nurturing in the male role, but they figure descent through the maternal line. As Sanday observes, "the matrilineal system was originally devised so that children would always have a family, food, and ancestral land."[48] She notes that although the Minangkabau certainly understand the male role in paternity, they view the father-child link as less reliable than the mother-child bond for fulfilling the central cultural purpose of providing care and security to the young.[49]

Significantly, the Minangkabau do not make an issue of paternity in the treatment of children or in relation to passing on male property. A Minangkabau elder, Nago Besar, put it this way:

Concerns about biological fatherhood deflect attention from the more important emphasis on the child's well-being. This is not to say that Minangkabau fathers don't play an important role in the lives of their children. They do, but the connection of father to child is not tied to the transmission of land and houses.[50]

Sanday compares Minangkabau thinking with the ideas of Hobbes and other philosophers who viewed social relations based on rankings of domination as the only alternative for maintaining social order. She observes, "since nurture (not dominion) is the primary social lesson that the Minangkabau take from nature, their construction of the social contract is geared toward institutions protecting the weak."[51] This is reflected in the observation that Minangkabau women hold rights to land and its products, while men have rights and access in this matrilineal system through their relationships with their sisters.

Another feature of Minangkabau society is that what helps foster social bonds is the exchange of men, or rather the giving in marriage of sons by mothers to other clans. But again, significantly, these bonds are not a matter of unilateral material exchanges such as bride-price or dowry. In line with the culture's partnership orientation, they are *reciprocal* exchanges where both the bride's and bridegroom's families contribute to the wedding feast. While maternal and paternal relatives play important roles in the wedding ceremony, there is special focus on the husband's mother. The special honoring of the paternal side is also important in ceremonies welcoming a newborn child. Sanday explains:

> The ceremony gives public recognition to the lifelong commitment of the paternal side to the child's interest. . . . A good connection between the clans is also considered necessary for the child's welfare. As a male *adat* expert told me, "Ceremonies maintain a good connection between families connected by marriage; if something happens to the father or the mother, the child is never forgotten."[52]

Contrasting Industrial Societies Orienting to Domination or Partnership

On the surface, Nazi Germany bears no resemblance to the Maasai and Taliban. But it has the same configuration of top-down control, an ideology of male supremacy, and institutionalized, socially idealized violence.

Reams have been published speculating about how a people who boasted great contributions to literature, music, philosophy, science, and other aspects of modern civilization could commit, support, or condone the atrocities of the Third Reich.[53] But little has been published about the underlying conditions that supported the German regression to authoritarianism and brutal violence.

The rise of Hitler has often been blamed on the punitive measures imposed on Germany after its defeat in World War I and the economic crisis in the short-lived Weimar Republic.[54] These were undoubtedly factors. But other nations have had severe economic problems and did not turn fascist.

A key factor in this turn to fascism is a nation where male dominance and authoritarian parent-child relations were still normative ideals.

When the Nazis were elected to rule Germany, they brought with them a revival of pagan myths about Aryan supermen who, as the German philosopher Friedrich Nietzsche argued, were entitled to rule over all women and most men.[55] The absolute authoritarianism celebrated in Nietzsche's prose went hand in hand with the "masculine" violence celebrated in Wagner's music.

Nazi propaganda asked men to become "real" men: truly "masculine" men who conquer and who rid the world of "inferiors." So the Nazi Wehrmacht went forth to conquer Europe, and from there the world, following their leaders' commands to commit the most meticulously organized and technologically efficient atrocities in recorded history.

At the same time that German men were instructed to reclaim their "masculinity," women were told that they were put on Earth to care for men—mind, body, and soul. Birth control clinics were closed, dissemination of birth control information was forbidden, and penalties for abortion were greatly stiffened. Women employed outside the home were blamed for male unemployment, inflation, and other economic ills and were exhorted to give up their jobs. Quotas of 10 percent limited women's access to higher education. Women lawyers were removed from judgeships and high state offices. Women doctors were allowed to practice medicine only if they merged their practice with that of their husband. Laws denied women tenure in jobs.[56]

As Joseph K. Folsom notes, the purpose of Nazi policy was not only to return women to their "traditional" place as wives and mothers economically dependent on the male head of household. It was also to take women out of professions and put them in low-paid occupations, thus promoting male supremacy in all relations.[57] After the war started, and women were needed in jobs men vacated to fight, as historian Claudia Koonz writes, "women were urged to be 'traditional' by reclaiming their economic importance." But in line with the Nazi's policy of male supremacy, their wages were officially kept lower than men's.[58]

Hitler declared as early as 1934 that "the message of woman's emancipation is a message discovered solely by the Jewish intellect and its content is stamped with the same spirit."[59] Or as a young Nazi leader put it, "the Jew has stolen women from us through the forms of sex democracy. We, the youth, must march out to kill the dragon so that we may again attain the most holy thing in the world, the woman as maid and servant."[60]

In Nazi Germany, as in Maasai and other cultures that orient closely to the domination system, "the ideal Nazi man was a fighter; the ideal Nazi woman, his mother."[61] "Soft" traits such as nonviolence and caregiving were appropriate only for "inferior" women and "effeminate" men.

A stark contrast to domination-oriented Nazi Germany is provided by a very different group of Western countries: the Nordic nations. While the Teduray and Minangkabau are Eastern and indigenous, the same partnership-oriented template can be seen in Western technologically developed, industrialized nations such as Denmark, Finland, Iceland, Norway, and Sweden.

Nordic nations have created societies with a high degree of political and economic equality in both the family and the state. They have a mix of free enterprise and central planning and were the first nations to move toward more industrial democracy, pioneering teamwork by self-directed groups to replace assembly lines where workers are mere cogs in the industrial machine.

As noted earlier, Nordic nations have succeeded in creating a generally good living standard for all, without the huge gaps between haves and have-nots characteristic of domination-oriented nations. According to the Gini coefficient, a widely used measure of social equality-inequality, all the Nordic countries are among the top 13 percent when it comes to social equality worldwide.[62] Finland is in first place globally in terms of equality. In Sweden, the average CEO of a company earns 89 times the average worker's pay, and in Norway and Denmark, respectively, CEOs take home 58 times and 48 times the amount of workers—which is a large difference, but dwarfs in comparison to the United States, where the average CEO earns 354 times more than workers.[63] Overall, on the United Nations' Inequality-Adjusted Human Development Index (IHDI) for 2015, which reflects a country's actual level of human development (with the amount of inequality within the country being taken into account), Finland ranks at 14 with a score of 0.843, while the United States lags behind, ranking at 20 with a score of 0.796. The other Nordic nations have IHDI rankings even lower than Finland, with Norway, Iceland, Sweden, and Denmark all ranking within the top 11 countries of the world for human development adjusted for inequality.[64]

This greater equality has sometimes been attributed to the relatively small and homogeneous populations of the Nordic nations. But smaller and even more homogeneous societies, such as certain oil-rich nations of the Middle East, orient closely to the domination system, with authoritarian regimes, large gaps between haves and have-nots, rigid male dominance, and rule through force or threat of force.

To understand why Nordic nations developed a more caring and equitable economy, we have to look beyond homogeneity and size to consider other factors. And one important factor is that in Denmark, Finland, Iceland, Norway, and Sweden there is much greater partnership between women and men. Women have held the highest political offices, and the percentages of Nordic women in parliament in recent years approaches parity with men, being generally around 40 percent, or about double the percentage in the United States.[65]

The former Prime Minister of Norway, Gro Harlem Brundtland born in 1939, reflects on the early influences of her life and the egalitarian and caring values that motivated her work, nationally and globally, to promote access to healthcare, better lives for all citizens, and sustainable development internationally. She explains,

> Gender equality was simply the norm in many areas of my young life. My mom participated in heated political discussions, taught herself to drive the car, and thought it the most natural thing in the world to carry a yoke with a three-gallon bucket of water hanging off each end. I was taught that women can achieve the same things in the world as men. These early years influenced me and created in me a fierce passion for justice, equity, health, and the greater world.[66]

As we will examine further in subsequent chapters, there is a strong connection between the status of women in a nation and both its general quality of life and economic success.[67] This is not only because women are half of humanity; it is also because as the status of women rises, so also does the value a society gives to stereotypically "feminine" traits and behaviors such as caring and caregiving—in women, men, and economic policy.

As the status of women rises, so does the status of traits and activities deemed unacceptable in men in domination-oriented cultures because they are associated with "inferior" femininity. This is a critical point: men in more partnership-oriented cultures no longer find it such a threat to their status—to their "masculinity"—to adopt more "soft" feminine traits and behaviors.

Along with the higher status of Nordic women came fiscal priorities that support "feminine" values and activities. So these more partnership-oriented nations pioneered caring policies, such as government-supported childcare, universal healthcare, and paid parental leave.

As Hilkka Pietila documents, largely as a result of these caring policies, countries that suffered from extreme poverty—including severe famines that led to waves of immigration to the United States—became prosperous. [68] This contradicts still another erroneous assumption about progressive Nordic social policies: that these policies were due to greater prosperity. In reality, as Pietila emphasizes, these policies were the *cause*, not the effect, of greater prosperity.[69]

While Nordic nations are sometimes called socialist, they actually have a thriving market economy as well as private property. Labeling them socialist because they have government policies that provide universal healthcare, childcare, and eldercare is a misnomer. What distinguishes these nations is not that the government is involved in the economy, which fascist governments such as Nazi Germany also were, but that these countries have many caring policies. Indeed, these more partnership-oriented nations often call them themselves "caring societies."[70]

Another important partnership feature of Nordic nations is that they pioneered legal measures and attitude change against the physical punishment and abuse of children. Sweden, Finland, and Norway in 1979, 1983, and 1987, respectively, were the first countries in the world to pass laws making corporal punishment of children illegal, and since that time, more than 30 other nations have followed suit, including Denmark in 1998 and Iceland in 2004.[71] In Finland, for example, the law states: "A child shall be brought up in the spirit of understanding, security and love. . . . [The child] shall not be subdued, corporally punished or otherwise humiliated . . . [and] growth towards independence, responsibility and adulthood shall be encouraged, supported and assisted."[72]

Passing of the law was accompanied by public awareness campaigns geared at changing attitudes and providing parents with nonviolent alternatives to engaging in physical punishment of children. Doug lived in Finland for almost 20 years and kept his eyes open for any acts of physical punishment of children, in homes and in public, and only once observed an adult strike a child. However, on closer investigation, it turned out that the parent and child were not ethnically Finnish. Psychologists Karin Österman and her colleagues surveyed Finns between the ages of 15 and 80 and found significantly lower rates of being beaten with an object or slapped among the respondents born after the passage of the law and the accompanying attitude change campaigns.[73]

Overall, the Nordic nations also have low homicide rates.[74] Some Nordic countries have well-supported men's movements against male violence toward women.[75] In discussing rape with Finnish men and women, Doug found that both sexes agreed that rape was a truly reprehensible crime and in fact was uncommon. One man said that if the woman says "no," Finnish men respect this. Another man said, "most men know how to get sex in the normal way"—by which he meant without coercion, threat, or violence. Finnish geographer Hille Koskela explains that, generally speaking, women feel safe at night: "It is quite common for women to go out without male company, and to stay out until the latest restaurants close at 4 a.m. and, as a consequence, the landscape of Finnish cities at night is not obviously gendered."[76] Doug teamed-up with Finnish sociologist Jukka-Pekka Takala to investigate how many lone women were out and about on the Helsinki streets at night. Forty-two percent of the people on the streets were women, and of the lone individuals, women constituted one third.[77] The various lines of data show the risks of rape and fear of rape are low in Finland.[78]

Nordic countries also have pioneered nonviolent conflict resolution, establishing peace studies programs and institutes early on, when most countries only had war academies. Denmark set up the Copenhagen Peace Research Institute, which is now part of the Danish Institute for International Studies, where researchers focus on such topics as nuclear weapons, climate change, and the challenge of the human impacts on the Earth in the Anthropocene.[79] Established in 1959, Norway hosts the Peace Research Institute of Oslo, which among other activities provides regular updates on peace and security issues as they affect women, as laid out in United Nations Security Council Resolution 1325 on women and security.[80]

Finland established the Tampere Peace Research Institute and, recently, a Master's program in Peace, Mediation, and Conflict Research. Former Finnish President Martti Ahtisaari was awarded the Nobel Peace Prize for his successful track record in mediating international conflicts in various parts of the globe. He set up the Crisis Management Initiative "that works to prevent and resolve violent conflicts through informal dialogue and mediation."[81] Sweden houses three peace studies programs, including the world famous Department of Peace and Conflict Research at Uppsala University.[82]

In addition, Nordic nations pioneered environmentally sound manufacturing approaches. In the Swedish "Natural Step," materials are recycled even after they reach the consumer to avoid pollution and waste.

Moreover, these nations contribute a larger percentage of their annual gross domestic product to international programs working for economic development, environmental protection, and human rights than other developed nations. This is another manifestation of greater empathy and care as the norm in these cultures—including empathy and care for people in far-away and very different places.

These Nordic practices and policies are *not* coincidental developments. They stem from the fact that the Nordic world orients more to the partnership than the domination configuration.

As the examples of the Moso, Teduray, Minangkabau, and Nordic nations show, partnership systems can be found in societies with very different subsistence modes, social structures, and religions orientations. And partnership-oriented structures, beliefs, policies, and relations support more egalitarian, gender-balanced, peaceful, empathetic, and caring ways of living than do domination-oriented systems.

As we will further detail in the next chapter, studies of nomadic forager band societies suggest that humanity's ancient orientation actually was toward partnership rather than domination over the many millennia of human evolution. This indicates that, whereas our flexible human species can accommodate to life in domination systems, our primal inclination bends toward partnership.

The *domination system* and the *partnership system* are social configurations that transcend conventional classifications such as religious versus secular, Eastern versus Western, or right versus left. Cross-culturally and throughout history, brutally repressive and violent societies exemplify the core configuration of the domination system, whether secular, like rightist-capitalist Nazi Germany in the West and Kim Jong-un's leftist-communist North Korea in the East, or religious, like the European Middle Ages or ISIS in the Middle East and Boko Haram in Africa (Table 6.1). More equitable and peaceful societies adhere more closely to the partnership system core configuration, whether ancient, such as during much of the deep nomadic forager past and prehistoric Çatalhöyük, or modern,

Table 6.1 A Comparison of the Primary Features of Domination and
Partnership Systems

	Domination System	Partnership System
1. Family and social structure	Authoritarian structure of ranking and *hierarchies of domination* in family and society. Top-down control of economic resources and politics. Children observe and experience inequality and inequity as the norm.	Democratic structure and sometimes *hierarchies of actualization*. Caring is economically valued. Egalitarian and equitable adult relations are the norm. Parenting is *not* authoritarian.
2. Gender roles and relations	Ranking of male half of humanity over female half. Rigid gender stereotypes, with "masculine" traits and activities such as toughness and conquest ranked over "feminine" ones such as caregiving and nonviolence	Equal valuing of the male and female halves of humanity. Fluid gender roles, with high valuing of empathy, caring, caregiving, and nonviolence in both women and men as well as in social and economic policy
3. Fear, abuse, and violence	High degree of fear and violence, from child beating to abuse by "superiors" in families, workplaces, and society	Low degree of fear, abuse, and violence. Respect for diversity and human rights
4. Narratives	Beliefs and stories justify and idealize domination and violence, which are deemed inevitable, moral, and desirable.	Beliefs and stories present empathic, mutually beneficial, nonviolent relations as normal, moral, and desirable.

such as Sweden, Norway, and Finland. No society is a pure partnership or
domination system, but the degree to which a culture orients to one or the
other shapes beliefs, social structures, and how the human brain develops.

Notes

1. Donald Brown, *Human Universals* (New York: McGraw-Hill, 1991).
2. Personal communication, Stuart Schlegel, November 1987.
3. Stuart Schlegel, *Tiruray Justice: Traditional Tiruray Law and Morality* (Berkeley: University of California Press, 1970), 31.
4. Stuart Schlegel, *Wisdom from a Rain Forest*. (Athens: University of Georgia Press, 1998), 111.
5. Schlegel, *Wisdom from a Rain Forest*, 112, emphasis in original.

6. Schlegel, *Wisdom from a Rain Forest*, 112.

7. Schlegel, *Wisdom from a Rain Forest*, 112.

8. Schlegel, *Wisdom from a Rain Forest*, 113.

9. Schlegel, *Wisdom from a Rain Forest*, 249.

10. Schlegel, *Wisdom from a Rain Forest*, 155.

11. Schlegel, *Wisdom from a Rain Forest*, 156.

12. Schlegel, *Wisdom from a Rain Forest*, 244.

13. Lamu Gatusa, "Matriarchal Marriage Patterns of the Mosuo of China," paper presented at the symposium *Societies of Peace—Past, Present, Future: Second World Congress of Matriarchal Studies,* Texas State University, San Marcos/Austin, Texas, September 29–October 2, 2005, translated by Wang Yun and Jutta Reid. Available online: http://www.second-congress-matriarchal-studies.com/gatusa.html.See also Chuan-kang Shih, *Quest for Harmony: The Moso Traditions of Sexual Union and Family Life* (Palo Alto, CA: Stanford University Press, 2009).

14. Heide Goettner-Abendroth, *Matriarchal Societies: Indigenous Cultures across the Globe* (New York: Peter Lang, 2012).

15. Junsheng Cai, "Myth and Reality: The Projection of Gender Relations in Prehistoric China," in *The Chalice and the Blade in Chinese Culture,* ed. Jiayin Min (Beijing: China Social Science Publishing House, 1995), 72.

16. Lamu Gatusa, "Matriarchal Marriage Patterns of the Mosuo of China."

17. Chuan-kang Shih and Mark Jenike, "A Cultural–Historical Perspective on the Depressed Fertility among the Matrilineal Moso in Southwest China," *Human Ecology* 30 (2002): 21–47, doi: 10.1023/A:1014579404548.

18. Shih and Jenike, "A Cultural–Historical Perspective on the Depressed Fertility."

19. Personal communication, October 2017, by Eisler and Fry with Margaret Koshal Reiyia, founder of Mara Learning & Development Centre in Maasai Mara, and Nelson O. Reiyia, founder of "I See Maasai Development Initiative" (ISMDI), focused on empowering women and especially ending traditions of female genital mutilation and child marriage. See, e.g., http://margaret-sakian-koshal.strikingly.com. In her book, Dorothy L. Hodgson, *Once Intrepid Warriors: Gender, Ethnicity, and the Cultural Politics of Maasai Development* (Bloomington: Indiana University Press, 2001) also notes the changes that have taken place from more traditional to more recent times and also that in this age-graded society, the age of women and men also plays an important role in gender relations.

20. Aud Talle, "Maasai," in *Encyclopedia of Sex and Gender, Volume 2,* eds. Carol R. Ember and Melvin Ember (New York: Kluwar Academic/Plenum Publishers, 2004), 611.

21. Hodgson, *Once Intrepid Warriors*.

22. Melissa Llewelyn-Davies, *Masai Women* (Video, 59 minutes, London: Granada Television International, 1974). Masai is a less-used alternate spelling of Maasai. See also Dorothy L. Hodgson, "Pastoralism, Patriarchy, and History: Changing Gender Relations among Maasai in Tanganyika 1890–1940," *Journal of African History* 40 (1999): 41–65, http://www.jstor.org/stable/183394.

23. Talle, "Maasai."

24. Talle, "Maasai,"

25. Talle, "Maasai," 613.
26. Talle, "Maasai," 615.
27. Talle, "Maasai."
28. Llewelyn-Davies, "Masai Women"; Talle, "Maasai."
29. Talle, "Maasai."
30. Llewelyn-Davies, "Masai Women"; Talle, "Maasai."
31. Llewelyn-Davies, "Masai Women."
32. Llewelyn-Davies, "Masai Women."
33. Hodgson, "Pastoralism, Patriarchy, and History," presents an intriguing argument that patriarchy among the Maasai was augmented under British colonial rule due to the introduction of a capitalist economic system. She writes (on pages 63–64): "Throughout the years, first the British government and then the Tanzanian government tried to encourage, bribe, coerce or force Maasai to perceive their cattle as commodities and sell them. The cumulative impact of the policies and practices examined in this article was significant. Gender-specific taxation forced men to seek a source of cash, and monetization and commoditization made them aware of a lucrative commodity in their own midst—livestock. Furthermore, as barter was replaced by commodity purchase, men usurped women's roles as traders; instead of women bartering livestock products, men began selling livestock to meet their growing cash needs. Capitalist values, which required the alienability of a product, privileged individual male control of cattle, collapsing the multiple, over-lapping use-rights of men and women in livestock into an idea of male 'ownership' of property." Hence Hodgson's conclusion (on page 65) is that, "Incorporation into the state system reinforced and enhanced male political authority and economic control by expanding the bases for political power and introducing new forms of property relations. Together, these processes shifted the contours of male-female power relations, resulting in the material disenfranchisement and conceptual devaluation of Maasai women as both women and pastoralists."
34. A social scientist who brings out some of these connections is the sociologist Fatima Mernissi. She writes how in Muslim North African society a man's prestige is linked "in an almost fatal way to the sexual behaviour of the women under his charge, be they his wives, sisters, or unmarried female relatives"; Fatima Mernissi, *Beyond the Veil: Male-Female Dynamics in Modern Muslim Society* (Bloomington: University of Indiana Press, 1987), 161. Mernissi, *Beyond the Veil*, 161, also notes how the differential socialization of boys and girls about sexuality is the source of great tension for both. Whereas men "are encouraged to expect full satisfaction of their sexual desires, and to perceive their masculine identity as closely linked to that satisfaction," women are from an early age "taught to curb their sexual drives" and even told about "the penis's 'destructive' effects."
35. Lila Abu-Lughod, *Veiled Sentiments* (Berkeley: University of California Pres, 1986), 158.
36. Abu-Lughod, *Veiled Sentiments*, 157.
37. Abu-Lughod, *Veiled Sentiments*, 158. As Abu-Lughod notes, the fundamentalist Muslim custom of requiring the veiling of women is another way of signaling

women's inferiority and hence the right and responsibility of superior males to control them. Veiling is not only a way of making women invisible as inferior dependents; the black veil, as she writes, also symbolizes women's "sexual shame" and "natural" moral inferiority (159). Not all Islamic scholars agree with Abu-Lughod's view. Neither would all Islamic women, who sometimes see in their veiling and seclusion a protection from contact with a male world that poses great dangers to them. This is an extreme variation of the dominator tenet that all women need a man to protect them—from other men—and hence that female dependency and subservience is only natural, given the "nature" of man. Ironically, as part of the Islamic nationalist independence movements, some women have even readopted the veil as a rejection of Western values and thus a symbol of "liberation." See, e.g., Minou Reeves, *Female Warriors of Allah: Women and the Islamic Revolution* (New York: Dutton, 1989). But as Abu-Lughod points out, the veil is black precisely because it symbolizes women's shame; in Bedouin society someone who has been shamed is said to have had his or her face blackened (Abu-Lughod, 138).

38. Abu-Lughod, *Veiled Sentiments,* 149.
39. Abu-Lughod, *Veiled Sentiments,* 150.
40. Abu-Lughod, *Veiled Sentiments,* 148.
41. Abu-Lughod, *Veiled Sentiments,* 157.
42. See, e.g., J. Rattray Taylor, *Sex in History* (New York: Ballantine Books, 1954). See also Anne Llewellyn Barstow, *Witchcraze: A New History of the European Witch Hunts* (London and San Francisco: Pandora, 1994); Frances Gies and Joseph Gies, *Marriage and the Family in the Middle Ages* (New York: Harper and Row, 1987); and Uta Ranke-Heineman, *Eunuchs for the Kingdom of Heaven: Women, Sexuality, and the Catholic Church,* trans. Peter Heinegg (New York: Doubleday, 1990). It was of course also a time when there were some partnership elements, but we are talking about norms and central tendencies, not exceptions.
43. Peggy Reeves Sanday, *Women at the Center* (Ithaca, NY: Cornell University Press, 2002), 148.
44. Sanday, *Women at the Center,* xi.
45. Sanday, *Women at the Center,* xxii.
46. Personal communication to Eisler from Peggy Reeves Sanday, January 30, 2002.
47. Sanday, *Women at the Center,* 22–24.
48. Sanday, *Women at the Center,* 24.
49. Sanday, *Women at the Center.*
50. Sanday, *Women at the Center,* 25.
51. Sanday, *Women at the Center,* 31.
52. Sanday, *Women at the Center,* 102.
53. See, e.g., David Welch, *The Third Reich* (New York: Routledge, 1993); Ervin Straub, *The Psychology of Good and Evil: Why Children, Adults, and Groups Help and Harm Others* (Cambridge, UK: Cambridge University Press, 2003); Ervin Straub, *The Roots of Goodness and Resistance to Evil* (New York: Oxford University Press, 2015).
54. See, e.g., Jean Monnet, *Memoirs* (New York: Doubleday, 1978).

55. Friedrich Nietzsche, *Thus Spoke Zarathustra* (Hollywood, FL: Simon and Brown, 2012).

56. Claudia Koon, "Mothers in the Fatherland: Women in Nazi Germany," in *Becoming Visible: Women in European History*, eds. Renate Bridenthal and Claudia Koonz (Boston: Houghton Mifflin, 1977), 464–466.

57. Joseph K. Folsom, *The Family and Democratic Society* (New York: Routledge, 1949).

58. Koonz, *Mothers in the Fatherland*, 466.

59. Adolf Hitler, quoted in *N.S. Frauenbuch* (Munich: J. F. Lehman, 1934), 10–11.

60. Gottfried Feder, quoted in "Die Deutsche Frau im Dritten Reich," *Reichstagskorrespondens der Bayrischen Volkspartai*, April 4, 1932.

61. Koonz, *Mothers in the Fatherland*, 447.

62. Central Intelligence Agency, "The World Fact Book," accessed March 13, 2018. Available online: https://www.cia.gov/library/publications/the-world-factbook/rankorder/2172rank.html. The United States, by comparison, ranks among the least equal countries, in the bottom 27 percent globally (rank 40/150).

63. Statista, "Pay Gap between CEOs and Average Workers in 2014, by Country," accessed March 13, 2018. Available online: https://www.statista.com/statistics/424159/pay-gap-between-ceos-and-average-workers-in-world-by-country/.

64. United Nations Development Program, "Human Development Reports—Table 3: Inequality-Adjusted Human Development Index," accessed April 28, 2018. Available online: http://hdr.undp.org/en/composite/IHDI. (See the column labeled *Difference from HDI rank* under *Inequality-adjusted HDI*).

65. Inter-Parliamentary Union, "Women in National Parliaments: The Situation as of January 1, 2018," accessed March 13, 2018. Available online: http://archive.ipu.org/wmn-e/classif.htm.

66. Gro Harlem Brundtland, "Why We Care," accessed March 13, 2018. Available online: http://reproductivehealth.aspeninstitute.org/Media/Details/0040/Gro-Harlem-Brundtland-Why-We-Care.

67. See, e.g., Riane Eisler, David Loye, and Kari Norgaard, *Women, Men, and the Global Quality of Life* (Pacific Grove, CA: Center for Partnership Studies, 1995); *Global Gender Gap Report 2017* (Geneva: World Economic Forum, 2017).

68. Hilkka Pietila, "Nordic Welfare Society—A Strategy to Eradicate Poverty and Build Up Equality: Finland as a Case Study," *Cooperation South* 2 (2001): 79–96.

69. Pietila, "Nordic Welfare Society."

70. For a detailed discussion, see Riane Eisler, *The Real Wealth of Nations: Creating a Caring Economics* (San Francisco: Berrett-Koehler, 2007).

71. Karin Österman, Kaj Björkqvist, and C. Wahlbeck, "Twenty-Eight Years after the Complete Ban of Physical Punishment in Finland: Trends and Psychosocial Concomitants," *Aggressive Behavior* 40 (2014): 568–581, doi: 10.1002/ab.21537.

72. Global Initiative to End All Corporal Punishment of Children, "Corporal punishment of children in Finland," last modified October 2017. Available online: http://www.endcorporalpunishment.org/wp-content/uploads/country-reports/Finland.pdf.

73. Österman et al., "Twenty-Eight Years."

74. Index Mundi, "Intentional Homicides (per 100,000 People)—Country Ranking," accessed April 28, 2018. Available online: https://www.indexmundi.com/facts/indicators/VC.IHR.PSRC.P5/rankings.

75. As two Nordic men, Jorgen Lorentzen and Per Are Lokke, wrote, "Many men have come to believe that violence against a woman, child, or another man is an acceptable way to control another person. By remaining silent about the violence, we allow other men to poison our environments. We also allow the picture of men as dangerous to stay alive.... Domestic violence is a problem within existing masculinity and it is we, as men, who have to stop it" (Jorgen Lorentzen and Per Are Lokke, "Men's Violence against Women: The Need to Take Responsibility," paper presented at the international seminar "Promoting Equality: A Common Issue for Men and Women," Palais de l'Europe, Strasbourg, France, June 17–18, 1997, p. 4).

76. Hille Koskela, "'Bold Walk and Breakings': Women's Spatial Confidence versus Fear of Violence," *Gender, Place, and Culture* 4 (1997): 301–319, doi: 10.1080/09663699725369.

77. Douglas P. Fry and Jukka-Pekka Takala, "Who's Afraid of Helsinki at Night?" Paper presented at the Conference of the European Sociological Association, Helsinki, Finland, August 28–September 1, 2001.

78. Douglas P. Fry, *The Human Potential for Peace: An Anthropological Challenge to Assumptions about War and Violence* (New York: Oxford University Press, 2006); Fry and Takala, "Who's Afraid of Helsinki at Night?"

79. See the Danish Institute for International Studies. Available online: http://www.diis.dk/en.

80. See the Peace Research Institute of Oslo. Available online: https://www.prio.org/News/Item/?x=2077.

81. See the Conflict Management Initiative. Available online: www.cmi.fi.

82. See the Department of Peace and Conflict Research at Uppsala University. Available online: http://www.pcr.uu.se/.

7

The Original Partnership Societies

Before about 12,500 years ago, the nomadic forager lifeway was ubiquitous. In the debates about the nature of human nature—whether we are more inclined toward war or peace, selfishness or altruism—nomadic forager societies are regularly evoked to draw inferences about human existence "in a state of nature" before the development of civilization.[1]

Nomadic foragers—also called nomadic hunter-gatherers—constitute the oldest form of human social organization, predating by far the agricultural revolution of about 10,000 years ago as well as the rise of pastoralists, tribal horticulturalists, chiefdoms, kingdoms, and ancient states. For most of humanity's existence, these ancestral foraging partnership societies lacked large population concentrations, permanently settled communities, stored plunderable resources, top-down leadership, distinct social rankings, and warfare.[2] These small, unwarlike, and egalitarian bands shifted camps regularly as they moved across the landscape in quest for food.

By contrast, another type of hunter-gatherers, usually called complex foragers, are generally hierarchical, settled, and have higher population densities than do nomadic foragers. Complex foragers tend to be found in areas of bountiful, consistent resources such as rich aquatic environments. Complex foragers of the northwest coast of North America, for example, shared certain features. They subsisted largely on marine resources such as highly productive salmon runs; had hierarchical class strata with chiefs, commoners, and sometimes slaves; had highly developed arts, rituals, and economies based on the redistribution of goods; and, last but not least, engaged in warfare.[3] Complex foragers are relatively rare in the worldwide ethnographic and archaeological records.[4]

Complex forager societies constituted the very first domination systems, and they arose relatively recently, being "most common after 12,500 BP, usually transitional between simple [nomadic/egalitarian] hunter-gathering and agricultural systems."[5] Not all transitional societies were domination systems. As noted earlier, the large Anatolian town of Çatalhöyük was partnership-oriented, with no signs of warfare for more than 1,000 years, no signs of major differences in status or wealth in both houses and burials, and gender equality as the norm.[6] But from diverse parts of the planet, archaeological sequences tell similar stories about the origin of domination systems from prior conditions of ubiquitous partnership. With development of greater social complexity, some societies, but certainly not all, embarked on a set of monumental changes in a domination direction.[7] These initial pre-agricultural changes toward social complexity provided the foundations for new social institutions and practices of domination, such as social classes, control of women by men, and slavery, features that are often assumed to be as old as humanity itself—but in fact constitute rather recent inventions.

Social Complexity and the Origins of Domination

There are a number of theories about how and why domination systems originated. One theory, which recently seems to have received some support from DNA studies of prehistoric European populations,[8] is based on the proposal by archeologist Marija Gimbutas that in Europe the shift was due to incursions of Indo-European pastoralists originating in the Eurasian steppes who brought with them strongman rule, male dominance, and warfare.[9] A more generally accepted theory is that this shift was due to the complexity complex. That is, settling down in one place, intensive resource use (often due to agriculture), accumulation of surpluses, population expansion, social hierarchies, definitive leadership, warfare, and sometimes slavery constituted a tremendous shift from the age-old human conditions of low population density, small-band life, nomadism, day-to-day foraging, egalitarianism in ethos and practice, and non-surplus-accumulating social life.[10]

The worldwide archaeological record offers a view into the evolutionary timeframe of partnership and domination. It shows that transitions from partnership to domination occurred at different locations at different times, and certainly did not take place everywhere.[11] As we have seen, a diversity of partnership-oriented societies have been documented across space and time, ranging from Minoan Crete that flourished from about 2000 BCE to 1500 BCE to the Teduray, Moso, and Minangkabau cultures considered in the Chapter 6, the Hopi of North America, and the contemporary Nordic countries of Europe. However, beginning as early as 12,500 years ago in parts of the Near East, and much later on the northwest coast of North

America, the Valley of Oaxaca in southern Mexico, and elsewhere, similar sequences of culture change accompanied transitions from partnership to domination.[12]

When it took place, the transition away from a nomadic forager lifestyle to a settled existence entailed many changes that are archaeologically apparent. For example, variability both in house size and burial features indicates that a social hierarchy existed, with high-status people living in larger homes and being interred more elaborately than those of lower social ranks. In other words, inequality leaves its marks in the archaeological record.

Various archaeological examples also show the birth of war in association with hierarchical systems. For instance, in the Near East between 12,000 and 10,000 years ago, nomadic foraging gave way to plant and animal domestication. In this region, there is no evidence of war or hierarchical social organization in the archaeological record at 12,000 years before the present, sparse evidence for war by about 9,500 years ago, and then clear evidence of spreading and intensifying warfare after that. Multiple kinds of data validate the fact that war in the Near East emerged from a condition of prior warlessness: the growing defensibility of settlement sites, increase of violence apparent in human skeletal remains, and rapid introduction of new artistic styles suggesting the imposition of a conquering group's cultural tradition in a new location.

Another archaeological case illustrates a similar sequence. Archaeologist Herbert Maschner chronicles changes in type and severity of violence and the rise of social complexity in an area of the northwest coast of North America.[13] Beginning at about 5,500 years ago and persisting over at least a couple millennia, skeletal trauma almost exclusively involved nonlethal injuries—and not many of these. This was a period of nomadic foraging. The rarity and nonlethality of the injuries, in conjunction with absolutely no other indicators of warfare, strongly imply the presence of incidents of interpersonal aggression rather than war. Later in this prehistoric sequence, evidence of war appears in correspondence with other domination elements such as social hierarchy and inequality. Maschner summarizes: "The first large villages appear, status differences become apparent, a heavy emphasis on marine subsistence develops, and warfare becomes visible in the archaeological record."[14]

Yet another example of the birth of a domination system comes from southern Mexico. Archaeologists Kent Flannery and Joyce Marcus find no evidence of group conflict or markers of social hierarchy among the egalitarian nomadic band societies that foraged in the Valley of Oaxaca for six millennia between 10,000 and 4,000 years ago.[15] This was a time of partnership. Toward the end of this period, the transition from nomadic foraging to hierarchical sedentary village life reliant on farming was underway. By 2,800 years before the present, three rival chiefdoms had developed, buffered from each other by unoccupied zones.

Archaeology shows that one chiefdom, San José Mogote, was then attacked and sacked. The survivors withdrew to a mountaintop called Monte Albán and constructed defensive walls that encircled the settlement. Eventually, Monte Albán emerged as the capital of the prehistoric Zapotec state. Hallmarks of such states, whether ancient or modern, are permanent armies with hierarchical command structures led by military specialists, which make military campaigns and protracted wars possible.[16] By about 2,300 years ago, the Zapotec state had obtained empire status by conquering and exacting tribute from neighboring peoples up to 150 km away. In summary, the archaeological time sequence for the Valley of Oaxaca again shows a long partnership period of egalitarian and peaceful nomadic forager lifestyle before the entrance of complexity with its settled, hierarchical social organization that eventually, in this case, developed state-level civilization with distinct social classes, a professional army, exploitation of labor, and torture and mutilation of war captives, along with hieroglyphic writing, massive temples, exquisite goldsmithery, and extensive astronomical knowledge.[17]

In light of these kinds of findings, whereas the development of agriculture is correctly heralded as a landmark event in world prehistory, bringing innumerable changes to the human species, the preagricultural revolution or, in other words, the emergence of social complexity in some places also can be viewed as a monumental transformation in human existence.[18] Prehistorian Donald Henry emphasizes the magnitude of the changes that often take place when nomadic partnership societies shift to settled, domination-based complex foraging, explaining that, "The replacement of . . . [nomadic forager] societies composed of small, highly mobile, materially impoverished, egalitarian groups by a society that was characterized by large, sedentary, materially rich and socially stratified communities represented a dramatic shift from an adaptive system that had enjoyed several million years of success."[19]

We want to highlight that this shift toward domination-oriented societies during the preagricultural and agricultural revolutions did not occur everywhere on the planet. But when the transition to domination did take place, it ushered in massive changes in relations between men and women, the way people lived, how they made a living, and their modes of interaction with one another.

The Recent Origins of War

Worldwide archaeology suggests that homicide has been around for a very long time but that warfare has not. Archaeologist Marilyn Roper reviews the skeletal finds for early humans—or hominins—over the last three million years, and she reaches the conclusion that sporadic homicides occurred in the deep past but not warfare.[20] In the absence of any corroborating evidence of warfare such as defensive sites, fortifications, mass graves showing trauma, or specialized weapons, the discovery of a single victim of lethal aggression does not justify a claim that war existed.[21] In the absence of other war indicators, skeletal trauma may likely represent a murder, a group-sanctioned execution, or a hunting or other accident, rather than war.[22]

Hisashi Nakao and his colleagues looked at all cases of skeletal violence in Japan across the mostly forager period beginning 13,000 years ago and extending into historical times less than 1,000 years ago.[23] Whereas Steven Pinker has assumed that high rates of warfare characterized nomadic forager prehistory, the data from Japan question this presumption because violent death averaged less than two percent over the entire period.[24] Absolutely no cases of lethal violence were discovered among the skeletons for the earliest 5,000-year period. Nakao and his colleagues point out that some, if not all, of the lethal trauma would have resulted from homicides and accidents rather than war. The authors conclude that their results are "inconsistent with arguments that warfare is inherent in human nature and was an important selection pressure."[25]

Worldwide, the archaeological site that possibly shows the earliest indications of war is a cemetery called Jebel Sahaba, dated between 11,600 and 14,300 years old.[26] Excavations of this ancient burial site in Sudanese Nubia near the Nile were originally reported to reflect a very high percentage of violent deaths in the skeletal population, and some scholars have attributed this violence to warfare or feuding. Other researchers have cautioned that homicides and executions cannot be ruled out. Additionally, the number of victims of violence almost certainly was overestimated in the original report because any association of a buried skeleton with stone flakes, chips, or scrapers in the nearby soil was seen as evidence of violent death, even in the absence of any skeletal trauma.[27]

Unambiguous indications of warfare only begin about 10,000 years ago, that is, after the preagricultural and agricultural revolutions were underway in some locations. A recently reported massacre on the ancient shores of Lake Turkana in Africa, dated to about 10,000 years ago, is a case in point.[28] Archaeologist Marta Mirazon Lahr and her colleagues note the presence of pottery, which is not typical of nomadic foragers, and they suggest that some degree of sedentism and food storage may be indicated. The location of this Lake Turkana violence is significant because social complexification tends to take place when a localized, consistent aquatic food supply allows population concentration in settlements, intensification of resource utilization, food storage, and increases in population density as preconditions for the development of warfare. This is documented in such places as the northwest coast of North America, the Kodak Archipelago in Alaska, and coastal Florida, as with the prehistoric Calusa, and possibly on the island of Isla Cedros off the coast of Baja California.[29] The *Washington Post* reports that, according to Robert Foley who coauthored the Lake Turkana massacre report, "the skeletons appear to have belonged to a group of hunter-gatherers living at the time on the lush, marshy edge of a lagoon where they used bone harpoons to fish and hunt. They were probably more sedentary than most foraging communities, as there are indications that the environment was quite rich."[30] Moreover, the abundant aquatic resources available at this relatively flat marshy area stood in contrast to most other parts of the steeply sloping lakeshore, making it a limited and valuable location for fishing in the shallow waters.[31]

Mark Allen and Terry Jones, in framing the chapters in a recent book that they co-edit, assert that war goes way back in prehistory to the earliest hominins—about five million years in other words.[32] However, Allen and Jones turn a blind eye to the fact that nearly all the archaeological chapters in their own book deal with violence or warfare within the last 10,000 years, that is, since the beginning of the Agricultural Revolution. And even the chapter by paleoanthropologist James Chatters that does consider data from more than 10,000 years ago contradicts the long-chronology view of warfare advocated by the book's editors.[33] Thus, Allen and Jones' assertion that the chapters in their book "support a long chronology for war and violence" is not supported by the evidence they themselves offer.[34]

As archaeologist Jonathan Haas writes, "there is negligible evidence for any kind of warfare anywhere in the world before about 10,000 years ago."[35] A recurring pattern can be seen across archaeological sequences from diverse geographical locations indicating that warfare as an element of domination systems lacks ancient roots. It originated various times in different locations as some, but by no means all, forager societies underwent shifts toward intensification of resource extraction and greater social complexity. Before this, for most of human evolutionary history, domination systems simply did not exist. A very significant conclusion emerges: human nature evolved under the long-standing era of partnership social organization; the human mind evolved in partnership contexts.

Extant Nomadic Foragers: Partnership par Excellence

For the overwhelming majority of the period that the genus *Homo* has existed, nomadic foraging constituted the ubiquitous human lifestyle. Consequently, to gain insights about the human past and human nature, a careful consideration of nomadic forager partnership societies is crucial.[36] As Bicchieri writes:

> For more than 99 percent of the approximately two million years since the emergence of a recognizable human animal, man has been a hunter and gatherer. . . . Questions concerning territorialism, the handling of aggression, social control, property, leadership, the use of space, and many other dimensions are particularly significant in these contexts. To evaluate any of these focal aspects of human behavior without taking into consideration the socioeconomic adaptation that has characterized most of the span of human life on this planet will eventually bias conclusions and generalizations. [37]

As discussed previously, the central features of partnership systems include (1) overall egalitarianism; (2) equality, respect, and partnership between women and men; (3) a nonacceptance of violence, war, abuse, cruelty, and exploitation; and (4) ethics that support human caring, prosocial cooperation, and flourishing.[38] We will now illustrate how the key features of partnership typify nomadic forager social life.

Overall Egalitarianism

Nomadic foragers are characterized as having egalitarian values, nonranked social structures, and high degrees of personal autonomy.[39] Forager specialist James Woodburn summarizes that "there are either no leaders at all or leaders who are very elaborately constrained to prevent them from exercising authority or using their influence to acquire wealth or prestige."[40] Anthropologist Eleanor Leacock concurs: "What is hard to grasp about the structure of the egalitarian band is that leadership as we conceive it is not merely 'weak' or 'incipient', as is commonly stated, but irrelevant."[41]

When the social order is egalitarian and thus a hierarchy of command is lacking, no one has the authority to order others to fight.[42] For example, anthropologist Mervin Meggitt explains that among the Walbiri of Australia there were neither military hierarchies nor "military leaders, elected or hereditary, to plan tactics and ensure that others adopted the plans." [43] Ethnographer John Cooper succinctly states of the Ona of South America that, "No man recognized authoritative headship of or accepted orders from any other."[44] Anthropologist Christopher Boehm describes nomadic foragers as "fiercely egalitarian."[45] In short, this lack of top-down leadership and the strong ethic of egalitarianism are recurring cultural features that have been documented ethnographically time and again for nomadic forager societies.[46]

Equality, Respect, and Partnership among Men and Women

Nomadic forager societies also tend to have high levels of gender egalitarianism compared with most other types of societies.[47] For example, among the Polar Eskimo, "men and women had more or less equal status."[48] Among the Ona of Tierra del Fuego, "the woman was largely her own mistress, particularly in such provinces of her own as child rearing, food gathering, and canoe managing. Some men domineered over their wives, but not a few husbands were under the thumbs of their spouses."[49] Leacock observes, "those who came to know the Montagnais more intimately saw women as holding 'great power.'"[50] Anthropologist Peter Gardner writes of the Paliyan of India, "Neither spouse can order the other and neither, by virtue of sex or age, is entitled to a greater voice in matters of mutual concern."[51] Anthropologists Kirk and Karen Endicott report that the Batek of Malaysia viewed "men and women as being different in various ways, but did not regard these differences as making either sex superior to the other."[52] Forager specialist Richard Lee writes, "women are a force to be reckoned with in Ju/ 'hoan society."[53]

Overall, women in nomadic forager societies can freely divorce and remarry.[54] For instance, anthropologist Gardner observed that Paliyan "spouses separate at the first quarrel, which results in the serial marriages. . . . One girl of fifteen rotated between three men, moving after each quarrel; she had experienced eight unions, each of which was referred to as a marriage."[55] In Montagnais bands, "divorce was easy and at the desire of either partner."[56]

Another reflection of the high level of gender egalitarianism and female autonomy that is *typical* of nomadic bands involves sexual relations. In many nomadic forager societies, women exercise considerable sexual independence.[57] Among the Batek, "people joked that affairs were fine unless the couple had their tryst on a major path. . . . Their attitude was that no one could control the sexuality of anyone else in premarital, marital, or extramarital contexts."[58] Anthropologist Allan Holmberg explains that Siriono "women enjoy about the same privileges as men. They get as much or more food to eat, and they enjoy the same sexual freedom."[59] Adultery is common among the Siriono and many other forager groups, yet it tends to be ignored if engaged in discreetly. Holmberg comments on the equality of the sexes in this regard:

> Generally speaking, great freedom is allowed in matters of sex. A man is permitted to have intercourse not only with his own wife or wives but also with her (their) sisters, real or classificatory. Conversely, a woman is allowed to have intercourse not only with her husband but also with his brothers, real and classificatory, and with the husbands and potential husbands of her own and classificatory sisters. Thus, apart from one's real spouse, there may be as many as eight or ten potential spouses with who one may have sex relations. There is, moreover, no taboo on sex relations between unmarried potential spouses, provided the women have

undergone the rites of maturity. Virginity is not a virtue. Consequently unmarried adults rarely, if ever, lack for sexual partners and frequently indulge in sex.[60]

Endicott and Endicott point out that another reflection of gender equality is when a society values both maternal and paternal descent.[61] Indeed, nomadic foragers usually figure descent bilaterally, that is, through both parental lines.[62] Knauft reports for a sample of 39 nomadic forager societies that 59 percent of them figure descent through both maternal and paternal lines.[63] Similarly, Doug discovered that 71 percent of a sample of nomadic forager societies had bilateral descent.[64]

Gender egalitarianism is also reflected in residence patterns. Drawing on the cultural codes of George Murdock, Knauft reports that only 26 percent of the nomadic foragers in his sample of 39 are classified as patrilocal—living with father's kin.[65] Among the Paliyan, at any given time, roughly equal numbers of persons shared camps with paternal and maternal relatives.[66] Marlowe refers to the typical forager residence pattern as multifocal, reflecting the fact that movement is the norm and nuclear families are to be found living with a variety of different relatives and nonrelatives over time.[67] The take-home point is that residence is flexible, does not significantly favor one gender's relatives over the other, but might slightly favor maternal kin over paternal relatives.[68] Thus, the gender equality criterion of partnership systems is solidly present across nomadic forager societies.[69]

Nonacceptance of Violence and War

The cherished virtues among nomadic foragers are nonmartial and include generosity, humility, and nonaggressiveness.[70] Doug and his colleague Patrik Söderberg examined the details of all incidences of lethal aggression ethnographically reported in a sample of 21 nomadic forager societies.[71] The ethnographic cases were derived from an existing cross-cultural sample to minimize the possibility of sampling bias, which can occur if ethnographic cases are simply self-selected.[72] Additionally, only the recommended ethnographic bibliography for this sample was used to obtain the highest-quality data on each society.[73] In this study, we did not classify lethal events as manslaughter, homicide, feud, or war beforehand, but rather examined the fundamental characteristics of the events such as the relationships of killers to victims, reasons for the killings, whether lethal events occurred within or between groups, and so on.[74] In this way, we let the specifics of the lethal aggression cases speak for themselves.

The core results are as follows.[75] Three societies had no reported lethal events at all. For the remaining 18 societies, there were a grand total of 148 lethal aggression events, with some societies having more than others. Men were almost always the perpetrators or co-perpetrators of lethal violence. One society, the Tiwi of Australia, was exceptionally violent, accounting for 47 percent (69/148), or nearly half, of all lethal events.[76] A majority of the 148 events, 55 percent, involved one perpetrator killing one victim. A one-killer, one-victim situation does not suggest war. Correspondingly, almost half of the societies, 10/21, had absolutely no lethal events perpetrated by more than one killer. After also considering the motives and circumstances of killing, which are interpersonal much of the time, we conclude overall that among nomadic forager societies, most incidents resulting in lethal aggression "may be classified as homicides, a few others as feuds, and a minority as war."[77]

Since nomadic foragers are so often assumed to fight over territory, it is noteworthy that boundaries are more typically controlled through permission-granting of resource use, rather than though outright fighting.[78] Kelly observes of nomadic forager societies that "a strong tendency toward permission-granting rather than active perimeter defense gives human land tenure its own particular character."[79] Anthropologist Eric Wolf points out that "to survive, a person periodically needs to gain access to resources in other locations, and he gains such access through ties of kinship, marriage, friendship, and exchange."[80] In agreement, forager specialists Lee and DeVore point out that local bands tend not to maintain exclusive rights to resources.[81] For example, Canadian Inuit men hunt where they choose without attempting to exclude other hunters.[82]

Moreover, the ethnographic descriptions suggest that the overwhelming majority of conflicts, disputes, and grievances in nomadic forager contexts do not lead to killings.[83] A common response to conflict in the nomadic forager world is for one or both parties to simply walk away, sometimes called "voting with one's feet" in the ethnographic literature, an easy option given the constantly changing membership of the bands.[84] Another typical nonviolent approach to conflict is discussion. Among the Ju/'hoansi, for example, "Differences are resolved by talk. Relatives and friends may intervene in quarrels between the husbands and wives and help them to stop the quarrel."[85] In nomadic forager society, an entire camp may act as mediators.[86] Alternatively, disgruntled persons may vent their feelings at night as the band clusters around campfires.[87] In conclusion, while some nomadic forager societies are remarkably peaceful and others less so in terms of interpersonal aggression, the cross-cultural evidence does not support an assumption that nomadic foragers are warlike.[88]

Ethics for Caring, Prosocial Behavior, Cooperation, and Flourishing

The overwhelming majority of nomadic forager social interaction involves prosocial behavior—initiating and reciprocating good deeds. An extensive survey of the ethnographic literature led Boehm to the conclusion that nomadic foragers value behaviors that are generous, cooperative, unbossy, and unarrogant.[89] The salient cultural values among Mardu Australian Aborigines, for instance, include unselfishness, kinship solidarity, sharing, amicability, and peace.[90]

Caring can be linked evolutionarily back to the basic mammalian pattern of nurturing dependent young, a tendency that is clearly evident in the order Primates and particularly in humans over the lengthy period of child dependency. Caring for offspring and other relatives is ubiquitous in human societies, but humans also regularly extend kindness and assistance to nonrelatives. De Waal points out, for example, the tremendous empathic potential not merely in humans but also in some primates and other species.[91]

As we saw in Chapter 3, the origin of human caring has long and strong evolutionary roots. It therefore should come as no surprise that caring is well represented among nomadic foragers. Anthropologist Sarah B. Hrdy documents how childcare extends well beyond parents in nomadic forager society.[92] "The fact that children depend so much on food acquired by others is one reason why those seeking human universals would do well to begin with sharing."[93]

Indeed, a prominent feature of the nomadic forager group is "an ethic of sharing that selectively extends to the entire group the cooperation and altruism found within the family."[94] A key example is that nomadic foragers share meat. Social life involves a network of obligations to cooperate, share, and participate in exchanges. The ubiquity of meat-sharing in nomadic forager society is unambiguous.[95] The Guayaki of South America, for example, have a practice that promotes sharing: a man cannot eat the flesh of an animal he has killed. This taboo makes each hunter mutually dependent within a camp and underscores the absolute necessity of sharing meat with others.[96]

The desert-dwelling African Ju/'hoansi, North American Shoshone, and Australian Walbiri survive by sharing. Wolf describes the pattern as follows:

> All three populations—[Ju/'hoansi or formerly the !Kung] San, Shoshoneans, Walbiri—live in environments where strategic resources are widely scattered and seasonably variable. To survive, a person periodically needs to gain access to resources in other locations, and he gains such access through ties of kinship, marriage, friendship, and exchange.[97]

Lee writes of the Ju/'hoansi: "If one has good relations with in-laws at different waterholes, one will never go hungry."[98] Leacock describes how among nomadic Montagnais foragers of Canada, sharing is the path to food security: "Owing to the uncertainty of the hunt, several families were necessarily dependent upon each other, thus providing [in Steward's words], 'a kind of subsistence insurance or greater security than individual families could achieve.'"[99] Anthropologist Gerald Wheeler notes a pattern among Australian Aborigines of sharing occasional windfalls, such as abundant harvests of nuts or berries. When a coastal group discovered a beached whale with enough meat to feed many people, the Aborigines lit signal fires and neighboring groups flocked to the beach to share in the leviathan-sized bounty.[100] The reciprocal sharing of periodic food abundances means that over time everyone gains more than had each group simply hoarded more than they could consume.

In previous work, Doug has suggested that sharing across different bands is promoted by at least three factors.[101] First, nomadic foragers are already accustomed to the norms for sharing within their own social circles, so it is psychologically and normatively congruent to extend sharing more generally. Second, nomadic foragers understand, and by example teach their children, the importance of reciprocal sharing: By sharing now, one will receive aid in the future.[102] Third, sharing among groups is promoted through kinship and friendship.[103] The typical pattern is for members of one group at any given point in time to have relatives and friends living in neighboring groups, which creates an overlapping network that promotes intergroup sharing and cooperation.[104] Thus, networks of relationships cut across bands, including at times bands from different language groups.[105] Shifting band composition also tilts decisions toward reciprocal sharing and away from hostile competition for scarce resources.[106] It is a culturally biased mistake to assume that human groups everywhere will favor a dog-eat-dog type of competition over cooperation and sharing.

More often than not, children are not explicitly taught moral values in nomadic band society, but instead simply learn prosocial sharing, helping, cooperating though observation, and imitation of their elders.[107] The Yahgan of Tierra del Fuego raise their children to be "good and useful human beings," and a similar sentiment can be inferred to exist in many other nomadic societies that emphasize caring and fairness orientations.[108]

Writing together, Geneviève Souillac and Doug have proposed that it may be particularly easy and rewarding for children to learn empathy, co-operation, helping, and sharing—in a word, prosocial behaviors.[109] As we have considered, engaging in cooperative activity can activate a neuro-chemical reward. "The strength of the neural response increases with the persistence of mutual cooperation over successive trials; it is cumulative and self-reinforcing" writes biological anthropologist Robert Sussman.[110] Such evolved neurophysiological responses may make it relatively easy for the developing individual to learn how to become "a good and useful human being."

Nonetheless, from time to time, people need to be reminded of group norms, values, and ethical behavior. Members of nomadic bands, with re-markable consistency, cooperate to sanction deviants and ideally lead them to correct their misbehavior. Rarely do cheaters prosper in small-scale in-terdependent societies because they get their comeuppance through criti-cism, ridicule, withdrawal of support, physical punishment, ostracism, and even execution if the crimes are serious.[111]

Since formal courts, police, and top-down leaders are nonexistent, no-madic foragers cooperate when faced with bullies or deviants. Boehm calls the phenomenon of the group collectively exercising social control against deviants a "reverse dominance hierarchy."[112] There may be an occasional upstart, but the nomadic forager group takes action to prevent domination by such deviants. Many different types of social control are exercised in no-madic forager society. For instance, Doug conducted an analysis of the 21 mobile forager societies and discovered that ridicule was mentioned for 13 societies; criticizing, scolding, or reprimanding for 12; delivering harangues, inflicting physical punishment, or instilling fear of sorcery in 11; ostracism, gossip, or supernatural threats in 10; execution in nine; shaming of deviants in eight; withdrawal of social support in five; and various other infrequent options (such as fear of illness, appeal to conscience, destroying property, or disapproving stares) in less than five societies.[113] To balance these largely negative methods of social control, it must be remembered that children are socialized to behave according to the prosocial norms and values of their society and usually do so into adulthood.

Partnership and Nomadic Foragers

In an opinion piece in the *Wall Street Journal*, physician and anthropologist Melvin Konner echoes writers such as Pinker or Allen and Jones in listing relatively recent (archaeologically) cases of mayhem to argue once again that war is as old as dirt, thus missing the "big picture" that the archaeologically recent birth of domination systems changed everything.[114] As documented previously, the warfare and inequalities that we see today, historically, and in recent prehistory are not representative of the deep past of nomadic partnerships on earth. The archaeological evidence demonstrates the prevalence of partnership systems over the evolutionary long haul. Of course, horrendous massacres; bloody feuds; acts of torture, mutilation, and abuse; the inhumanities and indignities of slavery; the appalling horrors of terrorism; and war of all shades are scattered across recent prehistory, chronicled in written history, and reported by the news media today. There is no denying this and no reason to deny the human capacity for violence. But we can go well beyond the easy narrative told by Konner, Pinker, Allen and Jones, and others that by compiling a litany of human barbarity they can "prove" war to be staunchly embedded in human nature.[115] This explanation for warfare is as fallacious as it is facile. The worldwide archaeological record and comparative nomadic forager studies combine to reveal how domination arose from an earlier condition of universal partnership. As forager specialists Richard Lee and Richard Daly express:

> [Nomadic foragers] lived in relatively small groups, without centralized authority, standing armies, or bureaucratic systems. Yet the evidence indicates that they have lived together surprisingly well, solving their

problems among themselves largely without recourse to authority figures and without a particular propensity for violence. It was *not* the situation that Thomas Hobbes, the great seventeenth-century philosopher,
described in a famous phrase as "the war of all against all."[116]

In summary, the recurring patterns across nomadic forager ethnographies
from around the world suggest that many elements of partnership systems—
social equality, gender egalitarianism, personal autonomy, sharing, caring,
and an absence of war—were typical of the evolutionary past when humanity lived as mobile foragers, whereas pervasive intergroup violence,
clear-cut social ranks, despotic rulers, sexism, and slavery were not. As the
words of economist John Gowdy remind us, partnership predates domination: "Judging from historical accounts of hunter-gatherers, for most of the
time humans have been on the planet we have lived in relative harmony
with the natural world and with each other. Our minds and cultures evolved
under these conditions."[117] In addition, as we have seen, findings from both
the social and neurological sciences are amassing more and more evidence
that humans are happier, healthier, and more fulfilled in partnership social
systems than in domination systems.

Lest this sound overly idyllic, of course, there are disputes and conflicts,
dislikes, and feelings of resentment, and when problems arise, the group
usually attempts to deal with them nonviolently, though occasionally these
interpersonal disputes lead to fights and even killings.[118] But at the primary
level, nomadic foragers socialize children to be, in the words of the Yahgan,
"good and useful human beings." And across nomadic forager ethnography,
central values instilled in the young are equality, humility, generosity, and
cooperation, so that the overwhelming majority of social interactions are
prosocial, cooperative, and caring.

Implications for Survival and Well-Being

We do not need to return to a nomadic foraging lifestyle to create a partnership world. Not only are many indigenous societies around the world
oriented toward partnership, as we have seen in cases such as the Moso,
Tiruray, and Minangkabau, but the socially and technologically complex
Nordic countries also are well on the way to creating partnership societies
within modern nations.

The main take-home lesson from a careful study of nomadic forager partnership societies, re-enforced by the recent Nordic experience, is that humans are capable of living in egalitarian social systems where neither sex dominates the other, where violence is minimized, and where prosocial co-operation and caring typify social life. This image is not a utopian fantasy but rather a set of potentials, if not inclinations, stemming from our evolutionary heritage.

Since partnership behaviors have been essential to survival for the millions of years that humans and their ancestors foraged for a living, the study of archaeology and nomadic forager societies raises an intriguing possibility. Given the long-standing evolutionary legacy of partnership, human minds and dispositions may be especially inclined toward the empathic, caring, egalitarian, prosocial, cooperative behaviors.

Humans are capable of cooperation as well as competition, sharing as well as selfishness, empathy as well as envy, and beneficence and well as bellicosity. Recognizing all these potentials has implications for security and survival in today's interdependent world. A partnership perspective highlights the evolved capacities of humans to get along with each other, to work together prosocially, and to resolve their disputes and differences without bloodshed.

Such partnership capacities, we suggest, have been critically important over the course of human evolution and are absolutely needed today. Competition does play a central role in Darwinian evolutionary thinking, and rightly so. But as the sharing of meat and the open access to resources across nomadic forager bands demonstrate, sometimes the best competitive strategy in a fitness-enhancing sense may be to cooperate in a behavioral sense.

Indeed, findings of numerous disciplines show that most human behavior actually is oriented toward getting along with others without violence, showing restraint against lethal aggression, cooperating toward shared goals, feeling empathy toward others, and resolving disputes peaceably, often with reconciliation and forgiveness as part of the process.[119] Moreover, studies from many quarters on health, happiness, and well-being substantiate that partnership systems are better for individuals, families, communities, and nations than domination systems, replete with their dehumanizing and destructive features. And given the serious challenges facing humanity in 21st century, working together for human survival is today urgent and mandatory.

On an interdependent planet facing major challenges, understanding the origins, natures, and impacts of partnership and domination systems on human lives and societies is crucial to human well-being and survival. Beliefs that humans are naturally competitive and aggressive can facilitate fear of others, distrust, and reluctance to work together. These assumptions can lead also to pessimism about creating more caring social institutions, achieving gender equality, eliminating gross inequities within nations and around the world, and maturing beyond the bullet and the bomb. By contrast, understanding the strong partnership underpinnings of human behavior offers a prescription for human survival and well-being. When the evolved prosocial and peaceable tendencies of humans are recognized along with the long-standing legacy of partnership systems, then the possibilities of creating, in the 21st century, true gender equality, rights, and opportunities, and of satisfying human needs, abolishing war, and handling disputes justly and without violence, all become viable.

In the chapters that follow we will look at progress in this direction, including actions we can jointly take. At the same time, we will examine obstacles in our way, starting with how people's early experiences can skew what they perceive as reality.

Notes

1. The quote is from Steven Pinker, *Better Angels of Our Nature: Why Violence Has Declined* (New York: Viking, 2011), xxiv; Jesse Graham et al., "Moral Foundations Theory: The Pragmatic Validity of Moral Pluralism," *Advances in Experimental Social Psychology* 47 (2013): 55–130.
2. R. Brian Ferguson, "The Prehistory of War and Peace in Europe and the Near East," in *War, Peace, and Human Nature: The Convergence of Evolutionary and Cultural Views*, ed. Douglas P. Fry (New York: Oxford University Press, 2013); Douglas P. Fry, *The Human Potential for Peace: An Anthropological Challenge to Assumptions about War and Violence* (New York: Oxford University Press, 2006); Douglas P. Fry and Patrik Söderberg, "Lethal Aggression in Mobile Forager Bands and Implications for the Origins of War," *Science* 341 (2013): 270–273, doi: 10.1126/science.1235675; Douglas P. Fry and Patrik Söderberg, "Supplemental Online Material for Lethal Aggression in Mobile Forager Bands and Implications for the Origins of War," *Science* 341 (2013): 270–273, doi: 10.1126/science.1235675; Douglas P. Fry and Geneviève Souillac, "The Original Partnership Societies: Evolved Propensities for Equality, Prosociality, and Peace," *Interdisciplinary Journal of Partnership Studies* 4

(2017): article 4, doi: 10.24926/ijps.v4i1.150; Bruce Knauft, "Violence and Sociality in Human Evolution," *Current Anthropology* 32, 4 (1991): 391–428, doi: 10.1086/203975.

3. Elman Service, *Profiles in Ethnology* (New York: Harper and Row, 1971); R. Brian Ferguson, "A Reexamination of the Causes of Northwest Coast Warfare," in *Warfare, Culture, and Environment*, ed. R. Brian Ferguson (Orlando, FL: Academic Press, 1984).

4. Lewis R. Binford, *Constructing Frames of Reference: An Analytical Method for Archaeological Theory Building Using Hunter-Gatherer and Environmental Data Sets* (Berkeley: University of California Press, 2001); Robert L. Kelly, *The Foraging Spectrum: Diversity in Hunter-Gatherer Lifeways* (Washington, DC: Smithsonian Institution Press, 1995), 302; George P. Murdock, "The Current Status of the World's Hunting and Gathering Peoples," in *Man the Hunter*, eds. Richard B. Lee and Irvin DeVore (Chicago: Aldine, 1968); Service, *Profiles in Ethnology*.

5. Knauft, "Violence and Sociality in Human Evolution," 392; see also Michael Alvard and L. Kuznar, "Deferred Harvests: The Transition from Hunting to Animal Husbandry," *American Anthropologist* 103 (2001): 295, doi: 10.1525/aa.2001.103.2.295; Mark Cohen, "Prehistoric Hunter-Gatherers: The Meaning of Social Complexity," in *Prehistoric Hunter-Gatherers: The Emergence of Cultural Complexity*, eds. T. Price and J. Brown (New York: Academic Press, 1985); Donald O. Henry, "Preagricultural Sedentism: The Natufian Example," in *Prehistoric Hunter-Gatherers: The Emergence of Cultural Complexity*, eds. T. Price and J. Brown (New York: Academic Press, 1985).

6. Ian Hodder, "Women and Men at Catalhoyuk," *Scientific American* 290 (2004): 77–83.

7. Ferguson, "The Prehistory of War and Peace"; Fry, *The Human Potential for Peace*; Jonathan Haas, "War," in *Encyclopedia of Cultural Anthropology, Volume 4*, eds. David Levinson and Melvin Ember (New York: Henry Holt and Company, 1996).

8. Wolfgang Haak, Josif Lazaridis, and David Reich, "Massive Migration from the Steppe Was a Source for Indo-European Languages in Europe," *Nature* 522 (2015): 207–211, doi: 10.1038/nature14317; Morten Allentoft, Martin Sikora, and Eske Willerslev, "Population Genomics of Bronze Age Eurasia," *Nature* 522 (2015): 167–172, doi: 10.1038/nature14507. See also John Novembre, "Human Evolution: Ancient DNA Steps into the Language Debate," *Nature* 522 (2015): 164–165, doi: 10.1038/522164a. These studies found a genetic affinity between samples from the central European culture known as Corded Ware, which existed from around 2500 BCE, and samples from the earlier Yamnaya steppe culture, which is best explained by a substantial westward expansion of the Yamnaya or their close relatives into central Europe, as proposed by the "steppe hypothesis" that Corded Ware cultures were a conduit for the dispersal of Indo-European languages into Europe.

9. Marija Gimbutas, *The Goddesses and Gods of Old Europe* (Berkeley: University of California Press, 1982); Marija Gimbutas, "The First Wave of Eurasian Steppe Pastoralists into Copper Age Europe," *Journal of Indo-European Studies* 5 (1977): 277–338.

10. Haas, "War."

11. Fry, *The Human Potential for Peace*.

12. Ferguson, "The Prehistory of War and Peace in Europe and the Near East"; Fry, *The Human Potential for Peace*; Haas, "War"; Henry, "Preagricultural Sedentism"; Kent Flannery and Joyce Marcus, "The Origin of War: New 14C Dates from Ancient Mexico," *Proceedings of the National Academy of Sciences (PNAS)* 100 (2003): 11, 801–811, 805, doi: 10.1073/pnas.1934526100; Kent Flannery and Joyce Marcus, *The Creation of Inequality: How Our Prehistoric Ancestors Set the Stage for Monarchy, Slavery, and Empire* (Cambridge, MA: Harvard University Press, 2012); Knauft, "Violence and Sociality in Human Evolution"; Herbert Maschner, "The Evolution of Northwest Coast Warfare," in *Troubled Times: Violence and Warfare in the Past*, eds. Debra Martin and David Frayer (Amsterdam: Gordon and Breach, 1997).

13. Maschner, "The Evolution of Northwest Coast Warfare."

14. Maschner, "The Evolution of Northwest Coast Warfare," 270.

15. Flannery and Marcus, "The Origin of War: New 14C Dates from Ancient Mexico."

16. S. P. Reyna, "A Mode of Domination Approach to Organized Violence," in *Studying War: Anthropological Perspectives*, eds. S. P. Reyna and R. E. Downs (Amsterdam: Gordon and Breach, 1994).

17. Fry, *The Human Potential for Peace*; Joseph Whitecotton, *The Zapotecs: Priests, Princes and Peasants* (Norman: University of Oklahoma Press, 1977).

18. Henry, "Preagricultural Sedentism."

19. Henry, "Preagricultural Sedentism," 365.

20. Marilyn Roper, "A Survey of the Evidence for Intrahuman Killing in the Pleistocene," *Current Anthropology* 10 (1969): 427–459, doi: 10.1086/201038.

21. Ferguson, "The Prehistory of War and Peace in Europe and the Near East."

22. Ferguson, "The Prehistory of War and Peace in Europe and the Near East"; Fry, *The Human Potential for Peace*.

23. Hisashi Nakao et al., "Violence in the Prehistoric Period of Japan: The Spatio-Temporal Pattern of Skeletal Evidence for Violence in the Jomon Period," *Biology Letters* 12 (2016): doi: 10.1098/rsbl.2016.0028.

24. Pinker, *Better Angels of Our Nature*.

25. Nakao et al., "Violence in the Prehistoric Period of Japan," 3.

26. Fry, *The Human Potential for Peace*; see also Daniel Antoine, Antoine Zazzo, and Renee Friedman, "Revisiting Jebel Sahaba: New Apatite Radiocarbon Dates for One of the Nile Valley's Earliest Cemeteries." Poster presented at the 82nd Annual Meeting of the American Association of Physical Anthropologists, Knoxville, TN, April 9–13, 2013. Abstract accessed March 6, 2018. Available online: http://meeting.physanth.org/program/2013/session25/antoine-2013-revisiting-jebel-sahaba-new-apatite-radiocarbon-dates-for-one-of-the-nile-valleys-earliest-cemeteries.html.

27. Ferguson, "The Prehistory of War and Peace in Europe and the Near East."

28. Marta Mirazon Lahr et al., "Inter-Group Violence among Early Holocene Hunter-Gatherers of West Turkana, Kenya," *Nature* 529 (2016): 394–398, doi: 10.1038/nature16477.

29. Mark W. Allen and Terry L. Jones, eds., *Violence and Warfare among Hunter-Gatherers* (Walnut Creek, CA: Left Coast Press, 2014); Matthew Des Lauriers,

"The Spectre of Conflict on Isla Cedros, Baja California, Mexico," in *Violence and Warfare among Hunter-Gatherers*, eds. Mark W. Allen and Terry L. Jones (Walnut Creek, CA: Left Coast Press, 2014); personal communication, Matthew Des Lauriers, August 16, 2015; Ben Fitzhugh, "The Evolution of Complex Hunter-Gatherers on the Kodiak Archipelago," *Senri Ethnological Studies* 63 (2003): 13–48; Fry, *The Human Potential for Peace*; Knauft, "Violence and Sociality in Human Evolution"; Maschner, "The Evolution of Northwest Coast Warfare."

30. Yanan Wang, "Discovery of Prehistoric Massacre May Point to Origins of Human Warfare," *Washington Post*, Science section, last modified January 21, 2016, accessed March 6, 2018. Available online: https://www.washingtonpost.com/news/morning-mix/wp/2016/01/21/discovery-of-prehistoric-massacre-may-point-to-origins-of-human-warfare/?utm_term=.906645897504.

31. Marta Mirazon Lahr, "The Ecology of Prehistoric Inter-Group Conflict in African Hunter-Gatherers." Paper presented at the symposium *Social Inequality before Farming?* University of Cambridge, UK, January 21–23, 2018.

32. Allen and Jones, *Violence and Warfare among Hunter-Gatherers*.

33. James Chatters, "Wild-Type Colonizers and High Levels of Violence among Paleoamericans," in *Violence and Warfare among Hunter-Gatherers*, eds. Mark W. Allen and Terry L. Jones (Walnut Creek, CA: Left Coast Press, 2014).

34. Allen and Jones, *Violence and Warfare among Hunter-Gatherers*, 354.

35. Haas, "War," 1360.

36. The archaeological record substantiates a nomadic hunting-and-gathering existence over humanity's evolutionary past. There were no villages or cities, no herding of animals, no horticulture, and no agriculture. The nomadic forager lifeway approximates conditions under which the genus *Homo* appeared about two million years ago and more recently under which modern *Homo sapiens* emerged roughly 40,000 to 50,000 years ago. The questions arise for ethnographically described mobile foragers: how much have they been influenced by external factors in recent history and hence to what degree can conclusions be drawn from such societies about human nature and the past? Following external contact, indigenous mobile forager societies have been affected by displacement, communicable disease, genocide, access to alcohol, firearms, state control, and so forth. Nonetheless, various patterns of social organization and behavior recur across nomadic foragers from different world regions. Compared with other types of societies (e.g., tribes, pastoralists, chiefdoms, kingdoms, and states) and despite various outside influences, an analysis of nomadic forager patterns provides the best basis for drawing inferences about the lifeways of ancestral humans and enduring features of humanity. In short, if we want a window to the past and insights about human nature, we should look for recurrent patterns across extant mobile foragers. For further discussion, see Fry, *The Human Potential for Peace*.

37. M. G. Bicchieri, ed., *Hunters and Gatherers Today* (Prospect Heights, IL: Waveland, 1972), iii, iv–v.

38. Kelly, *The Foraging Spectrum*, 293.

39. Christopher Boehm, *Hierarchy in the Forest: The Evolution of Egalitarian Behavior* (Cambridge, MA: Harvard University Press, 1999); Fry, *The Human Potential for*

Peace; Kelly, *The Foraging Spectrum*; Sheina Lew-Levy et al., "How Do Hunter-Gatherer Children Learn Social and Gender Norms? A Meta-Ethnographic Review," *Cross-Cultural Research* 52 (2017): 213–255, doi: 10.1177/1069397117723552; James Woodburn, "Egalitarian Societies," *Man* 17 (1982): 431–451.

40. Woodburn, "Egalitarian Societies," 444.
41. Eleanor Leacock, "Women's Status in Egalitarian Society: Implications for Social Evolution," *Current Anthropology* 19 (1978): 247–275, 249, doi: 10.1086/202074.
42. Boehm, *Hierarchy in the Forest*; Fry and Souillac, "The Original Partnership Societies"; Knauft, "Violence and Sociality in Human Evolution"; Richard B. Lee and Richard Daly, "Introduction: Foragers and Others," in *The Cambridge Encyclopedia of Hunters and Gatherers*, eds. Richard B. Lee and Richard Daly (Cambridge, UK: Cambridge University Press, 1999); Woodburn, "Egalitarian Societies."
43. Mervyn Meggitt, *Desert People: A Study of the Walbiri Aborigines of Central Australia* (Chicago: University of Chicago Press, 1965), 245.
44. John M. Cooper, "The Ona," in *Handbook of South American Indians, Volume 1, The Marginal Tribes*, ed. Julian H. Steward (Washington, DC: United States Printing Office, 1946), 116.
45. Boehm, *Hierarchy in the Forest*.
46. Cooper, "The Ona"; Peter Gardner, *Bicultural Versatility as a Frontier Adaptation among Paliyan Foragers of South India* (Lewiston, NY: Edwin Mellen Press, 2000); Leacock, "Women's Status in Egalitarian Society"; Richard B. Lee, *The !Kung San: Men, Women, and Work in a Foraging Community* (Cambridge, UK: Cambridge University Press, 1979); Meggitt, *Desert People*; Elizabeth M. Thomas, "Management of Violence among the Ju/wasi of Nyae Nyae: The Old Way and a New Way," in *Studying War: Anthropological Perspectives*, eds. S. P. Reyna and R. E. Downs (Amsterdam: Gordon and Breach, 1994); Woodburn, "Egalitarian Societies."
47. Karen L. Endicott, "Gender Relations in Hunter-Gatherer Societies," in *The Cambridge Encyclopedia of Hunters and Gatherers*, eds. Richard B. Lee and Richard Daly (Cambridge, UK: Cambridge University Press, 1999).
48. Rolf Gilberg, "Polar Eskimo," in *Handbook of North American Indians, Volume 5, Arctic*, volume ed. D. Damas, and series ed. W. C. Sturtevant (Washington, DC: Smithsonian Press, 1984), 585.
49. Cooper, "The Ona," 93.
50. Leacock, "Women's Status in Egalitarian Society," 191.
51. Peter Gardner, "The Paliyans," in *Hunters and Gatherers Today*, ed. M. G. Bicchieri (Prospect Heights, IL: Waveland, 1972), 422.
52. Kirk M. Endicott and Karen L. Endicott, *The Headman Was a Woman: Gender Egalitarianism among the Batek of Malaysia* (Long Grove, IL: Waveland, 2008), 25.
53. Richard B. Lee, *The Dobe Ju/'hoansi* (Fort Worth, TX: Harcourt Brace, 1993), 85.
54. Cooper, "The Ona"; Endicott, "Gender Relations in Hunter-Gatherer Societies"; Endicott and Endicott, *The Headman Was a Woman*; Gilberg, "Polar Eskimo"; Lee, *The Dobe Ju/'hoansi*; Fry and Souillac, "The Original Partnership Societies."
55. Gardner, "The Paliyans," 432.
56. Leacock, "Women's Status in Egalitarian Society," 192.

57. Endicott and Endicott, *The Headman Was a Woman*; Gardner, "The Paliyans"; Gardner, *Bicultural Versatility as a Frontier Adaptation.*
58. Endicott and Endicott, *The Headman Was a Woman*, 60.
59. Allan Holmberg, *Nomads of the Long Bow: The Siriono of Eastern Bolivia* (New York: American Museum of Natural History, 1969, originally published in 1950).
60. Holmberg, *Nomads of the Long Bow*, 165.
61. Endicott and Endicott, *The Headman Was a Woman.*
62. Alan Barnard, "Contemporary Hunter-Gatherers: Current Theoretical Issues in Ecology and Social Organization," *Annual Review of Anthropology* 12 (1983): 193–214, doi: 10.1146/annurev.an.12.100183.001205; Richard B. Lee and Irven DeVore, "Problems in the Study of Hunters and Gatherers," in *Man the Hunter*, eds. Richard B. Lee and Irven DeVore (Chicago: Aldine, 1968); Gardner, *Bicultural Versatility as a Frontier Adaptation*; Frank Marlowe, "Why the Hadza Are Still Hunter-Gatherers," in *Ethnicity, Hunter-Gatherers, and the "Other,"* ed. Susan Kent (Washington, DC: Smithsonian Institution Press, 2010).
63. Knauft, "Violence and Sociality in Human Evolution."
64. Fry, *The Human Potential for Peace.*
65. George P. Murdock, "Ethnographic Atlas: A Summary," *Ethnology* 6 (1967): 109–236; Knauft, "Violence and Sociality in Human Evolution."
66. Gardner, *Bicultural Versatility as a Frontier Adaptation.*
67. Marlowe, "Why the Hadza Are Still Hunter-Gatherers"; see also Mark Dyble et al., "Sex Equality Can Explain the Unique Social Structure of Hunter-Gatherer Bands," *Science* 348 (2015): 796–798, doi: 10.1126/science.aaa5139.
68. Frank Marlowe, *The Hadza Hunter-Gatherers of Tanzania* (Berkeley: University of California Press, 2010).
69. Endicott, "Gender Relations in Hunter-Gatherer Societies"; Endicott and Endicott, *The Headman Was a Woman*; Fry, *The Human Potential for Peace*; Ernestine Friedl, *Women and Men: An Anthropologist's View* (New York: Holt, Rinehart and Winston, 1975); Fry and Souillac, "The Original Partnership Societies"; M. Kay Martin and Barbara Voorhies, *Female of the Species* (New York: Columbia University Press, 1975).
70. Boehm, *Hierarchy in the Forest*; Fry, *The Human Potential for Peace.*
71. Fry and Söderberg, "Lethal Aggression in Mobile Forager Bands"; Fry and Söderberg, "Online Supplemental Material for Lethal Aggression in Mobile Forager Bands."
72. Murdock, "Ethnographic Atlas: A Summary"; George P. Murdock and Douglas White, "Standard Cross-Cultural Sample," *Ethnology* 8 (1969): 329–369; Douglas White, "Focused Ethnographic Bibliography: Standard Cross-Cultural Sample," *Behavior Science Research* 23 (1989): 1–145, doi: 10.1177/106939718902300102.
73. See White, "Focused Ethnographic Bibliography."
74. Fry and Söderberg, "Lethal Aggression in Mobile Forager Bands"; Fry and Söderberg, "Online Supplemental Material for Lethal Aggression in Mobile Forager Bands."
75. Fry and Söderberg, "Lethal Aggression in Mobile Forager Bands"; Fry and Söderberg, "Online Supplemental Material for Lethal Aggression in Mobile Forager Bands."

76. Fry and Söderberg discuss in "Supplemental Material for Lethal Aggression in Mobile Foraging Bands" the anomalous Tiwi case. They write:

> In comparison to the rest of the MFBS [Mobile Forager Band Societies], the Tiwi stand out as an exceptionally violent case, supplying 47 percent of the lethal events for the entire sample of 21 societies. The Tiwi also are one of the six MFBS in the Bowles (6) sample. Such an extreme outlier affected overall group means, as shown for instance in Table 1 and table S3. Unlike the other societies in the current sample, strings of back-and-forth revenge killings plague the Tiwi. A possible explanation is that the existence of social segmentation (28) in the form of a well-defined clan structure contributes to the high rate of violent death among the Tiwi.
>
> MFBS typically tend to be unsegmented or weakly segmented if compared to other social types in which subunits such as lineages and clans are common (7, 28). Kelly [(28), p. 47] explains that in unsegmented societies, "a homicide is consequently likely to be perceived and experienced as an individual loss shared with some kin rather than an injury to a group." As apparent in our data, close family members sometimes avenge the death of their loved-one by killing the actual killer, and in this type of unsegmented society, a revenge killing typically is the end of the matter (7). The second killing balances the first, as an individual affair, and life goes on without further bloodshed (e.g., see pairs of cases 36/37, 38/39, 50/51, 56/57, 107/108, 125/126). By contrast, in societies with well-developed social segments, lethal aggression tends to be perceived not only as a loss at the family level but also as an affront to the victim's patrilineage, clan, and so forth (28). Anyone in the killer's group may be targeted for revenge. The Tiwi cases show this pattern. They often try, in typical MFBS style, to target the actual killer, but in practice the members of a revenge expedition may settle for killing any male of the killer's group. Kelly (28) calls this phenomenon social substitutability, and in Tiwi society this phenomenon contributes to the strings of killings—blood feuds sometimes found in segmented societies. However, social segmentation and social substitutability are quite rare among MFBS; the Tiwi constitute the exception not the rule (7, 28). It can also be noted that in Tiwi society, there is a paucity of wives available to young men since most of the older men have multiple wives, a situation which may contribute to social tensions in the society.
>
> For the Tiwi with their clan structure (a feature that is atypical of MFBS), the majority of lethal events were between members of different clans, whereas for the rest of the MFBS in the sample, the majority of lethal events occurred within the local group (i.e., within the same band), as reflected in table S2. This represents a significant different ($\chi2 = 41.53$ (df = 2), p < .001; Cramer's V = .606, p < .001).

77. Fry and Söderberg, "Lethal Aggression in Mobile Forager Bands," 270.
78. Fry, *The Human Potential for Peace*; Kelly, *The Foraging Spectrum*; Julian Steward, "Causal Factors and Processes in the Evolution of Pre-Farming Societies," in *Man the Hunter*, eds. Richard B. Lee and Irven DeVore (Chicago: Aldine, 1968).
79. Kelly, *The Foraging Spectrum*, 192–193.
80. Eric Wolf, "Cycles of Violence: The Anthropology of War and Peace," in *Understanding Violence*, ed. David P. Barash (Boston: Allyn and Bacon, 2001), 196.
81. Lee and DeVore, "Problems in the Study of Hunters and Gatherers."

82. Asen Balikci, *The Netsilik Eskimo* (Garden City, NY: The Natural History Press, 1970).

83. Fry, *The Human Potential for Peace*.

84. Fry, *The Human Potential for Peace*.

85. Lorna Marshall, *The !Kung of Nyae Nyae* (Cambridge, MA: Harvard University Press, 1976), 177.

86. Fry, *The Human Potential for Peace*; Douglas P. Fry, "Human Nature: The Nomadic Forager Model," in *Origins of Altruism and Cooperation*, eds. Robert W. Sussman and C. Robert Cloninger (New York: Springer, 2011).

87. Douglas P. Fry, Gary Schober, and Kaj Björkqvist, "Evolutionary Restraints on Lethal Aggression in Animals and Humans," in *Nonkilling Societies*, ed. Joám Evans Pim (Honolulu: Center for Global Nonkilling, 2010).

88. Ferguson, "Pinker's List: Exaggerating Prehistoric War Mortality."

89. Boehm, *Hierarchy in the Forest*, 72.

90. Robert Tonkinson, *The Jigalong Mob: Aboriginal Victors of the Desert Crusade* (Menlo Park, CA: Cummings Publishing Company, 1974), 57, 65, 79.

91. Frans de Waal, *The Age of Empathy* (New York: Harmony, 2009).

92. Sarah B. Hrdy, *Mothers and Others: The Evolutionary Origins of Mutual Understanding* (Cambridge, MA: Harvard University Press, 2009); see also Lew-Levy et al., "How Do Hunter-Gatherer Children Learn Social and Gender Norms?"

93. Hrdy, *Mothers and Others: The Evolutionary Origins of Mutual Understanding*, 18.

94. Boehm, *Hierarchy in the Forest*, 67; see also Dyble et al., "Sex Equality Can Explain the Unique Social Structure of Hunter-Gatherer Bands."

95. Boehm, *Hierarchy in the Forest*, 183; Dyble et al., "Sex Equality Can Explain the Unique Social Structure of Hunter-Gatherer Bands"; Knauft, "Violence and Sociality in Human Evolution"; Richard B. Lee and Richard Daly, eds., *The Cambridge Encyclopedia of Hunters and Gatherers* (Cambridge, UK: Cambridge University Press, 1999); Frank Marlowe, "Why the Hadza Are Still Hunter-Gatherers"; for specific examples, see Pierre Clastres, "The Guayaki," in *Hunters and Gatherers Today*, ed. M. G. Bicchieri (Prospect Heights, IL: Waveland, 1972); Endicott and Endicott, *The Headman Was a Woman*, 48–49; and Woodburn, "Egalitarian Societies."

96. Clastres, "The Guayaki", 169.

97. Wolf, "Cycles of Violence," 196.

98. Lee, *The Dobe Ju/'hoansi*, 88.

99. Eleanor Leacock, "*The Montagnais 'Hunting Territory' and the Fur Trade,*" *Memoirs of the American Anthropological Association, American Anthropologist*, 56, no. 2, part 2 (1954) memoir number 78, 7.

100. Gerald C. Wheeler, *The Tribe, and Intertribal Relations in Australia* (London: John Murray, 1910), 67.

101. Fry, *The Human Potential for Peace*.

102. For recent documentation, see Lew-Levy et al., "How Do Hunter-Gatherer Children Learn Social and Gender Norms?"

103. Joseph Birdsell, "Australia: Ecology, Spacing Mechanisms and Adaptive Behaviour in Aboriginal Land Tenure," in *Land Tenure in the Pacific*, ed. R. Crocombe (New York: Oxford University Press, 1971); Wolf, "Cycles of Violence."

104. Coren Apicella et al., "Social Networks and Cooperation in Hunter-Gatherers," *Nature* 481 (2012): 497–502, doi: 10.1038/nature10736; Fry, *The Human Potential for Peace*; Tonkinson, *The Jigalong Mob*.

105. Birdsell, "Australia: Ecology, Spacing Mechanisms and Adaptive Behaviour in Aboriginal Land Tenure";E. Adamson Hoebel, *The Law of Primitive Man: A Study in Comparative Legal Dynamics* (Cambridge, MA: Harvard University Press, 1967).

106. Fry, *The Human Potential for Peace*.

107. Lew-Levy et al., "How Do Hunter-Gatherer Children Learn Social and Gender Norms?"

108. Martin Gusinde, *The Yaghan: The Life and Thought of the Water Nomads of Cape Horn*, trans. Frieda Schütze. In the electronic Human Relations Area Files, Yahgan, Doc. 1 (New Haven, CT: HRAF, 2003), accessed March 6, 2018. Available online: http://ehrafworldcultures.yale.edu/ehrafe/.

109. Douglas P. Fry and Geneviève Souillac, "The Relevance of Nomadic Forager Studies to Moral Foundations Theory: Moral Education and Global Ethics in the Twenty-First Century," *Journal of Moral Education* 42 (2013): 346–359, doi: 10.1080/03057240.2013.817328; see also Lew-Levy et al., "How Do Hunter-Gatherer Children Learn Social and Gender Norms?"

110. Robert W. Sussman, "Why the Legend of the Killer Ape Never Dies: The Enduring Power of Cultural Beliefs to Distort Our View of Human Nature," in *War, Peace, and Human Nature: The Convergence of Evolutionary and Cultural Views*, ed. Douglas P. Fry (New York: Oxford University Press, 2013), 105.

111. Fry, *The Human Potential for Peace*; Fry, "Human Nature: The Nomadic Forager Model"; Patrik Söderberg and Douglas P. Fry, "Anthropological Aspects of Ostracism," in *Ostracism, Exclusion, and Rejection*, eds. Kipling Williams and Steve Nida (New York: Routledge, 2017).

112. Boehm, *Hierarchy in the Forest*.

113. Fry, "Human Nature: The Nomadic Forager Model"; Fry and Söderberg, "Online Supplemental Material for Lethal Aggression in Mobile Forager Bands"; Söderberg and Fry, "Anthropological Aspects of Ostracism."

114. Melvin Konner, "For Peaceable Humans Don't Look to Prehistory," *Wall Street Journal*, last modified June 30, 2016, accessed March 6, 2018. Available online: http://www.wsj.com/articles/for-peaceable-humans-dont-look-to-prehistory-1467322723; see also Melvin Konner, "Human Nature, Ethnic Violence, and War," in *The Psychology of Resolving Global Conflicts: From War to Peace, Volume 1: Nature vs. Nurture*, eds. Mari Fitzduff and Chris E. Stout (Westport, CN: Praeger, 2006); and also see Allen and Jones, *Violence and Warfare among Hunter-Gatherers*; Pinker, *Better Angels of Our Nature*.

115. Konner, "Human Nature, Ethnic Violence, and War"; Konner, "For Peaceable Humans Don't Look to Prehistory"; see also Allen and Jones, *Violence and Warfare among Hunter-Gatherers*; see also Richard Wrangham and Luke Glowacki, "Intergroup Aggression in Chimpanzees and War in Nomadic Hunter-Gatherers," *Human Nature* 23 (2012): 5–29, doi: 10.1007/s12110-012-9132-1.

116. Lee and Daly, "Introduction: Foragers and Others," 1.

117. John Gowdy, "Hunter-Gatherers and the Mythology of the Market," in *The Cambridge Encyclopedia of Hunters and Gatherers*, eds. Richard B. Lee and Richard Daly (Cambridge, UK: Cambridge University Press, 1999), 397.

118. Fry, *The Human Potential for Peace*; Fry and Söderberg, "Online Supplemental Material for Lethal Aggression in Mobile Forager Bands"; Söderberg and Fry, "Anthropological Aspects of Ostracism."

119. De Waal, *The Age of Empathy*; Fry, *The Human Potential for Peace*.

8

Contracting or Expanding Consciousness

What we see and reality are not necessarily the same. Even the two physical qualities we take for granted as objective reality—space and time—are not absolute. Relative to the observer, as Einstein showed, both change significantly near the speed of light.[1]

As for the effect of culture on how we perceive reality, in some societies people blame illness on germs, while in others they believe illness is caused by a deity, witchcraft, or even a sudden fright. For instance, the Batek of Malaysia believe that the creator being, Tohan, would bring a fatal disease to someone who committed a serious offense, such as physically harming another person, and the Zapotec of Mexico believe that experiencing an unexpected fright, such as a snake dropping out of the house rafters, can cause a debilitating sickness called *susto*, requiring treatment by a curer.[2]

The recognition that what we consider reality is largely filtered through the lens of culture informs much of sociology, cultural anthropology, and social psychology. However, this is only part of the story.

As we glimpsed in Chapter 3, neuroscientist Antonio Damasio distinguishes between core consciousness, which we share with other species, and the expanded consciousness made possible by our human brain.[3] Expanded consciousness requires a large stored memory, the ability to reason, and the capacity to reflect on ourselves and our relationship with the environment. This in turn is connected with what Damasio calls the autobiographical self, which he notes "is not just dependent on, but is even regulated by, the environment."[4]

In other words, the extent to which expanded consciousness develops, or fails to develop, is *not* something we are born with. It is regulated by environmental influences, and hence by culture.

Selective Perception, Conformity, and Authority

Psychologists have studied what they call "selective perception" through clinical experiments going back several decades. In one of these experiments, Jerome Bruner and Leo Postman asked subjects to distinguish between normal and trick playing cards—and found that people tended to describe the trick cards in terms of categories familiar to them. For instance, when shown a black three of hearts, they generally perceived it as either a normal three of spades or a normal three of hearts.

Since subjects had been told some of the cards would fall into the category of trick cards, most eventually saw what was actually there. But it took them four times as long on average to identify a trick card than a normal card.[5]

In another experiment at a military post, a man was dressed in the blue Air Force uniform, but instead of the required—and familiar—blue nametag, his tag was green. After a five-minute interaction, the tag was covered up and subjects were asked what color it was. Eighty-seven percent responded it was blue—the expected color. These responses—based on familiar categories instead of what people actually saw—were also given in settings where people tended to look at the experimenter's nametag for identification.[6]

But familiarity is only one factor in selective perception. An even more powerful factor is the pressure to conform. This was shown some decades ago by psychologist Solomon Asch, who devised a series of experiments on social conformity wherein, unbeknown to an actual experimental subject within a group of confederates, all the other group members were following Asch's instructions to maintain falsely that the lengths of lines shown to the group were equal, even though the lines were clearly of different lengths. Having listened to the other group members express their erroneous conclusions, a majority of the experimental subjects agreed with them, even though this required them to deny what their own eyes told them.[7]

Other experiments have shown the power of pressure to obey authority. This was demonstrated in the experiments of psychologist Stanley Milgram. Having been told that they were participants in a teaching experiment, subjects were asked by a man in a white lab coat to administer powerful electric shocks to Milgram's confederates every time they made a "mistake." A majority obeyed the man's orders—even when Milgram's confederates screamed and said they were in terrible pain (though in actuality they were not receiving any shocks). So strong was the participants' inner pressure to obey the authority figure that, although many protested and were evidently disturbed by the pain they believed they were causing, they continued to deliver "shocks" to the end.[8]

The good news is that not everyone has the same need to conform or obey orders. In both Asch's and Milgram's experiments, a substantial minority did not conform or obey. Moreover, even one dissenter had a powerful effect on others.

Undoubtedly, a combination of factors account for the differences in how people behaved in these experiment. But one factor is the degree to which people are acculturated to subordinate their own perceptions and feelings to social pressures—particularly the pressure of external and internal figures of authority, as was shown in a later, but strangely ignored, study of participants in Milgram's experiments.[9]

Several months after his original experiments, Milgram and psychologist Alan C. Elms invited 40 of Milgram's experimental subjects to return to the Yale campus: 20 who had been fully obedient even with maximal cues for disobedience and 20 who had disobeyed even with maximal cues promoting obedience.[10] Elms interviewed and gave various personality tests to each participant. What he found, as he wrote in a 2009 article discussing experiments that replicated some of Milgram's findings, is that "fully obedient participants appeared rather consistently more authoritarian than disobedient participants on the original California F scale as well as on several biographical indices."[11]

The F scale consists of a set of tests measuring how compatible an individual is with fascist rule. It was developed after World War II by a group of scholars, most of them refugees from the Nazis, trying to understand how so many people could accept, and even participate in, the Holocaust, and why Hitler was followed, even loved, by so many Germans.

This takes us to the pioneering experiments of psychologist Else Frenkel-Brunswick, one of the developers of the F scale, and her findings that people who scored high on this scale generally came from families where deviation from norms was severely punished. Specifically, what Frenkel-Brunswick's research shows is that the people who scored high on this F scale had typically grown up with a great fear of punishment in families with powerful authority figures. She also found that people from these kinds of backgrounds—in her words, people from families where roles were "clearly defined in terms of dominance and submission"—tended to develop an "us versus them" mentality and to support strongman leaders.[12] In short, her findings not only foreshadowed Milgram's and Earl's later findings that people from authoritarian backgrounds tended to follow orders regardless of how much they hurt others, they also showed that these people were prone to vote for and support authoritarian leaders.

In a related set of studies, Frenkel-Brunswick further found that, in addition to their tendency to conform to authority, people from authoritarian families also tended to lack tolerance of ambiguity and have a strong aversion to complexity. In these highly stressful families, she writes, "certain aspects of experience have to be kept out of awareness . . . to reduce conflict and anxiety and to maintain stereotyped patterns."[13]

In one of her experiments, Frenkel-Brunswick showed her subjects the picture of a dog, followed by pictures of transitional stages as the dog transformed into a cat. In each case, the subject was asked to identify the image on the given card. Prejudiced people would continue to identify the picture as a dog, even when the characteristics of a cat became more and more apparent. As Frenkel-Brunswick put it, "There was a greater reluctance to give up the original object about which one had felt relatively certain and a tendency not to see what did not harmonize with the first [picture]."[14]

And that is not all. Recent brain experiments indicate that the experiences that lead to this mental rigidity actually leave their mark on the brain—and that these brain patterns appear to affect people's political orientations.

The Dominated Brain

In ongoing research, psychologists David Amodio, John Jost, and their colleagues study the perceptions and accompanying brain activities of people who identify themselves as either liberal or conservative.[15] In one experiment, the researchers instructed college students to tap a keyboard when they saw a letter "M" appear on a computer monitor, and to refrain from tapping when they saw a letter "W" appear. While they did this, encephalograph equipment recorded the activity in each participant's anterior cingulate cortex, a part of the brain that helps people shift gears when their habitual responses are inappropriate to a new situation.[16]

Because the letter "M" appeared four times more frequently than "W," participants became conditioned to tap the "M" key in a knee-jerk fashion.

However, the people who self-described themselves as conservatives erroneously tapped the "M" key when the "W" appeared more often than did self-identified liberals. And this behavioral difference was reflected in differences in anterior cingulate cortex activity patterns: the self-identified liberal subjects demonstrated significantly more activity than did the self-rated conservatives in this critical habit-changing region of the brain.

In other words, the brains of people who described themselves as liberals—people who have historically challenged traditional beliefs about what is or is not desirable and moral—were more flexible than were their more conservative counterparts. And those who described themselves as very conservative were even slower to shift away from preconceived or habitual ideas.

The Amodio and Jost research team did not ask subjects about their family backgrounds. But as Frenkel-Brunswick and others have shown, people who grow up in domination families are more likely to be conservative—in the sense of identifying with strong authority figures and supporting policies that are more punitive than caring. And, as experiments also show, such people have difficulty in letting go of preconceived assumptions.

The work of Frenkel-Brunswick, Amodio and Jost, and other psychologists leaves no doubt that there is a strong experiential component to how brain rigidities and flexibilities come about. Particularly relevant to how dominance-submission environments distort perceptions is this observation by Frenkel-Brunswick: "It is as if *any stimulus* [plays] the role of an authority to which the subject feels compelled to submit."[17]

Frenkel-Brunswick lists "an expectancy of self-negating submission and the inducement to repress non-acceptable tendencies" among factors contributing to this "rigidification." As a result, she notes, "we find a break and conflict between the different layers of personality. . . . Assumptions once made, no matter how faulty and out of keeping with reality because of a neglect of relevant aspects, are repeated over and over again and not corrected in the face of new evidence"[18] Or, in terms of our argument, the socialization to conform can be so severe that it stunts the capacity for expanded consciousness that makes it possible for us to accurately perceive and reflect upon ourselves in relation to changing environments.

Frenkel-Brunswick also repeatedly observed that this inability to recognize the need for changing one's perceptions, and the accompanying denial of reality, is part of a pattern of psychological dynamics. One of these dynamics is denial about childhood experiences and the displacement of fear and pain to culturally marginalized groups.

For children in abusive domination families, it is far too dangerous to disagree with their parents, let alone blame them for the pain they inflict. To do so would only add to the children's stress and pain because they are helpless to change their circumstances. So it is easier for such children to believe that they deserve this treatment than to accept that their pain is un-deserved and unfair. Hence the frequent idealization of punitive parents by their adult children, as well as the tendency of people brought up this way to idealize "strong" leaders and to scapegoat "weak" out-groups.

Children in these highly stressful environments grow up with a great deal of fear and suppressed anger, which is then often converted into preju-dice against out-groups. This was shown in other experiments by Frenkel-Brunswick, such as when she asked children to read a story in which one out of 11 featured children was African American (in the language of that time, Negro). When Frenkel-Brunswick asked questions about the story, she found that "children who scored high on prejudice mentioned the Negro boy significantly more often in an unfavorable context, even though the story said no more about him than that his father was a Negro and worked in a hotel."[19]

She also reported that the prejudiced children tended to recall a higher ratio of undesirable over desirable characteristics. "This result," she observed, "is in line with the general overemphasis on negative, hostile, and catastrophic features found in the clinical data, the interviews, and the Thematic Apperception Test scores of the highly ethnocentric subjects."[20] In other words, the overemphasis on hostility and danger conformed to the children's stressful experiences in the domination-oriented environments in which they were raised.

Brain science helps us understand these dynamics, showing that trau-matic or chronic stress alters the neurochemistry of the brain. As Robert Post, chief of the National Institute of Mental Health's Biological Psychiatry, writes, the impact of stress occurs on the cellular level in ways that recon-struct the brain, with long-lasting consequences for neural function and behavior.[21]

Stress tends to limit perceptual and behavioral options. This happens in part because stress often affects emotional memory in negative and limiting ways, as illustrated by the children Frenkel-Brunswick studied, whose over-emphasis on hostility and danger resulted from their stressful experiences.

As neuroscientist Debra Niehoff writes, "By progressively remodeling brain areas that participate in emotional memory, stress may slowly obliterate positive memories, leaving behind only the painful ones."[22]

Another frequent consequence of chronic stress is the development of a brain neurochemistry primed for violence or depression. In Niehoff's words, "More constructive coping responses are lost, and the brain fixates on an increasingly smaller portfolio of counterproductive reactions. With fewer and fewer alternatives, violence, depression, and fear stop being options and become a way of life."[23]

Laboratory studies of hamsters reveal what researchers call "subordinate stress" wherein young animals that were repeatedly attacked by adults developed an increased density of serotonin-containing fibers in the hypothalamus, a brain structure and chemical pathway involved in generating aggressive behavior. As adults, these animals were more submissive toward peers, but more aggressive toward younger or weaker animals.[24]

Studies show that continuous stress also can negatively affect those at the top of domination hierarchies. Baboons at the top of the domination hierarchy, for example, sometimes had elevated cortisol levels and nervously saw a threat behind every bush, in contrast to others who were calmer and less aggressive and hostile.[25]

Niehoff found that in humans stress has similar effects. "As stress wears away at the nervous system, risk assessment grows less and less accurate," she writes. "Minor insults are seen as major threats. Benign details take on a new emotional urgency. . . . Surrounded on all sides by real and imagined threats, the individual resorts to the time-honored survival strategies: fight, flight, or freeze."[26] Or as stress expert Bruce McEwen put it, "People say 'stress makes you stupid.' But what it really does is limit your options."[27]

Denial, Cruelty, and Politics

Another effect of stress is the suppression of empathy. Stress can make it harder to be conscious of others, or even fully conscious of oneself, as energy goes into ways of escaping from pain or at least becoming less aware of it. As Niehoff writes, "Empathy takes a back seat to relief from the numbing discomfort of a stress-deadened nervous system."[28]

This stress-related suppression of empathy helps explain how, generation after generation, parents can treat their children in cruel and abusive ways.

When parents profess love for their children at the same time that they mis-treat them, the protestations of love could be seen as hypocritical. However, Frenkel-Brunswick found a fragmentation of consciousness in people who as children were subjected to a great deal of fear and punishment.[29] Parents who love their children, having learned to fragment their consciousness, can treat their offspring in unempathic, stress- and pain-producing ways through denial. In denying their own harshness, parents also deny the mal-treatment they themselves suffered as children. And all this denial has been, and continues to be, a key psychological mechanism for domination sys-tems maintenance.

At the time Abraham was about to sacrifice Isaac to God, his culture gave fathers the right to kill their children. When Agamemnon sacrificed his daughter Iphigeneia so that the gods would grant him wind for his warships to sail, the same cultural rules were in place. Later, in the fabled Athenian civilization, fathers were legally entitled to decide whether a baby, usually a girl, should be abandoned on the town dung heap to starve to death or be torn apart by predators.

Although such practices are no longer culturally accepted, feeding girls less than boys and giving them less healthcare is still practiced in some parts of the world—often by the girls' mothers as well as fathers.[30] Even in cultures where we today find an uneasy mix of partnership and domination elements, we still often see parenting characterized by a mind-scrambling mix of caring and coercion. And the effects of this parenting are later expressed in society at large, including in how people vote and the policies they support.

In *The Politics of Denial*, social psychologists Michael Milburn and Sheree Conrad document how people who were abused as children are often drawn to political leaders who advocate a punitive social agenda. This, they note, serves as a means of deflecting repressed pain and anger against those perceived as weak and evil—exactly how they were taught to perceive themselves as children when their parents punished them.[31]

Milburn and Conrad point out that the conservative political agenda tends to focus on issues in which the common theme is punishment or retribution, such as capital punishment, heavy investment in prisons, use of military force in international affairs, and punishment of "immoral" women and gays. These issues, they write, often "serve as an arena for dis-placed childhood rage, fear, or helplessness, and an excuse for rationalizing the long-suppressed desire for retribution."[32]

As Milburn put it in a *Newsweek* interview after the photos of US torture of Iraqi prisoners at Abu Ghraib were published, "a major component in this politics of punishment is denial." Commenting on how Rush Limbaugh could dismiss these barbarities as no more "than what happens at the *Skull and Bones* initiation," and Senator James Inhofe could express outrage, *not* about the torture, but about the condemnation of it, Milburn pointed out that these reactions can be traced to harsh childhood punishments. These, he noted, often lead to identification with the "strong" and, along with this, to denial that there is anything wrong with those in control using force against those "who deserve it."[33]

Milburn and Conrad point out that this punitive politics of domination is especially pronounced in men. They attribute this to socialization processes that teach males to deny fear, pain, and empathy, focusing instead on anger and contempt as culturally proper masculine emotions.

The emotional and cognitive patterns stemming from the psychological mechanisms of denial and transference in both men and women help explain why throughout history, including in our own time, autocratic rulers have enjoyed the loyalty of so many people, even obtaining their love. In their 2018 book, *Raised to Rage: The Politics of Anger and the Roots of Authoritarianism*, Milburn and Conrad propose that these dynamics ultimately lie behind the election of Donald Trump as US President in 2016 and help explain the indifference of his constituents to the pain caused by many of his policies.[34]

Since children are helpless in the face of adults who ostensibly love them but treat them harshly, many children rely on denial and identify with the powerful and supposedly "good" adult rather than the weak, powerless, and allegedly "bad" child. As adults, children raised in such punitive contexts not only may fail to empathize with the pain caused by policies that harm people or neglect their basic needs but also identify with and support leaders who decree such policies.

A 2018 study from the Institute for the Study of Citizens and Politics sheds further light on the voters who brought Donald Trump to power. Based on an analysis of survey data from 1,200 representative voters, this study contradicts the common opinion that the people who voted for Trump were animated by economic hardship, as in the often-quoted assessment that they were the "forgotten" American white lower middle class. It seems that the primary motivation for many of these voters was *not* economic hardship, especially not individual financial hardship, but rather the

threat of loss of status or dominance. As the Director of the Institute, political scientist Diana C. Mutz, put it in her interview with the *New York
Times*, "It's not a threat to their own economic well-being; it's a threat to
their group's dominance in our country over all."[35]

Significantly, Dr. Mutz and her colleagues assessed what she termed a
"social dominance orientation," a psychological measure of a person's belief in hierarchy as necessary and inherent to a society. They found that
people who exhibit this orientation were more likely to move toward Mr.
Trump, reflecting their hope that the status quo be protected. Specifically,
voters who switched to Trump, the study found, were largely motivated by
what they perceived as the threat to white, Christian, male dominance by a
growing "brown" US population, foreigners, and women who they saw as
grabbing power away from white men.[36]

So even though many Trump supporters were Evangelical Christians,
they voted for a self-described sexual predator who, like many of them,
loved cheeseburgers and fries; felt superior to women, immigrants, and
foreigners (especially Muslims and the "unfair" Chinese); and promised
to put "America First"—a code phrase for restoring white male dominance. Moreover, Trump's "strong-man" stance, self-proclaimed success through bullying (as in his reality TV show "The Apprentice"), and
promises to cut aid to the "undeserving" and punish those who opposed
him (as in "lock her up") would also have served to deflect repressed
pain and anger from abusive childhoods into harsh policies against the
immigrants, women, and people of color whom Trump blamed for our
ills.[37]

Fortunately, there are, and have always been, those who consciously reject authoritarian and uncaring policies and relations. This is a testimony to
the powerful human yearning for caring, freedom, and equality—human
inclinations that, given half a chance, can overcome dysfunctional cultural
constructions.

But the psychosocial dynamics we have been examining also demonstrate that the flexibility of the human brain can be a two-edged sword.
Adjusting to domination cultures and subcultures, particularly to fear- and
force-based childhood experiences or the control of men over women,
tends to habituate people to accept, and even idealize, authoritarian control.
And when people experience life in a domination system, they tend not to
see that there exist more equitable and compassionate, and less stressful and
damaging, life options.

Constricting Consciousness and Normalizing Domination

Even in cultures and subcultures where there has been movement toward the partnership side of the continuum, our cultural heritage from more domination-oriented times continues to communicate the message that hierarchies of domination are normal, desirable, and inevitable. And this normalization of domination starts very early in life.

During the early years, when children's brains are literally being shaped by both experience and instruction, cherished fairy tales, myths, and cultural motifs idealize the dominators over the dominated, such as royalty over commoners, instilling in developing minds that the world is rightly divided into those on top and those on the bottom. These narratives, which are imbibed along with mothers' milk, almost invariably also present the control of females by males as normal, desirable, and even romantic.

In the West to this day, for example, *Cinderella*, *Sleeping Beauty*, and other tales told little children depict males as powerful and females as powerless. These stories, passed on from generation to generation, portray women not only as incapable of determining their own destinies but also as decorative possessions to be acquired by men. The hero is a prince or ruler who gets to possess a beautiful young girl as his wife (a model still replicated in popular culture today, as in the term "trophy wife").

When women in children's tales have some power, they are generally evil stepmothers or witches. So long before their critical faculties are in place, children learn the insidious lesson in folktales, books, and media that women should not be entrusted with power.

Even more perversely misogynous is the fabled Persian story of *Sheherazade* and her 1,000 Arabian tales. In this story, still included in many anthologies as romantic, a courageous and creative young woman, Sheherazade, saves her own life and that of countless other girls with inventive tales that distract a Persian king who for years raped a young girl every night and had her killed the next morning. As a reward for this accomplishment, in a bizarre "happy ending," Sheherazade gets to spend the rest of her life in the harem of this serial killer. There is not even a hint in the story that this royal monster should be punished for his crimes. On the contrary, he is rewarded with an entertaining and lovely new wife.

In other classic tales, such as *The Odyssey*, the hero's violence is idealized—as it still is in much of today's action entertainment. We learn how, wielding his lethal blade, Odysseus fights evil, which in the *Odyssey* is often embodied by sorceresses and female monsters. This theme of the female as villain also still lingers, as in the plot formula for the iconic James Bond films from *Diamonds Are Forever* to *Ocotpussy*. In all this normative literature, there are only the possibilities to dominate or be dominated. There is no partnership alternative.

Even the language we inherited from more rigid domination times constricts our ability to see partnership relations as a possibility. As Robert Ornstein writes in *The Psychology of Consciousness*, "Within a linguistic community, the common language provides an almost unconsciously agreed on set of categories for experience, and allows the speakers of that language to ignore experiences excluded by the common category system."[38]

This is a vital point. Language can be an instrument for excluding from consciousness even what we ourselves observe and experience. This is dramatically illustrated by the terms *matriarchy* (rule by mothers) and *patriarchy* (rule by fathers)—the only conventional categories that take into account how gender relations are constructed.

While at first glance matriarchy and patriarchy may seem like two contrasting categories, they actually describe the same way of structuring relations: both present rankings of domination—beginning with the ranking of half of our species over the other half—as the only possibility. Rather than expanding consciousness, these terms constrict consciousness, making it hard to imagine gender relations that are not based on dominating or being dominated.

Because there was no term for a relationship where women and men are equals, Riane coined the neologism *gylany*. It derives from the Greek *gyne* (woman) and *andros* (man) linked by the letter *l* for the Greek verb *lyo* (to set free) and *lyen* (to resolve). The letter *l* also indicates that the female and male parts of humanity are linked rather than ranked.[39] This new term provides a word for ideas and experiences that fall outside both matriarchy and patriarchy. Having this term can help us expand our consciousness.

Of course, much more than new terminology is needed to change old ways of perceiving and structuring "reality." For transformative change, we have to address the underlying dynamics of social systems—starting with the interconnections between the formative gender and parent-child relations and relations in society at large.

What happens in families and in the larger society is *not* a one-way process. Maintaining systems of domination entails interactive psychosocial dynamics that involve politics, economics, religion, and other institutions that severely limit partnership alternatives all through life. In other words, childhood experiences are not the simple cause of what later goes on in families and other institutions. Peer groups, education, religion, and other institutions interact with what children experience and observe in families, reinforcing one another.

Nonetheless, family socialization for relations of domination and submission is particularly effective. This is not only because early family experiences are so important. It is also, as we will see next, because these relations involve touch to the body—and it is through intimate touch that socialization is most powerful and enduring.

Notes

1. This change in perspective has not led, in general, to concerns that all is relative and subjective, and hence that nothing can be known. Most scientists still believe that there is a real world out there and that we can get to know more and more about it. But there is a movement from seeing a mechanistic world to seeing a more organic world of interacting dynamics in many fields. Heisenberg's Uncertainty Principle states that position and momentum cannot both be measured with precision; the greater the precision in the measurement of one, the greater the error in the other. This error is negligible for physical measurements of magnitudes greater than atomic; therefore, Heisenberg's Uncertainty Principle does not mean that we can't make accurate predictions based on observations of physical and cultural phenomena. But, following Einstein's lead, many mathematicians and scientists no longer see one objective reality. Instead of the mechanistic world of point masses moving in space—the moving point masses being from Galileo and Newton, and the space being Euclidean three-dimensional flat space—they see the world in terms of interacting energy fields. Albert Einstein, Leopold Infeld, and Banesh Hoffmann, "The Gravitational Equations and the Problem of Motion," *Annals of Mathematics* 39 (1938): 65–100, doi: 10.2307/1968714; George Gamow, *Thirty Years that Shook Physics: The Story of Quantum Physics* (New York: Doubleday, 1966).
2. Kirk M. Endicott and Karen L. Endicott, *The Headman Was a Woman: The Gender Egalitarian Batek of Malaysia* (Long Grove, IL: Waveland, 2008); Arthur Rubel and Carl O'Nell, *Susto: A Folk Illness* (Berkeley: University of California Press, 1991).
3. It may be that other species, such as whales, dolphins, and apes, also have some of this capacity.
4. Antonio Damasio, *The Feeling of What Happens: Body and Emotion in the Making of Consciousness* (New York: Harcourt, 1999), 229.
5. Jerome S. Bruner and Leo Postman, "On the Perception of Incongruity: A Paradigm," in *Readings in Perception*, eds. David Beardsley and Michael Wertheimer (Princeton, NJ: Van Nostrand, 1958), 648–663.

6. Jerome Bruner, Leo Postman, and John Rodriguez, "Expectation and the Perception of Color," *American Journal of Psychology* 64 (1951): 216–227, doi: 10.2307/1418668.

7. Solomon E. Asch, "Studies of Independence and Conformity: A Minority of One against a Unanimous Majority," *Psychological Monographs: General and Applied* 70 (1956): 1–70, doi: 10.1037/h0093718.

8. Stanley Milgram, "Behavioral Study of Obedience," *Journal of Abnormal and Social Psychology* 67 (1963): 371–378, doi: 10.1037/h0040525. Even though some of them have been replicated, Milgram's experiments have been controversial, and they have been criticized as unethical. See, e.g., Cari Romm, "Rethinking One of Psychology's Most Infamous Experiments," *Atlantic*, January 28, 2015. Available online: https://www.theatlantic.com/health/archive/2015/01/rethinking-one-of-psychologys-most-infamous-experiments/384913/. See also Gina Perry, *Behind the Shock Machine: The Untold Story of the Notorious Milgram Psychology Experiments* (New York: The New Press, 2013).

9. Alan Elms and Stanley Milgram, "Personality Characteristics Associated with Obedience and Defiance toward Authoritative Command," *Journal of Experimental Research in Personality* 1 (1966): 282–289.

10. Elms and Milgram, "Personality Characteristics Associated with Obedience."

11. Alan Elms, "Obedience Lite," *American Psychologist* 64 (2009): 32–36, doi: 10.1037/a0014473.

12. Else Frenkel-Brunswik, "Intolerance of Ambiguity as a Personality Variable," in *Readings in Perception*, eds. David C. Beardsley and Michael Wertheimer (Princeton, NJ: Van Nostrand, 1958), 664–685, 669.

13. Frenkel-Brunswik, "Intolerance of Ambiguity as a Personality Variable," 669–670.

14. Frenkel-Brunswik, "Intolerance of Ambiguity as a Personality Variable," 680.

15. John Jost and David Amodio, "Political Ideology as Motivated Social Cognition: Behavioral and Neuroscientific Evidence," *Motivation and Emotion* 36 (2012): 55–64, doi: 10.1007/s11031-011-9260-7; John Jost et al., "Political Neuroscience: The Beginning of a Beautiful Friendship," *Advances in Political Psychology* 35 (2014): 3–42, doi: 10.1111/pops.12162; Amy R. Krosch et al., "On the Ideology of Hypodescent: Political Conservatism Predicts Categorization of Racially Ambiguous Faces as Black," *Journal of Experimental Social Psychology* 49 (2013): 1196–1203, doi: 10.1016/j.jesp.2013.05.009.

16. David Amodio et al., "Neurocognitive Correlates of Liberalism and Conservatism," *Nature Neuroscience* 10 (2007): 1246–1247, doi: 10.1038/nn1979.

17. Frenkel-Brunswik, "Intolerance of Ambiguity as a Personality Variable," 680, emphasis in original.

18. Frenkel-Brunswik, "Intolerance of Ambiguity as a Personality Variable," 670–671. Frenkel-Brunswik notes that this fragmentation of consciousness contrasts sharply with the greater fluidity of transition and intercommunication between the different personality strata of a child in what she calls "the permissive home" (67). While she uses the term "permissive," which was used to describe nonauthoritarian families at the time she wrote, she does not say this is a home where there are no rules. Partnership families are not permissive in the laissez-faire sense: there are still

hierarchies of actualization, standards of desirable and undesirable behavior, and rules, in addition to modeling of empathy and caring. For a discussion of this, see Riane Eisler, *The Power of Partnership* (Novato, CA: New World Library, 2002).

19. Frenkel-Brunswik, "Intolerance of Ambiguity as a Personality Variable," 676.
20. Frenkel-Brunswik, "Intolerance of Ambiguity as a Personality Variable," 676. This phenomenon has also been extensively documented in trauma victims, who find themselves unable to leave behind their traumatic feelings. See, e.g., Bessel van der Kolk, *The Body Keeps the Score: Brain, Minds, and Body in the Healing of Trauma* (New York: Penguin, 2015).
21. Robert M. Post, "Transduction of Psychosocial Stress into the Neurobiology of Recurrent Affective Disorder," *American Journal of Psychiatry* 149 (1992): 999–1010, doi: 10.1176/ajp.149.8.999.
22. Debra Niehoff, *The Biology of Violence: How Understanding the Brain, Behavior, and Environment Can Break the Vicious Circle of Aggression* (New York: The Free Press, 1999), 187.
23. Niehoff, *The Biology of Violence*, 187.
24. Yvon Delville, Richard Melloni, and Craig Ferris, "Behavioral and Neurobiological Consequences of Social Subjugation during Puberty in Golden Hamsters," *Journal of Neuroscience* 18 (1998): 2667–2672, doi: 10.1523/JNEUROSCI.18-07-02667.1998.
25. See, e.g., Laurence R. Gesquiere et al., "Life at the Top: Rank and Stress in Wild Male Baboons," *Science* 333 (2011): 357–360, doi: 10.1126/science.1207120. See also Niehoff, *The Biology of Violence*, 175–177.
26. Niehoff, *The Biology of Violence*, 185.
27. Bruce McEwen quoted in Niehoff, *The Biology of Violence*, 186.
28. Niehoff, *The Biology of Violence*, 185.
29. Frenkel-Brunswik, *Readings in Perception*, 669–670.
30. Nicholas Kristof and Sheryl WuDunn, *Half the Sky: Turning Oppression into Opportunity for Women Worldwide* (New York: Vintage, 2010); Riane Eisler, "Protecting the Majority of Humanity: Toward an Integrated Approach to Crimes against Present and Future Generations," in *Sustainable Development, International Criminal Justice, and Treaty Implementation,* eds. Marie-Claire Cordonier Segger and Sébastien Jodoin (Cambridge, UK: Cambridge University Press, 2013).
31. Michael Milburn and Sheree Conrad, *The Politics of Denial* (Cambridge, MA: MIT Press, 1996).
32. Milburn and Conrad, *The Politics of Denial*, 53; see also Michael Milburn and Sheree Conrad, *Raised to Rage: The Politics of Anger and the Roots of Authoritarianism* (Cambridge, MA: MIT Press, 2018)and "Five Minutes with Michael Milburn and Sheree Conrad," *MIT Press,* September 30, 2016. Available online: https://mitpress.mit.edu/blog/five-minutes-michael-milburn-and-sheree-conrad.
33. Michael Milburn interviewed by Brian Braiker, "See No Evil—A Political Psychologist Explains the Roles Denial, Emotion and Childhood Punishment Play in Politics," *Newsweek,* last modified May 13, 2004, accessed March 18, 2018. Available online: http://nospank.net/n-m05r.htm. Also of interest, a biographer of Rush Limbaugh, Zev Chafets, in an interview in the *All Right Magazine* noted, "I was

impressed by the degree to which Rush's worldview was—and remains—shaped by his father. A large part of Rush's life has been dedicated to winning his father's respect and approval." "Interview with Zev Chafets, Author of Rush Limbaugh: *Army of One*." *All Right Magazine*, last modified on April 13, 2012. Available online: https://web.archive.org/web/20120413010651/http://www.allrightmagazine.com/exclusive-interviews/interview-with-zev-chafets-author-of-rush-limbaugh-army-of-one-4662/.

34. Milburn and Conrad, *Raised to Rage*. For a similar analysis, see also Riane Eisler, "Building an Integrated Progressive Agenda: The Post Election Crisis and Its Opportunities," Speech at the Cosmopolitan Club, New York City, 2017. Available online at http://rianeeisler.com/building-an-integrated-progressive-agenda-the-post-election-crisis-and-its-opportunities/.

35. Diana Mutz quoted in Niraj Chokshia, "Trump Voters Driven by Fear of Losing Status, Not Economic Anxiety, Study Finds," *New York Times*, April 24, 2018, https://www.nytimes.com/2018/04/24/us/politics/trump-economic-anxiety.html; Diana Mutz and Samuel Stouffer, "One Nation under Siege" and accompanying data. Working Paper, 2018. Article text will be posted after publication: http://iscap.upenn.edu/studies/one-nation-under-siege.

36. Chokshia, "Trump Voters Driven by Fear of Losing Status, Not Economic Anxiety, Study Finds."

37. Milburn and Conrad, *Raised to Rage*; Eisler, "Building an Integrated Progressive Agenda."

38. Robert Ornstein, *The Psychology of Consciousness* (Oxford, UK: Penguin, 1972), 40–41.

39. The term *gylany* was introduced in Riane Eisler, *The Chalice and the Blade: Our History, Our Future* (San Francisco: Harper & Row, 1987). See also Riane Eisler, "The Power of the Creative Word: From Domination to Partnership," in *The Tapestry of the Creative Word in Anglophone Literatures,* eds. Antonella Riem et al. (Udine, Italy: Forum Editrice, 2013).

9

Touch, Intimacy, and
Sexuality in Partnership and
Domination Environments

The idea that touch and sexuality have anything to do with partnership and domination systems may seem strange. But as physical anthropologist Ashley Montagu showed in his groundbreaking book *Touching*, how we are touched can powerfully affect how we feel, think, and act.[1]

The effects of touch are especially powerful in childhood. But touch is important throughout life. This is because, in the words of psychologist Dacher Keltner, "human skin has special receptors that transform patterns of tactile stimulation—a mother's caress or a friend's pat on the back—into indelible sensations as lasting as childhood smells."[2]

We communicate with one another through touch, starting from birth. As Keltner and others have found, we actually read other's intentions and emotions by how we are touched. In one of these experiment, scientists put strangers on two sides of a barrier so that they could not see each other but could touch each other through a hole. One person was asked to touch the other on the forearm several times, each time trying to convey one of 12 emotions—from anger, fear, and disgust to love, gratitude, and sympathy. When people were asked to describe the emotion they thought the person touching them was communicating, they successfully identified it to an amazing degree.[3]

Of course, our skin is not the only part of our body that registers what others are communicating. Many parts of our bodies are involved in receiving and transmitting sensory information. For instance, if someone threatens us, our heart and breathing rates increase, sending signals to our brain to confront or to flee. Studies also show that the heart often reacts to signals before our brains do.[4] Our glands, organs, and other bodily systems, too, respond to environmental stimuli and transmit messages to our brains.

All this is part of interactive feedback loops. Neurons communicate with one another and consolidate information.

Ultimately, the ways that people relate to others are processed through our bodies. And especially in parent-child relations and also later in sexual contexts, touching plays an important role in how feelings, thoughts, and even brains are shaped. Babies have to be touched to be fed, and even when they are not breastfed, they have to be cleaned, wiped, and carried. As Kenneth A. Wesson notes, at "nearly all early phases of one's development, a great deal is learned about the environment by the act of touching."[5]

Indeed, the skin can be seen as an extension of the brain itself. While the exact neurology of touch, and how it affects emotions and behavior, remains to be fully understood, we know that caring touch can trigger the release of oxytocin, bringing feelings of warmth and pleasure.[6] By contrast, uncaring and hurtful touch triggers the release of different neurochemicals, bringing feelings of pain, fear, and anger.[7]

The effect of touch on our nervous systems, as well as on our feelings and behaviors, is not just a temporary matter. As Montagu observed, the effects of touch start at birth and continue throughout life. How we are touched affects everything, including whether empathy and caring or fight/flight and dissociation patterns become habitual, and whether a morality of caring or coercion is considered normal.[8]

This is why, in order to maintain domination systems, coercive and hurtful touch is a powerful way of socializing people, whether they are those who dominate or those who are dominated. In this chapter, we explore how the patterns of touch, intimacy, and sexuality differ at the opposite ends of the domination-partnership continuum, and why understanding the societal variations in coercive and caring touch is important.

Domination: Binding More than the Feet

The practice of foot-binding was prevalent in prerevolutionary China, not only in the ruling classes but also in large sections of the population. From the age of around five to 13 or 14 years, little girls' feet were tightly bound until they were deformed into little stumps, making walking difficult and running impossible. This years-long ordeal not only impeded girls' natural growth; it also caused them excruciating pain. But it continued because men—those who held power—found these crippled feet sexually arousing and demanded it in their brides.

Foot-binding was a way of incapacitating women so that they could not escape their subordinate positions. But, as anthropologist C. Fred Blake writes in his study of this brutal practice, it did much more than that: foot-binding taught women to accept submission and self-sacrifice as the essence of their sense of self.[9]

On the fundamental level of neural pathways, foot-binding trained women from early childhood to mold their minds and bodies—and with this, what they imaged as their core identity or self—to the requirements of those in power. As is often the case with domination socialization, the main enforcer of this mutilation was the girl's own mother. Having herself had to mold her body, and her sense of self, to conform to these cruel requirements, a mother demanded from her daughters the sacrifice of their natural capacity to run, dance, and even walk without difficulty—as well as the terrible pain of years of oozing sores, bandages stiff with dried pus and blood, and sloughed-off gobs of flesh. It was a girl's mother who punished her for removing her bandages, and who insisted that men required this.

Most important, it was from her mother that a girl learned to accept that the same touch she associated with love should also be the coercive touch that caused her such terrible suffering. It was from her own mother—the person on whom she depended for not only survival but also caring—that she learned what Blake calls "the conflation of 'care' with 'pain.'"[10] She also learned, in the name of love, to do the same one day to her own daughters.

Foot-binding served still another function. It was a vehicle for women to deflect their rage and pain, *not* against those whose cruel wishes they implemented, but against other women—even against their own helpless daughters, whom they could dominate in the name of tradition. The only other chance that a woman had in the traditional Chinese household to dominate rather than be dominated was to become a mother-in-law, and thus also to have a younger woman under her control.

In short, foot-binding perpetuated the replication, from generation to generation, of the mind-and-body-numbing confluence of care with coercion and hurt. It perpetuated a system in which the human need for love is associated with submission to pain.

Caring and Coercion

The confluence of caring with coercion and pain is, to varying degrees, characteristic of domination childrearing. Sometimes, as is still the case in large world regions, we find more overt violence against girls, for example, the brutal genital mutilation inflicted on millions of girls in the Middle East and Africa, still considered moral and necessary by many parents.[11] Sometimes, as in some parts of the West, there may be more overt violence against boys, as when male children are hit to teach them the lesson that "boys don't cry." In some cases, the confluence of caring and hurt can be primarily psychological. But even then, because of how our bodies react to psychological abuse in the development of neural patterns, the mental becomes the physical at the neural level.[12]

All too often, both girls and boys are spanked, slapped, shaken, and even worse, when they cry.[13] One possible reason behind these traditional punishments is that cries unconsciously restimulate the buried pain of people who have been abused as children but were not able to protest, lest this lead to more punishment and pain. But whatever the reason, as we saw in Chapter 5, physical violence against children as a disciplinary measure is still considered normal and desirable by a majority of parents worldwide.[14]

Some cultures and subcultures teach parents not to be responsive to the pain of babies and children. Not so long ago, this was even recommended by psychologists such as John Watson, famous for his cruel conditioning experiments on his own son Albert, whom he deliberately frightened with loud noises until the nine-month-old baby cried in fear when he was shown objects with which the noises had been associated.[15] Still today, insensitivity to children's distress is promoted in Christian parenting guides telling parents not to spoil their children by responding to their pain, instead urging parents to cause children pain as a way of teaching them the parent's will is law. These guides admonish parents not to "overindulge" their children and instead follow "God's way"—which they say includes teaching "high-chair manners" by forcing babies as young as eight months to sit with their hands on their trays or laps, and squelching any fussiness through threats and violence.[16]

Justifying cruelty in the name of God or tradition is a way of conditioning people not to respond to the pain of others—in other words, to suppress their capacity for empathy. But domination parenting has an even more insidious effect: it teaches children who receive this treatment to associate love with coercion and pain. Hence, the conflation of the pleasure of caring with the pain of coercion is probably one of the most effective mechanisms for socializing people to submit willingly to domination as adults.[17]

Writing in the 1940s, psychologist Erich Fromm called this "the yearning for submission."[18] Fromm laid the 20th-century drift toward totalitarianism at the feet of modernity, arguing that while it has brought "modern man" more freedom, it made him more isolated so that he often wants to escape back into dependency and submission.[19] But the psychological tendency to submit to strong leaders is not just a modern phenomenon; it is a more general feature of domination systems.

Whether it is in modern or premodern times, the "yearning for submission" in domination systems goes deeper, to the kinds of psychological dynamics studied by Frenkel-Brunswick that we examined in Chapter 8. Indeed, we would argue that it was much more entrenched in earlier centuries, when "fealty" and "obedience" were the unquestioned norms.

What Fromm termed the yearning for submission can best be understood as the unconscious desire of people to replicate their early childhood relations with coercive parents who demanded strict obedience and love in exchange for protection and care. Not surprisingly, as adults such people tend to unconsciously drift toward dictatorial leaders who promise to protect and take care of them. They love these leaders even though, like their parents, they use fear and force to rule.

As we also saw in Chapter 8, people from highly punitive families tend to back punitive rather than caring social policies. In the United States, politicians with this orientation find money for prisons, but when it comes to funding care for children and other measures that have been shown to sharply decrease crime, they say there is no money. And a substantial number of people uncritically support such policies, having been culturally conditioned to devalue caring for children as "women's work," a subordination of women and the feminine that children are taught early on in domination systems so that it operates on an unconscious level.[20]

These political decisions are not based on rational considerations, much less facts. They are triggered by emotional programming, which in turn is connected with neural networks formed in response to socialization. Key to this socialization, which we inherited from more rigid domination times, is a modeling of lack of responsiveness to another's pain, as well as the linking of the good feelings of being cared for with domination and/or submission.

Sexual Intimacy and Domination

Like parenting, sexuality is distorted in domination systems. As Montagu writes:

> The mother's holding and cuddling of the child plays a very effective and important role in its subsequent sexual development. A mother who loves must enfold the child she loves. She must draw the child to her in a close embrace and, male or female, this is what the adult will want later and be able to demonstrate to anyone he loves. Children who have been inadequately held and fondled will suffer, as adolescents and adults, from an affect-hunger for such attention.[21]

As sexologists Masters and Johnson point out, sex creates a "pleasure bond" that supports mutuality in relations between men and women.[22] But sex as culturally defined in domination systems thwarts the full development of the pleasure bond, and hence the loving, equal, and cooperative relations it may help to facilitate. Instead, these social systems link sex with domination and submission. As Riane describes in *Sacred Pleasure,* male control of the female body is integral to the construction of sexuality in societies that orient closely to the domination system.[23]

Riane identifies what she calls the "erotization of domination" as a strategy that goes way back in history."[24] For example, the medieval Church made it a sin to have sexual intercourse in any way other than the man-on-top-and-woman-on-bottom position. Centuries later, this teaching was still exported to other cultures by Christian missionaries—hence the term "missionary position."

Another domination system strategy is to vilify women—especially women's sexuality—as dangerous to men. This is a common religious myth, which conflates the neutrally deadening emotion of fear with sexual desire, making it easier for men to dehumanize and violate women—as in the notion that it is a woman's fault if she is raped.

Still another strategy is to vilify sex itself and, with this, the human body. Greek and Roman philosophers, particularly the Stoics, already asserted that our bodies must be strictly controlled. But only later, with Saint Paul, and then more strictly with Saint Augustine in the fifth century, did the Christian idea that the body—particularly the body of woman—is corrupt, even demonic, begin to take hold. As religious historian Elaine Pagels points out, Augustine radically reinterpreted the biblical story of Adam, Eve, and the Fall to support the notion that the carnal is inherently evil.[25]

Augustine claimed that the Fall from Paradise—which was supposedly caused by woman's disobedience—made sex and the human body irreversibly corrupt.[26] This led to the Church doctrine, as Augustine wrote in the Christian classic, *The City of God,* that every child born of the sexual union of woman and man is born tainted with sin, which is sexually transmitted through the semen.[27]

The human body and human sexuality are, in Augustine's view, a carnal burden that truly spiritual men could only partly escape by tormenting their flesh.[28] Women, on the other hand, had no way to escape because, according to medieval Church doctrine, woman is by her nature the source of all carnal evil—and thus an eternal danger to man.[29]

We should add that while this fable is unique to Christian tradition, the idea that the human body—particularly woman's body—is an evil that must be strictly controlled by men is not. To varying degrees, this idea is found in Eastern, Western, and some indigenous religious mythologies designed to impose and maintain domination in political and sexual relations.

Today, we still see the idea that woman's sexuality is a terrible danger to men in some contemporary Muslim teachings that woman must conceal her body—even her face—to strip her from of any sexuality. We find it in even earlier Eastern religious teachers, for example, Zoroaster, who lived in Persia from 628 to 551 BCE, whose teachings were idealized by some Western philosophers, and even Mozart in his opera "The Magic Flute," where a powerful female figure is blamed for all evil. Zoroaster taught that man's soul is imprisoned by matter and that woman, whom he considered soulless, is the mother of all demons. He also claimed that cosmic darkness and evil were awakened by a female creature.[30]

In Buddhist mythology, one of the temptations the Buddha had to resist to attain enlightenment under the Bo tree was the temptation of lust and sensual pleasure. Accordingly, in some Buddhist sects, monks not only must be celibate but also are forbidden from all contact with women, even shaking their hands.

This view of woman as polluting and dangerous to man is a powerful rationale for the repression of female sexuality. And the repression of female sexuality is in turn a powerful model for all forms of repression by "superiors" of "inferiors."

The infamous sexual double standard we inherited is integral to the repression of female sexuality in societies that orient to the domination system. While rigidly controlling female sexuality, it gives license to male sexuality—including license to rape in war or if a woman supposedly provokes rape by not being under the "protection" of a man.

Even the medieval Church, which condemned sex as sinful in marriage except for reproduction, often condoned nonreproductive sex for men. It actually held that women must always be sexually available to their husbands, lest they seek sex elsewhere, and commanded women to do this, even if it cost their lives. As Archbishop Stephen Langton stated, "the wife must rather let herself be killed than her husband sin."[31]

Not only did the Church condone female sexual slavery, but it also did not prohibit its most blatant forms. For example, while it condemned some barbaric domination practices, it never condemned the custom of some European men of protecting their "honor" by forcing their wives to wear metal or wooden chastity belts that caused chronic irritation, infections, and unrelievable sexual arousal.[32] But just as the lives of wives were deemed less important than the sexual desires of their husbands, these women's pain, humiliation, and degradation were of no concern to the Church.

All these practices—and the Church's indifference to the suffering they caused—did not spring up in a vacuum. They came out of cultures where control by some over others was believed to be the God-given order of the world.

Totalitarianism and Fundamentalism

Because of this link between social repression and sexual repression, some earlier scholars, notably Wilhelm Reich, argued that there is a causal link between sexual repression and political repression. But this is an oversimplification.

The critical factor in the connection between political repression and sexual repression is *not* whether religious or other teachings repress male sexuality or whether sex is considered a male entitlement. Just as parent-child relations based on parental control of children's bodies through force and fear condition people to fit into a domination system, a cultural construction of sexuality based on control of women by men conditions people to regard the control of one individual or group by another as natural, even desirable.

The point to emphasize is that unless changes are made to the foundational gender and parent-child relations in domination systems, the same psychosocial patterns will continue, and domination systems will rebuild themselves. This is precisely what made possible the rise of both totalitarianism and religious fundamentalism.

As we saw, thinkers such as Fromm describe totalitarianism and the concomitant mass extermination of people as new phenomena characteristic of modern society, attributing our supposed "yearning for submission" to modern-day "alienation and anomie."[33] But totalitarianism is actually the application of modern technologies of destruction and repression to establish and maintain old traditions of domination.

The ideologies of totalitarian regimes such as the Nazis have been secular rather than religious.[34] At their core, however, is the same belief as in domination religious ideologies that authoritarian rule is natural and right.

German concentration camps, where millions of women, men, and children were enslaved, dehumanized, and murdered, were unprecedented in their bureaucratically organized horror. But if we look at the Assyrians, Aztecs, and Huns, we see that brutal atrocities are hardly new. Although more hideously efficient, the terror that characterized totalitarian regimes in modern times has its parallels in earlier means of domination. The Assyrians, for instance, lined the roads of conquered nations with people they crucified. The Spartans of ancient Greece were also masters at rule through terror: slaves could be killed at any moment without cause or trial.[35] Christian Crusaders massacred huge numbers of people, including, as in the Albigensian Crusades, fellow Christians whom the Church labeled heretics.[36]

Nor is the brainwashing of people in totalitarian regimes new. While strides have been made in the use of propaganda, many indoctrination techniques have their historical precedents. To illustrate, medieval Popes launched their Crusades through long, hypnotic torch-lit assemblies; a similar method was also used by Hitler.[37]

Neither was the push in Nazi Germany to impose a male-controlled family new. Hitler, like the German philosopher Nietzsche, linked rigid male dominance to an idealized Aryan past.[38] As soon as Hitler seized power, he set to work to strengthen male dominance over women and complained that masculine dominance had been watered down in the effeminate ("effete") Weimar republic as part of a Jewish plot to undermine Aryan power.[39]

When Stalin took over in the Soviet Union and imposed his ruthless totalitarian rule, he, too, called for a return to the traditional patriarchal family. Under Lenin, the Bolsheviks had made some attempts to change the old family structure, enacting laws to end the husband's legal domination. They decreed the equal division of property upon divorce and abolished the distinction between legitimate and illegitimate children. Women no longer had to go wherever their husbands willed them to go. These progressive laws, however, were never vigorously enforced. So there was no substantial change in the view that women should serve men and that the beating of women by their husbands, traditional in many Russian families, should not be prosecuted. However, it was only when Stalin came to power in 1924 that policies were enacted that openly supported the traditional male-dominated family. Stalin changed back inheritance laws to again give pre-eminence to the father as head of the family. Children born out of wedlock lost the right of paternal support. Abortion, which had been legalized in the 1920s, while at first only discouraged, was criminalized in 1936 under Stalin's regime.[40]

In a similar manner in Iran, when Ayatollah Khomeini instituted his fundamentalist Islamic regime in 1979, one of his first acts was to repeal family laws that had given women a modicum of rights. He reinstituted rigid male control over women in both the family and state and proclaimed the *chador*, the head-to-toe covering for women, to be the flag of his Islamic revolution.[41]

The Distortion of Sexuality

As we have glimpsed, the control of females by males in domination systems directly affects the construction of sexuality. Women's sexuality is repressed, while men generally have greater sexual freedom. For instance, in Nazi Germany, men were hardly forbidden sex. In fact, shortly before the Nazis' defeat, as a spur to his troops' flagging morale, Hitler promised that, like men in traditional Muslim societies or in more recent regimes such as the so-called Islamic Caliphate, decorated war heroes would be legally allowed to marry more than one woman.[42]

Similarly, in fundamentalist Iran—despite capital punishment for "immorality" such as homosexuality and prostitution—men also have a great deal of sexual freedom within religiously sanctioned limits. After the mullahs took control, for example, they institutionalized what they called "temporary marriage"—in essence, a religiously administered sexual trade in women to take the place of the prostitutes the mullahs executed when they closed the Iranian brothels.[43]

Likewise, the violent and repressive Samurai culture of Japan did not restrict male sexual freedom. As among the ancient Athenians, both heterosexual and homosexual relations were acceptable for Samurai warriors. But, as among the Greek warrior aristocracy, among the Samurai sexual relations between males were only considered proper if they were between *un*equals. The older warrior took the masculine role, and a young boy took the subordinate role that would otherwise be assigned to the woman.[44]

In other words, sexuality in domination societies is molded to fit the mandate that one person dominates and the other is dominated. So male sexuality, too, is distorted in domination systems.

Domination systems inculcate in males the belief that they are entitled to sex. The mass shootings of women in the United States and Canada by men who call themselves incel (involuntarily celibate) are a particularly violent manifestation of this belief.[45] But it is openly espoused by other men's groups, including not only some "alt right" organizations but also more mainstream ones, such as some college fraternities. For example, the Delta Kappa Epsilon fraternity at Yale University was suspended when a video of pledges chanting "No means yes! Yes means anal!" went viral; a Sigma Chi fraternity member at the College of William and Mary urged men to zero-in on women's vaginas and disregard "the 99% of horrendously illogical bullshit that makes up the modern woman"; and an email by the Kappa Alpha fraternity at the University of Richmond urged members to prepare for the "type of night that makes fathers afraid to send their daughters away to school."[46] This is the "aggrieved entitlement" afflicting some men today, expressed on a variety of websites on the so-called manosphere. Such attitudes are challenged by the MeToo movement when it exposes prominent men in politics, business, and other areas for dehumanizing women and assaulting them when they failed to comply with their sense of sexual entitlement.[47]

But while men in domination systems may gain a sense of power from their feelings of sexual entitlement, they, too, suffer from this system's construction—and constriction—of sexuality. When they are unable to exercise this power, they feel deprived of their identity as "real men," with its mandate that men demonstrate their dominance over women through sex. Male sexuality can also become disconnected from emotion, devoid of intimacy, and, as we will see, linked with violence. Indeed, it can become an obsessive sexuality where, as Kamel Daoud points out in *The New York Times*, there is so much focus on women's sexuality and the "need" of men to control it, that it becomes a torment, not only for women but also for men:

> One of the great miseries plaguing much of the so-called Arab world, and the Muslim world more generally, is its sick relationship with women. In some places, women are veiled, stoned and killed; at a minimum, they are blamed for sowing disorder in the ideal society. . . . Women are seen as a source of destabilization—short skirts trigger earthquakes, some say—and are respected only when defined by a property relationship, as the wife of X or the daughter of Y.[48]

Daoud goes on to observe how horribly pathological this distorted male sexuality can become: "Paradise and its virgins are a pet topic of preachers, who present these otherworldly delights as rewards to those who dwell in the lands of sexual misery. Dreaming about such prospects, suicide bombers surrender to a terrifying, surrealistic logic: The path to orgasm runs through death, not love."[49] This passage shows how the distortion of both male and female sexuality on "moral" grounds can be used by fundamentalist religious leaders to maintain rankings of domination in all relations—whether they are intimate or international.

Another way that fundamentalist leaders—whether Muslim or Christian—use sexuality to make domination seem moral is through their fierce opposition to reproductive freedom for women. This not only denies women autonomy over their own bodies but also justifies top-down control on the most basic bodily level. Denying women reproductive freedom is part of a larger fundamentalist political agenda to maintain, or in some cases to force return to, domination systems where *both* the male head of household and the male head of state have unquestioned control.

The previous examples show why, to effectively change political patterns of domination, we must go beyond analyses of the political sphere. To address fully Erich Fromm's question of why human beings by the millions, even in our supposedly emancipated age, seem to have "a yearning for submission" requires a systemic perspective.

Authoritarian families—where fear, violence, and the threat of pain impose and maintain domination—prepare people to fit into an authoritarian and violent social system, which mirrors the relationships within the family. And an authoritarian family structure parallels a cultural construction of sexuality that is built around coercion, control, and sometimes violence, rather than equality, respect, openness, tenderness, and love.

The Erotization of Violence and the Deadening of Empathy

In *Sacred Pleasure*, Riane introduces the term "erotization of violence" to describe how linking sex with violence serves to maintain male dominance and to impose and maintain a system based on rankings of domination. Like the confluence of caring with coercion in childhood relations, the constant linking of sexual arousal with violence conditions people to accept, and even be aroused by, violence. In addition, the linking of sex with violence serves to deaden or at least compartmentalize our human capacity for empathy.

As Frans de Waal documents in his book *The Age of Empathy*, the capacity to feel with or empathize with another is innate to both males and females.[50] As we saw in Chapters 2 and 3, along with our capacity to care for others, empathy has deep evolutionary roots.

While the biological mechanisms for empathy are still not clear, we have some interesting clues. One such clue came out of the discovery of what scientists call mirror neurons. This discovery came about accidentally, when scientists studying pig-tailed macaque monkeys were surprised to find that the same brain neuron activated when the monkey picked up a piece of food as when the experimenter picked up the food.[51]

Whether particular neurons perform the same function in the human brain is still a subject of controversy because the intrusive experiments done on monkeys are not permitted on humans. What we do know is that the vast majority of us are capable of putting ourselves in someone else's shoes. We also know that this capacity for identifying with others leads to a kind of emotional contagion where we feel what someone else is feeling, whether it is in real life or through books, films, and art.[52]

But whether this capacity for empathic identification with others is or is not expressed is another matter. As we have seen, domination systems block or at least compartmentalize this human capacity—and the erotization of violence is an effective way of doing so.

For instance, clinical experiments show that men who watch violent pornography are less likely to see rape as hurtful to women.[53] Daniel Linz, Edward Donnerstein, and Steven Penrod found that men exposed to only five X-rated movies linking sex and violence "came to have fewer negative emotional reactions to the films, to perceive them as significantly less violent, and to consider them significantly less degrading to women."[54]

We should add that pornography linking sex and violence is hardly new. For instance, Church-commissioned etchings of priests cutting off women's breasts to make them confess to being witches are grotesquely similar to some of the sadomasochistic pornography of our time.[55]

Of course, pornography is not the only way sex and violence have been culturally linked. We find this in a plethora of stories and images, from classical paintings of rapes (Lucrecia, Europa, and so on) to much of today's mass entertainment, including popular video games and action films. All this makes male violence not only acceptable but also sexually arousing.[56]

Psychologist Leonard Berkowitz describes this dynamic in his "stimulus-response association model"—a variation of the famous Pavlov findings that when dogs are conditioned to associate food with a ringing bell they will salivate when there is no food, just in response to the sound of the bell.[57] In addition, the research of Albert Bandura and Frances Menlove on modeling suggests an interactive, mutually reinforcing process where conditioning men to link sex with violence predisposes them to violence.[58]

This is by no means to say that everyone exposed to this conditioning will respond this way. But particularly for those men already predisposed to violence, the repeated cultural association of sexual pleasure with violence and cruelty will make it more difficult to overcome such tendencies.[59] As psychologist Barbara Krahé points out, violence against women must be viewed from a cultural/historical perspective that includes factors such as values, sex roles, and social structure.[60]

Maintenance of a domination system does not require that all men be violent. Just as in authoritarian regimes, relatively few men have to terrorize people to maintain their subordination; maintaining male dominance only requires that a certain number of men be violent against women. In both cases, it is enough to have intermittent violence to terrorize subordinate groups and thus effectively control attempts to change the status quo.

However, as we will examine in the next chapter, domination systems lead to a male identity that is equated with domination and violence. This is the case for a myriad of reasons, including the chronic warfare that is a hallmark of these systems.

The constant idealization and eroticization of male violence in video games is particularly revealing in this regard. As Lt. Col. Dave Grossman and Gloria DeGaetano point out in *Stop Teaching Our Kids to Kill: A Call to Action against TV, Movie and Video Game Violence*, these video games have been effectively used by the military to train men to kill.[61]

Already in 1978, William Arken and Lynne Dobrofsky published a study of American boot camp training that documents how linking sex and violence has long been used by the military to condition men to overcome what seems to be an innate human reluctance to kill. They reported that "the relationships of masculinity and violence, and masculinity and sex dominate formal as well as informal military socialization patterns." As they write, basic training not only trained men to be combatants in war; it also trained them to be combatants in the war of the sexes: "military discipline simultaneously embarrassed and reminded the recruit of his penis-as-power link."[62]

There have been changes in US boot camp training since the end of the draft and the increasing entry of women into the armed forces. But the headlines about rampant rape and sexual harassment in US forces indicate that a military culture that links war and the war of the sexes is still strong. US Congresswoman Jackie Speier calls attention to the disgraceful fact that "Women in the U.S. military are more likely to be raped by fellow soldiers than killed by enemy fire."[63] Additionally, the family members of returning male US combat veterans also are at increased risk of domestic abuse, including lethal violence.[64]

Of course, military training does not always successfully socialize men to be active combatants in the "war of the sexes"—or in war. But there's little question that military training reinforces the message that "real" men despise and suppress in themselves anything associated with what they are taught is "soft" or feminine—that is, feelings of empathy and caring.

When women are allowed into the armed forces, they, too, are trained to suppress "soft" feelings, again showing that what we are dealing with is *not* something inherent in men. As shown in the infamous Abu Ghraib photos of US guards and Iraqi prisoners, these women sometimes prove themselves "one of the boys" through the sexual humiliation and torture of helpless naked men.

It is men, however, who have systematically been trained to equate sex with coercion, conquest, and killing. While not all men are equally susceptible to this training, judging by the studies we just considered, even where the constant erotization of violence does not lead to violent behavior, it still deadens empathy. And so does the barrage of "action entertainment" that floods our airwaves, computers, smart phones, and homes with displays of violence and cruelty.

Such public displays of violence and cruelty are improvements, relatively speaking, over the brutal spectacles of public torture common in earlier, more rigid domination times, such as the ancient Roman circuses where gladiators fought to the death and people were fed to wild beasts for public entertainment. Even after the Middle Ages, public drawings and quartering, witch burnings, and other barbarities continued in the West, and it was not until after the 18th century Enlightenment that these displays of sadistic cruelty and horrible suffering were officially ended.

Unfortunately, there are still places where public displays of cruelty continue. In Saudi Arabia, for example, people watch public beheadings as well as amputations of hands for theft—practices that were also found in the West in earlier, more domination-oriented times. And it is not only in Saudi Arabia but also in other fundamentalist Muslim cultures that women suspected of sexual independence are slowly pelted with stones to suffer an excruciatingly painful death—sometimes in football stadiums where thousands of people watch.[65]

These exhibitions of horrendous cruelty serve the double purpose of terrorizing women and deadening empathy in both men and women. The effects of observing such brutality are not only cognitive and emotional but also neural. Not coincidentally, these Muslim fundamentalist regimes are also cultures that put enormous emphasis on policies that maintain or reinstate domination parent-child and male-female relations. So the link between normalizing relations based on the inflicting and suffering of bodily pain and fear- and force-based theocratic authoritarian regimes is implicitly recognized by the men who rule in these cultures.

It is time that those of us who want to leave the barbarities of our past behind also recognize these connections. As we will see in the next chapters, addressing these connections is essential if we are to have the foundation that supports respect for human rights and dignity in all relations.[66] But first, Box 9.1 explores how social media and other modern technologies pose further challenges to our human need for caring connection.

Box 9.1 The Impact of Digital Media on Touch, Intimacy, Sexuality—and More

Today, we face new developments that interfere with the caring connections we humans so want and need: digital media as a substitute for the touch and face-to-face contact that our species has relied on for millennia. This is particularly troubling in light of findings that teenagers use an average of nine hours of digital media per day and slightly younger "tweens" use an average of six hours per day.[67]

Already in 2011 the American Academy of Pediatrics issued a warning about the potential negative effects on children and teens of social media.[68] They point to sexting, cyberbullying, and other ways social media injure young people, tragically leading some youth to suicide. But even without such malicious uses, the Academy's warning notes that posts typically present a happy front so as to get more likes, with the result that viewers, especially teens who so heavily depend on peer approval, report feelings of inferiority, unhappiness, and low self-esteem.[69]

A large study of eighth-graders by Jean Twenge, author of iGen, found that heavy social media users, whom Twenge defines as spending three or more hours on social media, are 56 percent more likely to say they are unhappy, 27 percent more likely to be depressed, and 35 percent more likely to have a risk factor for suicide than those who use social media less.[70]

One study found that the more young people used Facebook, the worse they felt. The researchers text-messaged the subjects of this study five times per day for two weeks to examine how they were feeling moment to moment and how satisfied they were with their lives. The researchers discovered that the individuals who had used Facebook in the interval before the text reported feeling worse than others; additionally, the more a person used Facebook over the two-week study, the more that person's life satisfaction levels declined.[71] That frequent use of social media such as Facebook has negative effects is confirmed by studies showing that it tends to result in invidious comparisons, jealousy, and envy, which in turn lead to feelings of loneliness and depression.[72]

So rather than providing the caring connections that feel good, frequent social media use often actually contributes to a person feeling bad.

Or, as the authors of this study put it, "On the surface, Facebook provides an invaluable resource for fulfilling the basic human need for social connection. Rather than enhancing well-being, however, these findings suggest that Facebook may undermine it."[73]

This is not to say that digital technologies have no positive effects. They provide amazing ways of reaching people thousands of miles away, of exploring nature, raising ecological consciousness, and valuing different cultures and peoples. We can connect with one another by audio and video so that we can see each other even in another continent, build our own websites, and send messages in seconds that would take days if they were sent by letter. Digital media also provide access to huge amounts of information instantaneously, making it possible, for example, to do research online by just entering a key phrase—and getting results much more quickly than by going to libraries, finding the right books, and poring through reams of journals for relevant articles.

However, evaluating this information is another matter, especially for children and teens because their critical faculties have yet to be developed, but also to varying degrees for adults, as illustrated by the disinformation circulated and believed by so many in the United States during the 2016 election. Indeed, there is evidence that dependence on social media interferes with the ability to evaluate information not only because of information overload but also because this medium tends to distract and shorten attention spans, and hence cognitive capacities.

Many people, including teens and children, use their smartphones to avoid boredom, reading fewer books and instead turning to video games, social media, and texting. This can lead to an almost constant state of distraction, which, in addition to interfering with meaningful relationships, affects their ability to maintain attention and to concentrate deeply.

In 2017, 10 prominent researchers published an article in *Pediatrics* examining studies over the last 20 years on the relationship between multitasking and performance. They found that while some early studies indicated no or even positive effects on the cognitive performance of children and young adults, later studies show the opposite. A growing body of evidence demonstrates that heavy media multitaskers (MMTs), compared with lighter media multitaskers (LMTs), show differences in cognition (e.g., poorer memory), psychosocial behavior (e.g., increased impulsivity), and neural structure (e.g., reduced volume in the anterior cingulate cortex). The study in *Pediatrics* considers the issue of how multitasking with media during learning (in class or at home) can negatively affect academic outcomes. For example, college students learn less when dividing attention between listening to lectures and interacting with handheld devices. And just as MMT disrupts learning in a classroom setting, MMT and background media disrupt learning while doing homework.[74]

The researchers were careful to note that whether differences in underlying neural and cognitive traits lead to differing levels of MMT or vice versa is not yet clear. However, they emphasized the urgent need for further study, given that American youth spend an average of 7.5 hours per day every day on media (more time than any other activity); 29% of that time is spent juggling multiple media streams simultaneously; half of five- to eight-year-olds engage in MMT at least occasionally; even younger children spend two hours per day with screen media; and all this is not just an American phenomenon but one found in nations around the globe.[75]

Studies focused on the effects of cell phones even show that their mere presence can lead to reduced attention spans and poor performance, especially on tasks that require greater attention and cognitive abilities.[76] The mere possession of a cell phone also interferes with the quality of face-to-face interactions.[77]

But perhaps the most troublesome aspect of social media has been its addictive nature. According to a 2016 Common Sense report on technology addiction, in the United States half of teens feel addicted to their mobile devices, and the majority of parents (60 percent) feel their kids are addicted.[78] This should not surprise us because "likes" and other positive social media responses deliver bursts of dopamine, which as we have seen, is a neurotransmitter that provides sensations of pleasure, creating the same addictive loop responsible as other addictions, from cocaine to gambling.

In short, digital media affect cognitive function, the quality of face-to-face relationships, and even the neural networks of our brain. Moreover, and this seems not to have been studied to date, social media such as Facebook, Instagram, Snapchat, and texting are greatly reducing the actual time people, especially teenagers, spend together, which is probably a big factor in the loneliness and lack of satisfaction found in heavy digital media users.

Texting and other social media are increasingly a substitute for the touch and face-to-face contact that our species has relied on for millennia, and today's digital media also flood us with images of uncaring and violent touch through action entertainment, online pornography, and brutal video games.

As we have glimpsed and will further detail later, male socialization in domination systems relies heavily on the normalization, erotization, and idealization of violence. So the violence in social media entertainment and video games is not new. What is new is the extent to which this violence saturates this medium, its open access to children and teens, and its graphic and detailed portrayal of violence, including clips of school shootings and other real-life massacres.

Not only is all this exposure to violence desensitizing; many studies show that there is a link between media violence and increased aggression and violence, and this is also now being seen in girls.[79] Violent pornography may desensitize men to the violence of rape, and more generally public exhibitions of cruelty have dampened empathy throughout domination history. The same kinds of video games that are flooding young people's brains have been used by the military to condition soldiers to kill.[80]

On top of this are problems such as the hypersexualization of media content, the loss of privacy due to commercial data mining on the Internet and social media, identity theft, and malicious bots spreading false information. For example, a 2017 Australian study found that among 16-and 17-year-olds, three fourths of boys and one tenth of girls have watched an X-rated movie; three fourths were exposed accidentally to pornographic websites, and 38 percent of boys and two percent of girls deliberately accessed them.[81]

Moreover, with robotics (including sex dolls), artificial intelligence, and virtual reality already seeping into our lives, the problems being created through digital technologies will further accelerate in the very near future.

This takes us back to the larger issue of whether a culture orients to the domination or partnership side of the social scale, and what this means for all aspects of our lives. From this perspective, we can see that technological breakthroughs in themselves are not the problem, but rather how they are applied and how this in turn affects us. Will they continue to be used largely to distract, normalize violence, and dampen empathy, maintaining domination systems? Or will they be used mainly to foster consciousness, caring, and creativity, as well as truly satisfying interactions and connections?

Fortunately, there is growing awareness of the need for changes in digital media and for an ethic that ensures that digital breakthroughs do not result in commercial products that are harmful to us and to our children. For example, shareholders in Apple have urged the company to develop solutions for the "unintentional negative consequences" of iPhone use among kids, and a major Facebook investor has pressed the company to study its potential financial exposure for the platform's mental health consequences. A number of ex-Silicon company employees have founded the Center for Humane Technology, with the mission of pushing the digital industry toward "technology that protects our minds and replenishes society."[82]

These are manifestations of the trend toward corporate responsibility, which is part of the movement toward a partnership social and economic consciousness. However, real change, as we will address in the last chapter of this book, requires that we leave behind traditions of domination still embedded in our institutions, practices, and policies, including our economic structures and policies.

Notes

1. Ashley Montagu, *Touching* (New York: Columbia University Press, 1971).
2. Dacher Keltner, "The Compassionate Instinct," *Greater Good* (Spring 2004). Available online: http://greatergood.berkeley.edu/article/item/the_compassionate_instinct/.
3. Matthew J. Hertenstein et al., "Touch Communicates Distinct Emotions," *Emotion* 6 (2006): 528–533, doi: 10.1037/1528-3542.6.3.528.
4. See, e.g., Rollin McCraty, Mike Atkinson, and Raymond Trevor Bradley, "Electrophysiological Evidence of Intuition: Part 1, The Surprising Role of the Heart," *Journal of Alternative and Complementary Medicine* 10 (2004): 133–143, doi: 10.1089/107555304322849057.
5. Kenneth Wesson, "Memory and the Brain," *Independent Schools* 63 (2002): 89.
6. See, e.g., Kerstin Uvnas-Moberg and Maria Petersson, "Oxytocin, a Mediator of Anti-Stress, Well-Being, Social Interaction, Growth and Healing," *Zeitschrift fur*

Psychosomatische Medizin und Psychotherapie 51 (2005): 57–80, Retrieved in English from   https://pdfs.semanticscholar.org/0ac8/c14228b62b9c87636f5b6eb536a434 fd04de.pdf; C. Sue Carter, "Neuroendocrine Perspectives on Social Attachment and Love," *Psychoneuroendocrinology* 23 (1998): 779–818, doi: 10.1016/S0306-4530(98)00055-9; C. Sue Carter, "The Oxytocin-Vasopressin Pathway in the Context of Love and Fear," *Frontiers in Endocrinology* 8 (2017): article 356, doi: 10.3389/ Fendo.2017.00356; Darcia Narvaez, *Neurobiology and the Development of Human Morality: Evolution, Culture, and Wisdom* (New York: Norton, 2014).

7. Bruce D. Perry et al., "Childhood Trauma, the Neurobiology of Adaptation, and 'Use-Dependent' Development of the Brain: How 'States' become 'Traits,'" *Infant Mental Health Journal* 16 (1995): 271–291, doi: 10.1002/1097-0355(199524)16:4<271.

8. Montagu, *Touching*.

9. C. Fred Blake, "Foot-Binding in Neo-Confucian China and the Appropriation of Female Labor," *Signs* 19 (1994): 676–712, doi: 10.1086/494917.

10. Blake, "Foot-Binding in Neo-Confucian China," 682.

11. Riane Eisler, "Can International Law Protect Half of Humanity? A New Strategy to Stop Violence against Women," *Journal of Aggression, Conflict, and Peace Research* 7 (2015): 88–100, doi: 10.1108/JACPR-12-2013-0036.

12. Robyn Bluhm and Ruth Lanius, "Importance of the Developmental Perspective in Evolutionary Discussions of Post-Traumatic Stress Disorder," in *Ancestral Landscapes in Human Evolution*, eds. Darcia Narvaez et al. (New York: Oxford University Press, 2014); Darcia Narvaez, *Neurobiology and the Development of Human Morality*.

13. Riane Eisler, "Protecting the Majority of Humanity: Toward an Integrated Approach to Crimes against Present and Future Generations," in *Sustainable Development, International Criminal Justice, and Treaty Implementation*, eds. Marie-Claire Cordonier Segger and Sébastien Jodoin (Cambridge, UK: Cambridge University Press, 2013).

14. Emily Cuddy and Richard Reeves, "Report: Hitting Kids: American Parenting and Physical Punishment," *Brookings Institution*, last modified November 6, 2014. Available online: https://www.brookings.edu/research/hitting-kids-american-parenting-and-physical-punishment/. See also Eisler, "Protecting the Majority of Humanity"; Riane Eisler, "Protecting Children: From Rhetoric to Global Action," *Interdisciplinary Journal of Partnership Studies* 5 (2018): doi: 10.24926/ijps.v5i1.1125. Available at: https://pubs.lib.umn.edu/index.php/ijps/article/view/1125/1070.

15. John B. Watson and Rosalie Rayner, "Conditioned Emotional Reactions," *Journal of Experimental Psychology* 3 (1920): 1–14, doi: 10.1037/h0069608.

16. See, e.g., Hanna Rosin, "A Tough Plan for Raising Children Draws Fire: 'Babywise' Guides Worry Pediatricians and Others," *Washington Post*, last modified February 27, 1999, A01. Available online: https://www.highbeam.com/doc/1P2-571764. html, for a harrowing account of the damage done to children and parents by this approach.

17. See Riane Eisler, *Sacred Pleasure: Sex, Myth, and the Politics of the Body* (San Francisco: Harper Collins, 1995), for an in-depth discussion.

18. Erich Fromm, *Escape from Freedom* (New York: Macmillan, 1994).

19. Fromm, *Escape from Freedom*.
20. Riane Eisler, *The Real Wealth of Nations: Creating a Caring Economics* (San Francisco: Berrett-Koehler, 2007).
21. Montagu, *Touching*, 188.
22. William Masters, Virginia Johnson, and Robert Levin, *The Pleasure Bond: A New Look at Sexuality and Commitment* (Boston: Little, Brown, 1975).
23. Eisler, *Sacred Pleasure*.
24. Eisler, *Sacred Pleasure*.
25. Elaine H. Pagels, *Adam, Eve, and the Serpent* (New York: Vintage, 1988), 113.
26. St. Augustine, *City of God*, Book XIII, Chapter 14. Augustine's view held sway for a long time in the Catholic Church but is strongly criticized today, for example, in the writings of Matthew Fox.
27. Augustine wrote: "God, the author of all natures but not of their defects, created man good; but man, corrupt by choice and condemned by justice, has produced a progeny that is both corrupt and condemned. For, we all existed in that one man, since, taken together, we were the one man who fell into sin through the woman who was made out of him before sin existed. Although the specific form by which each of us was to live was not yet created and assigned, our nature was already present in the seed [semen] from which we were to spring. And because this nature has been soiled by sin and doomed to death and justly condemned, no man was to be born of man in any other condition." St. Augustine, *City of God*, Book XIII, Chapter 14.
28. Jamake Highwater, *Myth and Sexuality* (New York: Meridian/Penguin Books, 1990).
29. Jakob Sprenger, *The Malleus Maleficarum of Heinrich Kramer and James Sprenger* (New York: Dover, 1971).
30. Highwater, *Myth and Sexuality*, 95.
31. Uta Ranke-Heinemann, *Eunuchs for the Kingdom of Heaven: Women, Sexuality and the Catholic Church*, trans. Peter Heinegg (New York: Doubleday, 1990), 154.
32. Richard Lewinsohn, *A History of Sexual Customs*, trans. Alexander Mayce (New York: Fawcett, 1958), 133–134.
33. Fromm, *Escape from Freedom*.
34. For an analysis showing the similarities between religious theocracies and secular totalitarian states, including the idealization of supreme leaders, see Riane Eisler, *The Chalice and the Blade: Our History, Our Future* (San Francisco: Harper and Row, 1987).
35. Will Durant, *The Life of Greece* (New York: Simon and Schuster, 1966), 74.
36. Joseph Reese Strayer, *The Albigensian Crusades* (Ann Arbor: University of Michigan Press, 1992).
37. William L. Shirer, *The Rise and Fall of the Third Reich* (New York: Simon and Schuster, 1960).
38. Albury Castell, *An Introduction to Modern Philosophy* (New York: Macmillan, 1946).
39. Claudia Koonz, "Mothers in the Fatherland: Women in Nazi Germany," in *Becoming Visible: Women in European History*, eds. Renate Bridenthal and Claudia Koonz (Boston: Houghton Mifflin, 1977).
40. Sheila Robotham, *Women, Resistance, and Revolution* (New York: Vintage, 1974).

41. See, e.g., Elaine Sciolino, "Daughter of the Revolution Fights the Veil," *New York Times*, last modified April 2, 2003, accessed March 24, 2018. Available online: http://www.nytimes.com/2003/04/02/world/daughter-of-the-revolution-fights-the-veil.html.

42. Koonz, "Mothers in the Fatherland."

43. See, e.g., *Report on Child Brides under the Mullahs Rule in Iran*, National Council of Resistance of Iran (NCRI), Women's Committee 2015. Available online: http://women.ncr-iran.org/images/documents/child-brides-Iran-en.pdf, documenting how the brides in these "temporary marriages" that can last just an hour according to Iranian law are often children forced to marry by their families, and the Ayatollah Khomeini actually wrote, "A man is not permitted to have intercourse with his wife if she is under the age of nine but any other act such as touching out of lust and hugging are permitted even if the wife is an infant," in his book *Tahrir al Wasilah*.

44. Saikaku Ihara, *The Great Mirror of Male Love,* trans. Paul Schalow (Stanford, CA: Stanford University Press, 1990). Ihara highlights the contempt for women that was key to this practice. See also Eva Keuls, *The Reign of the Phallus: Sexual Politics in Ancient Athens* (Berkeley: University of California Press, 1993).

45. See, e.g., Gianluca Mezzofiore, "The Toronto Suspect Apparently Posted about an 'Incel Rebellion.' Here's What that Means." *CNN*, April 25, 2018. Available online: https://www.cnn.com/2018/04/25/us/incel-rebellion-alek-minassian-toronto-attack-trnd/index.html.

46. Libby Allnat, "Entitlement Leads to Sexual Assault," *State Press*, October 2, 2016. Available online: http://www.statepress.com/article/2016/10/spopinion-entitlement-and-sexual-assualt.

47. See, e.g., Michael Kimmel, *Angry White Men: American Masculinity at the End of an Era* (New York: Nation Books, 2013); Pardis Mahdavi, "How #MeToo Became a Global Movement," *Foreign Affairs,* March 6, 2018. Available online: https://www.foreignaffairs.com/articles/2018-03-06/how-metoo-became-global-movement.

48. Kamel Daoud, "The Sexual Misery of the Arab World," *New York Times*, accessed March 24, 2018. Available online: http://www.nytimes.com/2016/02/14/opinion/sunday/the-sexual-misery-of-the-arab-world.html?_r=0.

49. Daoud, "The Sexual Misery."

50. Frans de Waal, *The Age of Empathy: Nature's Lessons for a Kinder Society* (New York: Random House, 2009).

51. Giusseppe Di Pellegrino et al., "Understanding Motor Events: A Neurophysiological Study," *Experimental Brain Research* 91 (1992): 176–180, doi: 10.1007/BF00230027; Giacomo Rizzolatti et al., "Premotor Cortex and the Recognition of Motor Actions," *Cognitive Brain Research* 3 (1996): 131–141, doi: 10.1016/0926-6410(95)00038-0.

52. We say the vast majority of us have the capacity for empathy because some have what is known as empathy deficits; for example, autistic children seem to have a great deal of difficulty identifying with others. See, e.g., Frans de Waal, *The Bonobo and the Atheist: In Search of Humanism among the Primates* (New York: Norton, 2013), 138.

53. See, e.g., Seymour Feschbach and Bernard Malamuth, "Sex and Aggression: Proving the Link," *Psychology Today*, November 1978, 111, 116; Edward Donnerstein,

"Aggressive Erotica and Violence against Women," *Journal of Personality and Social Psychology* 39 (1980): 269–277, doi: 10.1037/0022-3514.39.2.269.

54. Daniel Linz, Edward Donnerstein, and Steven Penrod, "The Effects of Multiple Exposures to Filmed Violence against Women," *Journal of Communication* 34 (1984): 130–147, 130, doi: 10.1111/j.1460-2466.1984.tb02180.x. For a critical review see also Christopher Ferguson and Richard Hartley, "The Pleasure Is Momentary . . . The Expense Damnable? The Influence of Pornography on Rape and Sexual Assault," *Aggression and Violent Behavior* 14 (2009): 323–329, doi: 10.1016/j.avb.2009.04.008. Research suggests that no single causal variable lies behind sex-linked aggression but rather that multiple causal factors interact in the etiology of sexual violence, including "psychological factors, developmental experiences such as childhood sexual abuse, environmental factors and genetic and organic factors such as pre-natal neurodevelopment and neurocognitive impairment." (Kerensa Hocken and Neil Gredecki, "Thinking Outside of the Box: Advancements in Theory, Practice, and Evaluation in Sexual Offending Interventions," in *The Routledge International Handbook of Human Aggression: Current Issues and Perspectives*, eds. Jane L. Ireland, Philip Birch, and Carol A. Ireland (New York: Routledge, 2018).)

55. Margaret R. Miles, *Carnal Knowing: Female Nakedness and Religious Meaning in the Christian West* (Boston: Beacon Press, 1989).

56. Eisler, *Sacred Pleasure.*

57. Leonard Berkowitz, "Some Determinants of Impulsive Aggression: Role of Mediated Associations with Reinforcements for Aggression," *Psychological Review* 81 (1974): 165–176, doi: 10.1037/h0036094.

58. Albert Bandura and Frances Menlove, "Factors Determining Vicarious Extinction of Avoidance Behavior through Symbolic Modeling," *Journal of Personality and Social Psychology* 8 (1968): 99–108, doi: 10.1037/h0025260.

59. L. Rowell Huesmann, "An Integrative Theoretical Understanding of Aggression," in *Aggression and Violence: A Social Psychological Perspective*, ed. Brad Bushman (New York: Routledge, 2017).

60. Barbara Krahé, "Violence against Women," in *Aggression and Violence: A Social Psychological Perspective*, ed. Brad Bushman (New York: Routledge, 2017). The author points out that harm inflicted on women by men was considered the legitimate exercise of the right to domination and control.

61. Dave Grossman and Gloria DeGaetano, *Stop Teaching Our Kids to Kill: A Call to Action against TV, Movie and Video Game Violence* (New York: Crown Publishers, 1999).

62. William Arkin and Lynne Dobrofsky, "Military Socialization and Masculinity," *Journal of Social Issues* 34 (1978): 161, doi: 10.1111/j.1540-4560.1978.tb02546.x.

63. Jackie Speier, "Rapes of Women in Military 'a National Disgrace,'" *SF Gate,* last modified April 16, 2011. Available online: https://www.sfgate.com/opinion/article/Rapes-of-women-in-military-a-national-disgrace-2374845.php.

64. See, e.g., Stacy Bannerman, "High Risk of Military Domestic Violence on the Home Front," *SF Gate,* last modified April 7, 2014. Available online: http://www.sfgate.com/opinion/article/High-risk-of-military-domestic-violence-on-the-5377562.

php; Stacy Bannerman, "PTSD and Domestic Abuse: Husbands Who Bring the War Home," *Daily Beast*, last modified September 25, 2010. Available online: http://www.thedailybeast.com/articles/2010/09/25/ptsd-and-domestic-abuse-husbands-who-bring-the-war-home.html.

65. See, e.g., Farshad Hoseini, *List of Known Cases of Stoning to Death in Iran (1980-2010)*, accessed March 24, 2018. Available online: http://stopstonningnow.com/wpress/SList%20_1980-2010__FHdoc.pdf; Mike Wooldridge, "Iran's Grim History of Death by Stoning," *BBC News*, last modified July 9, 2010. Available online: http://www.bbc.com/news/10579121. For photos of stoning women to death from stadiums in Middle Eastern, Southeast Asian, and African nations, see https://www.google.com/search?q=stoning+women+in+football+stadium&biw=1363&bih=698&tbm=isch&tbo=u&source=univ&sa=X&ved=0ahUKEwje08e36I3QAhXpv1QKHVRaBZ8QsAQIMQ.

66. For more on this topic, see Riane Eisler, *The Power of Partnership* (Novato, CA: New World Library, 2002).

67. Vicky Rideout, *The Common Sense Census: Media Use by Tweens and Teens* (San Francisco: Common Sense Media, 2015). Available online: https://www.commonsensemedia.org/sites/default/files/uploads/research/census_researchreport.pdf.

68. Gwenn Schurgin O'Keeffe and Kathleen Clarke-Pearson, "The Impact of Social Media on Children, Adolescents, and Families," *Pediatrics* 127 (2011): 800–804, doi: 10.1542/peds.2011-0054.

69. O'Keeffe and Clarke-Pearson, "The Impact of Social Media on Children, Adolescents, and Families."

70. Jean M. Twenge, *iGen: Why Today's Super-Connected Kids Are Growing Up Less Rebellious, More Tolerant, Less Happy—and Completely Unprepared for Adulthood—and What That Means for the Rest of Us* (New York: Atria Books, 2017).

71. Ethan Kross et al., "Facebook Use Predicts Declines in Subjective Well-Being in Young Adults," *PLoS ONE* 8, 8 (2013): e69841, doi: 10.1371/journal.pone.0069841.

72. Christina Sagioglou and Tobias Greitemeyer, "Facebook's Emotional Consequences: Why Facebook Causes a Decrease in Mood and Why People Still Use It," *Computers in Human Behavior* 35 (2014): 359–363, doi: 10.1016/j.chb.2014.03.003; Edson C. Tandoc Jr., Patrick Ferrucci, and Margaret Duff, "Facebook Use, Envy, and Depression among College Students: Is Facebooking Depressing?" *Computers in Human Behavior* 43 (2015): 139–146, doi: 10.1016/j.chb.2014.10.053.

73. Kross et al., "Facebook Use Predicts Declines in Subjective Well-Being in Young Adults."

74. Melina R. Uncapher et al., "Media Multitasking and Cognitive, Psychological, Neural, and Learning Differences," *Pediatrics* 140 (2017): S62–S66, doi: 10.1542/peds.2016-1758D.

75. Uncapher et al., "Media Multitasking and Cognitive, Psychological, Neural, and Learning Differences."

76. Cary Stothart, Ainsley Mitchum, and Courtney Yehnert, "The Attentional Cost of Receiving a Cell Phone Notification," *Journal of Experimental Psychology* 41 (2015): 893–897, doi: 10.1037/xhp0000100; Adrian F. Ward et al., "Brain Drain: The Mere Presence of One's Own Smartphone Reduces Available Cognitive Capacity," *Journal of the Association for Consumer Research* 2 (2017): 140–154, doi: 10.1086/691462.

77. Andrew K. Przybylski and Netta Weinstein, "Can You Connect with Me Now? Showing Interference with Face-to-Face Contacts of Mere Presence of a Cell Phone," *Journal of Social and Personal Relationships* 30 (2012): 237–246, doi: 10.1177/0265407512453827.

78. Laurel J. Felt and Michael B. Robb, *Technology Addiction: Concern, Controversy, and Finding Balance* (San Francisco: Common Sense Media, 2016). Available online: https://www.commonsensemedia.org/sites/default/files/uploads/research/2016_csm_technology_addiction_executive_summary.pdf.

79. Barbara Krahe, "The Impact of Violent Media on Aggression," in *The Routledge International Handbook of Human Aggression: Current Issues and Perspectives*, eds. Jane L. Ireland, Philip Birch, and Carol A. Ireland (New York: Routledge, 2018), 319–330.

80. Dave Grossman and Gloria DeGaetano, *Stop Teaching Our Kids to Kill: A Call to Action against TV, Movie and Video Game Violence* (New York: Crown Publishers, 1999); Lt. Col. Dave Grossman, *On Killing: The Psychological Cost of Learning to Kill in War and Society* (New York: Little, Brown, 1995).

81. Michael Flood, "Exposure to Pornography among Youth in Australia," *Journal of Sociology* 43 (2017): 45–60, doi: 10.1177/1440783307073934. Available online: https://www.researchgate.net/publication/234028278_Exposure_to_Pornography_Among_Youth_in_Australia.

82. Todd Spangler, "Hooked on Hardware? Tech Giants Face Tough Questions over Device Addiction," *Variety*, accessed March 19, 2018. Available online: http://variety.com/2018/digital/features/smartphone-addiction-apps-apple-facebook-google-1202724489/.

10

Love, Violence, and
Socialization in Partnership and
Domination Environments

The mantra of Hollywood producers is that love stories only appeal to female audiences. To get males into theaters takes action entertainment, they say. So the big production dollars go to violent action films, not movies about love.

This devaluation of love as "feminine" also lies behind the fact that until recently scientists paid hardly any attention to the study of love. Even the new breed of systems scientists who began to emerge during the second part of the 20th century failed to include matters pertaining to the female half of our species in their supposedly inclusive analyses of social systems.[1] This constriction, distortion, and fragmentation of consciousness, based on the denial that women or topics pertaining to women are important, has been an obstacle to a true systems science.

The devaluation of half of humanity also holds for mass media; for example, in the disproportionate two-to-one ratio of male to female characters.[2] For instance, on the basis of a large-scale study that included 2.3 million articles from 950 news sources collected over a six-month period in 2016, Sen Jia and colleagues concluded that "the news media are still very much male-dominated, with an overall probability of 77.0 percent that an entity mentioned in the text is male, or 69.6 percent that a face image is male."[3] In both films and TV shows, women are still generally portrayed in gender-stereotypical ways and are cast in traditional sex roles, often in stories that normalize women as recipients of male violence.[4] As Julie Burton, head of the Women's Media Center, notes: "Inequality defines our media. Media tells us our roles in society—it tells us who we are and what we can be."[5]

And while today so-called "women's issues" are no longer shoved into a "women's section" of newspapers, they are not seen as meriting front-page coverage.

Yet, as we will explore in this chapter, leaving behind the devaluation of women and the "feminine" along with the stereotypical gender roles we inherited from more rigid domination times is key to cutting through the cycles of violence that do make the headlines.

Love and Mutuality

In *The Descent of Man,* Charles Darwin wrote 95 times of love. However, as evolutionary theorist David Loye notes, this was ignored in science for more than a century, and, even now, the indexes in many editions of this famous book list just a single entry for the word "love."[6] Not only has love been considered unimportant; as we saw in Chapter 3, most current evolutionary theories about love attribute it to selfishness in disguise.

Certainly, love is partly selfish. Being loved and loving make us feel good, so naturally we want to receive love as well as give it. Love can, therefore, be explained in part by self-centered motives. As psychologist Arthur Aron writes, love can be a way of "including others in the self."[7] But there is another aspect of love that philosophers, psychologists, and mystics have long identified: transcendence of self.

Love in a partnership context includes both these dynamics of inclusion and transcendence. One identifies with the loved one—with a child, a lover, a friend—thus including the other into one's sense of self. But because there is also empathy for the other, one also transcends the self in feeling what the other feels. So love can include placing the beloved's needs and welfare over one's own. Seeing the loved one happy and healthy in both body and spirit is a goal in itself.

In partnership-oriented cultures, where positive relations based on trust, respect, and mutual benefit are the norm, empathy can have freer rein. Empathy, as we saw in the last chapter, entails "feeling with the other." Empathy therefore makes it hard to impose and maintain top-down control through fear and punishment.

As we also have seen, humans are predisposed to empathic love—both to giving it and receiving it. Indeed, we receive powerful neurochemical rewards of pleasure for empathic love.[8] So the crucial issue is: What *conditions* support rather than inhibit the actualization of this human predisposition for empathy?

A study conducted at Emory University by anthropologist James Rilling and his colleagues shows that, given half a chance, the human capacity—indeed propensity—for empathy and mutuality will be expressed.[9] The Emory study used functional magnetic resonance imagery (fMRI) scans to monitor neural activity in young women playing a classic laboratory game called the Prisoner's Dilemma. The game gives players the choice of two different strategies to attain financial gain. In one strategy, the players can simply seek to win against another player. In the other strategy, they can choose mutual gain over merely winning.

The experimenters found, as Natalie Angier put it, that when the players chose mutualism over "me-ism," the mental circuitry associated with pleasurable neurochemical rewards came to life. The longer they chose mutual gain over winning, the more strongly the blood to the pathways of pleasure flowed.[10]

Specifically, choosing mutuality activated two brain areas rich in neurons responsive to dopamine. One was the anteroventral striatum, an area that includes the nucleus accumbens. This is sometimes called "the pleasure center" because experiments with rats have shown that when electrodes are placed in this area the animals will repeatedly press a bar to stimulate the electrodes, apparently receiving such pleasurable feedback that they will starve to death rather than stop pressing the bar in order to eat.[11] The other brain area activated was an area in the orbitofrontal cortex involved in both pleasure and impulse control.

One of the most important findings from this experiment was that the pleasure circuitry of the subjects was considerably less responsive when they knew they were playing against a computer rather than another person. In other words, mutuality and empathy, not merely monetary gain, activated the brain's "feel-good" circuitry.[12]

The participants in this study also found out that the choice of the more partnership-oriented alternative is not only more satisfying and pleasurable; in the long term, it is also more productive. Choosing the mutual gain strategy led to better financial results.[13]

But in environments orienting to the domination system, individuals often do not get to make these choices. So we are back to the conditions that make it possible for people to choose between different behaviors so as to experience more satisfying and productive ways to live—and how to create these.

Because domination settings do not offer these conditions, people tend to see winning or losing—in other words, dominating or being dominated—as the only alternatives. Psychologists Spencer Kagan and Millard Madsen put children into experimental game situations in which cooperation could lead to the greatest rewards.[14] They found that some children did not shift from a habitual win-or-lose competitive response to a cooperative orientation that would have benefited both players. What Kagan and Madsen also discovered is that cultural factors had a noteworthy influence; Mexican children living in Mexico acted more cooperatively than California-dwelling Mexican-American children, who in turn demonstrated more cooperative responses than did Anglo-Americans. Many Anglo-American children did not arrive at the understanding that they could gain greater rewards through cooperation than by striving to dominate their opponents. Kagan and Madsen conclude that "Anglo-American children behave irrationally: They remain in conflict to an extent which denies them toys for which they are striving."[15]

This win-lose mentality—characteristic of the domination system—in turn requires the suppression of empathy. Consequently, socialization, particularly the socialization of men, who are expected to win at all costs, has to blunt, warp, or at the extreme obliterate the human capacity to feel empathy.

Just as childrearing in domination systems consists of a mind-binding mix of caring and coercion, as we glimpsed in the last chapter, romantic or sexual love in domination systems is also associated with control. Sometimes men are said to kill out of love, as in Shakespeare's famous play *Othello*. But Othello smothers his wife Desdemona *not* out of love, but because he thinks he has lost exclusive possession of her body.

Alienation, Mutual Trust, and Intimacy

In strict domination settings, romantic love is often a mistrustful, tense affair where intimacy is fraught with ambivalence and danger. This underlying tension, as reflected to the extreme in *Othello*, stems from the supposition that relations consist of those who dominate and those who are dominated. So the closeness and intimacy of love itself threatens the web of control that maintains domination systems.

We saw this in Chapter 5 when we looked at domination cultures where expressions of love threaten a man's status—where even expressions of conjugal love in front of family members are equated with dependency—and hence compromise a man's right to control and receive respect. This devaluation of love and intimacy is again dramatically illustrated by a study from Western Africa of a society with strong hierarchies of domination.[16]

Drawing on data from several subgroups in Ghana, psychologists Glenn Adams, Joseph Adonu, and Stephanie Anderson found that marital and other family relations were characterized not only by lack of trust but also by fear of harm from those closely linked by marriage or kin.[17] Indeed, what the authors call "enemyship"—a relationship tainted by hatred and malice in which one person seeks another's downfall or tries to sabotage another's progress—was often attributed to close relations.[18]

Not surprisingly, intimacy was not particularly valued or sought, and disclosure of feelings was avoided in these circumstances. Yet paradoxically, most people placed great emphasis on relationships, particularly those based on marriage and kinship. Some studies even describe "an interdependent construction of the self" in which one's place in relationships is paramount.[19]

Adams and his colleagues reconciled these contradictions as follows: "we understand *interdependent* to refer, not to value orientations or desire for intimacy," but to "the extent to which people experience themselves to be embedded in fields of relational force."[20] That is, relations were very important *not* because they are desired, valued, and freely sought, but because they are culturally imposed and inescapable.

So "interdependence" actually had nothing to do with intimacy. On the contrary, because hierarchies of domination are threatened by intimacy, it had to be discouraged. "Because intimate contact between family members tends to foster a sense of social equality in what, given local constructions of self and social reality, are inherently unequal connections," Adams and his colleagues explain, "relationship ideology in many West African settings includes a number of practices—like avoidance between parents and children or proscriptions against addressing one's older relatives (including siblings) by name—that are designed to prevent such contact."[21] These alienating practices effectively interfere with the leveling effects of love and intimacy, creating a sense of impropriety, unease, and fear about closeness.

Of course, this connection between inequality and ambivalence or fear of closeness is *not* found only in West African settings with hierarchies of domination. It is a characteristic of *any* culture or subculture that strongly orients to the domination system. As Adams and his colleagues note, not long ago in the West, marriage was typically also one of "distance, deference, and patriarchy."[22]

To illustrate, Masterpiece Theater television programs about 19th-century British gender relations such as *The Forsythe Saga* dramatically show the contrast between earlier established norms and emerging romantic ones. In earlier Western gender relations, as Adams and his colleagues write, the expectation was "less about emotional closeness or intimate disclosure and more about (ideally) cheerful performance of relational obligations."[23] But in the 19th century, a romantic expectation of mutual respect and the giving and receiving of pleasure began to emerge, as reflected in the plot of *The Forsythe Saga* when Irene refuses to remain with her distant, punitive husband Soames and eventually finds closeness and happiness with another man.

We should add that a sense of obligation and responsibility is an important aspect of love in any setting. But if obligations and responsibilities are externally imposed by hierarchies of domination backed up by fear and punishments, they become a form of involuntary servitude, and relationships become an invisible prison.

As the *Forsythe Saga* illustrated, in recent centuries, along with cultural movement in a partnership direction, marital relations in the West began to change from "distance, deference, and patriarchy" to greater equality. People have become freer to express their feelings, expect emotional support, feel trust, and give and receive love without fear. As Adams and his colleagues also point out, "this sense of inherent equality" fostered both less hierarchical relationships and more trust and expectations of political independence and equality.[24]

So once again, cross-cultural and historical evidence demonstrates that love and intimacy have different meanings in different cultural contexts and that they are constructed differently in partnership or domination cultural settings. In a culture or subculture that orients more to the partnership side of the continuum, love also entails obligation and responsibility. But at the same time, it can provide real intimacy as well as a safe space for empathy, trust, self-expression, and personal growth.

The Normalization of Violence

Violence was—and all too often still is—condoned in marital relations where a man's "right" to possession of his wife's body is supported by custom and law, as dramatically portrayed in *Othello* by his murder of Desdemona and in *The Forsythe Saga* in the rape of Irene by her husband Soames. Researchers of family violence Ola Barnett and her colleagues point out that in the United States at least one married woman in 10 has been raped by her own husband.[25] Furthermore, "experts have also concluded that approximately twice as many women are raped by their husbands as by other men."[26]

Violence against children, too, as we saw in earlier chapters, is customary and legal in domination systems. Only a few hundred years ago violence seems to have been acceptable in the West. When Raffael Scheck studied the autobiographies of 70 people born in Germany between 1740 and 1840, he found that severe bodily restraints and violence were routine. Children were severely beaten, tied up, and locked in dark closets.[27] In *German Life and Manners as Seen in Saxony at the Present Day,* Henry Mayhew reported that the custom of swaddling that immobilizes babies for hours in their own excrement was also still common in Germany as late as 1864.[28]

This is not to say there was no caring even in the most rigid domination households. There were undoubtedly women and men who really loved each other. There were undoubtedly loving mothers and fathers who found pleasure in caring for their children. Indeed, since ours is a species that cannot survive infancy without some degree of caring, there had to be.

But there seems to be little question that in most households caring was contingent on strict obedience to authority and consciously or unconsciously tinged with fear of pain. There is also little question that throughout recorded history, until modern times (and in far too many places still today), violence –often in the name of sound pedagogy—has been central to what is still sometimes referred to as "traditional" childrearing.[29] There is disagreement as to how extreme and uniform this violence was. But we know that inflicting bodily pain on children for any kind of disobedience, and even as a corrective for what adults considered a faulty performance, was commonplace.

Even today, as noted earlier, violence against children is still accepted by many people. According to the US Centers for Disease Control and Prevention Adverse Childhood Experiences (ACE) study, one out of four American children was beaten by parents so severely that a mark was left on their body.[30]

A factor in this reliance on violence may be that the United States is more religious than most other Western nations. As David Walters points out in *Physical and Sexual Abuse of Children,* the Judeo-Christian tradition has condoned the use of physical punishment on children for a couple of millennia. As an illustration, Walters quotes *Proverbs,* "He that spareth the rod hateth his son: but he that loveth him chasteneth him betimes."[31] After reviewing the religious, literary, and legal history of the United States related to the treatment of children, Walters arrives at the conclusion that child abuse "is a logical outgrowth of our cultural heritage and predilection toward violence," but that it can be prevented if society commits to solving this problem.[32]

In domination systems, violence is also considered sound pedagogy in schools. Not so long ago, beatings, canings, and whippings were routine in the West. As late as the Enlightenment, according to historians Will and Ariel Durant, "flogging was *de rigueur.*" One 18th-century schoolmaster, they report, "reckoned that in fifty-one years of teaching he had given 124,000 lashes with a whip, 136,715 slaps with the hand, 911,527 blows with a stick, and 1,115,800 boxes on the ear." This may have been an extreme case, although the Durants cite it as an example of the prevalence of physical chastisement in a time when "stress was laid on obedience and industry."[33]

In many world regions physical punishments in schools are still routine, reflecting domination practices. Corporal punishment in schools is legal in 90 countries, and estimates are that at least 350 million students around the world face violence in their schools each year.[34] And, as we saw in Box 5.1, even today this violence can be very severe.

This is in sharp contrast to more partnership-oriented cultures, such as Nordic nations, where spanking at home and corporeal punishment in schools are now against the law.[35] In recent decades other countries, mostly in Europe and South America, have followed suit and outlawed corporal punishment.[36]

In the Nordic countries education emphasizes cooperative learning and teaches skills for nonviolent parenting. Children get free nutritious lunches; most children go to daycare and preschool, which receive strong government support; and students are encouraged to help other students rather than just compete with them—all factors contributing to their high standing in international surveys of math and literacy competence. Finland, for example, regularly places first in literacy among industrialized nations— way ahead of the United States.[37]

As noted earlier, peer groups also differ markedly depending on the degree of orientation to the partnership or domination side of the continuum. When domination dynamics take over, bullying behavior is facilitated.[38] This again creates the neurochemical patterns of stress, triggering disassociation or fight-or-flight responses, even to minor provocations. The good news is that antibullying programs are being introduced in various nations.[39] But this has only been happening in more recent times, along with movement in a partnership direction.

Males have often been trained to suppress consciousness to pain—one's own and the pain one causes to others—leading to psychological armoring and the accompanying suppression of empathy required to maintain rigid rankings of domination. For example, in the traditional military subculture, as we saw in the Chapter 9, men are taught to look down on not only women but also traits such as nonviolence and caring traditionally associated with women.

An illustration of denigrating women and their capacities for empathy, caring, and concern for others comes from US Army soldier Ethan McCord, who was stationed in Iraq. Fire from a US Apache helicopter had critically wounded two small children. On the ground, McCord had run, carrying the children's mangled bodies, to an evacuation vehicle. Once back at his base, badly shaken by the experience, he describes:

> I went to my room and tried to clean the children's blood from my uniform, fighting back tears, from what I had seen. My emotions were taking over. The very thing that the Army taught us not to do in war I was doing. My humanity and love for the human race were overcoming everything they taught me. My mind was reeling. . . . It was then that I decided that I needed to see a mental health counselor. [McCord goes to talk with a Staff Sergeant.] When I told him my feelings and how I was unable to deal "properly," in the Army sense, with what I had just witnessed, his response was, "You need to suck that shit up. Stop being a pussy and get the sand out of your vagina. If you go to mental health, there will be repercussions."[40]

Biology and Culture Interact

Whereas peaceful and nonwarring societies exist in which both sexes are to a high degree nonviolent, as a cross-cultural generalization, men are more physically aggressive than women. For example, cross-cultural studies show that with rare exceptions it is members of the male sex who ambush, feud, raid, and wage war in societies where intergroup aggression takes place.[41] Numerous studies also show nonlethal physical aggression to be more severe among males than among females.[42] A similar sex difference is also reflected in homicides, a finding that is consistent across countries, societies, and time periods.[43] According to a United Nations report, "some 95 percent of homicide perpetrators at the global level are also male; a share that is consistent across countries and regions, irrespective of the homicide typology or weapon used."[44]

It has sometimes been assumed that men are more violent than women because they have higher levels of the hormone testosterone.[45] While some studies have found a correlation between high male testosterone levels and violent behaviors, as neurobiologist Robert Sapolsky documents in his article "The Trouble with Testosterone," there is no *causal* relationship between testosterone and violence per se.[46]

Testosterone, like other hormones, does not automatically trigger a chemical message that initiates aggressive behavior. If this were the case, there would not be so much cultural variation in male violence, either across history or from one society to the next.

That a person's emotional reactions are affected by an interaction of biochemical states and social factors was shown in a classic experiment by social psychologists Stanley Schachter and Jerome Singer. They found that people who are biochemically aroused can be influenced to experience either anger or euphoria—depending on the social cues. In what was billed as a health experiment, male subjects were told they were getting a vitamin injection when they were actually given adrenaline (epinephrine), which causes significant hormonal arousal. The men were then divided into two groups and asked to wait until the "vitamin" took effect in separate rooms where the experimenters' confederates, who the subjects thought had also received the same injection, created two very different environments.

In one room, as the subjects began to feel the injection's effect and their hearts beat faster, the experimenters' confederates created an "anger condition." These men were asked to complete a form containing intimate and inappropriate questions while other research confederates angrily ripped up the questionnaire and loudly expressed anger and negativity. In the second room, the experimenters created a "euphoria condition." Here, as the injection took effect, the researchers' confederates were the essence of niceness and friendliness. They playfully threw paper airplanes in the air, shot crumpled balls of paper into a wastebasket, twirled in a hula hoop, and encouraged the experimental subjects to join in the fun.

These two opposite social cues made a huge difference in how the men with increased epinephrine levels responded. In the first group, the vast majority were angry and negative. In the second group, most were happy and giddy.[47]

This experiment vividly shows that how physical and emotional arousal is labeled—and therefore what actions are taken in response—can vary greatly in relation to environmental influences. It further shows that hormonal arousal alone does not predict aggression and violence. We must factor in social cues.[48]

Returning to testosterone, while it does not *cause* violent behavior, it may make learning violent behavior easier. According to Simon Baron-Cohen, director of the Autism Research Center at Cambridge University, testosterone seems to be implicated in a male tendency to be less empathic. When asked to judge when someone might have said something hurtful, girls score higher than boys from seven years of age onward. Women tend to be better at decoding nonverbal communication and picking up subtle nuances from tone of voice or facial expression. Baron-Cohen also cites findings that boys as young as 12 months make less eye contact than girls, which he attributes largely to differences in prenatal testosterone.[49]

Here, however, a note of caution is in order. As cognitive neuroscientist Cordelia Fine shows in her book *Delusions of Gender*, these kinds of findings may be the product of gender biases by experimenters. Fine documents that much of the literature on gender brain differences is deeply flawed.[50] As she writes, "when we take a closer look at the gender gap in empathizing, we find that what is being chalked up to hardwiring on closer inspection starts to look more like the sensitive tuning of the self to the expectations lurking in the social context."[51]

In any case, biology is not destiny. In the complex set of interactions among biological and environmental factors over the course of a person's development, behavioral patterns are heavily influenced by environmental forces. The extent to which males display violent behavior is heavily dependent on whether they have learned it and whether the social environment encourages and rewards or inhibits aggression and violence. The comparison of the Zapotec communities of San Andrés and La Paz in Box 10.1 illustrates this point at the community or cultural level.

Box 10.1 Two Zapotec Communities: Socialization for Domination or Partnership

Doug has conducted a comparative study of two neighboring Zapotec communities in southern Mexico that illustrates not only how physical punishment of children is passed on from one generation to the next in domination-oriented contexts but also how in partnership-focused settings, nonviolent forms of child discipline can become a transgenerational cultural pattern as well.[91] One of the Zapotec communities, San Andrés, reflects a domination orientation as contrasted with more partnership-oriented La Paz.

Although these two indigenous communities are from the same overall Zapotec culture, there are marked differences between them in terms of aggression and the nature of gender relations. "The frequency and intensity of 'horseplay,' fistfights, assaults, wife-beating, physical punishment of children, and murders all point to the same conclusion: San Andrés, while not extremely violent, has a substantially higher level of aggression than peaceful La Paz."[92] For example, the homicide rate is about five times higher in San Andrés than in La Paz.[93] And during fieldwork, wife beatings and child abuse were witnessed by Doug in San Andrés, but never in La Paz.[94]

San Andrés men exert their domination over wives and daughters through fear, restriction of movement, and sometimes force. For example, an elderly San Andrés man told Doug that "when I get very mad—well, the men, when they get very mad, they grab a stick and they hit them [their wives], but only two or three blows."[95] The pattern is very different in La Paz. Women enjoy an elevated status as potters, displaying an economically valuable skill that the men lack. The La Paz men are proud that the women know this special skill, which they pass from mother to daughter. La Paz women are far more independent and enjoy far greater freedom of movement than do their San Andrés counterparts. In La Paz, equality and respect cross gender lines and reflect the partnership-orientation apparent in this community.

The differing levels of aggression between San Andrés and La Paz correspond with methods used to socialize children.[96] Parents in San Andrés advocate the use of significantly more physical punishment than do parents in more peaceful La Paz. In domination-oriented San Andrés, the typical response to child disobedience, lack of respect, and other misbehavior is to hit or beat the child. As one father said, "Give him a blow so that he then obeys, right?" By contrast, the preferred socialization methods in partnership-focused La Paz involve purely verbal discussions to educate with words. One La Paz father said, "One must explain to the child with love, with patience, so that little by little the child understands you," and another told that the way to prevent and correct misbehavior in children should entail "trying to teach them . . . so that they have respect. Educate them!"

Given the very different social learning environments in these two Zapotec communities, it may come as no surprise that already by the three- to eight-year age range, the aggressiveness of the children also differs significantly. Children's aggression occurred significantly more often and lasted significantly longer in San Andrés than in La Paz.[97] Already at these young ages, children learn domination or partnership styles of interaction that mirror the behavior of adults in their respective communities. As anthropologist Clayton Robarchek explains more generally:

> The mirror in which the child sees himself reflected is the response of others to him, and these responses are guided by the fundamental assumptions and values of the society. . . . The child, then, comes to evaluate himself in terms of these cultural values and they become incorporated as aspects of his self-image.[98]

The comparison of these two Zapotec communities illustrates how methods of domination by men over women, and adults over children, are linked to aggression, fear, and control in San Andrés, whereas the cultural beliefs and values of La Paz that promote equality, respect, and nonviolence are tied to partnership relations. These two communities constitute two different learning environments for the growing child, one in which girls learn to be subordinate and boys learn to dominate them, and another in which children learn to respect members of the same and opposite sex and avoid the use of physical violence. In the words of a La Paz man on teaching his son the customs of the town, "if I have respect for others, well he imitates me. . . . Above all the father must make himself an example, by showing how to respect."[99] This lesson is very relevant today in any society wishing to reduce aggression and promote prosocial civility.

If we wish to reduce male aggression, we should explicitly focus on socializing males away from aggressive responses, rather than creating societies where male violence is culturally condoned, idealized, and systematically taught boys and men. Yet cultural modeling, teaching, and appreciation of violence are precisely the kind of socialization influences that help to maintain hierarchies of domination and reflect how boys are brought up in much of the world.

It is critically important to keep in mind the significant influence of socialization processes on human behavior—a point concretely illustrated by the high level of cultural variation that exists regarding the frequency and nature of expressed aggression in males. Some societies are violent, but others have extremely low rates of homicide, a paucity of violence, and do not engage in feuds or wars.[52]

The existence of peaceful societies such as the La Paz Zapotec, considered in Box 10.1, wherein neither men nor women fit the values and roles of the domination pattern, demonstrates that like girls, boys also can be raised to be caring and nonviolent. These societies show that any biological leanings that males as a sex might have for acting more aggressively than females can be overcome by the social environments we create. Males are not predestined to act aggressively.[53] Much depends on how masculinity is culturally defined, which differs greatly in domination- and partnership-oriented cultures or subcultures.

Violence, Masculinity, and Socialization

Violence, whether personal, intergroup, or international, can be dramatically reduced through socialization processes that are geared toward the development of empathic, social problem-solving, and self-regulation skills in both boys and girls and through belief systems and social institutions that support nonviolent conflict resolution and prosocial behaviors.[54] For example, in Chapter 6 we saw how the partnership-oriented Teduray of the Philippines developed elaborate social mechanisms for avoiding physical aggression and for preventing cycles of violence. The Teduray recognized that violence will occasionally erupt. But violence was not integral to male socialization. Nor did the Teduray have economic and political hierarchies of domination. Instead, elders—both female and male—mediated disputes.[55]

The Minangkabau of East Sumatra are also a partnership-oriented culture where mediation for violence prevention and nonescalation help to maintain a generally peaceable way of life. Nurturance is part of both the female and male roles. And, as among the Teduray, violence is not part of Minangkabau childrearing.

Among the La Paz Zapotec, boys are socialized into a male gender role that emphasizes the importance of respect, responsibility, and cooperation—values and behaviors that are conducive to partnership.[56] When confronted with conflict, La Paz boys are taught to avoid any open confrontation and instead to turn and walk away.[57] As adults, men typically either avoid or tolerate an unpleasant situation, or else formally file a grievance with the community authorities. Maintaining respect and acting nonviolently are principles of the highest order for La Paz Zapotec males. Correspondingly, the community experiences very low levels of physical aggression. In short, these cases show that the learning of nonviolence by males is clearly possible.[58]

Partnership-oriented societies generally reject and reduce structural and physical violence. As we discussed in Chapter 8, peace, social equality, and human well-being are valued over violence and militarism in the partnership-oriented Nordic nations of Denmark, Finland, Iceland, Norway, and Sweden. Recall that these Nordic nations were among the first countries worldwide to create peace studies programs at their universities, to have organizations of men against domestic violence, to promote social equality across society in ethos and practice, and to pass laws prohibiting the physical punishment of children under any circumstances. These Nordic nations have low crime rates, are often involved in international mediation, and are strong advocates of peace education.[59]

By contrast to the foregoing examples of partnership-oriented societies, in cultures that orient more to the domination side, violence is integral to male socialization—as illustrated by the Maasai rites that prepare boys to be warriors. Women in such cultures also tend to use violence against their children—like the Maasai's sexual mutilation of little girls traditionally performed by women. However, women in domination cultures are also socialized to care for life, rather than take life, and thus the most severe forms of violence are usually male-inflicted.[60]

In domination cultures, a central feature of male socialization is training boys to associate their identity with "not being like a woman." At the same time, males learn to equate "masculinity" with those traits and behaviors, including violence, required for domination.

In Western cultures, this male training for domination "masculinity" traditionally followed what psychologist Silvan Tomkins calls the "macho script for hypermasculine socialization."[61] Tomkins introduced "script theory," in which he proposed that personality is formed through an interaction over development of innate and cultural scripts that prepare men and women for culturally prescribed roles.

Tomkins and his colleague Donald Mosher point out that scripts for hypermasculine socialization are part of an ideology in which males are viewed as superior to females and emotions associated with masculinity are considered superior to those associated with femininity. Men are taught that the only "manly emotions" are the ones appropriate for those who dominate: disgust, anger, contempt. Men are also taught contempt for "inferior feminine" feelings, or at least that emotions such as distress, compassion, and empathy reside solidly in the female domain. Meanwhile, women are taught that "masculine" feelings are superior emotions but are off-limits for them.[62] During socialization, children are applauded for and rewarded by adults when they display behavior deemed appropriate to their gender, but humiliated and punished if they fail to conform to the expected gender-specific behaviors. This divergent socialization of boys and girls is most pronounced in families that condition children to fit into dominator-dominated rankings.

As Mosher and Tomkins note, in some families, parents fail to respond to a child's cries of distress with a comforting response—a caring reaction that would model empathy to the child. Instead, these parents, through their nonempathic reactions, model that suffering and distress in others, even loved ones, can be met uncompassionately by disinterest, mocking, or punishment.[63] In other words, in these families, "masculine" emotional responses are more valued than "feminine" ones.

Indeed, in domination-oriented families and societies, boys are taught that for males to express, or even feel, female "soft" emotions is shameful because such feelings are appropriate only for "inferior" girls and women, or for "sissies" or "effeminate" men. Hence, boys come to understand that they are being punished not just because they express such feelings but also because they are acting "feminine."

In 1972, US Presidential candidate Ed Muskie was reported to have cried while giving a press conference outside in a snowstorm. Whether or not the "tears" were actually melting snow, the event contributed to a perception that Muskie was not man enough to be president.[64]

Boys soon learn that there is a payoff for expressing "masculine" emotions—that while anger is forbidden to girls and women, for boys it is, as Mosher and Tomkins put it, "instrumental in securing desired goals." Mosher and Tomkins propose that through learning processes, "the unrelieved and intensified neural stimulation of painful distress is in boys transformed into the 'manly' emotion of anger."[65]

The co-director of the Harvard University Gender Research Project, Terrence Real, confirmed these dynamics.[66] He notes that little boys and little girls in the United States start off by being equally emotional, expressive, and dependent. But whereas females are generally allowed to remain emotionally expressive, males are subtly, or at times dramatically, socialized away from expressing their emotions and dependency needs.[67]

Boys, Dr. Real contends, suffer all their lives from this requirement that they disassociate themselves from soft emotions—and thus both literally and symbolically from their mothers.[68] For boys, he writes, "the development of their own sense of masculinity is not, as in most other forms of identity development, a steady movement toward something valued, as much as a repulsion from something devalued. Masculine identity development turns out to be not a process of development at all, but rather a process of elimination, a successive unfolding of loss."[69]

According to Real and his colleagues, this loss leads to a masculinity that by any sensible standard is mentally unhealthy, both individually and socially. Psychologist Ron Levant estimates that close to 80 percent of men suffer from mild to severe *alexithymia* or "muted feelings," which in turn lead to severe personal as well as social problems.[70]

Both violence and drug addiction have been associated with attempts to escape *alexithymia*—a desperate search for feeling, or as researchers put it, for "increased intensity." People whose ordinary psychic states are muffled and muted, who have dampened emotional experience, often seek relief from this alienation by trying to rev up dead feelings. Alcohol and drugs are one way of doing this—and in the United States men significantly outnumber women as drug addicts and alcoholics. Raging, risk-taking, and fighting are other ways men use to stimulate their neurochemicals in an attempt to "enliven" dead feelings.[71]

Socialized not to express or even acknowledge feelings of pain, fear, or any other vulnerability, boys in domination-oriented cultures or subcultures learn to externalize these feelings through action. While women are usually the majority of those diagnosed with depression, as noted earlier, men commit the overwhelming majority of violent crimes.[72] They also disproportionately initiate and perpetrate killings through homicides, lynchings, terrorist attacks, feuds, pogroms, and wars.[73]

Reducing Violence

All this violence is not inevitable. A culturally comparative perspective shows that a great deal of variation exists cross-culturally.[74] This cross-cultural variation in aggressive conflict is reflected in a sample of 90 societies studied by political scientist Marc Ross.[75] Ross' conflict score data can be ordered along a12-point peacefulness-to-aggressiveness continuum, which indicates that there are more societies at the peaceful end of the continuum than at the high conflict pole: 16 percent received the lowest or second lowest conflict score, whereas only 7 percent received the highest or second highest score.[76] Otherwise, with some rises and dips, the cultures are rather evenly distributed across the spectrum of conflict.

The peacefulness-to-aggressiveness continuum highlights the extensive range of societal possibilities, including the possibilities of creating peaceful societies (Box 10.2). Moreover, the fact that a society has a high level of physical aggression today does not preclude a shift toward peacefulness tomorrow. Shifts toward violence and shifts toward peacefulness have been ethnographically and historically documented to occur over years, generations, and centuries.[77] For example, anthropologists Clayton Robarchek and Carole Robarchek describe how the Waorani of Ecuador managed to decrease their extremely high rate of homicide by more than 90 percent in just a few years:

> The catalyst that began the transformation of the Waorani culture of war was the entry into Waorani territory of two North American Protestant missionary women accompanied by two Waorani women. . . . As bands became convinced that the feuding could stop, peace became a goal in its own right, even superseding the desire for revenge. . . . The killing stopped because the Waorani themselves made a conscious decision to end it.[78]

Box 10.2 Cross-Cultural Variability in Aggression and Peacefulness

It can be useful to conceptualize a cross-cultural peacefulness-to-aggressiveness continuum that highlights the strong effects of environmental factors on the learning of behavior. Some societies have achieved a very high level of internal peacefulness and some live without war, and hence they can be visualized as lying near the peacefulness end of the continuum.

A culturally comparative view indicates that the causes of aggression are multifaceted—including influences from such sources as learned values, socialization, social organization, economics and ecology, gender, and natural and sexual selection. Moreover, a study of peaceful and nonwarring societies suggests ways to reduce aggression within and among social groups—for instance, by restructuring institutions, promoting norms and values that favor peace over aggression, and socializing the young toward peaceful behavior.[100]

In the case of a highly social species with a long period of infant dependency, a high degree of behavioral plasticity, and reliance on learning and socialization, finding that aggression in humans is strongly affected by cultural experience should come as no surprise. Some of the most nonviolent societies described by anthropologists include the Batek of Malaysia, the Paliyan of India, the Saulteaux of North America, the Lepcha of Nepal, and various others.[101] People in internally peaceful societies use a variety of methods for dealing with conflicts without physical violence, such as resolving disputes through contests, discussions, mediation moots, and courts.[102] The anthropological literature also contains listings of nonwarring societies and descriptions of nonwarring peace systems.[103]

Intercultural variability in aggression is reflected in comparisons of homicide rates and other forms of physical aggression across societies. In nomadic forager societies, considered in Chapter 7, for instance, the incidences of ethnographically mentioned lethal events (whether manslaughter, homicide, feud, or warfare) ranged from zero to 69 per society, with an average of about seven per ethnographic case.[104] The cross-cultural variability of homicide is also shown in a study by Palmer, who was able to assign each of the 40 societies in his sample a homicide score that ranged between zero and 21, with the median score being 8.4.[105] Cross-national comparisons in recent years also reflect the intersocietal differences in homicide rates. For 2012, the homicide rates per 100,000, lowest to highest, for selected world cities were as follows: Singapore, 0.2; Hong Kong, 0.4; Reykjavik, Iceland, 0.5; Auckland, New Zealand, 0.7; Rome, 0.9; Paris, 1.8; New York, 5.1; Nairobi, 6.1; Juba, South Sudan, 12.0; Santo Domingo, Dominican Republic, 29.1; San Salvador, El Salvador, 52.5; and Panama City, Panama, 53.1.[106]

We can see that the cross-cultural variation in homicide rates is tremendous, for instance, with Panama City having about 665 times as many homicides as Singapore. Also, as noted in the chapter text, men across societies are more lethally violent than are women.

There are three conclusions to take away from the cross-cultural data. First, homicide and other forms of aggression vary tremendously across cultures, at the same time that a species sex difference is clearly notable, with men being far more lethal, as a group, than women. Second, nonviolent societies are represented in this cross-cultural spectrum. Therefore, third, it is in fact possible to create partnership-oriented peaceful societies and nonwarring systems. As Kenneth Boulding once quipped, "Anything that exists is possible."[107]

A similar case of a community plagued by murders and brutal attacks that managed to reduce rampant violence comes from a Chatino village in Mexico.[79] The community brought about land reforms and enacted new laws. In a movement initiated by village women who were fed up with losing their men to blood feuds, the community government strictly enforced a new ordinance that banned alcohol consumption and the packing of weapons. "These measures were effective and put an end to the blood feuding and factionalism in the village."[80]

Another case of violence reduction has been reported for the Enga of New Guinea.[81] After the introduction of shotguns and M-16 rifles resulted in a bloodbath, Enga elders reintroduced traditional mediation mechanisms to resolve conflicts without violence. The effect was to dramatically decrease the killing.[82]

The Waorani, Chatino, and Enga are examples of peoples who have supplanted violence with more peaceful ways to deal with social conflict, sometimes with remarkable rapidity. Such cases contradict the assumption that nothing can be done to reduce violence within a given society.

Additionally, the fact that numerous peaceful societies exist at all, as represented on the peaceful end of the peacefulness-to-aggressiveness continuum, shows that humans clearly have the capacity to create social systems that manifest very low levels of aggression. The ethnographic descriptions of peaceful societies prove that creating nonviolent social life is entirely within the human potential and not merely a utopian fantasy.[83]

Violence and Social Order

This takes us to the contention that violence is needed to maintain social order, as in the argument that the main function of government is to have a "monopoly" on violence.[84] While this top-down "law and order" approach is standard operating procedure for domination cultures, as we saw, cultures that orient to the partnership side of the continuum effectively maintain order and minimize violence through different means.

Violence is not used to maintain rigid rankings of domination in partnership systems, and in these settings socialization for male violence is minimal. By contrast, socialization favoring male violence is part and parcel of domination-oriented societies.

Domination-oriented societies provide socially approved channels for this violence, which in turn serve to maintain these kinds of systems. One such channel is the military. Of course, we realize that in a world that still orients heavily to the domination system, armed forces are needed for self-defense.[85] However, because the equation of "real" masculinity with "heroic" and "manly" violence sets up self-fulfilling prophecies of violence, this need would greatly diminish as societies worldwide shifted more to the partnership side of the continuum.

Unless we recognize the link between a male socialization for "not being like a woman"—that is, for despising the "soft" or stereotypically feminine not only in women but also in men themselves—we will continue to have value systems and social institutions that perpetuate cycles of warfare and terrorism. And we will also continue to see regressions to authoritarianism.

This leads to a second channel for male violence in domination systems: its use to maintain strongman rule. Indeed, in societies that socialize men to equate their masculine identity with domination and violence, top-down state or tribal control, and the accompanying use of fear and even terror can be justified as required to "maintain order"—that is, to prevent this violence from boiling over in ways that are not culturally accepted.

Authoritarian regimes only require that some men be willing to terrorize people to maintain their subordination. In the same way, it is enough to have intermittent violence to terrorize subordinate out-groups. The Soviet terror under Stalin and the Latin American, Asian, African, and Middle Eastern regimes that torture and kill to put or maintain "strongmen" in power provide modern examples of these domination systems dynamics. But we need only glance back into recorded history to see how ubiquitous terror has been in maintaining domination. Chu Yuan-Chang, the first emperor of the Chinese Ming dynasty, made a public ritual of the clubbing to death of high officials who seemed independent-minded or insufficiently sycophantic. When he thought he noticed a rebellious spirit in Nanking, he executed 15,000 people in one swoop.[86] The Spartans killed slaves as sport. Roman emperors had dissidents thrown to lions.[87]

Another outlet for men socialized to equate their masculinity with violence is the social condoning and even approval of family violence. This violence serves a number of purposes in domination-oriented societies.

The social approval of violence against women through "provoked" rapes, "deserved" beatings, and other brutal "traditional" practices is designed to keep women in a subordinate position. In addition, it is directly linked to these societies' great reliance on violence in solving conflicts, including international ones. The modeling of violence against women in homes is also an effective way of teaching men to be violent. As Valerie Hudson and her colleagues note, the first adults whom children observe regularly interacting are their parents, so when children witness violence against their mothers, they tend to imitate these behaviors—especially if they see that violence gets its perpetuators what they want. As Hudson and her colleagues write, "this increases the likelihood that they will experience low barriers to engaging in violence on an even larger scale, up to and including intrasocietal and interstate conflict." [88]

Of course, not all men are socialized to be violent in the domination system's "war of the sexes." And even among those who are, not all turn out to be violent. However, what children observe or experience in families where there is violence is a key part of the socialization to fit into a domination system.

This takes us to still another area where violence has been accepted in societies that orient to the domination side of the continuum. This is the "traditional" violence against children that is increasingly recognized as child abuse. Violence against children, as we have seen, is one form of violence by females that is condoned, and often encouraged, in cultures orienting to the domination system. This is because mothers are important socialization agents. However, the severest beatings are usually, though certainly not always, part of the male role.[89]

In either case, here again violence is modeled as acceptable, even moral. One result, as we saw in Chapter 8, is that all too often children who experience violence grow up identifying with those who cause them pain and later deflect their pain and rage toward "weak," "inferior," and "dangerous" out-groups.

Thus, various forms of violence—against children, spouses, members of different religions or ethnic groups—are interrelated. And such forms of violence are to varying degrees socially accepted in domination-oriented cultures.

Also accepted is the violence that then is required to control men so that their violence does not erupt in ways that are not socially condoned. In more "civilized" cultures, this violence is officially played down and, as much as possible, concealed. But in rigid domination cultures or subcultures, this vicious cycle of violence, male dominance, and repression is clearly visible.

We see this, for example, in rigidly male-dominated Iran, with its autocratic regime, sadistic punishments (such as flogging and stoning girls and women accused of adultery to death, or flogging and hanging boys accused of homosexuality) and support of terrorists trained to slaughter and intimidate others.[90] This is *not* because the society is Muslim, but rather is due to its domination-orientation wherein violence and the threat of violence are embedded in the social system.

Even in cultures with more partnership elements, there are still those who argue that the only way to reduce violence is through more violence—harsher punishments and more top-down controls. And if we view violence from within the perspective of the domination system, we can see how people are led to believe that "legitimate" force and fear of punishment—both temporal and divine—will bring violence under control.

Hence, in domination-oriented cultures, the question is not how to decrease violence, but how best to channel violence to keep the system operating while preventing it from erupting in ways that interfere with top-down control. And this entails the all-too-familiar military death squads, KGB-type organizations, storm troopers, and thugs who are willing to terrorize and kill.

Yet, while in a domination-oriented worldview the "solution" to violence is more violence, over the last centuries there have been growing efforts to reduce violence. We see this in the massive antiwar demonstrations of the 20th and early 21st centuries as well as in the nascent movement against rape, wife beating, child abuse, and other forms of intimate violence.

But to finally stop the domination system's macabre dance of death and destruction—not only of lives but of the human spirit—we must go further, as we will explore in the chapters that follow.

Notes

1. For example, although Kenneth Bausch, *The Emerging Consensus in Social Systems Theory* (New York: Springer, 2001) recounts valuable information, 99 percent of the systems theorists that his book describes are male, and the book completely ignores the immense, foundational area of social systems where the primary human relations take place.
2. Sen Jia et al., "Women Are Seen More than Heard in Online Newspapers," *PLoS ONE* 11 (2016): e0148434, doi: 10.1371/journal.pone.0148434.
3. Jia et al., "Women Are Seen More than Heard in Online Newspapers."
4. Julia T. Wood, "Gendered Media: The Influence of Media on Views of Gender," in *Gendered Lives: Communication, Gender, and Culture*, ed. Julia T. Wood (Belmont, CA: Wadsworth Publishing, 1994), 231–244; Hope Viner Samborn, "Media Bias against Women: Stuck in a Bygone Era," *Perspectives* 19 (2011): 1–4.
5. Adrienne LaFrance, "I Analyzed a Year of My Reporting for Gender Bias (Again)," *Atlantic*, last modified November 17, 2016, accessed March 23, 2018. Available online: https://www.theatlantic.com/technology/archive/2016/02/gender-diversity-journalism/463023/.
6. David Loye, *Darwin's Lost Theory,* (Carmel, CA: Benjamin Franklin Press, 2010).
7. Arthur Aron, Elaine N. Aron, and Christina Norman, "Self-Expansion Model of Motivation and Cognition in Close Relationships and Beyond," in *Blackwell Handbook of Social Psychology: Interpersonal Processes,* eds. Garth J. O. Fletcher and Margaret S. Clark (Oxford, UK: Blackwell Publishers, 2003), 478–503.
8. C. Sue Carter, "Neuroendocrine Perspectives on Social Attachment and Love," *Psychoneuroendocrinology* 23 (1998): 779–818, doi: 10.1016/S0306-4530(98)00055-9;

Ruth Feldman, "Oxytocin and Social Affiliation in Humans," *Hormones and Behavior* 61 (2012): 380–391, doi: 10.1016/j.yhbeh.2012.01.008; Paul J. Zak, Angela A. Stanton, and Sheila Ahmadi, "Oxytocin Increases Generosity in Humans," *PLoS ONE* 11 (2007) e1128, doi: 10.1371/journal.pone.0001128.

9. James K. Rilling et al., "A Neural Basis for Social Cooperation," *Neuron* 35 (2002): 395–405, doi: 10.1016/S0896-6273(02)00755-9. The subjects of the study were female. But, on the basis of past results, Rilling et al. concluded that neuroimaging studies of men playing the game would probably yield similar results. See also Alexander J. Stewart and Joshua B. Plotkin, "From Extortion to Generosity, Evolution in the Iterated Prisoner's Dilemma," *Proceedings of the National Academy of Sciences of the United States (PNAS)* 110 (2013): 15348–15353, doi: 10.1073/pnas.1306246110; James K. Rilling et al., "Opposing BOLD Responses to Reciprocated and Unreciprocated Altruism in Putative Reward Pathways," *NeuroReport* 15 (2004): 1–5; James K. Rilling et al., "Neural Correlates of Social Cooperation and Non-Cooperation as a Function of Psychopathy," *Biological Psychiatry* 61 (2007): 1260–1271, doi: 10.1016/j.biopsych.2006.07.021; James K. Rilling, "The Neurobiology of Cooperation and Altruism," in eds. Robert W. Sussman and C. Robert Cloninger, *Origins of Altruism and Cooperation* (New York: Springer, 2011), 295–306.

10. Natalie Angier, "Why We're So Nice: We're Wired to Cooperate," *New York Times*, last modified July 23, 2002. Available online: https://www.nytimes.com/2002/07/23/science/why-we-re-so-nice-we-re-wired-to-cooperate.html.

11. David J. Linden, *The Compass of Pleasure: How Our Brains Make Fatty Foods, Orgasm, Exercise, Marijuana, Generosity, Vodka, Learning, and Gambling Feel So Good* (New York: Viking, 2011).

12. Rilling et al., "A Neural Basis for Social Cooperation."

13. Rilling et al., "A Neural Basis for Social Cooperation."

14. Spencer Kagan and Millard Madsen, "Cooperation and Competition of Mexican, Mexican-American, and Anglo-American Children of Two Ages under Four Instruction Sets," *Developmental Psychology* 5 (1971): 32–39, doi: 10.1037/h0031080; Spencer Kagan and Millard Madsen, "Experimental Analyses of Cooperation and Competition of Anglo-American and Mexican Children," *Developmental Psychology* 6 (1972): 49–59, doi: 10.1037/h0032219.

15. Kagan and Madsen, "Experimental Analyses of Cooperation and Competition," 58.

16. Glenn Adams, Joseph Adonu, and Stephanie Anderson, "The Cultural Grounding of Closeness and Intimacy," in *Handbook of Closeness and Intimacy*, eds. Debra J. Mashek and Arthur Aron (New York: Psychology Press, 2004), 321–342.

17. Adams et al., "The Cultural Grounding of Closeness and Intimacy," 327.

18. Although nearly absent as a topic of study in psychological science, a concern with enemyship is prominent in studies of West Africa; for example, the percentage of respondents who claim enemies—"people who hate you, personally, to the extent of wishing for your downfall or trying to sabotage your progress"—is several times greater in a variety of settings in the West African country of Ghana than in a variety of settings in the United States (Adams et al., "The Cultural Grounding of Closeness and Intimacy," 327).

19. Adams et al., "The Cultural Grounding of Closeness and Intimacy," 332.

20. Adams et al., "The Cultural Grounding of Closeness and Intimacy," 317.

21. Adams et al., "The Cultural Grounding of Closeness and Intimacy," 326.

22. Adams et al., "The Cultural Grounding of Closeness and Intimacy," 331.

23. Adams et al., "The Cultural Grounding of Closeness and Intimacy," 331.

24. Adams et al., "The Cultural Grounding of Closeness and Intimacy," 330–331, also noted that "the emphasis on closeness and intimacy in contemporary North American settings is not natural or inevitable, but is instead a relatively recent development associated with the rise of affective individualism: constructions of self and social reality characterized not only by an ontological sense of separate, autonomous, and equal individuals, but also a positive value on exploration and expression of one's unique, personal feelings."

25. Ola Barnett, Cindy Miller-Perrin, and Robin Perrin, *Family Violence across the Lifespan: An Introduction* (Thousand Oaks, CA: Sage, 1997), 190.

26. Barnett et al., *Family Violence*, 190.

27. Raffael Scheck, "Childhood in German Autobiographical Writings, 1740-1820," *Journal of. Psychohistory* 15, 1 (Summer 1987): 391–422.

28. As Mayhew writes, babies were "wound up, in Heaven knows how many ells of bandages, from the feet right, and tight, up to the neck," as if they were mummies, with the bandages only removed once, at most twice a day. (Lloyd DeMause, "Schreber and the History of Childhood," *Journal of Psychohistory* 15, 1 (Summer 1987): 423–430, 426).

29. See, e.g., Alice Miller, *For Your Own Good: Hidden Cruelty in Child-Rearing and the Roots of Violence*, trans. Hildegarde Hannum and Hunter Hannum (New York: Farrar, Straus and Giroux, 1990); David R. Walters, Physical and Sexual Abuse of Children: Causes and Treatment (Bloomington, IN: Indiana University Press, 1975).

30. Vincent J. Felitti, Robert F, Andra, Dale Nordenberg, David F. Williamson, Alison Spitx, Valerie Edwards, Mary P. Koss, and James S. Marks, "Relationship of Childhood Abuse and Household Dysfunction to Many of the Leading Causes of Death in Adults: The Adverse Childhood Experiences (ACE) Study." *American Journal of Preventive Medicine* 14 (1998): 245–258, doi: 10.1016/S0749-3797(98)00017-8.

31. Walters, *Physical and Sexual Abuse of Children*, 11; see also Christopher G. Ellison and John P. Bartkowski, "Religion and the Legitimation of Violence: Conservative Protestantism and Corporal Punishment," in *The Web of Violence: from Interpersonal to Global*, eds. Jennifer Turpin and Lester R. Kurtz (Urbana: University of Illinois Press, 1997).

32. Walters, *Physical and Sexual Abuse of Children*, 4, 23.

33. Will Durant and Ariel Durant, *The Age of Voltaire* (New York: Simon & Schuster, 1980), 400.

34. Randeep Kaur interview, in "Millions Face School Violence across Asia," *Australia Broadcasting Corporation (ABC)*, last modified October 8, 2008. Available online: http://www.abc.net.au/ra/programguide/stories/200810/s2385881.htm. See also Global Initiative to End All Corporal Punishment of Children. Available

online: http://www.endcorporalpunishment.org and United Nations: *School Violence and Bullying: Global Status Report*. (Paris: United Nations Educational, Scientific and Cultural Organization, 2017). Available online: http://unesdoc.unesco.org/images/0024/002469/246970e.pdf.

35. Karin Österman, Kaj Björkqvist, and Kristian Wahlbeck, "Twenty-Eight Years after the Complete Ban on the Physical Punishment of Children in Finland: Trends and Psychosocial Concomitants," *Aggressive Behavior* 40 (2014): 568–581, doi: 10.1002/ab.21537.

36. Global Initiative to End All Capital Punishment of Children, "Countdown to Universal Prohibition," accessed December 3, 2016. Available online: http://www.endcorporalpunishment.org/progress/countdown.html.

37. Lizette Alvarez, "Educators Flocking to Finland, Land of Literate Children," *New York Times*, last modified April 9, 2004. Available online: http://www.nytimes.com/2004/04/09/world/suutarila-journal-educators-flocking-to-finland-land-of-literate-children.html.

38. Dan Olweus, "Tackling Peer-Victimization with a School-Based Intervention Program," in *Cultural Variation in Conflict Resolution: Alternatives to Violence*, eds. Douglas P. Fry and Kaj Björkqvist (Mahwah, NJ: Erlbaum, 1997); Dan Olweus, "Cyber Bullying: A Critical Overview," in *Aggression and Violence: A Social Psychological Perspective* (New York: Routledge, 2017), 225–240.

39. Olweus, "Tackling Peer-Victimization with a School-Based Intervention Program"; Dan Olweus and Jan Helge Kallestad, "The Olweus Bullying Prevention Program: Effects of Classroom Components at Different Grade Levels," in *Indirect and Direct Aggression*, ed. Karin Österman (Frankfurt am Main: Peter Lang, 2010), 115–131.

40. Ethan McCord, "Innocence Lost: Ethan McCord Recounts Aftermath of Iraqi Civilian Massacre, UNPC 7/24/2010," accessed December 3, 2016. Available online: https://www.youtube.com/watch?v=3ihPGtcHjNk.

41. Victoria K. Burbank, "Female Aggression in Cross-Cultural Perspective," *Behavior Science Research* 21 (1987): 70–100, doi: 10.1007/BF01420987; Douglas P. Fry, "Anthropological Perspectives on Aggression: Sex Differences and Cultural Variation," *Aggressive Behavior* 24 (1998): 81–95, doi: 10.1002/(SICI)1098-2337(1998)24:2<81; Douglas P. Fry, *The Human Potential for Peace: An Anthropological Challenge to Assumptions about War and Violence* (New York: Oxford University Press, 2006).

42. Burbank, "Female Aggression in Cross-Cultural Perspective"; Fry, "Anthropological Perspectives on Aggression"; Fry, *The Human Potential for Peace*; Eleanor Maccoby and C. Jacklin, *The Psychology of Sex Differences* (Stanford, CA: Stanford University Press, 1974).

43. Victoria Burbank, *Fighting Women: Anger and Aggression in Aboriginal Australia* (Berkeley: University of California Press, 1994); Martin Daly and Margo Wilson, *Homicide* (New York: Aldine de Gruyter, 1988); Douglas P. Fry and Patrik Söderberg, "Lethal Aggression in Mobile Forager Bands and Implications for the Origins of War," *Science* 341 (2013): 270–273, doi: 10.1126/science.1235675; United Nations Office on Drugs and Crime, "Global Study on Homicide, 2013: Trends, Context, Data,"

accessed on March 23, 2018. Available online: https://www.unodc.org/documents/data-and-analysis/statistics/GSH2013/2014_GLOBAL_HOMICIDE_BOOK_web.pdf.

44. United Nations Office on Drugs and Crime, "Global Study on Homicide, 2013," 13. Meanwhile, not a single ethnographic example has been found where the females of the society kill more frequently than the males. However, this should not be interpreted to mean that women never engage in physical aggression. Based on a study of 137 societies worldwide, Burbank, "Female Aggression in Cross-Cultural Perspective," documents that, in the majority of the sample, women attacked other persons. Burbank also discovered that the most common reason for physical attacks by women involved competition over a man. The overall conclusion from a cross-cultural vantage point is thus that, whereas women are capable of committing acts of physical violence, the female of the species tends to be less violent than the male.

45. Both women and men have some amounts of each other's hormones. But women on average have about 40 nanograms of testosterone per deciliter of blood, and men on average have anywhere from 300 to 1,000 nanograms of testosterone per deciliter, or 10 times a woman's concentration.

46. Robert M. Sapolsky, *The Trouble with Testosterone and Other Essays on the Biology of the Human Predicament* (New York: Touchstone, 1998); see also Robert M. Sapolsky, *Behave: The Biology of Humans at Our Best and Worst* (New York: Penguin Press, 2017), 99–107. A Norwegian study, for example, found that testosterone did not drive aggression. It only magnified a boy's readiness to respond vigorously to threats and provocation (Dan Olweus et al., "Circulating Testosterone Levels and Aggression in Adolescent Males: A Causal Analysis," *Psychosomatic Medicine* 50, 3 (1988): 261–272); Angela Turner, "Genetic and Hormonal Influences on Male Violence," in *Male Violence*, ed. John Archer (New York: Routledge, 1994). Turner notes that environmental factors have a strong influence in humans and concludes that "There are clearly no simple genetic or hormonal factors that can explain the variation in aggressive and antisocial behavior between individuals or the differences in such behavior between males and females," 247.

47. Stanley Schachter and Jerome E. Singer, "Cognitive, Social and Psychological Determinants of Emotional State," *Psychological Review* 69 (1962): 379–399, doi: 10.1037/h0046234.

48. Even in birds, whose behavior is tied much more to hormonal control than in humans, the environment makes a big difference. If you inject androgen into a male bird, there will be no aggression unless another male is present and is acting in a particular fashion and the environment is familiar.

49. Simon Baron-Cohen, *The Essential Difference: Male and Female Brains and the Truth about Autism* (New York: Basic Books, 2003).

50. Cordelia Fine, *Delusions of Gender: How Our Minds, Society, and Neurosexism Create Difference* (New York: Norton, 2011).

51. Fine, *Delusions of Gender*, 13.

52. Karen P. Ericksen and Heather Horton, "'Blood Feuds': Cross-Cultural Variations in Kin Group Vengeance," *Behavior Science Research* 26 (1992): 57–85, doi: 10.1177/

106939719202600103; Fry, "*The Human Potential for Peace*"; Keith F. Otterbein, "Internal War: A Cross-Cultural Study," *American Anthropologist* 70 (1968): 277–289, doi: 10.1525/aa.1968.70.2.02a00040; Keith Otterbein, *The Evolution of War: A Cross-Cultural Study* (New Haven, CT: Human Relations Area Files Press, 1970).

53. Kirk Endicott and Karen Endicott, *The Headman Was a Woman: The Gender Egalitarian Batek of Malaysia* (Long Grove, IL: Waveland, 2008).

54. For examples of foraging societies that do not rely on ranking to maintain order, that on the contrary, appear to be more peaceful because they do not have "strongman" rule, see Douglas P. Fry, ed., *War, Peace, and Human Nature* (New York: Oxford University Press, 2013), especially Chapter 14 about the Hadza of Tanzania.

55. Stuart Schlegel, *Wisdom from a Rainforest* (Athens: University of Georgia Press, 1998).

56. Carl W. O'Nell, "Hostility Management and the Control of Aggression in a Zapotec Community," *Aggressive Behavior* 7 (1981): 351–366, doi: 10.1002/1098-2337(1981)7:4<351.

57. Douglas P. Fry, "Maintaining Social Tranquility: Internal and External Loci of Aggression Control," in *The Anthropology of Peace and Nonviolence*, eds. Leslie E. Sponsel and Thomas Gregor (Boulder, CO: Lynne Rienner, 1994), 133–154; Douglas P. Fry, "Multiple Paths to Peace: The 'La Paz' Zapotec of Mexico," in *Keeping the Peace: Conflict Resolution and Peaceful Societies around the World*, eds. Graham Kemp and Douglas P. Fry (New York: Routledge, 2004), 73–87.

58. Edwin G. Burrows, *Flower in My Ear: Arts and Ethos on Ifaluk Atoll* (Seattle: University of Washington Press, 1963); Endicott and Endicott, *The Headman Was a Woman*; Kirk Endicott, "Peaceful Foragers: The Significance of the Batek and the Moriori for the Question of Innate Human Nature," in *War, Peace, and Human Nature: The Congruence of Evolutionary and Cultural Views*, ed. Douglas P. Fry (New York: Oxford University Press, 2013), 243–261; Graham Kemp and Douglas P. Fry, eds., *Keeping the Peace: Conflict Resolution and Peaceful Societies around the World* (New York: Routledge, 2004); Peter M. Gardner, "Respect and Nonviolence among Recently Sedentary Paliyan Foragers," *Journal of the Royal Anthropological Institute* (N. S.) 6 (2000): 215–236, doi: 10.1111/1467-9655.00013; Peter M. Gardner, *Bicultural Versatility as a Frontier Adaptation among Paliyan Foragers of South India* (Lewiston, NY: Edwin Mellen Press, 2000); Peter M. Gardner, "Respect for All: The Paliyans of South India," in *Keeping the Peace: Conflict Resolution and Peaceful Societies around the World*, eds. Graham Kemp and Douglas P. Fry (New York: Routledge, 2004), 53–71; Peter M. Gardner, "South Indian Forages' Conflict Management in Comparative Perspective," in *War, Peace, and Human Nature: The Congruence of Evolutionary and Cultural Views*, ed. Douglas P. Fry (New York: Oxford University Press, 2013), 297–314; Ashley Montagu, ed., *Learning Non-Aggression: The Experience of Non-Literate Societies* (New York: Oxford University Press, 1978); Clayton A. Robarchek, "The Image of Nonviolence: World View of the Semai Senoi," *Federated Museums Journal* (Malaysia) 25 (1980): 103–117.

59. See, e.g., Institute for Economics and Peace, *Global Peace Index 2017*. Available online: http://maps.visionofhumanity.org/#/page/indexes/global-peace-index; John

F. Helliwell, Richard Layard, and Jeffrey D. Sachs, *World Happiness Report 2018* (New York: Sustainable Development Solutions Network. 2018). Available online: https://s3.amazonaws.com/happiness-report/2018/WHR_web.pdf; Central Intelligence Agency, "World Factbook." Available online: https://www.cia.gov/library/publications/the-world-factbook/rankorder/2091rank.html.

60. Daly and Wilson, *Homicide*; Fry, *The Human Potential for Peace*.
61. Donald L. Mosher and Silvan S. Tomkins, "Scripting the Macho Man: Hypermasculine Socialization and Enculturation," *Journal of Sex Research* 25 (1988): 60–84, doi: 10.1080/00224498809551445. Tomkins stresses how the macho script originated from a society which accepted slavery as well as living by the sword and writes that it is our heritage from nomadic societies of perceived scarcity.
62. Mosher and Tomkins, "Scripting the Macho Man."
63. Mosher and Tomkins, "Scripting the Macho Man," 66.
64. Elisabeth Goodridge, "Front-Runner Ed Muskie's Tears (or Melted Snow?) Hurt His Presidential Bid," *U.S. News,* last modified January 17, 2008. Available online: https://www.usnews.com/news/articles/2008/01/17/72-front-runners-tears-hurt.
65. Mosher and Tomkins, "Scripting the Macho Man," 67.
66. Terrence Real, *I Don't Want to Talk about It: Overcoming the Secret Legacy of Male Depression.* (New York: Scribner, 1997).
67. Real, *I Don't Want to Talk about It*, 123.
68. As Real documents, research does *not* support the widely held belief that the presence of a father is the essential component for healthy male development. He writes: "Recent studies indicate that boys raised by women, including single women and lesbian couples, do not suffer in their adjustment; they are not appreciably less 'masculine'; they do not show signs of psychological impairment. What many boys without fathers inarguably do face is a precipitous drop in their socioeconomic status. When families dissolve, the average standard of living for mothers and children can fall as much as 60 percent, while that of the man usually rises. . . . The key component of a boy's healthy relationship to his father is affection, not 'masculinity.' The boys who fare poorly in their psychological adjustment are not those without fathers, but those with abusive or neglectful fathers. Contrary to the traditional stereotype, a sweet man in an apron who helps out with the housework may be just the nurturant kind of father a boy most needs." (Real, *I Don't Want to Talk about It,* 141.)
69. Real, *I Don't Want to Talk about It,* 131.
70. Real, *I Don't Want to Talk about It,* 146.
71. Real, *I Don't Want to Talk about It,* 146–147.
72. Real, *I Don't Want to Talk about It,* 147.
73. Daly and Wilson, *Homicide*; Fry, *The Human Potential for Peace*.
74. Fry, *The Human Potential for Peace*.
75. Marc Howard Ross, *The Culture of Conflict: Interpretations and Interests in Comparative Perspective* (New Haven, CT: Yale University Press, 1993).
76. Fry, *The Human Potential for Peace*.
77. Fry, *The Human Potential for Peace*.

78. Clayton A. Robarchek and Carole J. Robarchek, "Waging Peace: The Psychological and Sociocultural Dynamics of Positive Peace," in *Anthropological Contributions to Conflict Resolution*, eds. Alvin W. Wolfe and Honggang Yang (Athens: University of Georgia Press, 1996), 64–80; See also Clayton Robarchek and Carole Robarchek, *Waorani: The Contexts of Violence and War* (Fort Worth: Harcourt Brace, 1998).

79. James B. Greenberg, *Blood Ties: Life and Violence in Rural Mexico* (Tucson: University of Arizona Press, 1989).

80. Greenberg, *Blood Ties*, 231.

81. Polly Wiessner and Nitze Pupu, "Toward Peace: Foreign Arms and Indigenous Institutions in a Papua New Guinea Society," *Science* 337 (2012): 1651–1654, doi: 10.1126/science.1221685.

82. Wiessner and Pupu, "Toward Peace."

83. Bruce D. Bonta, *Peaceful Peoples: An Annotated Bibliography* (Metuchen, NJ: Scarecrow Press, 1993); Bruce D. Bonta, "Conflict Resolution among Peaceful Societies: The Culture of Peacefulness," *Journal of Peace Research* 33 (1996): 403–420, doi: 10.1177/0022343396033004003; Bruce D. Bonta, "Cooperation and Competition in Peaceful Societies," *Psychological Bulletin* 121 (1997): 299–320, doi: 10.1037/0033-2909.121.2.299; Bruce D. Bonta, "Peaceful Societies Prohibit Violence," *Journal of Aggression, Conflict, and Peace Research* 5 (2013): 117–129, doi: 10.1108/JACPR-01-2013-0002; Bruce D. Bonta and Douglas P. Fry, "Lessons for the Rest of Us: Learning from Peaceful Societies," in *The Psychology of Resolving Global Conflicts: From War to Peace, Volume I, Nature vs. Nurture*, eds. Mari Fitzduff and Chris E. Stout (Westport, CT: Praeger Security International, 2006), 175–210; Fry, *The Human Potential for Peace*; Douglas P. Fry, "Life without War," *Science* 336 (2012): 879–884, doi: 10.1126/science.1217987.

84. Ayn Rand, *The Virtue of Selfishness* (New York: Signet, 1964).

85. A viable security system based on the concepts of collective security, human security, human rights protection, and international law is sorely needed on our interdependent planet. Consideration of approaches that focus not merely on national defense but also on global collective security can be found in Douglas P. Fry, "Cooperation for Survival: Creating a Global Peace System," in *War, Peace, and Human Nature: Convergence of Evolutionary and Cultural Views*, ed. Douglas P. Fry (New York: Oxford University Press, 2013); Kent Shifferd, Patrick Hiller, and David Swanson, *A Global Security System: An Alternative to War* (World Beyond War, 2017); Richard Falk, *Power Shift: On the New Global Order* (London: Zed Books, 2016); Mary Kaldor, *Human Security* (Cambridge, UK: Polity Press, 2007), and Geneviève Souillac, *A Study in Transborder Ethics: Justice, Citizenship, and Civility* (Brussels: Peter Lang, 2012).

86. Marc Cartwright, "Hongwu Emperor," *Ancient History Encyclopedia*, posted February 13, 2019. Available online: https://www.ancient.eu/Hongwu_Emperor/

87. Riane Eisler, *Sacred Pleasure: Sex, Myth, and the Politics of the Body* (San Francisco: Harper Collins, 1995); Riane Eisler, *The Chalice and the Blade: Our History, Our Future* (San Francisco: Harper and Row, 1987).

88. Valerie M. Hudson et al., "The Heart of the Matter: The Security of Women and the Security of States," *International Security* 33 (2008/2009): 7–45, 23–26. Available online: http://belfercenter.ksg.harvard.edu/publication/18797/heart_of_the_matter.html.

89. See, e.g., Laura McCloskey and Riane Eisler, "Family Structure and Family Violence and Nonviolence," in *Encyclopedia of Violence, Peace, and Conflict* (San Diego: Academic Press, 1999), 1–11. The authors note that the common denominator in family violence is its use to impose socially sanctioned relations of domination and submission. They write: "if a society, or family, orients strongly to the dominator model—in which relations are based primarily on rankings of domination—patterns of violence will be necessary to maintain these rankings. By contrast, in families and societies orienting primarily to the partnership model—where relations are based primarily on linking, with hierarchies of actualization maintained by enabling rather than disabling power—the teaching of empathy, caring, and the exchange of mutual benefits can be central in the socialization process" (11). In Alice Miller's *For Your Own Good,* Miller gives as an example Adolf Hitler's abuse by his father and his contempt for his mother not being able to protect him from his father's brutality.

90. See, e.g., Saeed Kamili Dehghan and Ian Black, "Iranians Still Facing Death by Stoning Despite 'Reprieve.'" *Guardian,* last modified July 8, 2010. Available online: https://www.theguardian.com/world/2010/jul/08/iran-death-stoning-adultery; "Human Rights Violations on the Basis of Sexual Orientation, Gender Identity, and Homosexuality in the Islamic Republic of Iran," submission to the 103rd Session of the United Nations Human Rights Committee (October 17–November 4, 2011), International Gay and Lesbian Human Rights Commission (IGLHRC). Available online: https://www.iglhrc.org/sites/default/files/Iran%20Shadow%20Report%202011.pdf.

91. Douglas P. Fry, "Female Aggression among the Zapotec of Oaxaca, Mexico," in *Of Mice and Women: Aspects of Female Aggression,* eds. Kaj Björkqvist and Pirkko Niemalä (Orlando, FL: Academic Press, 1992); Douglas P. Fry, "'Respect for the Rights of Others Is Peace': Learning Aggression versus Non-Aggression among the Zapotec," *American Anthropologist* 94 (1992): 621–639, doi: 10.1525/aa.1992.94.3.02a00050; Douglas P. Fry, "Intergenerational Transmission of Disciplinary Practices and Approaches to Conflict," *Human Organization* 52 (1993): 176–185, doi: 10.17730/humo.52.2.5771276435620789; Douglas P. Fry, "Multiple Paths to Peace: The 'La Paz' Zapotec of Mexico," in *Keeping the Peace: Conflict Resolution and Peaceful Societies around the World,* eds. Graham Kemp and Douglas P. Fry (New York: Routledge, 2004); Carl O'Nell, "Hostility Management and the Control of Aggression in a Zapotec Community," *Aggressive Behavior* 7 (1981): 351–366, doi: 10.1002/1098-2337(1981)7:4<351; Carl O'Nell, "Some Primary and Secondary Effects of Violence Control among the Nonviolent Zapotec," *Anthropological Quarterly* 59 (1986): 184–190, doi: 10.2307/3317333; Carl O'Nell, "The Non-Violent Zapotec," in *Societies at Peace: Anthropological Perspectives,* eds. Signe Howell and Roy Willis (New York: Routledge, 1989).

92. The community names San Andrés and La Paz are pseudonyms; Fry, "'Respect for the Rights of Others Is Peace,'" 628.

93. Fry, "'Respect for the Rights of Others Is Peace.'"

94. Fry, "'Respect for the Rights of Others Is Peace'"; Fry, "Intergenerational Transmission of Disciplinary Practices and Approaches to Conflict"; Douglas P. Fry, "Multiple Paths to Peace."

95. Fry, "Female Aggression among the Zapotec of Oaxaca, Mexico," 192.

96. Fry, "Intergenerational Transmission of Disciplinary Practices and Approaches to Conflict."

97. Fry, "'Respect for the Rights of Others Is Peace'"; Douglas P. Fry, *The Human Potential for Peace: An Anthropological Challenge to Assumptions about War and Violence* (New York: Oxford University Press, 2006).

98. Clayton, Robarchek, "The Image of Nonviolence: World View of the Semai Senoi." *Federated Museums Journal (Malaysia)* 25 (1980): 103–117.

99. Fry, "Intergenerational Transmission of Disciplinary Practices and Approaches to Conflict," 183.

100. Douglas P. Fry, "Life without War," *Science* 336 (2012): 879–884, doi: 10.1126/science.1217987.

101. Kirk Endicott, "Peaceful Foragers: The Significance of the Batek and the Moriori for the Question of Innate Human Nature," in *War, Peace, and Human Nature: The Congruence of Evolutionary and Cultural Views*, ed. Douglas P. Fry (New York: Oxford University Press, 2013); Kirk Endicott and Karen Endicott, *The Headman Was a Woman: The Gender Egalitarian Batek of Malaysia* (Long Grove, IL: Waveland, 2008); Peter M. Gardner, *Bicultural Versatility as a Frontier Adaptation among Paliyan Foragers of South India* (Lewiston, NY: Edwin Mellen Press, 2000); Peter M. Gardner, "Respect for All: The Paliyans of South India," in *Keeping the Peace: Conflict Resolution and Peaceful Societies around the World*, eds. Graham Kemp and Douglas P. Fry (New York: Routledge, 2004); A. Irving Hallowell, "Aggression in Saulteaux Society," in *Culture and Experience*, ed. A. Irving Hallowell (Philadelphia: University of Pennsylvania Press, 1974); Geoffrey Gorer, *Himalayan Village: An Account of the Lepchas of Sikkim*, 2nd edition (New York: Basic Books, 1967).

102. Bruce D. Bonta, "Conflict Resolution among Peaceful Societies: The Culture of Peacefulness," *Journal of Peace Research* 33 (1996): 403–420, doi: 10.1177/0022343396033004003; Bruce D. Bonta, "Cooperation and Competition in Peaceful Societies," *Psychological Bulletin* 121 (1997): 299–320, doi: 10.1037/0033-2909.121.2.299; Bruce D. Bonta, "Peaceful Societies Prohibit Violence," *Journal of Aggression, Conflict, and Peace Research* 5 (2013): 117–129, doi: 10.1108/JACPR-01-2013-0002; Douglas P. Fry, *The Human Potential for Peace: An Anthropological Challenge to Assumptions about War and Violence* (New York: Oxford University Press, 2006); Signe Howell and Roy Willis, eds., *Societies at Peace: Anthropological Perspectives* (New York: Routledge, 1989); Graham Kemp and Douglas P. Fry, eds., *Keeping the Peace: Conflict Resolution and Peaceful Societies around the World* (New York: Routledge, 2004); Ashley Montagu, ed., *Learning Non-Aggression: The Experience of Non-Literate Societies* (New York: Oxford University Press, 1978).

103. Bruce D. Bonta and Douglas P. Fry, "Lessons for the Rest of Us: Learning from Peaceful Societies," in *The Psychology of Resolving Global Conflicts: From War to Peace, Volume I, Nature vs. Nurture*, eds. Mari Fitzduff and Chris E. Stout (Westport, CT: Praeger Security International, 2006); Fry, *The Human Potential for Peace*; Fry, "Life without War"; Douglas P. Fry and Geneviève Souillac, "Peace by Other Means: Reflections from the Indigenous World," *Common Knowledge* 22 (2016): 8–24; Geneviève Souillac and Douglas P. Fry, "Anthropology: Implications for Peace," in *The Palgrave Handbook on Disciplinary and Regional Approaches to Peace*, eds. Oliver P. Richmond, Sandra Pogodda, and Jasmine Ramovic (New York: Palgrave Mcmillan, 2016).

104. Douglas P. Fry and Patrik Söderberg, "Lethal Aggression in Mobile Forager Bands and Implications for the Origins of War," *Science* 341 (2013): 270–273, doi: 10.1126/science.1235675.

105. Stuart Palmer, "Murder and Suicide in Forty Non-Literate Societies," *Journal of Criminal Law, Criminology, and Police Science* 56 (1965): 320–324, doi: 10.2307/1141241.

106. United Nations Office on Drugs and Crime, "Global Study on Homicide, 2013," Table 8.4. Available online: http://www.marteau.pro/wp-content/uploads/2013/08/UNODC-Global-Study-on-Homicide.pdf.

107. "Peaceful Societies: Alternatives to Violence and War," University of Alabama at Birmingham, accessed March 23, 2018. Available online: https://cas.uab.edu/peacefulsocieties/.

11

The Real Culture Wars

Every day, our newsfeeds bombard us with stories of cultural conflict world-wide. In the United States, the ongoing "culture wars" pit religion against humanists, feminists, other "God-less" secularists, and now also Muslims. In the Middle East, Muslim Shiites fight Muslim Sunnis, and vice versa. In Southeast Asia, the hostility is between Hindus and Muslims.

But the actual cultural conflict is not between religion and secularism or between different religious sects. Neither is it between modernity and traditionalism, East and West, nor South and North.

The real cultural conflict is *within* all these sectors. It is the conflict between those who believe dominating and being dominated are the only alternatives, and those trying to move toward a less painful, less violent, more humane way of life.

As we already glimpsed, a key battleground in this struggle are the cultural stories or myths that define what is, or is not, normal, moral, and possible. The popular meaning of a myth is a falsehood, probably because so many old myths were proved false by science. But cultural myths, in the words of Mircea Eliade, express what is seen by society as the truth and, beyond this, as "a story that is precious because it is sacred, exemplary, and significant."[1] In other words, cultural myths express what people at a particular time and place believe to be the ultimate or gospel truth.

Myths are embedded in our minds and shape consciousness through what scientists call mental representations. The neurochemical coding schemes by which mental representations are stored and processed are now being studied through neuroimaging and other techniques. But it is generally agreed that internalized representations play a major role in people's perceptions, beliefs, emotions, and actions.[2]

In children's brains, the neural networks needed for more mature functioning are not yet in place, so children have little biological capacity for reflecting on themselves and their environments. Therefore, many mental representations are unconsciously internalized, indeed virtually imprinted, into children's minds before they are able to evaluate them. This is why the stories we learn as children are so important.

Since we inherited many cultural myths from authoritarian, rigidly male-dominated, chronically violent times, the message of many stories is still that rankings of domination backed up by fear and force are inevitable. We saw this in Chapter 8, when we briefly looked at some of our most beloved fairy tales: stories that portray males as powerful and females as powerless, idealize royal rule and princely prerogatives, and generally present inequality as normal and desirable.

Fortunately, we also have stories that present relations of mutuality and caring as desirable and normal. In recent decades, these have included many children's stories where "common people" do wonderful things and both girls and boys are active and empowered.

The problem is that often these two kinds of stories are found side by side, with little guidance about the messages they convey. Here, again, the analytical tools of the partnership system and domination system can help us sort things out so that we can identify which myths to leave behind and which to highlight and disseminate in order to advance the movement toward partnership.[3]

Ancient Partnership and Domination Myths

Some of the most powerful myths in every culture deal with universal questions. One basic question is: What does it mean to be human? As there are two halves of humanity, another basic question is: What does it mean to be a woman or a man? But while these questions are universal, how they are answered is very different depending on the degree to which a culture orients to either end of the domination-partnership continuum.[4]

Since there has been movement over the last centuries toward partnership, today many partnership and domination myths exist side by side. This makes for a confusing mix, particularly because most of us have lacked the integrative framework of the partnership-domination continuum to explain such contradictory accounts. Conflicting myths, however, are not new. We already find contradictory accounts of human nature and what it means to be female or male in the most sacred Western text: the Bible.

Probably the best-known biblical story about human origins is the story of how God created Adam and Eve. Yet the Bible actually has two very different stories about the origins of these two halves of humanity. In the first version, both woman and man are created simultaneously in God's image: "male and female created he them" (Genesis 1:27). By contrast, in the much more famous second tale, the primordial woman is a mere afterthought: God whips Eve out of Adam's rib to give him a "helpmate" (Genesis 2:18-23).

The first story suggests a matter that Riane extensively examines in *The Chalice and the Blade* and other works: that Western religious traditions stem from earlier, more partnership-oriented cultures.[5] The second version, which biblical scholars tell us was added later as part of a massive editing to justify theocratic rule, establishes one of the core elements of the domination system: the ranking of males over females.[6]

This constantly retold story not only presents the first woman as a secondary creation; it also blames Eve for nothing less than humanity's expulsion from Paradise. God decrees that henceforth woman be subservient to man as punishment for Eve's disobedience (Genesis 3). One could hardly ask for a better justification for male dominance than blaming woman for all of humanity's ills.

The Adam and Eve story also justifies a second core element of the domination system: the legitimacy of top-down control, including mind control. This tale tells us that what led to the Fall from Paradise is that Eve decided to find out what is right or wrong independently by eating from the Tree of Knowledge herself. The lesson is clear. Not only must we do what we are told; we must also think only what we are told, or we will be severely punished.

Since a snake counsels Eve to disobey Yahweh, and Eve in turn counsels Adam to do so, another lesson is that both women and snakes give evil counsel. Here, too, we find a radical departure from earlier myths in which women and serpents are associated, not with bad advice, but rather with wise, even prophetic, counsel.[7]

We can still vividly see this association in the art of the Minoan civilization that flourished in the Mediterranean island of Crete until circa 1400 BCE. Here, archeologists have excavated figures of priestesses in oracular trances with snakes coiled around their arms.[8] Even in later, more domination-oriented Greek times, the famous oracle of Delphi, consulted by statesmen pondering important decisions, was still a priestess who put herself in an oracular trance working with snakes—clearly a legacy from an earlier era.

Also reversing earlier myths and realities is the second-best-known story in the Old Testament: the tale of Cain and Abel, in which Cain, the farmer, kills Abel, the herder (Genesis 4).[9] This story of brother killing brother provides a powerful legitimization of a third core element of the domination system: it presents violence, even fratricide, as yet another aspect of our "flawed human nature."

In summary, the underlying message of these powerful biblical myths is that core components of the domination system—male dominance, top-down control, and chronic violence—are inevitable. This said, we want to emphasize that these kinds of religious stories were *not* introduced by the ancient Hebrews. As detailed in *The Chalice and the Blade*, they go back much further.[10] For example, the Mesopotamian myth *Enuma Elish* tells us that a new war god, Marduk, killed the Mother Goddess Tiamat, and out of her dismembered body created earth and heaven.[11]

Nor are religious stories idealizing male dominance and violence exclusive to the West. Similar myths are found in the major world religions. For instance, a famous Hindu story celebrates how the supreme Hindu deity, Vishnu, was saved from death in his crib when a girl baby was deliberately put in his place so that she would be killed instead.[12] This story, too, teaches the superior worth of males. In another famous Hindu story, the Mahabarahta, deities slash each other to pieces, presenting violence as a means to resolve conflicts, with the victors presumably in the right.

To some people, such tales may seem just a reflection of reality. Violence, they say, *is* just human nature and men *are* superior to women. But then we have to ask what kind of reality is reflected by earlier myths that are so different from the religious stories we have been examining.

What kinds of realities do ancient myths about powerful female deities who bring humanity the gifts of life, wisdom, and justice reflect? A millennia-old Sumerian tablet refers to the Goddess Nammu as "the Mother who gave birth to heaven and earth." Another Sumerian prayer exalts the glorious Queen Nana as "the Mighty Lady, the Creatress." In both Sumerian and later Babylonian legends, we find accounts of how women and men were created simultaneously or in pairs by a female deity. From another Sumerian tablet we learn that the Goddess Nanshe of Lagash was worshiped as "She who knows the orphan, knows the widow, seeks justice for the poor and shelter for the weak." In tablets from nearby Erech, we read that the Goddess Nidaba was known as "The Learned of the Holy Chambers, She who teaches the Decrees."[13] Even later, the Greek Goddess

Demeter, like the Egyptian Goddess Isis, was known as a lawgiver and sage, a Great Mother dispensing wisdom, counsel, and justice.

The same questions about what kinds of realities earlier myths reflect are raised by the Chinese *Tao Te Ching*. This ancient work tells of a time when the *yin*, or feminine principle, was not yet ruled by the male principle, or *yang*: a more peaceful and just time when the wisdom of the mother was still honored. Similarly, in the Bible we read that henceforth woman is to be subservient to man. "Henceforth" clearly points to an earlier time before this was the case.

All these are clues to a more partnership-oriented time in prehistory.[14] Regarding our distant past, as we considered in Chapter 7, a strong case can be made for a partnership orientation being the default over millions of years of human evolutionary prehistory.[15] But we have been conditioned to gloss over all this, or simply to ignore it, because it does not fit into the prevailing paradigm.

The Conflict within Religions

For much of history, the only acceptable worldview was religious, and to a much larger extent than is generally recognized, many religious teachings—both Eastern and Western—have served to establish and maintain domination systems. Yet if we closely look at religious teachings, here, too, we find the conflict between partnership and domination writ large.

At the core of most world religions are teachings that we should be empathic and caring.[16] The equivalent of the Golden Rule is found not only in Judaism and Christianity but also in all major religions. And the critical role of reciprocity as a moral precept for human interaction in societies around the world has been emphasized by thinkers as diverse as Darwin and Confucius.[17]

Like Isaiah in the Old Testament or Jewish Bible, Jesus preached that we do unto others as we want them to do unto us. Jesus taught that the meek, humble, and weak would someday inherit the earth. He spoke of children in tender ways: "suffer the little children to come onto me for theirs is the kingdom of Heaven." In both his words and actions Jesus rejected the subservient and separate position assigned women and even freely associated with them—a form of heresy in his time. Jesus also forcefully denounced the ruling classes of his time—the rich and powerful, and the religious authorities—for oppressing and exploiting the people. Indeed, it was this challenge to domination that eventually led to his death.

The earliest Christians were Jewish sects who espoused nonviolence.[18] They were generally egalitarian, and, as religious historian Elaine Pagels writes, some sects "prayed to both a divine Father and Mother."[19]

According to the Gnostic Gospels, some of which are older than the official Christian Gospels written almost 100 years after Jesus died, Mary Magdalene was an important leader in the early Christian movement. Even the official New Testament tells us that women were leaders in early Christian communities. Many of the first churches were in the homes of widows who had some measure of independence. Women in these communities were able to baptize, which meant, as the later Christian cleric Tertullian complained, that they could act as bishops.[20] All this reflects the partnership nature of early Christianity.[21]

However, by the year 200, Christianity was well on its way to becoming the kind of rigidly top-down, male-dominated system Jesus had rebelled against. And after Emperor Constantine's conversion to Christianity in 360, as Pagels documents in her book *The Gnostic Gospels*, "Christian bishops, previously victimized by the police, now commanded them."[22] This is why the Gnostic Gospels, which generally reflected the egalitarian and peaceful character of Jesus's followers, had to be buried, lest they be discovered and destroyed. That did not mean that all of Jesus's teachings were abandoned. But "orthodox" Church structure and dogma now largely followed a domination orientation.

The myth that woman is inferior and dangerous—a belief propagated by the Fall from Paradise story as well as the Greek myth of how Pandora unleashed all human ills from her box by being too curious—was constantly used to justify the subordination and brutalization of women. The medieval *Malleus Maleficarum* went even further. Published in 1486 and blessed by Pope Innocent VIII, this manual for hunting, torturing, and killing witches stated that woman by her nature is "the source of all carnal evil." By conservative estimates, 100,000 European women were publicly tortured to death by representatives of the Church—a slaughter of huge proportions, considering the small population of Europe at that time.[23]

The teaching that woman is sinful and dangerous to man also reinforced the high level of mistrust and fear characteristic of domination systems. Every human has to have contact with a woman to be born and, in a time before formula feeding, years of close contact with a woman were a requisite of survival. But if the giver and nurturer of life is evil and cannot be trusted, how can *anyone* be trusted? In this and other ways, the religious dogma of the "divinely ordained" ranking of one half of humanity over the other half not only had terrible effects for women and girls but also had extremely negative effects for men and boys. For one thing, this male superior/female inferior model of our species provides a mental map for viewing all relations between people who are different in terms of domination and submission. This view and its violent reflection in the seemingly endless persecutions of Jews and other "heretics," as well as constant wars between Christians and Muslims, Catholics and Protestants, and so forth, has further skewed consciousness in a domination direction for much of recorded history.

From Religion to Science

Modern science eventually brought a dramatic break from religious dogma. However, much remained unchanged. Modern science, as the historian of science David Noble documents in his book *A World without Women*, emerged from the medieval monastic culture.[24] The early cleric-scientists were monks interested in using science to support orthodox theology. As illustrated by Galileo's nearly fatal run-in with the Inquisition, these "establishment scientists" and their religious masters were dedicated to eradicating "heresies"—and their proponents. They avoided, prohibited, and severely punished purveyors of any findings that did not fit with the dictates of those in power.

These early scientists excluded and devalued women and anything stereotypically considered feminine. As Noble writes, modern science "first took root in an exclusively male—and celibate, homosocial, and misogynous—culture, all the more so because a great many of its early practitioners belonged also to the ascetic mendicant orders."[25] From its first flowering in the 12th and 13th centuries, he observes, "the culture of science was the culture of the ecclesiastic academy, and hence a world without women."[26]

The cleric-scientists were unmarried, and presumably childless, or at least not involved in taking care of their children. The love these clerics sometimes talked about was abstract. Both women and sexuality were viewed with disdain, even horror. Bodily pleasure was severely constrained. And so was consciousness. All this is documented by Noble and other scholars, such as Margaret Wertheim in her book *Pythagoras' Trousers: God, Physics, and the Gender Wars.*[27]

But the overly abstract, detached, misogynist character of Western science stems not only from its origin in a monastic context that excluded and abhorred women; it also comes from its development in the context of cultures that oriented to the domination system. The domination configuration of top-down rule, rigid male dominance, and the use of violence against dissenters and opponents was at the core of medieval European society as well as its "orthodox" Church.

In the late Middle Ages, the rediscovery of Greek philosophy began to greatly affect European thinking. But while this inspired scientific and artistic developments, it did little to change traditions of domination. A fact, lost behind the customary worship of the Age of Pericles as the seedbed of democracy, is that ancient Athens was in basic respects a domination system: a slave society where the majority of the population—women and slaves of both sexes—had few if any rights.[28] Despite the occasional inclusion of women in the academies of Plato and Pythagoras, and even a few academies founded by women such as the poet Sapho, the female hemisphere of humanity was excluded from the male worlds of political participation, economic power, and even education. Completing the domination configuration is that the Athenians were also chronically at war.

The Athenians had rigidly segregated "women's quarters" at the back of homes. As for the famous Greek symposia (which were actually a combination of conversation and drunken orgies), the only women admitted were prostitutes, along with an occasional *hetaera* or courtesan.[29]

Though the Greeks, like their Minoan predecessors from whom they borrowed much of their civilization, created beautiful works of architecture and art, much of the latter dealt with "heroic" battles, in sharp contrast to Minoan art. As for philosophy, while Socrates in one of his dialogues satirized the fact that men married child brides so as to better control their wives, we only have to recall Aristotle's famous syllogism that slaves were meant to be slaves because they were born slaves and women were meant to be subordinate or they would have been born free men.

The European Renaissance, too, oriented primarily to the domination side of the continuum. This should not surprise us because its artistic, scientific, and philosophical flowering was largely inspired by the rediscovery of Greek traditions.[30] Nonetheless, there was during this period some movement in a partnership direction, including a somewhat higher status of women, as exemplified by the emergence of a number of prominent female artists. Yet even then, with few exceptions, women were excluded from higher education and scientific pursuits. And to ensure this, women did not advance after the Renaissance primogeniture was instituted.[31]

Some years later, the Reformation seemed to challenge the old order. But when the breakdown of the feudal system brought the European peasant revolts of the 1500s, Martin Luther sided with the landowners, urging them to "strangle the peasants like mad dogs"—for which he was rewarded with the protection and patronage of the nobles who, thanks to the Reformation, acquired many Church estates.[32] And under Luther and Calvin, women continued to be rigidly controlled.[33]

As the years passed, there was somewhat more social mobility, and religious teachings were increasingly challenged by science. But violence continued unabated, the gap between ruler and ruled and haves and have-nots continued to be huge, and while some women took advantage of the cultural destabilization of the times, as they had during the Middle Ages when men went off to the Crusades, their subordinate status remained basically unchanged.[34]

Even after the 17th- and 18th-century Enlightenment, when Voltaire and his colleagues embarked on the Encyclopedia project to replace religious myths with scientific findings, and philosophers like John Locke and Jean-Jacques Rousseau declared that men have inalienable rights to life, liberty, and property, these rights were only for men—and then only for a minority of selected men.[35] As in the "democracy" of ancient Athens, only free, property-owning men of the Enlightenment period were enfranchised. As for the rights of women, despite all his writings about freedom and equality, Rousseau asserted that girls must be taught early on that they are subordinate to men.[36]

From Philosophy to Psychology

In the 19th and 20th centuries, challenges to traditions of domination grew exponentially. Yet at the same time, brand new theories from both philosophy and science sprang up to again claim that top-down control, male dominance, and chronic violence are inevitable.

One of the most influential modern proponents of domination and submission as inherent—especially in relations between men and women—was the "father" of modern psychology: Sigmund Freud. Freud was a brilliant man whose insights about the power of the unconscious greatly enriched our understanding of human behavior. He also had the courage to speak against slavish belief in religious dogma, which he saw as superstitions originating in what he called the ignorant times of the childhood of humanity.[37] But although Freud's outspoken goal was to replace a religious worldview with a more liberated scientific one, many of his theories merely replaced religious stories that justify domination with new secular ones.

According to Christian dogma, good, represented by the Judeo-Christian God, and evil, symbolized by darkness, Satan, the serpent, and the carnal female, vie for "man's immortal soul." According to Freud, the same battle rages, only now it is a psychological battle between the *superego* or conscience and the *id* as the dark and primitive side of the psyche that must be suppressed.[38] Freud's position, like that of the religious doctrine of original sin, was that human nature is dangerous and must be controlled. In the human psyche, that control must be exercised through the coercive action of the superego; in society, it must be exercised through the coercive action of those in positions of authority.

Freud not only theorized; he also made up compelling myths. In Freud's works, as in the Bible, we read an origins story that supports the view that strict inner and outer controls are essential. In books such as *Totem and Taboo, Group Psychology*, and *Moses and Monotheism*, Freud maintained that civilization is based on guilt because we *are* guilty: society began with a heinous "primal" crime.[39] And while Freud's primal crime story differs in detail from the stories of Eve and Adam's Fall and the fratricide of Abel by Cain, its core messages are identical.

As in Genesis, the action in Freud's tale opens with an all-powerful male figure in control. This figure is not a deity, but a brutal strongman who tyrannizes his sons and keeps all the women for himself. Wanting access to the women, his sons kill him. But heinous as this crime was, according to Freud, it was also necessary because without it, civilization could not have come about.[40] Even though in this story the murder is the killing of a father by his sons, rather than the killing of brother by brother, violence is again presented as inevitable.

And that is only the beginning. In Freud's "scientific" scheme of things, the "archaic heritage" of this primal crime continues as part and parcel of every male psyche, where it is unconsciously remembered in the mind of every man ever born. Inexorably transmitted from generation to generation, it plays itself out in what Freud famously named the "Oedipus Complex": a son's wish to murder his father and his desire to sexually possess his mother.[41]

As in Judeo-Christian dogma, Freud's story blames woman for "man's" ills. Just as in the earlier religious cosmology where Eve is responsible for Adam's sin, in Freud's myth, woman is the underlying cause of the primal patricide.[42] So whether it is due to original sin or primal crime, humanity is doomed by its guilt. Man's guilt is for what he thinks and does. Woman's guilt is for what she is.[43] Authoritarian control—of women, and also of men—is a necessity.

On top of this, Freud updated the religious dogma of woman's inferiority with a new "scientific" explanation. According to Freud's much-quoted theory of "penis envy," being penis-less, woman is an incomplete, and hence inferior, man. This "deficiency," according to Freud, is something for which every woman blames her mother. As for the mother, Freud maintained she could never value her daughters as much as her sons—for "a mother is only brought unlimited satisfaction by her relation to a son."[44] Freud further asserted that among other "psychical peculiarities of mature femininity" are a lesser sense of justice and less capacity for reason than men, physical vanity (as a "late compensation for their original sexual inferiority"), shame (a "concealment of genital deficiency"),[45] and a "female castration" or "masculinity complex" in which woman rebelliously refuses "to recognize the unwelcome fact "that she has no penis."[46]

There is only one solution, Freud went on, to the girl's "disappointing" realization that she has no penis. Since this deficiency, not her severely limited social options, which he never mentions, has such stunting effects on her, the only way woman can compensate for her haltered psychic development is to fulfill her "feminine destiny" by bearing her husband children, preferably sons.[47] In other words, woman's only "natural destiny" is to serve man as the reproducer of "his kind" because, according to Freudian theory, the development of the unique qualities that make us human is biologically impossible for women.

Of course, what Freud described are not the female or male psyches, but psyches shaped by the dynamics of dominator socialization. If the women who came to him for help—upper-middle-class, turn-of-the-century Europeans and Americans—suffered from neuroses and "hysteria," if they were less intellectually developed than men, if they envied men the greater freedoms and opportunities associated with maleness, it was because they had been taught to limit and distort their human potentials to fit into the dominator mold for women. And if the men Freud observed in his practice struggled with murderous competitiveness toward other men—even their fathers—and if they were unable to relate to women—even their mothers—as human beings, seeing women only in terms of their sexual and reproductive roles, it was because they also had been taught to fit into the domination-oriented culture of 19th- and early-20th-century Europe and America. The "permanent limits" that Freud ascribed to human society and the human psyche in fact described the domination psyche.

The Cultural Push toward Partnership and the Domination Resistance

During the second half of the 20th century, especially in the tumultuous 1960s when there was a strong push toward partnership, many psychologists rejected Freud's static psychological model of "man." Rather than offering therapies to help people "adjust," as in the once popular Freudian psychoanalysis, they began to emphasize the realization of our human potentials— what humanist psychologists such as Abraham Maslow call *growth* rather than *defense* needs.[48]

Gradually, brand new fields, such as women's studies and men's studies, began to emerge, reexamining what it means to be a woman or a man. Human rights, and later more particularly, women's and children's human rights, began to gain attention.

Scholars amassed large bodies of evidence showing that many traits that had been assumed to be innate gender-specific characteristics actually are the product of socialization.[49] The new field of relational-cultural psychology, inspired by the work of psychiatrist Jean Baker Miller, focused on growth-fostering cultures and relationships as central to human development, and disconnection as the source of psychological problems.[50] It emphasized the centrality to individual and social health of so-called "feminine" traits and activities such as forging caring connections of love and empathy.

Feminist writers and a number of other scholars drew connections between attitudes toward gender and shifts in social values and behaviors. For example, social psychologist David McClelland found that time periods when the emphasis in popular culture is to downgrade what he called "affiliation"—more "feminine" peaceful and compassionate values—and re-idealize "power"—more "masculine" or "hard" values—presage wars. Similarly, psychologist David Winter found that time periods when Don Juan "lady-killer"-type fiction proliferates predict warfare and regression to repression.[51]

The inauguration of university curricula such as peace, gender, and multicultural studies over recent decades further reflects, and fosters, changes in consciousness. In recent years, efforts have proliferated to change educational methods in a partnership direction and to bring into the curriculum narratives that offer a more complete and accurate picture of human possibilities, including more gender-balanced, diverse content.[52]

Scholars have reexamined "traditional childrearing" because research showed that customs such as spanking and other violence and abuse are not only harmful but also generally ineffective, even as means of controlling children's behavior. A whole literature on more mutually respectful, authoritative rather than authoritarian parenting has sprung up to help parents learn more caring and less coercive ways of relating to children, often taking into account new findings from neuroscience.[53]

Neuroscience, developmental psychology, anthropology, the study of relational dynamics, and related fields have contributed new data that challenge propositions that humans are hardwired for selfishness and violence, and to the contrary, show that we are predisposed toward mutuality and caring.[54] The traumatic, often lifelong effects from childhood abuse or later experiences such as rape or combat have increasingly become recognized and studied, as has their frequency.[55]

Yet the integration of new findings into mainstream culture, including schools and university curricula, is meeting with resistance. And much of what is taught as truth and knowledge still presents domination systems as normal, even desirable, despite mounting evidence to the contrary.

History still focuses on men, especially on the men of the ruling classes and their bloody conflicts. Economics focuses on conventional categories such as capitalism, socialism, and communism and generally ignores the life-support systems of nature. Also generally ignored are the life-supporting activities of nurturing and caregiving in households that in domination systems are assigned almost exclusively to women—even though these activities are not only essential but also make enormous economic contributions.[56] And so strong is the devaluation of women and anything stereotypically considered feminine that while feminist scholars have for centuries written about the social implications of the status of women, these works, too, are excluded from the canon, relegated to the academic wasteland of "women's studies."

None of this should surprise us because, as we have seen, fear of change is built into brains socialized to fit into dominations systems. Still, even though it remains largely on the social and cultural periphery, the push toward partnership continues to gain momentum. Indeed, the fierce pushback against dismantling domination structures and beliefs is evidence of the inroads being made by the partnership thrust.

The Struggle for Our Minds and Our Future

The struggle for the human mind is today playing itself out in all aspects of culture—both mainstream and alternative. This struggle between those trying to move to a more peaceful, equitable, and sustainable future and those trying to push us back to more rigid patterns of domination is the *real* culture war.

While the outcome of this struggle still hangs in the balance, there is little question that during the last few centuries, as the disequilibrium caused by the shift from agrarian to industrial and then postindustrial technologies destabilized existing economic and social arrangement, the movement toward partnership has gained unprecedented momentum.[57] Indeed, beneath the seemingly random events of modern history is one progressive movement after another, each challenging entrenched traditions of domination.[58]

The 17th and 18th centuries brought challenges to the "divinely ordained" right of kings to rule over their "subjects," and monarchies were, at least in some world regions, replaced by republics. In the same centuries, men's "divinely ordained right" to rule over the women and children in the "castles" of their homes began to be challenged.

The 19th century brought further movements against economic oppression and domination: the antislavery and abolitionist movements challenged the "divinely ordained right" of one race to dominate and even enslave another, and an organized feminist movement challenged traditions of male dominance. The 20th-century civil rights and anticolonial movements, the indigenous liberation movements, and the women's liberation and women's rights movements also challenged traditions of domination.

Challenges to domination traditions are behind the economic justice and antiviolence movements, whether it is the peace movement or the more recent movement to expose the global pandemic of violence against women and children that is still in many places justified on traditional or religious grounds. The environmental movement is a challenge to man's once celebrated "conquest of nature"—another tradition of domination.

But modern history also shows that these movements have been fiercely, often violently opposed. And this opposition is not only on the ground but also in our minds. This struggle is usually presented in terms of left versus right, secular versus religious, eastern versus western, southern versus northern, or liberal versus conservative, and so on. But from the vantage point of the Biocultural Partnership-Domination Lens, the actual struggle is between partnership and domination. For instance, some people who call themselves conservatives consider male dominance normal. But other conservatives do not. The same is true of attitudes toward gay and transsexual rights, which are supported by some conservatives and opposed by others. Some liberals strongly oppose images and stories that degrade and devalue women, but other liberals defend pornography and action entertainment wherein violence and domination are depicted as manly.

Wherever we turn, we see this point-counterpoint of the partnership thrust and the domination resistance transcending old cultural categories. Another example is the struggle over population growth and its link to environmental problems, poverty, and violence. For a while, there was strong forward movement to halt exponential population growth, such as the shift in discourse from the first international population meeting in Bucharest in 1974 (where women were barely mentioned) to later meetings where discussions shifted to so-called women's issues (not only free access to family planning but also equal educational and occupational opportunities so that women's security and status no longer depend on giving birth to men's sons). But then the Vatican and a number of Muslim nations mounted a strong counter-push, claiming that reducing population growth is a Western imperialist conspiracy of genocide against poor and more populous nations. After this, population became a taboo topic for a majority of liberals—despite the fact that empirical data from the Worldwatch Institute and other scientific sources clearly show that we are rapidly exceeding our planet's carrying capacity.[59]

The point-counterpoint between partnership and domination can also be seen within the New Age movement. On the partnership side, we see the spread of meditation and other ways of accessing wisdom independently of top-down religious hierarchies. On the domination side, we find people flocking to gurus and slavishly following their teachings. There are New Age workshops on new myths and role models for women and men. At the same time, domination myths are dressed up in New Age clothes; for instance, a popular retelling of the story of "Iron John," who like other dominator heroes must kill before he gets to mate.[60] While there is concern about environmental and peace issues, in another iteration of the denial characteristic of dominator psychological dynamics, more attention is paid to crystals, past-life regressions, and aromatics than to pressing social, economic, and ecological problems. Still, partnership-supporting myths such as Daniel Quinn's story *Ishmael* are popular, and books such as Christiane Northrup's *Women's Bodies, Women's Wisdom* and John Robbins' *Reclaiming Our Health* not only address the New Age interest in alternative lifestyles and healing but also show how patterns of domination get in the way.

We see this same point-counterpoint in political struggles around the world. For instance, during the Arab Spring, Egyptians nonviolently toppled the domination regime of Hosni Mubarak. But then they elected an Islamic fundamentalist regime that was again brutally authoritarian and pushed women further back into their "traditional" subservient place. All this, again, demonstrates that real democracy and equality require a significant shift to the partnership side of the continuum, including leaving behind traditions of male dominance in families and society.

Wherever we look, we can see the struggle between partnership and domination playing itself out in various aspects of culture. For example, while the movement against the large economic inequalities inherent in domination systems is gaining momentum worldwide, the reconcentration of wealth in the new global fiefdoms of transnational corporations is also underway. Yet even within these corporations are people who recognize that the move from domination to partnership is essential. Corporations were patterned on the traditional domination or military model of top-down chains of command. Nonetheless, there is the growing perception that rigid top-down structures—whether they are centrally planned socialist bureaucracies or capitalist corporate bureaucracies—are inefficient in an era of rapid technological and economic change. There is also growing recognition that ecologically sound practices, as well as greater teamwork and more nurturing or stereotypically "feminine" management styles, are urgently needed.

Even in religion, once a major weapon for justifying and maintaining domination systems, there is a movement toward partnership teachings and actions. While fundamentalist leaders use religious writings to justify authoritarianism, male dominance, and violence, other religious leaders emphasize teachings of empathy, equality, and nonviolence—and use their resources to implement these teachings.

Universal standards for human rights are gaining ground. There is mounting recognition that it is absurd to split off the rights of the majority of humanity from "human rights" as just "women's rights" and "children's rights."[61] Thousands of grassroots groups are making a powerful social justice argument to challenge inequality, oppression, and discrimination. The global women's movement is growing by leaps and bounds, as is the movement for environmental sustainability.

Yet at the same time, the belief in the inevitability of rigid rankings of domination persists. And so, too, does denial, which, as we have seen, is characteristic of brains socialized to fit into domination systems—including the denial of human-caused climate change.

Today, both because technological breakthroughs continue to destabilize beliefs and institutions, and because advanced technologies in service of conquest and domination could take us to an evolutionary dead end, the struggle for our future is coming to a head. Yet the outcome of this struggle is far from certain. As we will see in the next chapter, informed and conscious human action will be the determining factor.

Notes

1. Mircea Eliade, *Myth and Reality,* trans. William R. Trash (London: Allen and Unwin, 1964), 122.
2. Neuroscientists and psychologists write about "mental representations" we each carry in our brains. Some of these representations, for example, images of how our limbs and other body parts move, are built into the neural structure of our brains. Most of them, however, come about as we store and process sensory inputs and feelings. These sensory inputs and feeling do not come only from what we directly experience and observe; the stories we are taught about reality are a key factor in the mental representations we carry.
3. For exercises used in high school and university classes to identify partnership and domination heroes and heroines, see Riane Eisler and David Loye, *The Partnership Way,* revised edition (Pacific Grove, CA: Center for Partnership Studies, 1998).

4. Riane Eisler, *The Chalice and the Blade: Our History, Our Future* (San Francisco: Harper Collins, 1987); Riane Eisler, *Sacred Pleasure: Sex, Myth, and the Politics of the Body—New Paths to Power and Love* (San Francisco: Harper Collins, 1995); Riane Eisler, *Tomorrow's Children: A Blueprint for Partnership Education in the 21st Century* (Boulder, CO: Westview Press, 2000); Riane Eisler, *The Power of Partnership: Seven Relationships that Will Change Your Life* (Novato, CA: New World Library, 2002); Riane Eisler, *The Real Wealth of Nations: Creating a Caring Economics* (San Francisco, Berrett-Koehler, 2007).

5. Eisler, *The Chalice and the Blade.*

6. *The Dartmouth Bible*, annotated by Roy Chamberlain and Herman Feldman, with the counsel of an advisory board of biblical scholars (Boston: Houghton Mifflin, 1950), 78–79.

7. For an analysis of Greek art and literature for clues to earlier, more partnership-oriented times, see Adele Anggard, *A Humanitarian Past: Antiquity's Impact on Present Social Conditions* (Phoenix, AZ: Author-House, 2014).

8. See, e.g., Nicolas Platon, *Crete* (Geneva: Nagel Publishers, 1966).

9. The biblical portrayal of farmer killing herder is particularly interesting as a reversal of earlier realities in light of findings indicating that prehistoric horticultural settlers were practically wiped out by pastoralist invaders in lands around the Mediterranean. See, e.g., Wolfgang Haak, Josif Lazaridis, and David Reich, "Massive Migration from the Steppe Was a Source for Indo-European Languages in Europe," *Nature* 522 (2015): 207–211, doi: 10.1038/nature14317; Morten E. Allentoft, Martin Sikora, and Eske Willerslev, "Population Genomics of Bronze Age Eurasia," *Nature* 522 (2015): 167–172, doi: 10.1038/nature14507; John Novembre, "Human Evolution: Ancient DNA Steps into the Language Debate," *Nature* 522 (2015): 164–165, doi: 10.1038/522164a. See also Marija Gimbutas, "The First Wave of Eurasian Steppe Pastoralists into Copper Age Europe," *Journal of Indo-European Studies* 5 (Winter 1977): 277–338; Riane Eisler, *The Chalice and the Blade.*

10. Eisler, *The Chalice and the Blade.*

11. David Leeming and Jake Page, *Goddess: Myths of the Female Divine* (New York: Oxford University Press, 1996).

12. These kinds of myths are often justified as conveying spiritual teachings about good and evil, and the argument is made that they should not be taken literally. But there are many ways of communicating spiritual teachings that would not involve idealizing violence or killing female babies.

13. Later female deities are commonly associated with violence; for example, the Greek Goddess Athene is associated with war, and the Mesopotamian Ishtar/Astarte also becomes a goddess of war as well as, in some places, a goddess of human sacrifice—features that, as the religious historian E. O. James pointed out, are absent from earlier female deities.

14. For detailed discussions about more partnership-oriented cultures, especially in the areas around the Mediterranean, see Eisler, *The Chalice and the Blade,* and Eisler, *Sacred Pleasure.*

15. In addition to Chapter 7, see also Douglas P. Fry and Geneviève Souillac, "The Original Partnership Societies: Evolved Propensities for Equality, Prosociality, and Peace," *Interdisciplinary Journal of Partnership Studies* 4, 1 (2017): doi: 10.24926/ijps. v4i1.150.

16. Dalai Lama, *Beyond Religion: Ethics for a Whole World* (Boston: Mariner Books/ Houghton Mifflin, 2011).

17. Dalai Lama, *Beyond Religion*; Charles Darwin, *The Descent of Man* (New York: Prometheus, 1998), 131; Douglas P. Fry, "Reciprocity: The Foundation Stone of Morality," in *Handbook of Moral Development*, eds. Melanie Killen and Judith G. Smetana (Mahwah, NJ: Lawrence Erlbaum, 2006), 399–422; David Loye, *Rediscovering Darwin* (Carmel, CA: Romanes Press, 2018); David Loye, *Moral Sensitivity* (unpublished manuscript); on Confucius, see Charles C. Helwig, "Rights, Civil Liberties, and Democracy Across Cultures," in *Handbook of Moral Development*, eds. Melanie Killen and Judith G. Smetana (Mahwah, NJ: Lawrence Erlbaum, 2006), 185–210, 200.

18. Keith Akers, *The Lost Religion of Jesus: Simple Living and Nonviolence in Early Christianity* (New York: Lantern Books, 2000); Brian Griffith, *Correcting Jesus: 2000 Years of Changing the Story* (Minneapolis, MN: Exterminating Angel Press, 2009); see also Mark Kurlansky, *Nonviolence: The History of a Dangerous Idea* (New York: The Modern Library, 2008).

19. Elaine Pagels, *The Gnostic Gospels* (New York: Random House, 1979), 52–53. For archeological evidence that the ancient Hebrews venerated a female deity and that this was the most prevalent form of worship, stretching well into monarchic times, see Raphael Patai, *The Hebrew Goddess* (New York: Avon, 1978).

20. Pagels, *The Gnostic Gospels*, 63.

21. See Kurlansky, *Nonviolence*.

22. Pagels, *The Gnostic Gospels*; Kurlansky, *Nonviolence*.

23. Anne Llewellyn Barstow, *Witchcraze: A New History of the European Witch Hunts* (London: Pandora, 1994), 63.

24. David Noble, *A World without Women: The Christian Clerical Culture of Western Science* (New York: Knopf, 1992).

25. Noble, *A World without Women*, 163.

26. Noble, *A World without Women*, 163.

27. Margaret Wertheim, *Pythagoras' Trousers: God, Physics, and the Gender Wars* (New York: Norton, 1997).

28. Eva Kuels, *The Reign of the Phallus* (Berkeley, CA: University of California Press, 1993).

29. Kuels, *The Reign of the Phallus*.

30. Will Durant, *The Renaissance: A History of Civilization in Italy from 1304-1576 A.D.* (New York: Fine Communications, 1997).

31. Both before and during the Renaissance, there were writings challenging the vilification of women, such as Christine de Pisan's (1364–c.1430) decrying the misogyny of European society.

32. Edmund E. Wilson, *To the Finland Station: A Study in the Writings and Acting of History [The Revolutionary Tradition in Europe and the Rise of Socialism]* (New York: Doubleday, 1953), 202.

33. See, e.g., Rosemary R. Reuther, *Sexism and God Talk: Toward a Feminist Theology Anniversary Edition* (Boston: Beacon Press, 1993).

34. See, e.g., Renate Bridenthal and Claudia Koonz, *Becoming Visible: Women in European History* (Boston: Houghton Mifflin, 1977).

35. See, e.g., Susan Moller Okin, *Women in Western Political Thought* (Princeton, NJ: Princeton University Press, 1979); Sheila Robotham, *Women, Resistance, and Revolution* (New York: Vintage, 1974); Linda Kerber, *Women of the Republic: Intellect and Ideology in Revolutionary America* (Chapel Hill: University of North Carolina Press, 1980).

36. See, e.g., Jean Jacques Rousseau, *The Confessions of Jean Jacques Rousseau, 1712-1778, Book I* (New York: The Modern Library, 1945).

37. Sigmund Freud, *Moses and Monotheism,* trans. K. Jones (New York: Vintage Books, 1955).

38. The id, Freud asserted, "is the dark, inaccessible part of our personality. Instinctual cathexes seeking discharge—that, in our view, is all there is to the id." Sigmund Freud, *New Introductory Lectures on Psychoanalysis*, trans and ed. James Strachey (New York: Norton, 1965), 66. "The super-ego," on the other hand, "is the representative for us of every moral restriction, the advocate of a striving toward perfection— it is, in short, as much as we have been able to grasp psychologically of what is described as the higher side of human nature." Freud, *New Introductory Lectures on Psychoanalysis*, 59.

39. Sigmund Freud, *Totem and Taboo,* trans. James Strachey (New York: Norton, 1990); Sigmund Freud, *Group Psychology and an Analysis of the Ego*, trans. James Strachey (New York: Norton, 1990); Freud, *Moses and Monotheism*.

40. Freud, *Moses and Monotheism*. As Herbert Marcuse pointed out in *Eros and Civilization*, Freud also wanted to demonstrate that brutal and despotic male dominance was the original or natural human state. The sons wanted freedom from tyrannical strongman rule, so their crime was the prerequisite to civilization. However, as Marcuse noted, the reason Freud gives for why the sons rebel and kill the father was not his despotism and cruelty: it was that he monopolized the male prerogative that is rightfully theirs as men by keeping for himself dominion over all the women of the primal horde. Herbert Marcuse, *Eros and Civilization: A Philosophical Inquiry into Freud* (New York: Norton, 1955), 54, 156.

41. Freud, *Moses and Monotheism,* 155.

42. Freud, *Moses and Monotheism,* 157.

43. Freud, *Moses and Monotheism*, 157.

44. Freud, *New Introductory Lectures on Psychoanalysis,* 99–119.

45. Freud, *New Introductory Lectures on Psychoanalysis,* 192.

46. Freud, *New Introductory Lectures on Psychoanalysis,* 193.

47. Freud, *New Introductory Lectures on Psychoanalysis,* 193.

48. Abraham H. Maslow, *Toward a Psychology of Being*, 3rd edition (New York: Wiley, 1998).
49. See, e.g., Carol Gilligan, *In a Different Voice* (Cambridge, MA: Harvard University Press, 2009); Myra Sadker and David Sadker, "Sexism in the Schoolroom of the '80s," *Psychology Today* (1985): 54–57; Kate Peirce, "Socialization of Teenage Girls through Teen-Magazine Fiction: The Making of a New Woman or an Old Lady?" *Sex Roles* 29 (1993): doi: 10.1007/BF00289996; Michael Kimmel, "The Contemporary 'Crisis' of Masculinity in Historical Perspective," in *The Making of Masculinities: The New Men Studies*, ed. Harry Brod (Boston: Allen & Unwin, 1987).
50. Jean Baker Miller and Irene P. Stiver, *The Healing Connection: How Women Form Relationships in Therapy and in Life* (Boston: Beacon Press, 1997). For information about Jean Baker Miller's relational/cultural psychology, see http://www.wellesley.edu/JBMTI/aboutus.html.
51. David McLelland, *Power* (New York: Irvington, 1980); David Winter, *The Power Motive* (New York: The Free Press, 1973).
52. Some of these developments are detailed in Riane Eisler, *Tomorrow's Children*.
53. See, e.g., Licia Rando, *Caring and Connected Parenting Guide*. Available online: www.saiv.org.
54. See, e.g. Frans de Waal, *The Age of Empathy: Nature's Lessons for a Kinder Society* (New York: Harmony Books, 2009); Dasher Keltner, *Born to Be Good* (New York: Norton, 2009); Darcia Narvaez, *Neurobiology and the Development of Human Morality: Evolution, Culture, and Wisdom* (New York: Norton, 2014); James K. Rilling, "Neuroscientific Approaches and Applications within Anthropology," *Yearbook of Physical Anthropology* 51 (2008): 2–32, doi: 10.1002/ajpa.20947; James K. Rilling et al., "Opposing BOLD Responses to Reciprocated and Unreciprocated Altruism in Putative Reward Pathways," *NeuroReport* 15 (2004) 1–5; Eric B. Keverne, "Epigenetics: Significance of the Gene-Environment Interface for Brain Development," in *Pathways to Peace: The Transformative Power of Children and Families*, eds. James F. Leckman, Catherine Panter-Brick, and Rima Salah (Cambridge, MA: MIT Press, 2014), 65–77; William T. Harbaugh, Ulrich Mayr, and Daniel Burghart, "Neural Responses to Taxation and Voluntary Giving Reveals Motives for Charitable Donations," *Science* 316 (2007): 1622–1625, doi: 10.1126/science.1140738; Farida Anwar, Douglas P. Fry, and Ingrida Grigaityte, "Reducing Aggression and Violence," in *Aggression and Violence: A Social Psychological Perspective*, ed. Brad J. Bushman (New York: Routledge, 2017), 307–320; Fry and Souillac, "The Original Partnership Societies"; Douglas P. Fry, ed., *War, Peace, and Human Nature: The Convergence of Evolutionary and Cultural Views* (New York: Oxford University Press, 2013).
55. See, e.g., Bessel van der Kolk, *The Body Keeps the Score: Brain, Minds, and Body in the Healing of Trauma* (New York: Penguin, 2015); Donna Jackson Nakazawa, *Childhood Disrupted: How Your Biography Becomes Your Biology, and How You Can Heal* (New York: Atria Books, 2016).
56. See Eisler, *The Real Wealth of Nations*. See also www.caringeconomy.org.
57. Eisler, *The Chalice and the Blade*.

58. Eisler, *Sacred Pleasure*.
59. For an important film on this issue, see *Mother: Caring for 7 Billion*, directed by Christophe Fauchere (Tiroir a Films Productions, 2013).
60. Robert Bly, *Iron John* (Boston: Da Capo Press, 2015).
61. See, e.g., Riane Eisler, "Human Rights: Toward an Integrated Theory for Action," *Human Rights Quarterly* 9 (1987): 287–308, and Riane Eisler, "Protecting the Majority of Humanity: Toward an Integrated Approach to Crimes against Present and Future Generations" in *Securing the Rights of Future Generations: Sustainable Development and the Rome Statute of the International Criminal Court*, eds. Marie-Claire Cordonier Segger, Maja Goepel, and Sébastien Jodoin (Cambridge, UK: Cambridge University Press, 2013).

12

A New Beginning

We hope that the research described in the previous chapters has convinced you that "is" does not equal "must be"—that the cycles of violence and injustice that cause so much suffering and misery in our world are not inevitable. We are not talking about building a perfect world, but we are not doomed to be insensitive, cruel, and destructive. On the contrary, neuroscience shows that empathy, caring, and creativity are core human traits. But whether these genetic possibilities are developed and expressed, or stunted and inhibited, largely depends on whether the cultures we grow up in orient to the domination or partnership end of the scale.

How we raise our children and what they experience and observe, especially in the relations between women and men, leave a profound and fundamental mark on children's brains that translate into the values they carry into adulthood and the kind of society they forge. The domination systems that have characterized so many past and present societies can indeed be transformed into partnership systems. More peaceful, equitable, and sustainable societies are possible.

In a time of global warming and other dire ecological challenges, we cannot continue the once hallowed "conquest of nature." When terrorists and rogue states have acquired or are trying to acquire nuclear, chemical, and biological weapons whose destructive power make Hiroshima and Nagasaki look like fireworks, resorting to violence to settle international disputes can be disastrous. Without transformative social change, our children face a decidedly grim future, or perhaps no future at all.

Building foundations for a peaceful and equitable world requires awareness that across cultures and history, two very different social configurations repeatedly emerge. We have considered in this book how partnership and domination systems are underlying social possibilities that affect nothing less than our brains, actions, relationships, values, customs, and institutions. Partnership has a very long evolutionary history and has asserted itself in various places and times. The challenge is to nurture partnership where it exists today, to coax it into existence where it does not, and to protect its sustainability against the re-emergence or spread of domination. We conclude this book with a call to action.

Our History, Our Future

The most important pattern in modern times is the ebb and flow of organized challenges to traditions of domination. Yet over the last four hundred years, the focus of progressive social movements has been primarily on changing economic and political aspects of domination systems. Far less attention has been given to changing traditions of domination and violence in parent-child and gender relations, despite all the evidence that it is through experiencing and observing these primary relations that children learn either to avoid violence and abuse or to accept and even idealize it.

Conventional social analyses have failed to take this foundational matter into account, even though the impact of early experiences on how people think, feel, and act, including what kinds of leaders and policies they favor, has been amply verified. As we have seen, neuroscience shows that early relationships with caretakers profoundly affect brain development and thus set the stage for future beliefs and behaviors.

As we have explored in this book, our human capacities for consciousness, empathy, caring, and nonviolence are suppressed and distorted in domination systems, starting in early childhood. These psychosocial dynamics explain why those who want to push us back to a more autocratic, violent, and unjust social structure uniformly work to maintain or impose rigid domination in gender and parent-child relations. Yet, ironically, for many people who consider themselves progressives, women's and children's rights are still peripheral. It is therefore essential that we see the connection between what is considered normal in gender and generational relations and whether societies are peaceful or violent, equitable or inequitable, caring or punitive.

We have seen that cross-culturally and through history, societies marked by the domination system have the following interacting core characteristics:

- Top-down authoritarian rule in both the family and society;
- The subordination of women to men and greater valuing of stereotypically "masculine" traits and activities;

- A high degree of institutionalized violence, from wife- and child-beating to warfare and terrorism, as fear and force ultimately maintain domination;
- The belief that rankings of domination are divinely or naturally ordained and that the threat or use of violence to impose or maintain them is normal and moral.

In contrast, we find a very different interactive configuration in societies that orient toward partnership. These societies:

- Favor egalitarian and democratic organization in both the family and society;
- Value men and women equally and embody stereotypically feminine caring and nonviolence in socioeconomic policy and social relations;
- Promote nonviolence in social life and relationships, whether within families, communities, or among nations;
- Believe that mutual respect and accountability are part of human nature.

Understanding these two configurations and the multitude of effects they foment is essential for making enlightened decisions for human well-being. We need to promote the partnership configuration to build a more equitable, caring, and sustainable future. The first step is constructing the foundations for this partnership future, starting with the following interactive, mutually supporting four cornerstones.

The First Cornerstone: Childhood

The human brain enters the world as a work in progress. Its circuits and patterns of activity are shaped by the experiences an individual has for the next 20 years (or more): by abuse that causes a child to be hypervigilant and suspicious, or by kindness that creates the neurological circuits that underlie trust; by experiences of sharing and caring that shape neural networks that support empathy, or by experiences that lead to brains that make people chronically defensive, domineering, and uncaring.

While there may be genetic differences in our predispositions for empathy and caring, studies show that offspring of violent parents can become empathic and caring if brought up in empathic and caring family environments. However, if early experiences are violent, children learn that violence directed by the powerful against the powerless is acceptable and a legitimate way of dealing with conflicts or problems. If family relations based on disrespect and abuse are considered normal, they provide mental and emotional models for also condoning violations of basic rights in other relations.

Some people grow up to reject such family patterns, but many do not. In epigenetic terms, neural pathways laid down during development influence intelligence, creativity, dispositions toward violent or nonviolent behavior, empathy or insensitivity, independence or overconformity, and other fundamental traits. Coercive, inequitable, and violent childrearing is therefore foundational to the imposition and maintenance of a coercive, inequitable, and chronically violent social organization.

The problem, as we have seen, is that there is a global pandemic of abuse and violence against children. The staggering rates of abuse and violence against children worldwide constitute widespread, abhorrent, and systemic violations of human rights that cause enormous harm and trauma, kill untold numbers of unreported victims, and leave lifelong post-traumatic effects on the survivors.

The question that arises is why these crimes have been given so little attention not only in scholarly and public discourse but also in the thousands of volumes that have by now been written about human rights. These omissions have served a purpose, whether intended or not. They perpetuate the widespread belief that what happens in families and to children is of little if any real social importance. Another reason for the silence about violations of children's human rights is that religious scriptures condone the use violence against children, as in the famous adage, "spare the rod and spoil the child." To this day, many traditions of abuse and violence are justified on religious grounds.

Over the last decades, violence against children has been increasingly reported rather than accepted as normal and justifiable, reflecting movement away from domination toward partnership. A salient international example is the United Nations Convention on the Rights of the Child, adopted in 1989: "State Parties shall take all appropriate legislative, administrative, social and educational measures to protect the child from all forms of physical or mental violence, injury or abuse, neglect or negligent treatment, maltreatment or exploitation, including sexual abuse, while in the care of parent(s), legal guardian(s) or any other person who has the care of the child."[1]

In 2006, a special report commissioned by the Secretary General of the United Nations emphasized that there can be "no compromise in challenging violence against children. Children's uniqueness—their potential and vulnerability, their dependence on adults—makes it imperative that they have more, not less, protection from violence." It urged member states "to fulfill their human rights obligations and other commitments to ensure protection from all forms of violence," and noted that "no violence against children is justifiable; all violence against children is preventable."[2]

On the national level, as we have considered, a global movement to ban corporal punishment of children is underway. Sweden became the first country to outlaw slapping and spanking as a means of discipline in families back in 1979.[3] Since then, other countries have enacted some version of this prohibition: Finland (1983), Norway (1987), Austria (1989), Cyprus (1994), Italy (1996), Denmark (1997), Latvia (1998), Croatia (1999), Bulgaria (2000), Germany (2000), Israel (2000), Iceland (2003), Ukraine (2004), Romania (2004), Hungary (2005), Greece (2007), Netherlands (2007), and New Zealand (2007).[4] Between 2008 and 2016, another 20 nations put similar laws on their books, including Moldovia, Costa Rica, Lichtenstein, Luxembourg, Argentina, Brazil, Slovenia, and Ireland.[5]

Such laws are important steps in the movement toward the partnership side of the social scale. They are expressions of social values that do not accept the use of corporal punishment of children. But much more is necessary.

The Biocultural Partnership-Domination Lens allows us to see that childhood experiences profoundly affect feelings, thinking, and behavior later in life. To change foundational early relations and experiences to promote human well-being, we urgently need a global campaign against abuse and violence in childhood. Such a campaign should have the following components:

- *Education*: Raising awareness of the consequences—personal and global—of domination as contrasted with partnership childhood relations, as well as education that provides the knowledge and skills necessary for empathic, sensitive, nonviolent, authoritative rather than authoritarian childrearing.[6] Since studies show that empathy and compassion can be taught, school curricula should include these vital skills. From preschool to graduate school, education worldwide should teach caring for life: for self, for others, and for nature.[7]

- *Law*: Enacting and enforcing laws that criminalize violence against children in families, as well as passing legislation that mandates funds and education to support nonviolent, empathic, and caring childrearing.
- *Mass media*: Enacting reforms so that children are not exposed to representations of violence as a means of resolving conflicts and to "comedies" where family members abuse and humiliate each other.
- *Spiritual and religious*: Engaging spiritual and religious leaders to take a strong stand against the intimate violence that perpetuates cycles of violence in relations.[8]
- *International law*: Expanding the purview of international law to protect children worldwide.[9] The Rome Statute, especially Article 7 on Crimes against Humanity, enables the International Court to prosecute government officials responsible for widespread, abhorrent, and systemic violations of human rights or those failing to prevent these.[10] While the Rome Statute has been applied primarily to situations in war or conflict zones, the intent of the statute is to protect certain groups from genocide and widespread, abhorrent, and systemic violations of human rights. However, as it now stands, the Rome Statute does not list *children* under protected groups. Therefore, we propose expanding the interpretation of relevant sections of the Rome Statute to include widespread and systemic practices that cause children great suffering or serious injury to physical or mental health, and amending the Rome Statute to include children under the description of protected groups.[11]

The Second Cornerstone: Gender

Many crimes against children target girls: female infanticide, genital mutilation/cutting, withholding food and healthcare, child marriage, sexual abuse, and sex trafficking (recall Box 5.1).[12] Systemic violence against girls and women has been extensively documented worldwide, yet in many places, egregious human rights violations are condoned on cultural or religious grounds and go unprosecuted. For example, so-called honor killings accounted for one-third of the murders of women in Jordan in 1999.[13]

These murders are considered justified even in cases of sexual assault, as in the case of a 16-year-old girl who was killed because her brother raped her. Neither the family members who murdered the girl nor her rapist brother were punished for their crimes.[14]

Similarly, throwing acid in a girl's face for spurning a suitor and other customary violence to punish girls and women go unprosecuted in some regions. Beating a woman to chastise her for not obeying her husband is culturally accepted in some societies, and often is not questioned by the women themselves.

According to the United Nations Population Fund, one in five women worldwide will be a victim of rape or attempted rape in her lifetime. As highlighted in the recent MeToo campaign, a high frequency of sexual assault and sexual harassment is only beginning to be publicly recognized. Thanks to the global women's movement, the extent and gravity of these systemic violations of human rights are increasingly acknowledged and reported. However, this recognition is quite new.[15]

This again raises a question: Why have abuse and violence against women and girls not been on the agenda as egregious human rights violations long before now? A major reason for this silence is that we have been taught through history, philosophy, social practice, politics, religion, and other cultural institutions that the female part of humanity is not important. The social categories we have culturally inherited also pay sparse if any attention to women. Women's rights are still only a sidebar in most human rights discussions. Moreover, as with violence against children, violence against women is condoned in some of our world's sacred scriptures.

Nonetheless, there has been progress in recent decades. Notable examples are the United Nations Convention on the Elimination of all Forms of Discrimination against Women, adopted by the United Nations General Assembly in 1979, and the United Nations Declaration on the Elimination of Violence against Women, adopted in 1993.[16] However, there is still a general lack of awareness of how the social construction of the roles and relations of women and men not only affects women's and men's individual life options but also affects social institutions—from families, education, and religion to politics, law, and economics—as well as a society's guiding values.

These psychosocial dynamics become evident through the lens of the Biocultural Partnership-Domination Lens. We then see, for instance, why domination-leaning cultures and subcultures with strong in-group versus out-group beliefs and practices, such as racism and anti-Semitism, are also those where people learn early on to equate differences, beginning with the difference between male and female, with superiority or inferiority, with dominating or being dominated.

This domination pattern comes to be seen as normal and natural, and even desirable and moral. Yet, as we have seen, the subordination and de-valuation of women and the "feminine" have actually caused enormous harm not only to women but also to all of humanity.

In reality, the status of women is a powerful predictor of a society's ge-neral quality of life. This was first documented in *Women, Men, and the Global Quality of Life*, a study based on statistics from 89 nations conducted by the Center for Partnership Studies.[17] Subsequently, this finding was rep-licated in the 2000 *World Values Survey*, the largest international survey documenting how attitudes correlate with economic development and democratic or authoritarian political structure.[18] Studies also show that the nations with the lowest gender gaps (such as Norway, Sweden, and Finland) are regularly in the top ranks of the World Economic Forum's *Global Competitiveness Reports*.[19]

Values are human creations, they are learned, and they can be changed through both formal and informal education. It is crucial to teach children that stereotypically feminine traits, such as caring and nonviolence, are core human traits found in both women and men.

In more and more societies today, there is movement toward real part-nership in all spheres of life between women and men, along with a blurring of rigid gender stereotypes. More and more people are recognizing that ster-eotypical women's work, such as taking care of children and maintaining a clean and healthy home, can be performed by both sexes. Men are nur-turing babies, and women are entering positions of economic and political leadership. But this movement remains slow and localized, and in some cultures and subcultures it is fiercely opposed by, among others, religious fundamentalists.

What is needed is greater recognition by scholars, policymakers, and the public that gender is a powerful organizing social principle that shapes institutions and social values. Also urgently needed is a global campaign for equitable and nonviolent gender relations backed by the world's progressive leaders. This campaign would consist of the same five components listed earlier for the campaign against abuse and vio-lence in childhood relations: education, law, media, engaging religious and spiritual leaders, and expanding the purview of international law to protect girls and women worldwide. We propose that the Rome Statute should be interpreted or amended to include gender as a protected category.[20] This is an important means of expanding consciousness in a partnership direction that can lead to urgently needed changes in policies and behaviors.

As long as women hold a small minority of political positions, we cannot really talk of representative democracy. As long as boys and men learn to equate "real masculinity" with violence and control—be it through "heroic" epics, war toys, and violent TV, films, and video games—we cannot realistically expect to end the arms build-ups that are today bankrupting our world and the terrorism and aggressive warfare that in our age of nuclear and chemical warfare threaten our survival. Nor can we realistically expect an end to racism, anti-Semitism, and other ugly isms as long as children learn, before their critical faculties are in place, to accept a model of our species in which one kind of person dominates another.

The global women's movement is an essential step toward a partnership world. We must also support the newer men's movement that is reexamining and reconstructing masculinity, spreading the understanding that domination also has robbed men of their full humanity.[21]

The Third Cornerstone: Economics

Current economic systems are endangering our natural life-support systems. The gap between haves and have-nots has been widening among and often within nations. Poverty seems intractable, speculation is rampant, and so are insensitive and ultimately destructive financial practices.

We need a new way of structuring economics that goes beyond capitalism and socialism.[22] This does not mean we should do away with markets or central planning. Trade and markets have helped millions of people move from poverty to the middle class, and central planning in the form of caring government policies has reduced inequality, as illustrated by in the partnership-oriented Nordic nations. What is needed is leaving the domination elements of both capitalism and socialism behind, strengthening their partnership elements, and building a new economic system that can meet our unprecedented global challenges.

Capitalism and socialism came out of early industrial times, in the 1700s and 1800s, and we are now well into the postindustrial age. Both are antiquated. And both have perpetuated traditions of top-down economics.

If we reexamine the critique of capitalism as unjust and exploitive from the perspective of the partnership-domination continuum, we see that it is actually a critique of the beliefs, institutions, and relationships inherent in domination systems—be they ancient or modern. Long before capitalist billionaires amassed fortunes, Egyptian pharaohs and Chinese emperors hoarded their nations' wealth. Indian potentates received tributes of silver and gold, while lower castes lived in abject poverty. In Asia, Africa, and the Middle East, warlords pillaged, plundered, and terrorized their people. European feudal lords killed their neighbors and oppressed their subjects. And fast-forwarding to today, we can see that capitalist "trickle-down economics" is a replay of earlier traditions where, as in feudal times, those on the bottom are supposed to content themselves with the scraps dropping from the opulent tables of the rich. In short, what we are dealing with is just one more version of an economics of domination.

As for the two large-scale applications of socialism, in the former USSR and China, they, too, created top-down economics. In 1983, Eisler saw this first hand in Russia, where the officials on top ate caviar and drank champagne while the mass of people had to stand in line for hours for the most basic necessities. And these two major applications of socialism not only brutally suppressed freedom and human rights; they also had horrendous environmental problems, as we still see in China today.

When first capitalism and then socialism emerged, there were already some challenges to rankings of domination. Indeed, capitalism challenged mercantilism, or top-down economic control by kings and their agents. Then, socialism challenged the top-down control of the capitalist bourgeoisie, especially of the industrial "robber barons."

However, neither capitalism nor socialism challenged the fact that during the 18th century and most of the 19th century, men's rule over the women and children in their families was the norm—so much so that women and their work were legally the property of their husbands. Accordingly, attempts by thinkers such as Adam Smith and subsequently Karl Marx to devise a more equitable economic system were confined to the public sphere from which women were largely barred by law and custom. And, to this day, neither capitalist nor socialist theory pays attention to the critical matter of whether intrahousehold economic distribution is equitable or inequitable, despite studies showing that this profoundly affects quality of life as well as children's well-being and development.[23]

Both capitalism and socialism reflect and perpetuate domination thinking about what is, and is not, important and valuable. When Smith and Marx developed their economic theories, gender stereotypes in which women and "women's work" were viewed as less important than men and "men's work" were even more rigid than they are today. Caring for people, starting in early childhood, and keeping a clean and healthy home environment were relegated in their economic theories to "reproductive" rather than "productive" work. Similarly, in their theories, there is no mention of the importance of caring for nature. Indeed, for both Smith and Marx, nature was just to be exploited.

Both capitalism and socialism have perpetuated a gendered system of valuations in which anything associated with women and the "feminine"—such as caring, caregiving, and nonviolence—is deemed inferior to anything associated with men and the "masculine." This is the system of values still taught in economic schools and treatises, where to this day the "women's work" of caring for people is barely mentioned. And this is despite findings from neuroscience that caring for people, starting in early childhood, is key to producing the "high-quality human capital" essential for the postindustrial knowledge-service economy.

Of course, as long as caring is culturally devalued, we cannot realistically expect caring social and economic policies designed to promote human well-being and protection of the natural environment. We have to change this cultural and historical bias against the importance of caring.

The massive technological dislocation we see all around us is a crisis. But it is also an opportunity to redefine what is and is not productive work.

A first step is to change how we measure economic health. Current measures such as GDP and GNP include as "productive" work those activities that harm and take life, such as selling guns and cigarettes with their resulting health and funeral costs—all of which are great for GDP and GNP. But they fail to count as productive the hard work of people who care for children, the sick, the elderly, and others at home, and accord very low value to this work in the market.

We need a caring economics. We realize that some people will do a double-take just hearing the terms *caring* and *economics* in the same sentence. But think of what a terrible comment that is on how we have been socialized to accept that uncaring values must drive economics.

In reality, caring is very economically effective. Caring economic practices and policies pay big dividends—not only in human and environmental terms but also in financial terms.[24]

Many studies show that caring companies do better. For example, companies that are regularly listed in *Working Mother* or *Fortune500* as the best firms to work for have a substantially higher return to their investors.[25] Moreover, as we saw when we looked at countries such as Sweden, Finland, and Norway, investing in caring policies pays extremely well for nations.

Caring policies are essential not only for human and environmental reasons but also for economic ones. If we are to have the "high-quality human capital" needed for the postindustrial knowledge-service era, we must recognize what both psychology and neuroscience tell us: human development largely depends on the kind of care and early education children receive. We therefore need strong social support for the caregiving work performed in both the market and the household economic sectors. In addition, with our exponentially growing elderly population, good training and adequate rewards for care work are necessities.

There are trends in this direction. Many West European nations offer monetary assistance and education for parenting, along with government-subsidized paid parental leave, healthcare, and high-quality early childhood education. Satellite economic indicators are beginning to count the economic value of this work. The Swiss government found that if the unpaid work in households were included, it would constitute 40 percent of the reported Swiss GDP.[26] An Australian study, using not only replacement value (which is low, given the devaluation of this "women's work") but also "opportunity cost" (the earnings a caregiver forfeits when s/he does care work in the home) found it would be even higher, at 50 percent of the reported GDP.[27]

In this spirit, initiatives such as Center for Partnership Studies' Caring Economy Campaign developed "Social Wealth Economic Indicators" that go beyond GDP to include environmental conditions as well as levels of health, education, and poverty—and give special attention to the status of women and children as predictors of both quality of life and long-term economic success. The Center's Caring Economics Campaign is designed to help policymakers and the public recognize the importance of moving to a caring economics.[28] Social Wealth Economic Indicators that demonstrate the economic value of the work of caring—whether performed by women or men, and whether in workplaces or homes—are essential to guide government and business policies in the directions sorely needed in our knowledge-service age.

Social Wealth Economic Indicators also guide policies to break through cycles of poverty more effectively worldwide. It makes no sense to talk of poverty in generalities when the mass of the world's poor are women and children. Even in the United States, according to US Census statistics, women over the age of 65 are twice as likely to be poor as men over 65.[29] Most of these women are, or were, caregivers. The persistent failure to give real value to the "women's work" of caregiving helps explain why poverty and hunger have proved so intractable. Among ways this can be changed are establishing caregiver tax credits and Social Security and subsidies for childcare.

Development policies also need to shift their focus to women. Studies confirm that in most of the developing world, women allocate far more of their resources to their families than men do, especially to care and education for children, which is key to both human and economic development.[30]

We urgently need new economic and social inventions that give value to caring and caregiving work in both the market and nonmarket economic sectors. For example, national programs train soldiers to kill—and guarantee them pensions for decades after they leave the armed services. By contrast, there are no national programs for training women and men to care effectively for children and no pensions for their childrearing work.

Caring for other human beings, particularly our children and our elderly, is socially essential and personally meaningful. Support for this vital work can be obtained by taxing activities that harm and take life or that add no real value to human existence—for example, substantially taxing weapons, cigarettes, and short-term trading in stock markets worldwide.

As automation, robotics, and artificial intelligence replace more and more jobs previously performed by people, we must redefine "productive work" and focus on the essential work of caring for and educating people, starting in early childhood. Redefining and revaluing what is productive in this way will also imbue work with meaning—something often lacking in a domination system, where it is primarily motivated by fear and the artificial creation of scarcities.

However, to change economics fundamentally, we cannot focus only on economic systems. As illustrated in Box 12.1, the shift from domination to partnership requires that we change policies and practices in all four cornerstones.

Box 12.1 The Four Cornerstones of Partnership: Examples of Policies and Practices

Childhood
- Delegitimize violence against children as immoral and dysfunctional. Unite behind campaigns to end violence and abuse of children worldwide. Promote caring authoritative rather than authoritarian parenting that empowers rather than disempowers, teaching care and nonviolence.
- Ensure healthcare and good nutrition for all children. Show the personal, economic, social, and environmental benefits from these policies.
- Support and improve public education and promote environmentally conscious gender-balanced multicultural education to help young people learn to respect themselves, others, and the environment and to co-create a healthy, equitable future.
- Provide high-quality childcare and caregiver training. Award high status and economic benefits for the essential work of caregiving, whether done by women or men, in families or in the marketplace.

Gender
- Change cultural beliefs that the male half of humanity is entitled to control the female half in families and societies. Unlink masculinity from domination and violence and femininity from subordination and obedience. Stop violence against women, girls, and LGBTQ communities.
- Change social priorities so that activities stereotypically associated with women are valued. Teach that caring and nonviolence are essential in men, women, and social policy.
- Bring gender-balanced education into schools to change mindsets that value one kind of person more than others. Support partnership education as foundational to ending sexism, racism, and other dominator isms.
- Recognize gender equity as key to building a more peaceful, just, and caring world.

- Promote women in decision-making and bring partnership-oriented women and men from diverse racial and ethnic groups into policy-making positions to support more caring, empathic, and effective policies, including family planning and reproductive choice.

Economics

- Enact environmentally and socially responsible business standards and rules; work for partnership charters for domestic and international corporations as well as in economic and environmental treaties; reward prosocial policies and practices with tax breaks and other benefits and penalize irresponsible ones.
- Enact public campaign financing and other measures to free policymakers to work for an equitable, environmentally sustainable, and caring economic system.
- Show the economic value of caring for people and nature; ensure that caring work is adequately rewarded.
- Use new measures of economic productivity that focus on quality of life, human development, and environmental sustainability.
- Support development of a caring economics or *partnerism* to meet the unprecedented technological, economic, and environmental challenges of our times.

Narratives and Language

- Increase awareness of partnership systems and domination systems as contrasting configurations and show and promote the numerous benefits of partnership over domination.
- Discard cultural narratives that promote domination. Strengthen the understanding that human nature is flexible and includes powerful capacities for empathy, caring, and creativity. Show that self-interest and concern for others can coexist and therefore are not opposites.
- Ensure that the voice of partnership and diversity informs formal and informal education, and counter false stories in social media.

- Use education to raise awareness of beliefs, myths, and stories that promote either domination or partnership, and show the consequences of each system.
- Create and disseminate narratives that support men and women worldwide in regaining their full spectrum of human capacities and possibilities. Recognize the value of caring, caregiving, and nonviolence in both women and men.
- Promote partnership morality and ethics in all relations. Nurture the spiritual courage required to challenge domination and create a partnership world.

The Fourth Cornerstone: Narratives and Language

As we have illustrated, the message of many stories we inherited from earlier times is that dominating and being dominated are the only social possibilities. The gradual proliferation of stories about relations built on mutual benefit, mutual respect, and mutual accountability signals a real revolution in consciousness. But for this revolution in consciousness to succeed, we need a concerted social change effort in the arts, music, and literature as well as science and education.

A real revolution in consciousness requires use of the Biocultural Partnership-Domination Lens to deconstruct domination narratives and replace them with partnership ones, across society and especially in the socialization and education of children. It requires changes in language, stories, and curricula as well as in what is presented as normal and desirable in the mass media worldwide (Table 12.1).

A major issue for our future is what kinds of narratives will be spread through the much-touted virtual reality already advancing on the technological horizon. Other major issues are the standards that guide biotechnology and bioengineering, as well as how artificial intelligence is programmed. If guided by an ethos of partnership, these kinds of technological breakthroughs could vastly improve our lives. If guided by an ethos of domination, our own and future generations of humanity face grim prospects.

Table 12.1 Examples of Domination and Partnership
Vocabularies

Domination/Control	Partnership/Respect
Family values	Valuing families
Educational accountability	Educational responsibility
Capitalist economics	Caring economics
Free market	Fair market
Compassionate conservative	Caring democracy
Traditional values	Humane traditions
Globalization	Global responsibility
Traditional morality	Moral sensitivity
Women's work	Caring work
Politically correct	Personally caring
Matriarchy	Partnership system or *gylany*
Patriarchy	Domination system
Conquest of nature	Harmony with nature

Partnership-oriented stories about spirituality and morality are also essential. We must show that spirituality can be a path to creating a better world right here on Earth instead of an escape from "this veil of tears" to otherworldly realms. Rather than being used to coerce, dominate, and all too often kill, morality must be imbued with caring and love.

Clearly, all of us must continue, and intensify, our various efforts for positive environmental, economic, and social change. These efforts, however, will not succeed unless they are supported by new narratives, especially new scientific theories about our past and present and the possibilities for our future.[31]

Conclusion

The struggle for our future is between those trying to move toward partnership and those pushing us back to rigid rankings of domination. If we are to build a future where all children can realize their capacities for consciousness, caring, and creativity—the capacities that make us fully human—we have to start constructing the foundations for this future now.

In this book, we argue that humans are equipped with a broad range of genetic possibilities, from maintaining domination systems to developing partnership systems. The Biocultural Partnership-Domination Lens describes the conditions that support the expression of our human capacities for insensitivity, cruelty, and destructiveness, or alternately, for consciousness, caring, and creativity.

Moving to a world that orients primarily to partnership rather than domination is essential in our time when high technology guided by an ethos of domination could take us to an evolutionary dead end. It will require time to change established beliefs and structures. It will take perseverance to challenge domination and violence in intimate and international relations. And it will take courage.

It takes courage to actively oppose injustice and cruelty in all spheres of life, not only in the public sectors of politics, law, and business but also in the private realms of parent-child, gender, and sexual relationships. It may not be popular, and may even be dangerous, to do this because domination and violence in intimate and intergroup relations are encoded in some religious and ethnic traditions. But it must be done.

None of us can do everything. But each of us can do something to help build the solid foundations for a more equitable, peaceful, and caring partnership world. Our future and that of coming generations depends on this—starting with what we do today.

Notes

1. United Nations High Commissioner for Refugees, "Convention on the Rights of the Child." Available online: http://www.unhcr.org/en-us/protection/children/50f941fe9/united-nations-convention-rights-child-crc.html.
2. United Nations News, "Annan Welcomes Study on Violence against Children that Calls for Urgent Global Action," last modified October 11, 2006. Available online: www.un.org/apps/news/story.asp?NewsID=20225&Cr=child&Cr1.
3. Before the enactment of their antispanking laws, opinion polls from 1965 showed that 53% of the Swedish people considered physical punishment indispensable. An antispanking campaign during 1970s resulted in a shift to 30% of the population believing that physical punishment was indispensable. By 1994, survey results show that a majority (89%) of Swedes were opposed to every form of physical punishment. Subsequent research (2000) indicates that the percentage of the population opposing all forms of physical punishment has risen to 92%, and among today's generations of parents and the generation to come, there is a greater abhorrence

of physical punishment. *Save the Children: Annual Report 2001 70th Anniversary Issue* (Westport, CT: Save the Children, 2001). The first antispanking law in the world: Stockholm, Sweden. See "Breaking Down the Walls of Silence" online: www. wallsofsilence.com.

4. No Spank, "Countries Where Spanking Is Prohibited by Law in the Home, at School, Everywhere!" last modified March 2007. Available online: www.nospank.net/ totalban.htm.

5. Global Initiative to End All Capital Punishment of Children, "Countdown to Universal Prohibition," accessed December 3, 2016. Available online: http://www. endcorporalpunishment.org/progress/countdown.html.

6. Two excellent resources are Licia Rando, *The Caring and Connected Parenting Guide: A Guide to Raising Connected Children from Birth to 4 Years* (Pacific Grove, CA: Center for Partnership Studies, 2010), available free in English and Spanish at www.saiv.org or www.centerforpartnership.org; and Julie de Azevedo Hanks, "Bringing Partnership Home: A Model of Family Transformation," *Interdisciplinary Journal of Partnership Studies*, 2 (Spring 2015): doi: 10.24926/ijps.v2i1.100.

7. Riane Eisler, *Tomorrow's Children: A Blueprint for Partnership Education in the 21st Century* (Boulder, CO: Westview Press, 2000).

8. This is the mission of the Spiritual Alliance to Stop Intimate Violence (SAIV) that Eisler co-founded with Nobel Peace Laureate Betty Williams, accessed May 7, 2018. Available online: www.saiv.org.

9. Riane Eisler, "Protecting the Majority of Humanity: Toward an Integrated Approach to Crimes against Present and Future Generations," in *Sustainable Development, International Criminal Justice, and Treaty Implementation,* eds. Sebastien Jodoin and Marie-Claire Cordonier Segger (Cambridge, UK: Cambridge University Press, 2013).

10. The Rome Statute (sometimes called the International Criminal Court Statute or the Rome Statute of the International Criminal Court) established the International Criminal Court (ICC). It was adopted at a diplomatic conference in Rome on July 17, 1998, entered into force on July 1, 2002, and has been used in a number of high-profile cases such as the trial of the Serbian leader for war crimes.

11. Eisler, "Protecting the Majority of Humanity."

12. Eisler, "Protecting the Majority of Humanity."

13. "Speak Truth to Power: Telling Stories to Effect Change," *Public Broadcasting Service*, accessed May 7, 2018. Available online: http://www.pbs.org/speaktruthtopower/ rana.html.

14. "Speak Truth to Power: Telling Stories to Effect Change."

15. To illustrate, Riane Eisler's early article "Human Rights: Toward an Integrated Theory for Action," *Human Rights Quarterly* 9 (1987): 287–308, doi: 10.2307/761877, was the first article ever published by the *Human Rights Quarterly* on what has since become known as "women's rights as human rights."

16. United Nations, "Convention on the Elimination of All Forms of Discrimination against Women," December 18, 1979. Available online: https://treaties.un.org/doc/ Publication/MTDSG/Volume%20I/Chapter%20IV/IV-8.en.pdf;   United   Nations,

"Declaration on the Elimination of Violence against Women," December 20, 1993. Available online: http://www.un.org/documents/ga/res/48/a48r104.htm.

17. Riane Eisler, David Loye, and Kari Norgaard, *Women, Men, and the Global Quality of Life* (Pacific Grove, CA: Center for Partnership Studies, 1995).

18. Ron Inglehart, Pippa Norris, and Christian Welzel, "Gender Equality and Democracy," *Comparative Sociology* 1 (2002): 321–346. doi: 10.1163/156913302100418628.

19. Robert Hausmann, Laura D. Tyson, and Saadia Zahidi, *The Global Gender Gap Report* (Geneva: The World Economic Forum, 2011).

20. Eisler, "Protecting the Majority of Humanity."

21. See e.g., Michael S. Kimmel, "The Contemporary 'Crisis' of Masculinity in Historical Perspective," in *The Making of Masculinities: The New Men Studies*, ed. Harry Brod (Boston: Allen & Unwin, 1987); Michael S. Kimmel and Thomas E. Mosmiller, eds., *Against the Tide: Pro-Feminist Men in the United States 1776-1990* (Boston: Beacon Press, 1992).

22. Riane Eisler, *The Real Wealth of Nations: Creating a Caring Economics* (San Francisco: Berrett-Koehler, 2007).

23. For a discussion of this vital, though generally ignored, economic matter, see Eisler, *The Real Wealth of Nations*; Riane Eisler, "Economics as if Caring Matters," *Challenge* 55, (2012): 58–86, doi: 10.2753/0577-5132550203.

24. Eisler, *The Real Wealth of Nations*.

25. Eisler, *The Real Wealth of Nations*.

26. Ueli Schiess and Jacqueline Schön-Bühlmann, *Satellitenkonto Haushaltsproduktion Pilotversuch für die Schweiz* (Neuchâtel, Switzerland: Statistik der Schweiz, 2004).

27. See Economic Security for Women, "The Australian Care Economy." Available online: http://www.security4women.org.au/projects/the-australian-care-economy.

28. The Center for Partnership Studies Caring Economy Campaign offers resources, online training webinars, and advocacy opportunities at www.centerforpartnership.org or www.caringeconomy.org.

29. United States Census Bureau, *Selected Highlights from 65+ in the United States: 2005 Appendix* (Washington, DC: US Census Bureau).

30. See, e.g., Judith Bruce and Cynthia B. Lloyd, "Finding the Ties that Bind: Beyond Headship and Household," in *Intrahousehold Resource Allocation in Developing Countries: Models, Methods, and Policy*, eds. Lawrence Haddad, John Hoddinott, and Harold Alderman (Baltimore: International Food Policy Research Institute, The Johns Hopkins University Press, 1997).

31. To this end, in 2014 the Center for Partnership Studies helped launch the *Interdisciplinary Journal of Partnership Studies*, an online, peer-reviewed, open-access journal housed at the University of Minnesota. Its mission is to share scholarship and create connections "for cultural transformation to build a world in which all relationships, institutions, policies and organizations are based on principles of partnership." The *Interdisciplinary Journal of Partnership Studies*. Available online: https://pubs.lib.umn.edu/index.php/ijps/index.

Acknowledgments

Many people have contributed to this book, which has gone through a number of iterations. Earlier manuscript drafts were strengthened through reviews by biologist Mary E. Clark and psychologist/primatologist Frans de Waal and by the dedicated editing of Helen Knode. Science writer Sharon Begley was also of help, as were psychologist Daniel S. Levine, primatologist Barbara Smuts, anthropologists Stuart Schlegel and Peggy Sanday, neuroscientist Lucy R. Brown, social psychologist David Loye, as well as Melissa Stone, Loren Alison, and Andrea Eisler. We express our gratitude to all of them.

We next want to give our thanks to the many contributions made to the final version of the book by neuroscientist C. Sue Carter, anthropologist Kirk Endicott, psychologist Sheina Lew-Levy, anthropologist Paul "Jim" Roscoe, primatologist/neuroscientist Robert Sapolsky, and peace and global ethics scholar Geneviève Souillac. We also want to thank Loren Alison, Julia Alison, Ann Amberg, Michelle Bird, Frances Collins, Leah Gowron, Carla Goldstein, Kacey Keith, Matt Lett, Brie Mathers, Sara and Manfred Melchior, Sara Saltee, and Claire Souillac.

Our editor at Oxford University Press, Joan Bossert, merits our special thanks, as do Phil Velinov, Jennifer Rod, and Ayshwarya Ramakrishnan.

We would like to acknowledge the collaboration and creative synergy between us as joint authors of this book. It has truly been a pleasure working together, and we have each learned a great deal in the process.

Last, but certainly not least, we want to thank our spouses for their wonderful support and great patience with us during the writing of this book. Riane's partner David Loye has been an invaluable source of care, insight, and knowledge, and so also has Doug's partner Geneviève Souillac. They continue to inspire us.

Riane Eisler and Douglas P. Fry
April 2019

Bibliography

"20 Years Ago Today: Brookfield Zoo Gorilla Helps Boy Who Fell into Habitat." *Chicago Tribune.* August 15, 2016. Available online: http://www. chicagotribune.com/news/ct-gorilla-saves-boy-brookfield-zoo-anniversary-20160815-story.html.

Abbott, Alison. "Obesity Linked to Grandparental Diet: Mice Eating High-Fat Foods Confer Changes on at Least Two Subsequent Generations." *Nature* (2008): doi: 10.1038/news.2008.1240.

Abu-Lughod, Lila. *Veiled Sentiments: Honor and Poetry in a Bedouin Society.* Berkeley: University of California Press, 1986.

Adams, Glenn, Joseph Adonu, and Stephanie Anderson. "The Cultural Grounding of Closeness and Intimacy." In *Handbook of Closeness and Intimacy,* edited by Debra J. Mashek and Arthur Aron, 321–342. New York: Psychology Press, 2004.

Akers, Keith. *The Lost Religion of Jesus: Simple Living and Nonviolence in Early Christianity.* New York: Lantern Books, 2000.

"'Alarming' Rise in Boko Haram Child Suicide Bombers." *Al Jazeera,* last modified April 12, 2017. Available online: http://www.aljazeera.com/news/2017/04/rise-boko-haram-child-suicide-bombers-170412041301650.html.

Allen, Mark W., and Terry L. Jones, editors. *Violence and Warfare among Hunter-Gatherers.* Walnut Creek, CA: Left Coast Press, 2014.

Allen, Paula Gunn. *The Sacred Hoop: Recovering the Feminine in American Indian Traditions.* Boston: Beacon Press, 1992.

Allentoft, Morten E., Martin Sikora, and Eske Willerslev. "Population Genomics of Bronze Age Eurasia." *Nature* 522 (2015): 167–172. doi: 10.1038/nature14507.

Allnat, Libby. "Entitlement Leads to Sexual Assault." *The State Press.* October 2, 2016. Available online: http://www.statepress.com/article/2016/10/spopinion-entitlement-and-sexual-assualt.

Alvard, Michael S., and L. Kuznar. "Deferred Harvests: The Transition from Hunting to Animal Husbandry." *American Anthropologist* 103 (2001): 295–311. doi: 10.1525/aa.2001.103.2.295.

Alvarez, Lizette. "Educators Flocking to Finland, Land of Literate Children." *New York Times,* last modified April 9, 2004. Available online: http://www.

nytimes.com/2004/04/09/world/suutarila-journal-educators-flocking-to-finland-land-of-literate-children.html.

Amodio, David, John Jost, S. Master, and C. Yee. "Neurocognitive Correlates of Liberalism and Conservatism." *Nature Neuroscience* 10 (2007): 1246–1247. doi: 10.1038/nn1979.

Anda, Robert, Vincent Felitti, James Bremner, John Walker, Charles Whitfield, Bruce Perry, Shanta Dube, and Wayne Giles. "The Enduring Effects of Abuse and Related Adverse Experiences in Childhood." *European Archives of Psychiatry and Clinical Neuroscience* 256 (2016): 174–186. doi: 10.1007/s00406-005-0624-4.

Anderson, Steven, A. Bechara, H. Damasio, D. Tranel, and A. Damasio. "Impairment of Social and Moral Behavior Related to Early Damage in Human Prefrontal Cortex." *Nature Neuroscience* 2 (1999): 1032–1037. doi: 10.1038/14833.

Anggard, Adele. *A Humanitarian Past: Antiquity's Impact on Present Social Conditions.* Phoenix, AZ: Author-House, 2014.

Angier, Natalie. "Why We're So Nice: We're Wired to Cooperate." *New York Times*, last modified July 23, 2002. Available online: https://www.nytimes.com/2002/07/23/science/why-we-re-so-nice-we-re-wired-to-cooperate.html.

Angier, Natalie. "No Time for Bullies: Baboons Retool Their Culture." *New York Times*, April 13, 2004. Available online: http://www.nytimes.com/2004/04/13/science/no-time-for-bullies-baboons-retool-their-culture.html.

Angoff, William. "The Nature-Nurture Debate, Aptitudes, and Group Differences." *American Psychologist* 43 (1988): 713–720. doi: 10.1037/0003-066X.43.9.713.

Antoine, Daniel M., Antoine Zazzo, and Renee Friedman. "Revisiting Jebel Sahaba: New Apatite Radiocarbon Dates for One of the Nile Valley's Earliest Cemeteries." Poster presented at the 82nd Annual Meeting of the American Association of Physical Anthropologists. Knoxville, TN, April 9–13, 2013. Abstract accessed March 6, 2018. Available online: http://meeting.physanth.org/program/2013/session25/antoine-2013-revisiting-jebel-sahaba-new-apatite-radiocarbon-dates-for-one-of-the-nile-valleys-earliest-cemeteries.html.

Anwar, Farida, Douglas P. Fry, and Ingrida Grigaityte. "Reducing Aggression and Violence." In *Aggression and Violence: A Social Psychological Perspective*, edited by Brad J. Bushman, 307–320. New York: Routledge, 2017.

Apicella, Coren, Frank Marlowe, James C. Fowler, and Nicholas Christakis. "Social Networks and Cooperation in Hunter-Gatherers." *Nature* 481 (2012): 497–502. doi: 10.1038/nature10736.

Ark of Hope for Children. "Child Trafficking Statistics," last updated July 31, 2017. Available online: https://arkofhopeforchildren.org/child-trafficking/child-trafficking-statistics.

Arkin, William, and Lynne Dobrofsky. "Military Socialization and Masculinity." *Journal of Social Issues* 34 (1978): 161. doi: 10.1111/j.1540-4560.1978.tb02546.x.

Arnold, Matthew. "Dover Beach." In *Seven Centuries of Verse: English and American*, edited by A. J. M. Smith, 476. New York: Scribner, 1967.

Aron, Arthur, Elaine Aron, and Christina Norman. "Self-Expansion Model of Motivation and Cognition in Close Relationships and Beyond." In *Blackwell Handbook of Social Psychology: Interpersonal Processes*, edited by Garth Fletcher and Margaret Clark, 478–503. Oxford, UK: Blackwell Publishers, 2003.

Asch, Solomon. "Studies of Independence and Conformity: A Minority of One against a Unanimous Majority." *Psychological Monographs: General and Applied* 70 (1956): 1–70. doi: 10.1037/h0093718.

Assagioli, Roberto. *Psychosynthesis: A Manual of Principles and Techniques.* New York: Viking Press, 1965.

Augustine, *City of God*, Book XIII, Chapter 14.

Bajak, Aleszu. "The Prenatal Impacts of Violence." Available online: http://undark.org/2016/05/26/pregnancy-violence-homicide-brazil/.

Balikci, Asen. *The Netsilik Eskimo.* Garden City, NY: The Natural History Press, 1970.

Bandura, Albert, and Frances Menlove. "Factors Determining Vicarious Extinction of Avoidance Behavior through Symbolic Modeling." *Journal of Personality and Social Psychology* 8 (1968): 99–108. doi: 10.1037/h0025260.

Bannerman, Stacy. "PTSD and Domestic Abuse: Husbands Who Bring the War Home." *Daily Beast*, last modified September 25, 2010. Available online: http://www.thedailybeast.com/articles/2010/09/25/ptsd-and-domestic-abuse-husbands-who-bring-the-war-home.html.

Bannerman, Stacy. "High Risk of Military Domestic Violence on the Home Front." *SF Gate,* last modified April 7, 2014. Available online: http://www.sfgate.com/opinion/article/High-risk-of-military-domestic-violence-on-the-5377562.php.

Barkow, Jerome, Leda Cosmides, and John Tooby, editors. *The Adapted Mind: Evolutionary Psychology and the Generation of Culture.* New York: Oxford University Press, 1992.

Barnard, Alan. "Contemporary Hunter-Gatherers: Current Theoretical Issues in Ecology and Social Organization." *Annual Review of Anthropology* 12 (1983): 193–214. doi: 10.1146/annurev.an.12.100183.001205.

Barnett, Ola, Cindy Miller-Perrin, and Robin Perrin. *Family Violence across the Lifespan: An Introduction.* Thousand Oaks, CA: Sage.

Baron-Cohen, Simon. *The Essential Difference: Male and Female Brains and the Truth about Autism.* New York: Basic Books, 2003.

Barstow, Anne Llewellyn. *Witchcraze: A New History of the European Witch Hunts.* London: Pandora, 1994.

Barth, Jurgen, Lilian Bermetz, E. Heim, Sven Trelle, and Thomy Tonia. "The Current Prevalence of Child Sexual Abuse Worldwide: A Systematic Review and Meta-analysis." *International Journal of Public Health* 58 (2013): 469–483. doi: 10.1007/s00038-012-0426-1.

Bath, Alison. "Despite Opposition, Paddling Students Allowed in 19 States." *USA Today,* April 23, 2012. Available online: http://usatoday30.usatoday.com/news/nation/story/2012-04-22/school-corporal-punishment/54475676/1.

Bausch, Kenneth. *The Emerging Consensus in Social Systems Theory.* New York: Springer, 2001.

Beckerman, Stephen, Pamela Erickson, James Yost, Jhanira Regalado, Lilia Jaramillo, Corey Sparks, Moises Iromenga, and Kathryn Long. "Life Histories, Blood Revenge, and Reproductive Success among the Waorani of Ecuador." *Proceedings of the National Academy of Sciences (PNAS)* 106 (2009): 8134–8139. doi: 10.1073/pnas.0901431106.

Bekoff, Marc, and Jessica Pierce. *Wild Justice: The Moral Lives of Animals.* Chicago: University of Chicago Press, 2009.

Benedict, Ruth. *The Chrysanthemum and the Sword: Patterns of Japanese Culture.* Boston: Houghton Mifflin, 1946.

Berkowitz, Leonard. "Some Determinants of Impulsive Aggression: Role of Mediated Associations with Reinforcements for Aggression." *Psychological Review* 81 (1974): 165–176. doi: 10.1037/h0036094.

Bicchieri, M. G., editor. *Hunters and Gatherers Today.* Prospect Heights: IL: Waveland, 1972.

Binford, Lewis R. *Constructing Frames of Reference: An Analytical Method for Archaeological Theory Building Using Hunter-Gatherer and Environmental Data Sets.* Berkeley: University of California Press, 2001.

Birdsell, Joseph B. "Australia: Ecology, Spacing Mechanisms and Adaptive Behaviour in Aboriginal Land Tenure." In *Land Tenure in the Pacific,* edited by R. Crocombe, 334–361. New York: Oxford University Press, 1971.

Bjorklund, David F., and Anthony D. Pellegrini. *The Origins of Human Nature: Evolutionary Developmental Psychology*. Washington, DC: American Psychological Association, 2002.

Blackstone, William. *Commentaries on the Laws of England*. Oxford: Clarendon Press, 1765.

Blake, C. Fred. "Foot-Binding in Neo-Confucian China and the Appropriation of Female Labor." *Signs* 19 (1994): 676–712. doi: 10.1086/494917.

Bligh-Glover, William, Tamara Killi, Laura Shapiro-Kulnane, Ginny Dilley, Lee Friedman, Elizabeth Balrai, Grazyna Raikowska, and Craig Stockmeir. "The Serotonin Transporter in the Midbrain of Suicide Victims with Major Depression." *Biological Psychiatry* 47 (2000): 1015–1024. doi: https://doi.org/10.1016/S0006-3223(99)00313-3.

Bluhm, Robyn, and Ruth A. Lanius. "Importance of the Developmental Perspective in Evolutionary Discussions of Post-Traumatic Stress Disorder." In *Ancestral Landscapes in Human Evolution*, edited by Darcia Narvaez, Kristin Valentino, Agustin Fuentes, James J. McKenna, and Peter Gray, 286–302. New York: Oxford University Press, 2014.

Bly, Robert. *Iron John*. Boston: Da Capo Press, 2015.

Boehm, Christopher. *Hierarchy in the Forest: The Evolution of Egalitarian Behavior*. Cambridge, MA: Harvard University Press, 1999.

Bohman, M. "Predispositions to Criminality: Swedish Adoption Studies in Retrospect." In *Genetics of Criminal and Anti-social Behavior*, edited by G. Bock and J. Goode, 99–114. Chichester, UK: Wiley, 1996.

"Bono: 'There's a Difference Between Cosying Up to Power and Being Close to Power.'" *Guardian*, September 21, 2013. Available online: http://www.theguardian.com/music/2013/sep/22/bono-campaigner-u2-global-poverty.

Bonta, Bruce. *Peaceful Peoples: An Annotated Bibliography*. Metuchen, NJ: Scarecrow Press, 1993.

Bonta, Bruce. "Conflict Resolution among Peaceful Societies: The Culture of Peacefulness." *Journal of Peace Research* 33 (1996): 403–420. doi: 10.1177/0022343396033004003.

Bonta, Bruce. "Cooperation and Competition in Peaceful Societies." *Psychological Bulletin* 121 (1997): 299–320. doi: 10.1037/0033-2909.121.2.299.

Bonta, Bruce. "Peaceful Societies Prohibit Violence." *Journal of Aggression, Conflict, and Peace Research* 5 (2013): 117–129. doi: 10.1108/JACPR-01-2013-0002.

Bonta, Bruce, and Douglas P. Fry. "Lessons for the Rest of Us: Learning from Peaceful Societies." In *The Psychology of Resolving Global Conflicts: From War to Peace, Volume I, Nature vs. Nurture*, edited by Mari Fitzduff and Chris E. Stout, 175–210. Westport, CT: Praeger Security International, 2006.

Bowlby, John. *The Roots of Parenthood*. London: National Children's Home, 1953.

Bowlby, John. "The Nature of the Child's Tie to His Mother." *International Journal of Psychoanalysis* 39 (1958): 350–373.

Bowlby, John. *Attachment: Attachment and Loss, Volume 1*. New York: Basic Books, 1969.

Bridenthal, Renate, and Claudia Koonz. *Becoming Visible: Women in European History*. Boston: Houghton Mifflin, 1977.

Brown, Donald. *Human Universals*. New York: McGraw-Hill, 1991.

Bruce, Judith, and Cynthia B. Lloyd. "Finding the Ties that Bind: Beyond Headship and Household." In *Intrahousehold Resources Allocation in Developing Countries: Methods, Models, and Policy*, edited by Lawrence Haddad, John Hoddinott, and Harold Alderman, 213–228. Baltimore: International Food Policy Research Institute and Johns Hopkins University Press, 1997.

Brundtland, Gro Harlem. "Why We Care." Accessed March 13, 2018. Available online: http://reproductivehealth.aspeninstitute.org/Media/Details/0040/Gro-Harlem-Brundtland-Why-We-Care.

Bruner, Jerome, and Leo Postman. "On the Perception of Incongruity: A Paradigm." In *Readings in Perception*, edited by David C. Beardsley and Michael Wertheimer, 648–663. Princeton, NJ: Van Nostrand, 1958.

Bruner, Jerome, Leo Postman, and John Rodriguez. "Expectation and the Perception of Color." *American Journal of Psychology* 64 (1951): 216–227. doi: 10.2307/1418668.

Burbank, Victoria. "Female Aggression in Cross-Cultural Perspective." *Behavior Science Research* 21 (1987): 70–100. doi: 10.1007/BF01420987.

Burbank, Victoria. *Fighting Women: Anger and Aggression in Aboriginal Australia*. Berkeley: University of California Press, 1994.

Burlingham, Dorothy, and Anna Freud, *Infants without Families*. Oxford: Allen and Unwin, 1944.

Burrows, Edwin. *Flower in My Ear: Arts and Ethos on Ifaluk Atoll*. Seattle: University of Washington Press, 1963.

Buss, David. *Evolutionary Psychology: The New Science of the Mind*. Boston: Allyn and Bacon, 1999.

Buss, David. *The Murderer Next Door: Why the Mind Is Designed to Kill*. New York: Penguin Press, 2005.

Cadoret, Remi, Edward Throughton, Jeffrey Bagford, and George Woodworth. "Genetic and Environmental Factors in Adoptee Antisocial Personality." *European Archives of Psychiatry and Clinical Neuroscience* 239 (1990): 231–240. doi: 10.1007/BF01738577.

Cadoret Remi, Edward Troughton, Thomas O'Gorman, and Ellen Heywood. "Alcoholism and Antisocial Personality: Interrelationships, Genetic and Environmental Factors." *Archives of General Psychiatry* 42 (1985): 161–167. doi: org/10.1001/archpsyc.1985.01790250055007.

Cadoret, Remi, William Yates, Edward Troughton, George Woodworth, and Mark Stewart. "Genetic-Environmental Interaction in the Genesis of Aggressivity and Conduct Disorders." *Archives of General Psychiatry* 52 (1995): 916–924. doi: 10.1001/archpsyc.1995.03950230030006.

Cai, Junsheng. "Myth and Reality: The Projection of Gender Relations in Prehistoric China." In *The Chalice and the Blade in Chinese Culture: Gender Relations and Social Models,* edited by Min Jiayin, 34–90. Beijing: China Social Sciences Publishing House, 1995.

Callaway, Ewen. "Fearful Memories Haunt Mouse Descendants: Genetic Imprint from Traumatic Experiences Carries through at Least Two Generations." *Nature* (2013). doi:10.1038/nature.2013.14272. Available online: http://www.nature.com/news/fearful-memories-haunt-mouse-descendants-1.14272.

Calvin, William. *The Throwing Madonna: Essays on the Brain.* New York: McGraw-Hill, 1983.

Cantor, Karen, and Camilla Kjaerilff. *The Danish Solution.* Singing Wolf Documentaries, 00:58:00, 2010. Accessed May 2, 2018. Available online: http://www.snagfilms.com/films/title/the_danish_solution.

Carter, C. Sue. "Neuroendocrine Perspectives on Social Attachment and Love." *Psychoneuroendocrinology* 23 (1998): 779–818. doi: 10.1016/S0306-4530(98)00055-9.

Carter, C. Sue. "The Chemistry of Child Neglect: Do Oxytocin and Vasopressin Mediate the Effects of Early Experience?" *Proceedings of the National Academy of Sciences (PNAS)* 102 (2005): 18247–18248. doi: 10.1073/pnas.0509376102.

Carter, C. Sue, and Stephen W. Porges. "Peptide Pathways to Peace." In *Pathways to Peace: The Transformative Power of Children and Families,* edited by James F. Leckman, Catherine Panter-Brick, and Rima Salah, 43–64. Cambridge, MA: MIT Press, 2014.

Caspi, Avshalom, Joseph McClay, Terrie Moffitt, Jonathan Mill, Judy Martin, Ian Craig, Alan Taylor, and Richie Poulton. "Role of Genotype in the Cycle of Violence in Maltreated Children." *Science* 297 (2002): 851–854. doi: 10.1126/science.1072290.

Castell, Albury. *An Introduction to Modern Philosophy.* New York: Macmillan, 1946.

Central Intelligence Agency. "World Factbook." Available online: https://www. cia.gov/library/publications/the-world-factbook/rankorder/2091rank.html.

Chagnon, Napoleon. "Life Histories, Blood Revenge, and Warfare in a Tribal Population." *Science* 239 (1988): 985–992. doi: 10.1126/science.239.4843.985.

Chagnon, Napoleon. *Yanomamö.* Fort Worth, TX: Harcourt Brace Jovanovich, 1992, 4th edition.

Champagne, Frances. "Epigenetics of Mammalian Parenting." In *Ancestral Landscapes in Human Evolution: Culture, Childrearing and Social Wellbeing,* edited by Darcia Narvaez, Kristin Valentino, Agustin Fuentes, James J. McKenna, and Peter Gray, 18–37. New York: Oxford University Press, 2014.

Chaplin, Tristan, Hsin-Hao Yu, Juliana Soares, Ricardo Gattass, and Marcello Rosa. "A Conserved Pattern of Differential Expansion of Cortical Areas in Simian Primates." *Journal of Neuroscience* 33 (2013): 15120–15125. doi: 10.1523/JNEUROSCI.2909-13.2013.

Chatters, James. "Wild-Type Colonizers and High Levels of Violence among Paleoamericans." In *Violence and Warfare among Hunter-Gatherers,* edited by Mark W. Allen and Terry L. Jones, 70–96. Walnut Creek, CA: Left Coast Press, 2014.

Chenoweth, Erica, and Maria Stephan, *Why Civil Resistance Works: The Strategic Logic of Nonviolent Conflict.* New York: Columbia University Press, 2011.

Cho, Mary, Courtney DeVries, Jessie Williams, and C. Sue Carter. "The Effects of Oxytocin and Vasopressin on Partner Preferences in Male and Female Prairie Voles (*Microtus ochrogaster*)." *Behavioral Neuroscience* 113 (1999): 1071–1079. Available online: http://dx.doi.org/10.1037/0735-7044.113.5.1071.

Chokshia, Niraj. "Trump Voters Driven by Fear of Losing Status, Not Economic Anxiety, Study Finds." *New York Times.* April 24, 2018. Accessed May 6, 2018. Available online: https://www.nytimes.com/2018/04/24/us/politics/trump-economic-anxiety.html.

"Cincinnati Zoo Gorilla Shooting: Mum of Rescued Boy Questioned by Police in Child Neglect Investigation." *Mirror,* June 2, 2016. Available online: https://www.mirror.co.uk/news/world-news/cincinnati-zoo-gorilla-shooting-mum-8106015.

Clastres, Pierre. "The Guayaki." In *Hunters and Gatherers Today,* edited by M. G. Bicchieri, 138–174. Prospect Heights, IL: Waveland, 1972.

Cloud, John. "Epigenetics: Why Your DNA Isn't Your Destiny." *Time,* January 6, 2010. Available online: http://www.time.com/time/health/article/0,8599,1951968,00.html.

Cohen, Mark N. "Prehistoric Hunter-Gatherers: The Meaning of Social Complexity." In *Prehistoric Hunter-Gatherers: The Emergence of Cultural Complexity*, edited by T. D. Price and J. A. Brown, 99–119. New York: Academic Press, 1985.

Coltrane, Scott. "Father-Child Relationships and the Status of Women: A Cross-Cultural Study." *American Journal of Sociology* 93 (1988): 1060–1095. doi: 10.1086/228864.

Committee on the Rights of the Child (CRC). *The Right of the Child to Protection from Corporal Punishment and Other Cruel or Degrading Forms of Punishment* [articles 19, 28(2) and 37, interalia], CRC/C/GC/8, para 11. General Comment No. 8, 2006.

Cooper, John M. "The Ona." In *Handbook of South American Indians, Volume 1, The Marginal Tribes*, edited by Julian H. Steward, 107–125. Washington, DC: United States Printing Office, 1946.

"Corporal Punishment in Public Schools." *CNN*, last modified August 20, 2008. Available online: http://www.cnn.com/2008/US/08/20/corporal.punishment/#cnnSTCOther1.

Côté, Stéphane, Paul Piff, and Robb Willer. "For Whom Do the Ends Justify the Means? Social Class and Utilitarian Moral Judgment." *Journal of Personality and Social Psychology* 104 (2013): 490–503. doi: 10.1037/a0030931.

Csikszentmihalyi, Mihaly. *Flow: The Psychology of Optimal Experience*. New York: Harper Collins, 1990.

Cuddy, Emily, and Richard V. Reeves. "Report: Hitting Kids: American Parenting and Physical Punishment." *Brookings Institution*, last modified November 6, 2014. Available online: https://www.brookings.edu/research/hitting-kids-american-parenting-and-physical-punishment/.

Dabrowski, Kazimierz. *Positive Disintegration*. Boston: Little, Brown, 1964.

Dalai Lama. *Beyond Religion: Ethics for a Whole World*. Boston: Mariner Books/Houghton Mifflin, 2011.

Daly, Martin, and Margo Wilson. *Homicide*. New York: Aldine de Gruyter, 1988.

Damasio, Antonio. *Descartes' Error*. New York: Grosset/Putnam, 1994.

Damasio, Antonio. *The Feeling of What Happens: Body and Emotion in the Making of Consciousness*. New York: Harcourt, 1999.

Damon, William. *Moral Child: Nurturing Children's Natural Moral Growth*. New York: Free Press, 1990.

Daoud, Kamel. "The Sexual Misery of the Arab World." *New York Times*. Accessed March 24, 2018. Available online: http://www.nytimes.com/2016/02/14/opinion/sunday/the-sexual-misery-of-the-arab-world.html?_r=0.

The Dartmouth Bible. Annotated by Roy Chamberlain and Herman Feldman. Boston: Houghton Mifflin, 1950.

Darwent, John, and Christyann Darwent. "Scales of Violence across the North American Arctic." In *Violence and Warfare among Hunter-Gatherers,* edited by Mark W. Allen and Terry L. Jones, 182–203. Walnut Creek, CA: Left Coast Press, 2014.

Darwin, Charles. *Origin of Species: By Means of Natural Selection of the Preservation of Favoured Races in the Struggle for Life.* New York: Norton, 1958, Mentor paperback edition, originally published in 1859.

Darwin, Charles. *The Descent of Man.* Princeton, NJ: Princeton University Press, 2010, originally published in 1871.

Dawkins, Richard. *The Selfish Gene.* New York: Oxford University Press, 1976 and 1989 editions.

Day, R. L., Kevin Laland, and F. John Odling-Smee. "Rethinking Adaptation: The Niche-Construction Perspective." *Perspectives in Biology and Medicine* 46 (2003): 80–95. doi: 10.1353/pbm.2003.0003.

Deacon, Terrence. *The Symbolic Species: The Co-evolution of Language and the Brain.* New York: Norton, 1998.

de Azevedo Hanks, Julie. "Bringing Partnership Home: A Model of Family Transformation." *Interdisciplinary Journal of Partnership Studies* 2 (2015): Spring. doi: 10.24926/ijps.v2i1.100.

Deci, Edward, and Richard M. Ryan. *Intrinsic Motivation and Self-Determination in Human Behavior.* New York: Plenum Press, 1985.

Dehghan, Saeed Kamili, and Ian Black. "Iranians Still Facing Death by Stoning Despite 'Reprieve.'" *Guardian,* last modified July 8, 2010. Available online: https://www.theguardian.com/world/2010/jul/08/iran-death-stoning-adultery.

Delville, Yvon, Richard Melloni, and Craig Ferris. "Behavioral and Neurobiological Consequences of Social Subjugation during Puberty in Golden Hamsters." *Journal of Neuroscience* 18 (1998): 2667–2672. doi: 10.1523/JNEUROSCI.18-07-02667.1998.

DeMause, Lloyd. "Schreber and the History of Childhood." *Journal of Psychohistory* 15 (1987): 423–430.

Dentan, Robert K. "Notes on Childhood in a Nonviolent Context: The Semai Case (Malaysia)." In *Learning Non-Aggression: The Experience of Non-Literate Societies,* edited by Ashley Montagu, 94–143. New York: Oxford University Press, 1978.

Des Lauriers, Matthew R. "The Spectre of Conflict on Isla Cedros, Baja California, Mexico." In *Violence and Warfare among Hunter-Gatherers,* edited by Mark W. Allen and Terry L. Jones, 204–222. Walnut Creek, CA: Left Coast Press, 2014.

de Waal, Frans. *Peacemaking among Primates*. Cambridge, MA: Harvard University Press, 1989.

de Waal, Frans. *Good Natured: The Origins of Right and Wrong in Humans and Other Animals*. Cambridge, MA: Harvard University Press, 1996.

de Waal, Frans. *The Ape and the Sushi Master*. New York: Basic Books, 2001.

de Waal, Frans. *The Age of Empathy*. New York: Harmony, 2009.

de Waal, Frans. *The Bonobo and the Atheist: In Search of Humanism among the Primates*. New York: Norton, 2013.

de Waal, Frans, and Frans Lanting. *Bonobo: The Forgotten Ape*. Berkeley: University of California Press, 1997.

de Waal, Frans, Kristin Leimgruber, and Amanda R. Greenberg. "Giving Is Self-Rewarding for Monkeys." *Proceedings of the National Academy of Sciences (PNAS)* 105 (2008): 13685–13689. doi: 10.1073/pnas.0807060105.

Dias, Brian, and Kerry Ressler. "Parental Olfactory Experience Influences Behavior and Neural Structure in Subsequent Generations." *Nature Neuroscience* 17 (2014): 89–96. doi: 10.1038/nn.3594.

Dijkstra, Bram. *Idols of Perversity: Fantasies of Feminine Evil in Fin-de-Siècle Culture*. Oxford: Oxford University Press, 1986.

Di Pellegrino, Giusseppe, Luciano Fadiga, Leonardo Fogassi, Vittorio Gallese, and Giacomo Rizzolatti. "Understanding Motor Events: A Neurophysiological Study." *Experimental Brain Research* 91 (1992): 176–180. doi: 10.1007/BF00230027.

Dixon, Robyn. "In Parts of Africa, People with Albinism Are Hunted for Their Body Parts. The Latest Victim: A 9-Year-Old Boy." *Los Angeles Times*, last modified June 15, 2017. Available online: http://www.latimes.com/world/africa/la-fg-malawi-albinos-hunted-2017-story.html.

Dobshansky, Theodosius. *The Biology of Ultimate Concern*. New York: Meridian, 1969.

Dobzhansky, Theodosius. *Genetics and the Origin of Species*. New York: Columbia University Press, 1982, originally published in 1937.

"Dolphins Save Swimmers from Shark Attack." *Guardian*. November 23, 2004. Available online: https://www.theguardian.com/world/2004/nov/23/1.

Dondi, Marco, Francesca Simion, and Giovanna Caltran. "Can Newborns Discriminate Between Their Own Cry and the Cry of Another Newborn Infant?" *Developmental Psychology* 35 (1999): 418–426, doi: 10.1037/0012-1649.35.2.418.

Donnerstein, Edward. "Aggressive Erotica and Violence against Women." *Journal of Personality and Social Psychology* 39 (1980): 269–277. doi: 10.1037/0022-3514.39.2.269.

Draper, Patricia. "The Learning Environment for Aggression and Anti-Social Behavior among the !Kung (Kalahari Desert, Botswana, Africa)." In *Learning Non-Aggression: The Experience of Non-Literate Societies*, edited by Ashley Montagu, 31–53. New York: Oxford University Press, 1978.

Dudenhoefer, Anne-Lynn. "Understanding the Recruitment of Child Soldiers in Africa." *ACCORD*, August 16, 2016. Available online: http://www.accord.org.za/conflict-trends/understanding-recruitment-child-soldiers-africa/.

Dunbar, Robin, Louise Barrett, and John Lycett. *Evolutionary Psychology*. Oxford: Oneworld Press, 2007.

Dunbar, Robin, Chris Knight, and Camilla Power, editors. *The Evolution of Culture: An Interdisciplinary View*. New Brunswick, NJ: Rutgers University Press, 1999.

Dunn, Elizabeth, Lara Aknin, and Michael Norton. "Spending Money on Others Promotes Happiness." *Science* 319 (2008): 1687–1688. doi: 10.1126/science.1150952.

Durant, Will. *The Life of Greece*. New York: Simon and Schuster, 1966.

Durant, Will, and Ariel Durant. *The Age of Voltaire*. New York: Simon and Schuster, 1980.

Durant, Will. *The Renaissance: A History of Civilization in Italy from 1304-1576 a.d.* New York: Fine Communications, 1997.

Dyble, Mark, Gul Deniz Salali, Nikhil Chaudhary, A. Page, D. Smith, J. Thompson, Lucio Vinicius, Ruth Mace, and Andrea Migliano. "Sex Equality Can Explain the Unique Social Structure of Hunter-Gatherer Bands." *Science* 348 (2015): 796–798, doi: 10.1126/science.aaa5139.

Economic Security for Women. "The Australian Care Economy." Available online: http://www.security4women.org.au/projects/the-australian-care-economy.

Ehrenberg, Rachel. "Motherly Love Coddles the Brain." *Science*. August 2, 2004. Available online: http://www.sciencemag.org/news/2004/08/motherly-love-coddles-brain.

Einstein, Albert, Leopold Infeld, and Banesh Hoffmann. "The Gravitational Equations and the Problem of Motion." *Annals of Mathematics* 39 (1938): 65–100. doi: 10.2307/1968714.

Eisler, Riane. *The Chalice and the Blade: Our History, Our Future*. San Francisco: Harper and Row, 1987.

Eisler, Riane. "Human Rights: Toward an Integrated Theory for Action." *Human Rights Quarterly* 9 (1987): 287–308.

Eisler, Riane. *Sacred Pleasure: Sex, Myth, and the Politics of the Body*. San Francisco: Harper Collins, 1995.

Eisler, Riane. "Cultural Transformation Theory: A New Paradigm for History." In *Macrohistory and Macrohistorians*, edited by Johan Galtung and Sohail Inayatullah, 141–150. Westport, CT: Praeger Publishers, 1997.

Eisler, Riane. *Tomorrow's Children: A Blueprint for Partnership Education in the 21st Century*. Boulder, CO: Westview Press, 2000.

Eisler, Riane. "A Time for Partnership." In *SAGA: Best New Writings on Mythology, Volume 2*, edited by Jonathan Young, 147–153. Ashland, OR: White Cloud Press, 2001.

Eisler, Riane. *The Power of Partnership: Seven Relationships that Will Change Your Life*. Novato, CA: New World Library, 2002.

Eisler, Riane. *The Real Wealth of Nations: Creating a Caring Economics*. San Francisco: Berrett-Koehler, 2007.

Eisler, Riane. "Our Great Creative Challenge: Rethinking Human Nature—and Recreating Society." In *Everyday Creativity and New Views of Human Nature*, edited by Ruth Richards, 261–286. Washington, DC: APA Books, 2007.

Eisler, Riane. "Economics as if Caring Matters." *Challenge* 55 (2012): 58–86. doi: 10.2753/0577-5132550203.

Eisler, Riane. "Protecting the Majority of Humanity: Toward an Integrated Approach to Crimes against Present and Future Generations." In *Sustainable Development, International Criminal Justice, and Treaty Implementation*, edited by Marie-Claire Cordonier-Segger and Sébastien Jodoin, 305–326. Cambridge, UK: Cambridge University Press, 2013.

Eisler, Riane. "Human Possibilities: An Integrated Systems Approach." *Journal of Global Education* 69 (2013): 269–289. doi: 10.1080/02604027.2013.803361.

Eisler, Riane. "The Power of the Creative Word: From Domination to Partnership." In *The Tapestry of the Creative Word in Anglophone Literatures*, edited by Antonella Riem, Maria Renata Dolce, Stephano Mercanti, and Caterina Colombra, 33–47. Udine, Italy: Forum Editrice, 2013.

Eisler, Riane. "Human Possibilities: The Interaction of Biology and Culture." *Interdisciplinary Journal of Partnership Studies* 1 (2014): 3. doi: 10.24926/ijps. v1i1.88.

Eisler, Riane. "Can International Law Protect Half of Humanity? A New Strategy to Stop Violence against Women." *Journal of Aggression, Conflict, and Peace Research* 7 (2015): 88–100. doi: 10.1108/JACPR-12-2013-0036.

Eisler, Riane. "Societal Contexts for Family Relations: Development, Violence and Stress." In *Contexts for Young Child Flourishing: Evolution, Family and Society*, edited by Darcia Narvaez, Julia M. Braungart-Rieker, Laura E. Miller-Graff, Lee T. Gettler, and Paul D. Hastings, 61–78. New York: Oxford University Press, 2016.

Eisler, Riane. "Building an Integrated Progressive Agenda: The Post-Election Crisis and Its Opportunities." *Speech delivered at the Cosmopolitan Club*, New York, NY, 2017. Available online at http://rianeeisler.com/building-an-integrated-progressive-agenda-the-post-election-crisis-and-its-opportunities/.

Eisler, Riane. "Protecting Children: From Rhetoric to Global Action." *Interdisciplinary Journal of Partnership Studies* 5 (2018): Article 7. doi: 10.24926/ijps.v5i1.1125.

Eisler, Riane, and Daniel Levine. "Nurture, Nature, and Caring: We Are Not Prisoners of Our Genes." *Brain and Mind* 3 (2002): 9–52. doi: 10.1023/A:1016553723748.

Eisler, Riane, and David Loye. *The Partnership Way*. Pacific Grove, CA: Center for Partnership Studies, 1998, revised edition.

Eisler, Riane, David Loye, and Kari Norgaard. *Women, Men, and the Global Quality of Life*. Pacific Grove, CA: Center for Partnership Studies, 1995.

Eisler, Riane, and Teddie M. Potter. *Transforming Interprofessional Partnerships: A New Framework for Nursing and Partnership-Based Health Care*. Indianapolis, IN: Sigma Theta Tau, 2014.

Eliade, Mirce. *Myth and Reality*. Translated by William Trash. London: Allen and Unwin, 1964.

Ellison, Christopher, and John Bartkowski. "Religion and the Legitimization of Violence: Conservative Protestantism and Corporal Punishment." In *The Web of Violence: From Interpersonal to Global*, edited by Jennifer Turpin and Lester R. Kurtz, 45–67. Urbana: University of Illinois Press, 1997.

Elms, Alan. "Obedience Lite." *American Psychologist* 64 (2009): 32–36. doi: 10.1037/a0014473.

Elms, Alan, and Stanley Milgram. "Personality Characteristics Associated with Obedience and Defiance toward Authoritative Command." *Journal of Experimental Research in Personality* 1 (1966): 282–289.

Embry, Dennis. "Nurturing the Genius of Genes: The New Frontier of Education, Therapy, and Understanding the Brain." *Brain and Mind* 3 (2002): 101–132. doi: 10.1023/A:1016509908727.

Endicott, Karen L. "Gender Relations in Hunter-Gatherer Societies." In *The Cambridge Encyclopedia of Hunters and Gatherers*, edited by Richard B.

Lee and Richard Daly, 411–418. Cambridge, UK: Cambridge University Press, 1999.

Endicott, Kirk M. "Peaceful Foragers: The Significance of the Batek and Moriori for the Question of Innate Human Violence." In *War, Peace, and Human Nature: The Convergence of Evolutionary and Cultural Views*, edited by Douglas P. Fry, 243–261. New York: Oxford University Press, 2013.

Endicott, Kirk M., and Karen L. Endicott. *The Headman Was a Woman: Gender Egalitarianism among the Batek of Malaysia*. Long Grove, IL: Waveland, 2008.

Ericksen Karen, and Heather Horton. "'Blood Feuds': Cross-Cultural Variations in Kin Group Vengeance." *Behavior Science Research* 26 (1992): 57–85. doi: 10.1177/106939719202600103.

Falk, Richard. *Power Shift: On the New Global Order*. London: Zed Books, 2016.

Fauchere, Christophe. *Mother: Caring for 7 Billion*. DVD, Blue Ray, 69 minutes, Tiroir A Film Productions, 2013.

Federal Bureau of Investigation. *FBI Law Enforcement Bulletin, Human Sex Trafficking* (March 2011). Available online: https://www.hsdl.org/ ?abstract&did=6872.

Federal Interagency Forum on Aging-Related Statistics. *Older Americans 2016 Key Indicators of Well-Being*. Washington, DC: US Government Printing Office, 2016. Available online: http://www.agingstats.gov/docs/LatestReport/ OA2016.pdf.

Feldman, Ruth. "Oxytocin and Social Affiliation in Humans." *Hormones and Behavior* 61 (2012): 380–391. doi: 10.1016/j.yhbeh.2012.01.008.

Feldman, Ruth, A. Vengrober, and R. Ebstein. "Affiliation Buffers Stress: Cumulative Genetic Risk in Oxytocin-Vasopressin Genes Combines with Early Caregiving to Predict PTSD in War-Exposed Young Children." *Translational Psychiatry* 4 (2014): e370. doi: 10.1038/tp.2014.6.

Felitti, Vincent. "Adverse Childhood Experiences and Adult Health." *Academic Pediatrics* 9 (2009): 131–132. doi: 10.1016/j.acap.2009.03.001. Available online: http://static1.squarespace.com/static/500ee7f0c4aa5f5d4c9fee39/t/ 53ecfab7e4b03cc699a85f97/1408039607750/Adverse+Childhood+Experienc es+and+Adult+Health.pdf.

Felitti, Vincent, R. Anda, D. Nordenberg, D. Williamson, A. Spitz, V. Edwards, M. Koss, and M. Marks. "Relationship of Childhood Abuse and Household Dysfunction to Many of the Leading Causes of Death in Adults: The Adverse Childhood Experiences (ACE) Study." *American Journal of Preventive Medicine* 14 (1998): 245–258. doi: 10.1016/S0749-3797(98)00017-8.

Felt, Laurel, and Michael Robb. *Technology Addiction: Concern, Controversy, and Finding Balance*. San Francisco: Common Sense Media, 2016. Available online: https://www.commonsensemedia.org/sites/default/files/uploads/re-search/2016_csm_technology_addiction_executive_summary.pdf.

Ferguson, Christopher, and Richard Hartley. "The Pleasure Is Momentary . . . The Expense Damnable? The Influence of Pornography on Rape and Sexual Assault." *Aggression and Violent Behavior* 14 (2009): 323–329. doi: 10.1016/j.avb.2009.04.008.

Ferguson, R. Brian. "A Reexamination of the Causes of Northwest Coast Warfare." In *Warfare, Culture, and Environment*, edited by R. Brian Ferguson, 267–328. Orlando, FL: Academic Press, 1984.

Ferguson, R. Brian. *Yanomami Warfare: A Political History*. Santa Fe, NM: School of American Research Press, 1995.

Ferguson, R. Brian. "The Prehistory of War and Peace in Europe and the Near East." In *War, Peace, and Human Nature: Convergence of Evolutionary and Cultural Views*, edited by Douglas P. Fry, 191–240. New York: Oxford University Press, 2013.

Ferguson, R. Brian. "Pinker's List: Exaggerating Prehistoric War Mortality." In *War, Peace, and Human Nature: Convergence of Evolutionary and Cultural Views*, edited by Douglas P. Fry, 112–131. New York: Oxford University Press, 2013.

Ferguson, Jennifer, Larry Young, Elizabeth Hearn, Martin Matzuk, Thomas Insel, and James Winslow. "Social Amnesia in Mice Lacking the Oxytocin Gene." *Nature Genetics* 25 (2000): 284–288, doi:10.1038/77040.

Fernandez, Manny. "Lessons on Love, from a Rabbi Who Knows Hate and Forgiveness." *New York Times*, January 4, 2009. Available online: https://www.nytimes.com/2009/01/05/nyregion/05rabbi.html.

Fernea, Robert. "Putting a Stone in the Middle: The Nubians of Northern Africa." In *Keeping the Peace: Conflict Resolution and Peaceful Societies around the World*, edited by Graham Kemp and Douglas P. Fry, 105–121. New York: Routledge, 2004.

Feschbach, Seymour, and Bernard Malamuth. "Sex and Aggression: Proving the Link." *Psychology Today*, November 1978.

Fine, Cordelia. *Delusions of Gender: How Our Minds, Society, and Neurosexism Create Difference*. New York: W. W. Norton, 2011.

Fisher, Helen, Arthur Aron, and Lucy Brown. "Romantic Love: An fMRI Study of a Neural Mechanism for Mate Choice." *Journal of Comparative Neurology* 493 (2005): 58–62. https://doi.org/10.1002/cne.20772.

Fitzhugh, Ben. "The Evolution of Complex Hunter-Gatherers on the Kodiak Archipelago." *Senri Ethnological Studies* 63 (2003): 13–48.

"Five Minutes with Michael Milburn and Sheree Conrad." *MIT Press*. September 30, 2016. https://mitpress.mit.edu/blog/five-minutes-michael-milburn-and-sheree-conrad.

Flannery, Kent V., and Joyce Marcus. "The Origin of War: New 14C Dates from Ancient Mexico." *Proceedings of the National Academy of Sciences (PNAS)* 100 (2003): 11801–11805. doi: 10.1073/pnas.1934526100.

Flannery, Kent V., and Joyce Marcus. *The Creation of Inequality: How Our Prehistoric Ancestors Set the Stage for Monarchy, Slavery, and Empire*. Cambridge, MA: Harvard University Press, 2012.

Flood, Michael. "Exposure to Pornography among Youth in Australia." *Journal of Sociology* 43 (2017): 45–60. doi:10.1177/1440783307073934. Available online: https://www.researchgate.net/publication/234028278_Exposure_to_Pornography_Among_Youth_in_Australia.

Folbre, Nancy, and Julie A. Nelson. "For Love or Money—Or Both?" *Journal of Economic Perspectives* 14 (2000): 123–140. doi: 10.1257/jep.14.4.123.

Folsom, Joseph. *The Family and Democratic Society*. New York: Routledge, 1949.

Francis, Darlene, Josie Diorio, Dong Liu, and Michael Meaney. "Nongenomic Transmission across Generations of Maternal Behavior and Stress Responses in the Rat." *Science* 286 (1999): 1155–1158. doi: 10.1126/science.286.5442.1155.

French, Howard. "Tokyo Journal: The Japanese, It Seems, Are Outgrowing Japan." *New York Times*, February 1, 2001. Available online: http://www.nytimes.com/2001/02/01/world/tokyo-journal-the-japanese-it-seems-are-outgrowing-japan.html.

Frenkel-Brunswik, Else. "Intolerance of Ambiguity as a Personality Variable." In *Readings in Perception*, edited by David Beardsley and Michael Wertheimer, 664–685. Princeton, NJ: Van Nostrand, 1958.

Freud, Sigmund. *Moses and Monotheism*. Translated by K. Jones. New York: Vintage Books, 1955.

Freud, Sigmund. *New Introductory Lectures on Psychoanalysis*. Translated and edited by James Strachey. New York: Norton, 1965.

Freud, Sigmund. *Totem and Taboo*. Translated by James Strachey. New York: Norton, 1990.

Freud, Sigmund. *Group Psychology and an Analysis of the Ego*. Translated by James Strachey. New York: Norton, 1990.

Friedl, Ernestine. *Women and Men: An Anthropologist's View*. New York: Holt, Rinehart and Winston, 1975.

Fromm, Erich. *Escape from Freedom*. New York: Macmillan, 1994.

Fry, Douglas P. "The Evolution of Aggression and the Level of Selection Controversy." *Aggressive Behavior* 6 (1980): 69–89. doi: 10.1002/1098-2337(1980)6:1<69.

Fry, Douglas P. "Female Aggression among the Zapotec of Oaxaca, Mexico." In *Of Mice and Women: Aspects of Female Aggression*," edited by Kaj Björkqvist and Pirkko Niemalä, 187–199. Orlando, FL: Academic Press, 1992.

Fry, Douglas P. "'Respect for the Rights of Others Is Peace': Learning Aggression versus Non-Aggression among the Zapotec." *American Anthropologist* 94 (1992): 621–639. doi: 10.1525/aa.1992.94.3.02a00050.

Fry, Douglas P. "Intergenerational Transmission of Disciplinary Practices and Approaches to Conflict." *Human Organization* 52 (1993): 176–185. doi: 10.17730/humo.52.2.5771276435620789.

Fry, Douglas P. "Maintaining Social Tranquility: Internal and External Loci of Aggression Control." In *The Anthropology of Peace and Nonviolence*, edited by Leslie E. Sponsel and Thomas Gregor, 133–154. Boulder: Lynne Rienner, 1994.

Fry, Douglas P. "Anthropological Perspectives on Aggression: Sex Differences and Cultural Variation." *Aggressive Behavior* 24 (1998): 81–95. doi: 10.1002/(SICI)1098-2337(1998)24:2<81.

Fry, Douglas P. "Conflict Management in Cross-Cultural Perspective." In *Natural Conflict Resolution*, edited by Filippo Aureli and Frans de Waal, 334–351. Berkeley: University of California Press, 2000.

Fry, Douglas P. "Multiple Paths to Peace: The 'La Paz' Zapotec of Mexico." In *Keeping the Peace: Conflict Resolution and Peaceful Societies around the World*, edited by Graham Kemp and Douglas P. Fry, 73–87. New York: Routledge, 2004.

Fry, Douglas P. *The Human Potential for Peace: An Anthropological Challenge to Assumptions about War and Violence*. New York: Oxford University Press, 2006.

Fry, Douglas P. "Reciprocity: The Foundation Stone of Morality." In *Handbook of Moral Development*, edited by Melanie Killen and Judith Smetana, 399–422. Mahwah, NJ: Erlbaum, 2006.

Fry, Douglas P. "Anthropological Insights for Creating Nonwarring Social Systems." *Journal of Aggression, Conflict and Peace Research* 1 (2009): 4–15. doi: 10.1108/17596599200900008.

Fry, Douglas P. "Human Nature: The Nomadic Forager Model." In *Origins of Altruism and Cooperation*, edited by Robert W. Sussman and C. Robert Cloninger, 227–247. New York: Springer, 2011.

Fry, Douglas P. "Anthropology, War, and Peace: Hobbesian Beliefs within Science, Scholarship, and Society." In *Dangerous Liaisons*, edited by Laura A. McNamara and Robert A. Rubinstein, 185–201. Santa Fe, NM: School for Advanced Research Press, 2011.

Fry, Douglas P. "Life without War." *Science* 336 (2012): 879–884. doi: 10.1126/science.1217987.

Fry, Douglas P., editor. *War, Peace, and Human Nature: Convergence of Evolutionary and Cultural Views*. New York: Oxford University Press, 2013.

Fry, Douglas P. "Cooperation for Survival: Creating a Global Peace System." In *War, Peace, and Human Nature: Convergence of Evolutionary and Cultural Views*, edited by Douglas P. Fry, 543–558. New York: Oxford University Press, 2013, 543–558.

Fry, Douglas P. "The Evolution of Cooperation: What's War Got to Do with It?" *Reviews in Anthropology* 42 (2013): 102–121. doi: 10.1080/00938157.2013.788351.

Fry, Douglas P. "The Evolutionary Logic of Human Peaceful Behavior." In *Peace Ethology: Behavioral Processes and Systems of Peace*, edited by Peter Verbeek and Benjamin A. Peters, 249–265. New York: Wiley and Sons, 2018.

Fry, Douglas P., Bruce D. Bonta, and Karolina Baszarkiewicz. "Learning from Extant Cultures of Peace." In *Handbook on Building Cultures of Peace*, edited by Joseph de Rivera, 11–26. New York: Springer, 2008.

Fry, Douglas P., and Marta Miklikowska. "Culture of Peace." In *Psychological Components of Sustainable Peace,* edited by Morton Deutsch and Peter Coleman, 227–243. New York: Springer, 2012.

Fry, Douglas P., Gary Schober, and Kaj Björkqvist. "Evolutionary Restraints on Lethal Aggression in Animals and Humans." In *Nonkilling Societies*, edited by Joám Evans Pim, 101–128. Honolulu: Center for Global Nonkilling, 2010.

Fry, Douglas P., and Patrik Söderberg. "Lethal Aggression in Mobile Forager Bands and Implications for the Origins of War." *Science* 341 (2013): 270–273. doi: 10.1126/science.1235675.

Fry, Douglas P., and Patrik Söderberg. "Supplemental Online Material for Lethal Aggression in Mobile Forager Bands and Implications for the Origins of War." *Science* 341 (2013): 270–273. doi: 10.1126/science.1235675.

Fry, Douglas P., and Patrik Söderberg. "Myths about Hunter-Gatherers Redux: Nomadic Forager War and Peace." *Journal of Aggression, Conflict and Peace Research* 6 (2014): 255–266. doi: 10.1108/JACPR-06-2014-0127.

Fry, Douglas P., and Geneviève Souillac. "The Relevance of Nomadic Forager Studies to Moral Foundations Theory: Moral Education and Global Ethics in the Twenty-First Century." *Journal of Moral Education* 42 (2013): 346–359. doi: 10.1080/03057240.2013.817328.

Fry, Douglas P., and Geneviève Souillac. "Peace by Other Means: Reflections from the Indigenous World." *Common Knowledge* 22 (2016): 8–24.

Fry, Douglas P., and Geneviève Souillac. "The Original Partnership Societies: Evolved Propensities for Equality, Prosociality, and Peace." *Interdisciplinary Journal of Partnership Studies* 4 (2017): article 4. doi: 10.24926/ijps.v4i1.150.

Fry, Douglas P., and Jukka-Pekka Takala. "Who's Afraid of Helsinki at Night?" Paper presented at the Conference of the European Sociological Association, Helsinki, Finland, August 28–September 1, 2001.

Fuentes, Agustin. "Cooperation, Conflict, and Niche Construction in the Genus *Homo*." In *War, Peace, and Human Nature: Convergence of Evolutionary and Cultural Views*, edited by Douglas P. Fry, 78–94. New York: Oxford University Press, 2013.

Galtung, Johan. "Cultural Violence." *Journal of Peace Research* 27 (1990): 291–305. doi: 10.1177/0022343390027003005.

Galtung, Johan, and Tord Höivik. "Structural and Direct Violence: A Note on Operationalization." *Journal of Peace Research* 8 (1971): 73–76. doi: 10.1177/002234337100800108.

Gamow, George. *Thirty Years that Shook Physics: The Story of Quantum Physics.* New York: Doubleday, 1966.

Gardner, Lytt. "Deprivation Dwarfism." *Scientific American* 227 (1972): 76–82. doi: 10.1038/scientificamerican0772-6.

Gardner, Peter. "The Paliyans." In *Hunters and Gatherers Today*, edited by M. G. Bicchieri, 404–447. Prospect Heights, IL: Waveland, 1972.

Gardner, Peter. "Respect and Nonviolence among Recently Sedentary Paliyan Foragers." *Journal of the Royal Anthropological Institute (N. S.)* 6 (2000): 215–236. doi: 10.1111/1467-9655.00013.

Gardner, Peter. *Bicultural Versatility as a Frontier Adaptation among Paliyan Foragers of South India.* Lewiston, NY: Edwin Mellen Press, 2000.

Gardner, Peter. "Respect for All: The Paliyans of South India." In *Keeping the Peace: Conflict Resolution and Peaceful Societies around the World*, edited by Graham Kemp and Douglas P. Fry, 53–71. New York: Routledge, 2004.

Gardner, Peter. "South Indian Forages' Conflict Management in Comparative Perspective." In *War, Peace, and Human Nature: The Congruence of Evolutionary and Cultural Views*, edited by Douglas P. Fry, 297–314. New York: Oxford University Press, 2013.

Gatusa, Lamu. "Matriarchal Marriage Patterns of the Mosuo of China." Paper presented at the symposium *Societies of Peace—Past, Present, Future: Second World Congress of Matriarchal Studies*. Texas State University, San Marcos/ Austin, Texas, September 29—October 2, 2005. Translated by Wang Yun and Jutta Reid. Available online: http://www.second-congress-matriarchal-studies.com/gatusa.html.

Gerhardt, Sue. *Why Love Matters: How Affection Shapes a Baby's Brain*. New York: Routledge, 2015.

Gesquiere, Laurence, Niki Learn, M. Carolina Simao, Patrick Onyango, Susan Alberts, and Jeanne Altmann. "Life at the Top: Rank and Stress in Wild Male Baboons." *Science* 333 (2011): 357–360. doi: 10.1126/science.1207120.

Gettler, Lee, Thomas McDade, Alan Feranil, and Christopher Kuzawa. "Longitudinal Evidence that Fatherhood Decreases Testosterone in Human Males." *Proceedings of the National Academy of Sciences (PNAS)* 108 (2011): 16194–16199. doi: 10.1073/pnas.1105403108.

Ghiglieri, Michael. *The Dark Side of Man: Tracing the Origins of Violence*. Reading, MA: Perseus, 1999.

Ghiselin, Michael. *The Economy of Nature and the Evolution of Sex*. Berkeley: University of California Press, 1974.

Giddens, Anthony. *The Constitution of Society*. Berkeley: University of California Press, 1984.

Giddens, Anthony. *The Transformation of Intimacy: Sexuality, Love, and Eroticism in Modern Societies*. Stanford, CA: Stanford University Press, 1992.

Gies, Frances, and Joseph Gies. *Marriage and the Family in the Middle Ages*. New York: Harper and Row, 1987.

Gilberg, Rolf. "Polar Eskimo." In *Handbook of North American Indians, Volume 5, Arctic*, volume edited by D. Damas, and series edited by W. C. Sturtevant, 577–594. Washington, DC: Smithsonian Press, 1984.

Gilligan, Carol. *In a Different Voice*. Cambridge, MA: Harvard University Press, 2009.

Gimbutas, Marija. "The First Wave of Eurasian Steppe Pastoralists into Copper Age Europe." *Journal of Indo-European Studies* 5 (1977): 277–338.

Gimbutas, Marija. *The Goddesses and Gods of Old Europe*. Berkeley: University of California Press, 1982.

Global Gender Gap Report 2017. Geneva: World Economic Forum, 2017.

Global Initiative to End All Capital Punishment of Children. "Countdown to Universal Prohibition." Accessed December 3, 2016. Available online: http://www.endcorporalpunishment.org/progress/countdown.html.

Global Initiative to End All Corporal Punishment of Children. Available on-line: http://www.endcorporalpunishment.org.

Global Initiative to End All Corporal Punishment of Children. "Corporal Punishment of Children in Finland." Last modified October 2017. Available online: www.endcorporalpunishment.org/assets/docs/states-reports/ Finland.docx.

Goettner-Abendroth, Heide. *Matriarchal Societies: Indigenous Cultures across the Globe*. New York: Peter Lang, 2012.

Goldschmidt, Walter. *The Bridge to Humanity: How Affect Hunger Trumps the Selfish Gene*. New York: Oxford University Press, 2005.

Goleman, Daniel. "Researchers Trace Empathy's Roots to Infancy." *New York Times* (1989). Available online: http://www.nytimes.com/ 1989/03/28/science/researchers-trace-empathy-s-roots-to-infancy. html?pagewanted=all&src=pm.

Goodman, Alan H., and Thomas L. Leatherman. *Building a New Biocultural Synthesis: Political-Economic Perspectives on Human Biology*. Ann Arbor: University of Michigan Press, 1998.

Goodridge, Elisabeth. "Front-Runner Ed Muskie's Tears (or Melted Snow?) Hurt His Presidential Bid." *U.S. News,* last modified January 17, 2008. Available online: https://www.usnews.com/news/articles/2008/01/17/ 72-front-runners-tears-hurt.

Gorer, Geoffrey. *Himalayan Village: An Account of the Lepchas of Sikkim*. New York: Basic Books, 1967.

Gottlieb, Gilbert. *Synthesizing Nature-Nurture*. Mahwah, NJ: Erlbaum, 1997.

Gourhan, Andre Leroi, *Prehistoire de l'Art Occidental*. Paris: Edition D'Art Lucien Mazenod, 1971.

Gowdy, John. "Hunter-Gatherers and the Mythology of the Market." In *The Cambridge Encyclopedia of Hunters and Gatherers*, edited by Richard B. Lee and Richard Daly, 391–398. Cambridge, UK: Cambridge University Press, 1999.

Graham, Jesse, Jonathan Haidt, Sena Koleva, Matt Motyl, Ravi Iyer, Sean P. Wojcik, and Peter H. Ditto. "Moral Foundations Theory: The Pragmatic Validity of Moral Pluralism." *Advances in Experimental Social Psychology* 47 (2013): 55–130.

Greenberg, James. *Blood Ties: Life and Violence in Rural Mexico*. Tucson: University of Arizona Press, 1989.

Griffith, Brian. *Correcting Jesus: 2000 Years of Changing the Story*. Minneapolis, MN: Exterminating Angel Press, 2009.

Grossman, Dave. *On Killing: The Psychological Cost of Learning to Kill in War and Society*. New York: Little, Brown, 1995.

Grossman, Dave, and Gloria DeGaetano. *Stop Teaching Our Kids to Kill: A Call to Action against TV, Movie and Video Game Violence*. New York: Crown Publishers, 1999.

Guenther, Mathias. "War and Peace among Kalahari San." *Journal of Aggression, Conflict and Peace Research* 6 (2014): 229–239. doi: 10.1108/JACPR-02-2014-0005.

Gusinde, Martin. *The Yaghan: The Life and Thought of the Water Nomads of Cape Horn*. Translated by Frieda Schütze. In the electronic Human Relations Area Files, Yahgan, Doc. 1. New Haven, CT: HRAF, 2003. Accessed March 6, 2018. Available online: http://ehrafworldcultures.yale.edu/ehrafe/.

Haak, Wolfgang, Josif Lazaridis, and David Reich. "Massive Migration from the Steppe Was a Source for Indo-European Languages in Europe." *Nature* 522 (2015): 207–211. doi: 10.1038/nature14317.

Haas, Jonathan. "War." In *Encyclopedia of Cultural Anthropology, Volume 4*, edited by David Levinson and Melvin Ember, 1357–1361. New York: Henry Holt and Company, 1996.

Haas, Jonathan. "The Origins of War and Ethnic Violence." In *Ancient Warfare: Archaeological Perspectives*, edited by J. Carman and A. Harding, 11–24. Gloucestershire, UK: Sutton Publishing, 1999.

Haas, Jonathan. "Warfare and the Evolution of Culture." In *Archaeology at the Millennium: A Sourcebook*, edited by G. Feinman and T. D. Price, 329–350. New York: Kluwer Academic/Plenum, 2001.

Haas, Jonathan, and Matthew Piscitelli. "The Prehistory of Warfare: Misled by Ethnography." In *War, Peace, and Human Nature: Convergence of Evolutionary and Cultural Views*, edited by Douglas P. Fry, 168–190. New York: Oxford University Press, 2013.

Haidt, Jonathan. *The Righteous Mind: Why Good People Are Divided by Politics and Religion*. New York: Pantheon, 2012.

Hallowell, A. Irving. "Aggression in Saulteaux Society." In *Culture and Experience*, edited by A. Irving Hallowell, 277–290. Philadelphia: University of Pennsylvania Press, 1974.

Harbaugh, William, Ulrich Mayr, and Daniel Burghart. "Neural Responses to Taxation and Voluntary Giving Reveals Motives for Charitable Donations." *Science* 316 (2007): 1622–1625. doi: 10.1126/science.1140738.

Harlow, Harry. "The Nature of Love." *American Psychologist* 13 (1958): 673–685. doi: 10.1037/h0047884.

Harlow, Harry, and Margaret Harlow. "Social Deprivation in Monkeys." *Scientific American* 207 (1962): 136–50. Available online: http://www.jstor.org/stable/24936357.

Harris, La Donna, and Jacqueline Wasilewski. "Indigeneity, an Alternative Worldview: Four R's (Relationship, Responsibility, Reciprocity, Redistribution) vs. Two P's (Power and Profit). Sharing the Journey towards Conscious Evolution." *Systems Research and Behavioral Science* 21 (2004): 489–503. doi: 10.1002/sres.631.

Hausmann, Robert, Laura Tyson, and Saadia Zahidi. *The Global Gender Gap Report*. Geneva: The World Economic Forum, 2011.

Hegel, G. W. F. *Phenomenology of Spirit*. Translated by A. V. Miller. Oxford: Clarendon Press, 1977, originally published in 1807.

Heiskala, Risto. "How to Be a Virtuous Male/Female: The Politics of Gender in Advertisements in Some Finnish Magazines in 1955 and 1985." *Semiotica* 87 (1991): 381–409.

Helliwell, John, Richard Layard, and Jeffrey Sachs, editors. *World Happiness Report 2018*. New York: Sustainable Development Solutions Network, 2018. Available online: https://s3.amazonaws.com/happiness-report/2018/WHR_web.pdf.

Helwig, Charles. "Rights, Civil Liberties, and Democracy across Cultures." In *Handbook of Moral Development*, edited by Melanie Killen and Judith Smetana, 185–210. Mahwah, NJ: Erlbaum, 2006.

Henry, Donald. "Preagricultural Sedentism: The Natufian Example." In *Prehistoric Hunter-Gatherers: The Emergence of Cultural Complexity*, edited by T. D. Price and J. A. Brown, 365–384. New York: Academic Press, 1985.

Henry, J., and S. Wang. "Effects of Early Stress on Adult Affiliative Behavior." *Psychoneuroendocrinology* 23 (1998): 863–875. doi: 10.1016/S0306-4530(98)00058-4.

Henry, Meghan, Alvaro Cortes, and Sean Morris. *The 2013 Annual Homeless Assessment Report (AHAR) to Congress: Part 1 Point-in-Time Estimates of Homelessness*. Washington, DC: US Department of Housing and Urban Development, 2013. Available online: https://www.hudexchange.info/resources/documents/ahar-2013-part1.pdf.

Hertenstein, Matthew, Dacher Keltner, Betsy App, Brittany A. Bulleit, and Ariane R. Jaskolka. "Touch Communicates Distinct Emotions." *Emotion* 6 (2006): 528–533. doi: 10.1037/1528-3542.6.3.528.

Highwater, Jamake. *Myth and Sexuality*. New York: Meridian/Penguin Books, 1990.

Hobbes, Thomas. *Leviathan: Or the Matter, Forme and Power of a Commonwealth Ecclesiastical and Civil*. Oxford: Basil Blackwell, 1946, originally published in 1651.

Hocken, Kerensa, and Neil Gredecki. "Thinking Outside of the Box: Advancements in Theory, Practice, and Evaluation in Sexual Offending Interventions." In *The Routledge International Handbook of Human Aggression: Current Issues and Perspectives*, edited by Jane L. Ireland, Philip Birch, and Carol A. Ireland, 302–315. New York: Routledge, 2018.

Hodder, Ian. "Women and Men at Catalhoyuk." *Scientific American* 290 (2004): 77–83.

Hodgson, Dorothy. "Pastoralism, Patriarchy, and History: Changing Gender Relations among Maasai in Tanganyika 1890–1940." *Journal of African History* 40 (1999): 41–65. http://www.jstor.org/stable/183394.

Hodgson, Dorothy. *Once Intrepid Warriors: Gender, Ethnicity, and the Cultural Politics of Maasai Development*. Bloomington: Indiana University Press, 2001.

Hoebel, E. Adamson. *The Law of Primitive Man: A Study in Comparative Legal Dynamics*. Cambridge, MA: Harvard University Press, 1967.

Holmberg, Allan. *Nomads of the Long Bow: The Siriono of Eastern Bolivia*. New York: American Museum of Natural History, 1969.

Hoseini, Farshad. *List of Known Cases of Stoning to Death in Iran (1980-2010)*. Accessed March 24, 2018. Available online: http://stopstonningnow.com/wpress/SList%20_1980-2010__FHdoc.pdf.

"How to Find Help Treating a Trauma-Related Problem." *PsychGuides.com*. Available online: http://www.psychguides.com/guides/trauma-symptoms-causes-and-effects/.

Howell, Signe, and Roy Willis, editors. *Societies at Peace: Anthropological Perspectives*. New York: Routledge, 1989.

Hrdy, Sarah B. *Mothers and Others: The Evolutionary Origins of Mutual Understanding*. Cambridge, MA: Harvard University Press, 2009.

Hudson, Valerie, Mary Caprioli, Bonnie Ballif-Spanvill, Rose McDermott, and Chad F. Emmett. "The Heart of the Matter: The Security of Women and the Security of States." *International Security* 33 (2008/2009): 7–45. Available online: http://belfercenter.ksg.harvard.edu/publication/18797/heart_of_the_matter.html.

Hudspeth, William, and Karl Pribram. "Psychophysiological Indices of Cerebral Maturation." *International Journal of Psychophysiology* 12 (1992): 19–29. doi: 10.1016/0167-8760(92)90039-E.

Huesmann, L. Rowell. "An Integrative Theoretical Understanding of Aggression." In *Aggression and Violence: A Social Psychological Perspective*, edited by Brad Bushman, 3–21. New York: Routledge, 2017.

Human Rights Violations on the Basis of Sexual Orientation, Gender Identity, and Homosexuality in the Islamic Republic of Iran. Submission to the 103rd Session of the United Nations Human Rights Committee (October 17—November 4, 2011), International Gay and Lesbian Human Rights Commission (IGLHRC). Available online: https://www.iglhrc.org/sites/default/files/Iran%20Shadow%20Report%202011.pdf.

Ihara, Saikaku. *The Great Mirror of Male Love.* Translated by Paul Schalow. Stanford, CA: Stanford University Press, 1990.

Index Mundi. "Intentional Homicides (per 100,000 People)—Country Ranking." Accessed April 28, 2018. Available online: https://www.indexmundi.com/facts/indicators/VC.IHR.PSRC.P5/rankings.

Inglehart, Ron, Pippa Norris, and Christian Welzel. "Gender Equality and Democracy." *Comparative Sociology* 1 (2002): 321–346. doi: 10.1163/156913302100418628.

Insel, Thomas. "Oxytocin—A Neuropeptide for Affiliation: Evidence from Behavioral, Receptor Autoradiographic, and Comparative Studies." *Psychoneuroendoctrinology* 17 (1992): 3–35. doi: https://doi.org/10.1016/0306-4530(92)90073-G.

Insel, Thomas, James Winslow, Xuoxin Wang, and Larry Young. "Oxytocin, Vasopressin, and the Neuroendocrine Basis of Pair Bond Formation." In *Vasopressin and Oxytocin. Advances in Experimental Medicine and Biology*, edited by Hans Zingg, Charles Bourque, and Daniel Bichet, 215–224. Boston: Springer, 1998.

Institute for Economics and Peace. *Global Peace Index 2017.* Available online: http://maps.visionofhumanity.org/#/page/indexes/global-peace-index.

"Interesting Facts about Finland: Finland Guide." *Eupedia.* Available online: http://www.eupedia.com/finland/trivia.shtml.

International Committee of the Red Cross. "Geneva Conventions and Commentaries." Available online: https://www.icrc.org/en/war-and-law/treaties-customary-law/geneva-conventions. United Nations, General Assembly, Universal Declaration of Human Rights (1948). Available online: http://www.un.org/en/universal-declaration-human-rights/.

International Programme on the Elimination of Child Labour (IPEC). "What Is Child Labour." Available online: http://www.ilo.org/ipec/facts/lang--en/index.htm.

Inter-Parliamentary Union. "Women in National Parliaments: The Situation as of January 1, 2018." Accessed March 13, 2018. Available online: http://archive.ipu.org/wmn-e/classif.htm.

"Interview with Zev Chafets, Author of Rush Limbaugh: *Army of One*." *All Right Magazine*. Last modified on April 13, 2012. Available online: https://web.archive.org/web/20120413010651/http://www.allrightmagazine.com/exclusive-interviews/interview-with-zev-chafets-author-of-rush-limbaugh-army-of-one-4662/.

Iwaniec, Dorota. *The Emotionally Abused and Neglected Child*. Chichester, UK: Wiley and Sons, 2006.

Jablonka, Eva, and Gal Raz. "Transgenerational Epigenetic Inheritance: Prevalence, Mechanisms, and Implications for the Study of Heredity and Evolution." *Quarterly Review of Biology* 84 (2009): 131–176. doi: 10.1086/598822.

Jaenisch, R., and A. Bird. "Epigenetic Regulation of Gene Expression: How the Genome Integrates Intrinsic and Environmental Signals." *Nature Genetics* 33 (2003): 245–254. doi: 10.1038/ng1089.

Jia, Sen, Thomas Lansdall-Welfare, Saatviga Sudhahar, Cynthia Carter, and Nello Cristianini. "Women Are Seen More than Heard in Online Newspapers." *PLoS One* 11 (2016): e0148434. doi: 10.1371/journal.pone.0148434.

Jiang, Yan, et al. "Epigenetics in the Nervous System." *Journal of Neuroscience* 28 (2008): 11753–11759. doi: 10.1523/JNEUROSCI.3797-08.2008.

Jones, Teresa, and Robert Greenough. "Ultrastructural Evidence for Increased Contact between Astrocytes and Synapses in Rats Reared in a Complex Environment." *Neurobiology of Learning Memory* 65 (1996): 48–56.

Jost, John, and David Amodio. "Political Ideology as Motivated Social Cognition: Behavioral and Neuroscientific Evidence." *Motivation and Emotion* 36 (2012): 55–64. doi: 10.1007/s11031-011-9260-7.

Jost, John, H. Hannah Nam, David Amodio, and Jay Van Bavel. "Political Neuroscience: The Beginning of a Beautiful Friendship." *Advances in Political Psychology* 35 (2014): 3–42. doi: 10.1111/pops.12162.

Kagan, Spencer, and Millard Madsen. "Cooperation and Competition of Mexican, Mexican-American, and Anglo-American Children of Two Ages under Four Instruction Sets." *Developmental Psychology* 5 (1971): 32–39. doi: 10.1037/h0031080.

Kagan, Spencer, and Millard Madsen. "Experimental Analyses of Cooperation and Competition of Anglo-American and Mexican Children." *Developmental Psychology* 6 (1972): 49–59. doi: 10.1037/h0032219.

Kaldor, Mary. *Human Security*. Cambridge, UK: Polity Press, 2007.

Kano, Takayoshi. "The Bonobos' Peaceable Kingdom." *Natural History* 99 (1990): 62–70.

Kant, Immanuel. *Foundations of the Metaphysics of Morals and What Is Enlightenment.* Translated by Lewis White Beck. New York: Macmillan, 1990, originally published in 1785.

Kaplow, Julie, and Cathy Spatz Widom. "Age of Onset of Child Maltreatment Predicts Long-Term Mental Health Outcomes." *Journal of Abnormal Psychology* 116 (2007): 176–187. doi: 10.1037/0021-843X.116.1.176.

Kawai, Masao. "Newly-acquired Pre-cultural Behavior of the Natural Troop of Japanese Monkeys on Koshima Island." *Primates* 6 (1965): 1–30. doi: 10.1007/BF01794457.

Kelly, Raymond. *Warless Societies and the Origin of War.* Ann Arbor: University of Michigan Press, 2000.

Kelly, Robert L. *The Foraging Spectrum: Diversity in Hunter-Gatherer Lifeways.* Washington, DC: Smithsonian Institution Press, 1995.

Keltner, Dacher. "The Compassionate Instinct." *Greater Good*, Spring 2004. Available online: http://greatergood.berkeley.edu/article/item/the_compassionate_instinct/.

Keltner, Dasher. *Born to Be Good.* New York: Norton, 2009.

Keltner, Dacher, Aleksandr Kogan, Paul Piff, and Sarina Saturnet. "The Sociocultural Appraisals, Values, and Emotions (SAVE) Framework of Prosociality: Core Processes from Gene to Meme." *Annual Review of Psychology* 65 (2014): 425–460. doi: 10.1146/annurev-psych-010213-115054.

Kemp, Graham, and Douglas P. Fry, editors. *Keeping the Peace: Conflict Resolution and Peaceful Societies around the World.* New York: Routledge, 2004.

Kendall, Virginia, and T. Markus Funk. *Child Exploitation and Trafficking: Examining Global Enforcement and Supply Chain Challenges and U.S. Responses.* (Lanham, MD: Rowman and Littlefield Publishers, 2016), 79.

Kerber, Linda. *Women of the Republic: Intellect and Ideology in Revolutionary America.* Chapel Hill: University of North Carolina Press, 1980.

Keuls, Eva. *The Reign of the Phallus: Sexual Politics in Ancient Athens.* Berkeley: University of California Press, 1993.

Keverne, Eric B. "Epigenetics: Significance of the Gene-Environment Interface for Brain Development." In *Pathways to Peace: The Transformative Power of Children and Families*, edited by James F. Leckman, Catherine Panter-Brick, and Rima Salah, 65–77. Cambridge, MA: MIT Press, 2014.

Keverne, Eric B., Nicholas Martensz, and Bernadette Tuite. "Beta-endorphin Concentrations in Cerebrospinal Fluid of Monkeys Are Influenced by

Grooming Relationships." *Psychoneuroendocrinology* 14 (1989): 155–161. doi: 10.1016/0306-4530(89)90065-6.

Kim, Pilyoung, Gary Evans, Michael Angstadt, S. Shaun Ho, Chandra Sripada, James Swain, Israel Liberzon, and K. Luan Phan. "Effects of Childhood Poverty and Chronic Stress on Emotion Regulatory Brain Function in Adulthood." *Proceedings of the National Academy of Sciences (PNAS)* 110 (2013): 18442–18447. doi: 10.1073/pnas.1308240110.

Kimmel, Michael. "The Contemporary 'Crisis' of Masculinity in Historical Perspective." In *The Making of Masculinities: The New Men Studies*, edited by Harry Brod, 121–124. Boston: Allen and Unwin, 1987.

Kimmel, Michael, and Thomas Mosmiller, editors. *Against the Tide: Pro-Feminist Men in the United States 1776-1990*. Boston: Beacon Press, 1992.

Kimmel, Michael. *Angry White Men: American Masculinity at the End of an Era*. New York: Nation Books, 2013.

Klein Jeffrey, Rodney Swain, Kim Armstrong, Ruth Napper, Theresa Jones, and William Greenough. "Selective Synaptic Plasticity within the Cerebellar Cortex following Complex Motor Skill Learning." *Neurobiology of Learning and Memory* 69 (1998): 274–289.

Knauft, Bruce. "Violence and Sociality in Human Evolution." *Current Anthropology* 32 (1991): 391–428. doi: 10.1086/203975.

Kohn, Alfie. *No Contest: The Case against Competition*. New York: Houghton Mifflin, 1986.

Konner, Melvin. "Human Nature, Ethnic Violence, and War." In *The Psychology of Resolving Global Conflicts: From War to Peace, Volume 1: Nature vs. Nurture*, edited by Mari Fitzduff and Chris E. Stout, 1–40. Westport, CT: Praeger, 2006.

Konner, Melvin. "For Peaceable Humans Don't Look to Prehistory." *Wall Street Journal*, last modified June 30, 2016. Accessed March 6, 2018. Available online: http://www.wsj.com/articles/for-peaceable-humans-dont-look-to-prehistory-1467322723.

Koppensteiner, Martin Foureaux, and Marco Manacorda. "Violence and Birth Outcomes: Evidence from Homicides in Brazil." *Journal of Development Economics* 119 (2016): 16–33.

Koonz, Claudia. "Mothers in the Fatherland: Women in Nazi Germany." In *Becoming Visible: Women in European History*, edited by Renate Bridenthal and Claudia Koonz, 445–473. Boston: Houghton Mifflin, 1977.

Kosfeld, Michael, Markus Heinrichs, Paul J. Zak, Urs Fischbacher, and Ernst Fehr. "Oxytocin Increases Trust in Humans." *Nature* 435 (2005): 673–676. doi: 10.1038/nature03701.

Koskela, Hille. "'Bold Walk and Breakings': Women's Spatial Confidence versus Fear of Violence." *Gender, Place, and Culture* 4 (1997): 301–319. doi: 10.1080/ 09663699725369.

Krahé, Barbara. "Violence against Women." In *Aggression and Violence: A Social Psychological Perspective*, edited by Brad Bushman, 241–258. New York: Routledge, 2017.

Krahé, Barbara. "The Impact of Violent Media on Aggression." In *The Routledge International Handbook of Human Aggression: Current Issues and Perspectives*, edited by Jane Ireland, Philip Birch, and Carol Ireland, 319–330. New York: Routledge, 2018.

Kramer, Samuel Noah, and John Maier. *Myths of Enki, The Crafty God.* New York: Oxford University Press, 1989.

Kraus Michael, Stephane Cote, and Dacher Keltner. "Social Class, Contextualism, and Empathic Accuracy." *Psychological Science* 21 (2010): 1716–1723. doi: 10.1177/0956797610387613.

Kristof, Nicholas, and Sheryl WuDunn. *Half the Sky: Turning Oppression into Opportunity for Women Worldwide.* New York: Vintage, 2010.

Krosch, Amy, Leslie Berntsen, David Amodio, John Jost, and Jay Van Bavel. "On the Ideology of Hypodescent: Political Conservatism Predicts Categorization of Racially Ambiguous Faces as Black." *Journal of Experimental Social Psychology* 49 (2013): 1196–1203. doi: 10.1016/j.jesp.2013.05.009.

Kross, Ethan, Philippe Verduyn, Emre Demiralp, Jiyoung Park, David Seungjae Lee, Natalie Lin, Holly Shablack, John Jonides, and Oscar Ybarra. "Facebook Use Predicts Declines in Subjective Well-Being in Young Adults." *PLoS ONE* 8 (2013): e69841, doi: 10.1371/journal.pone.0069841.

Kuels, Eva. *The Reign of the Phallus.* Berkeley: University of California Press, 1993.

Kuhn, Thomas S. *The Structure of Scientific Revolutions.* Chicago: University of Chicago Press, 1970.

Kukolja, Tihomir. "Saving Witch Children in Nigeria." *HuffPost*, last modified June 17, 2014. Available online: https://www.huffingtonpost.com/tihomir-kukolja/witch-children-in-nigeria_b_5149931.html.

Kurlansky, Mark. *Nonviolence: The History of a Dangerous Idea.* New York: Modern Library, 2008.

Kuroda, Suehisa. "Social Behavior of the Pygmy Chimpanzees." *Primates* 21 (1980): 181–197. doi: 10.1007/BF02374032.

LaFrance, Adrienne. "I Analyzed a Year of My Reporting for Gender Bias (Again)." *Atlantic*, last modified November 17, 2016. Accessed March 23,

2018. Available online: https://www.theatlantic.com/technology/archive/
2016/02/gender-diversity-journalism/463023/

Lahr, Marta Mirazon. "The Ecology of Prehistoric Inter-Group Conflict
in African Hunter-Gatherers." Paper presented at the symposium *Social
Inequality before Farming?* University of Cambridge, UK, January
21–23, 2018.

Lahr, Marta Mirazon, et al. "Inter-Group Violence among Early Holocene
Hunter-Gatherers of West Turkana, Kenya." *Nature* 529 (2016): 394–398.
doi: 10.1038/nature16477.

Lambrot, R., C. Xu, S. Saint-Phar, G. Chountalos, T. Cohen, M. Paquet, M.
Suderman, M. Hallett, and S. Kimmins. "Low Paternal Dietary Folate Alters
the Mouse Sperm Epigenome and Is Associated with Negative Pregnancy
Outcomes." *Nature Communications* 4 (2013): article 2889. doi: 10.1038/
ncomms3889.

Leacock, Eleanor. "The Montagnais 'Hunting Territory' and the Fur
Trade." *Memoirs of the American Anthropological Association, American
Anthropologist,* 56, no. 2, part 2 (1954): memoir number 78.

Leacock, Eleanor. "Women's Status in Egalitarian Society: Implications for Social
Evolution." *Current Anthropology* 19 (1978): 247–275. doi: 10.1086/202074.

Lebra, Joyce Chapman, Joy Paulson, and Elizabeth Powers, editors. *Women in
Changing Japan.* Stanford, CA: Stanford University Press, 1978.

Lee, Richard B. *The !Kung San: Men, Women, and Work in a Foraging
Community.* Cambridge, UK: Cambridge University Press, 1979.

Lee, Richard B. *The Dobe Ju/'hoansi.* Fort Worth, TX: Harcourt Brace, 1993.

Lee, Richard B. "Hunter-Gatherers on the Best-Seller List: Steven Pinker
and the 'Bellicose School's' Treatment of Forager Violence." *Journal of
Aggression, Conflict, and Peace Research* 6 (2014): 216–228. doi: 10.1108/
JACPR-04-2014-0116.

Lee, Richard B., and Richard Daly. "Introduction: Foragers and Others." In *The
Cambridge Encyclopedia of Hunters and Gatherers,* edited by Richard B. Lee
and Richard Daly, 1–19. Cambridge, UK: Cambridge University Press, 1999.

Lee, Richard B., and Richard Daly, editors. *The Cambridge Encyclopedia of
Hunters and Gatherers.* Cambridge, UK: Cambridge University Press, 1999.

Lee, Richard B., and Irven DeVore. "Problems in the Study of Hunters and
Gatherers." In *Man the Hunter,* edited by Richard B. Lee and Irven DeVore,
3–12. Chicago: Aldine, 1968.

Leeming, David, and Jake Page. *Goddess: Myths of the Female Divine.*
New York: Oxford University Press, 1996.

Levine, Daniel, Samuel J. Leven, and Paul S. Prueitt. "Integration, Disintegration, and the Frontal Lobes." In *Motivation, Emotion, and Goal Direction in Neural Networks*, edited by Daniel S. Levine and Samuel Leven, 301–335. Mahwah, NJ: Erlbaum, 1992.

Lew-Levy, Sheina, Noa Lavi, Rachel Reckin, Jurgi Cristóbal-Azkarate, and Kate Ellis-Davies. "How Do Hunter-Gatherer Children Learn Social and Gender Norms? A Meta-Ethnographic Review." *Cross-Cultural Research* 52 (2017): 213–255. doi: 10.1177/1069397117723552.

Lewin, Kurt. *Field Theory in Social Science*. New York: Harper & Row, 1951.

Lewinsohn, Richard. *A History of Sexual Customs*. Translated by Alexander Mayce. New York: Fawcett, 1958.

Lewontin, R. C. "The Units of Selection." *Annual Review of Ecology and Systematics* 1 (1970): 1–18. doi: 10.1146/annurev.es.01.110170.000245.

Lincoln, Bruce. "The Indo-European Myth of Creation." *History of Religions* 15 (1975): 121–145. doi: 10.1086/462739.

Linden, David. *The Compass of Pleasure: How Our Brains Make Fatty Foods, Orgasm, Exercise, Marijuana, Generosity, Vodka, Learning, and Gambling Feel So Good*. New York: Viking, 2011.

Linz, Daniel, Edward Donnerstein, and Steven Penrod. "The Effects of Multiple Exposures to Filmed Violence against Women." *Journal of Communication* 34 (1984): 130–147. doi: 10.1111/j.1460-2466.1984.tb02180.x.

Lizot, Jacques. "On Warfare: An Answer to N. A. Chagnon." Translated by Sarah Dart. *American Ethnologist* 21 (1994): 845–862. doi: 10.1525/ae.1994.21.4.02a00100.

Llewelyn-Davies, Melissa. *Masai Women*. Video, 59 minutes, London: Granada Television International, 1974.

Lorentzen, Jorgen, and Per Are Lokke. "Men's Violence against Women: The Need to Take Responsibility." Paper presented at the international seminar "Promoting Equality: A Common Issue for Men and Women." Palais de l'Europe, Strasbourg, France, June 17–18, 1997.

Low, Bobbie. "An Evolutionary Perspective on War." In *Behavior, Culture, and Conflict in World Politics*, edited by W. Zimmerman and H. Jacobson, 13–55. Ann Arbor: University of Michigan Press, 1993.

"Low Levels of Neurotransmitter Serotonin May Perpetuate Child Abuse across Generations." *Science Daily*, November 2, 2006. Available online: https://www.sciencedaily.com/releases/2006/11/061102092229.htm.

Loye, David. "The Moral Brain." *Brain and Mind* 3 (2002): 133–150. doi: 10.1023/A:1016561925565.

Loye, David. *Darwin's Lost Theory*. Pacific Grove, CA: Benjamin Franklin Press, 2007.

Loye, David. *Rediscovering Darwin: The Rest of Darwin's Theory and Why We Need It Today*. Pacific Grove, CA: Romanes Press, 2018.

Luby, Joan, Deanna Barch, Andy Belden, Michael Gaffrey, Rebecca Tillman, Casey Babb, Tomoyuki Nishino, Hideo Suzuki, and Kelly Botteron. "Maternal Support in Early Childhood Predicts Larger Hippocampal Volumes at School Age." *Proceedings of the National Academy of Sciences (PNAS)* 109 (2012): 2854–2859. doi: 10.1073/pnas.1118003109.

Lumey, L. "Decreased Birthweights in Infants after Maternal in utero Exposure to the Dutch Famine of 1944-1945." *Paediatrics and Perinatal Epidemiology* 6 (1992): 240–253. doi: 10.1111/j.1365-3016.1992.tb00764.x.

Maccoby, Eleanor, and C. Jacklin, *The Psychology of Sex Differences*. Stanford, CA: Stanford University Press, 1974.

MacLean, Paul. *The Triune Brain in Evolution: Role in Paleocerebral Functions*. New York: Springer, 1990.

MacLean, Paul. "Women: A More Balanced Brain?" *Zygon* 31 (1996): 421–439.

Maestripieri, Dario, Kai McCormack, Stephen Lindell, J. Dee Higley, and Mar Sanchez. "Influence of Parenting Style on the Offspring's Behaviour and CSF Monoamine Metabolite Levels in Crossfostered and Noncrossfostered Female Rhesus Macaques." *Behavioural Brain Research* 175 (2006): 90–95. doi: 10.1016/j.bbr.2006.08.002.

Mahdavi, Pardis. "How #MeToo Became a Global Movement." *Foreign Affairs*. March 6, 2018. Available online: https://www.foreignaffairs.com/articles/ 2018-03-06/how-metoo-became-global-movement.

Marcuse, Herbert. *Eros and Civilization: A Philosophical Inquiry into Freud*. New York: Norton, 1955.

Marinatos, Nanno. *Minoan Religion: Ritual, Image, and Symbol*. Columbia, SC: University of South Carolina Press, 1993.

Marlowe, Frank. "Why the Hadza Are Still Hunter-Gatherers." In *Ethnicity, Hunter-Gatherers, and the "Other,"* edited by Susan Kent, 247–275. Washington, DC: Smithsonian Institution Press, 2010.

Marlowe, Frank. *The Hadza Hunter-Gatherers of Tanzania*. Berkeley: University of California Press, 2010.

Marmot, Michael, G. Smith, S. Stansfeld, C. Patel, F. North, J. Head, I. White, E. Brunner, and A. Feeney. "Health Inequalities among British Civil Servants: The Whitehall II Study." *Lancet* 337 (1991): 1387–1393.

Marsh, Jason. "Why Inequality Is Bad for the One Percent." *Greater Good*, last modified September 25, 2012. Available online: http://greatergood.berkeley.edu/article/item/why_inequality_is_bad_for_the_one_percent.

Marshall, Lorna. *The !Kung of Nyae Nyae.* Cambridge, MA: Harvard University Press, 1976.

Martin, M. Kay, and Barbara Voorhies. *Female of the Species.* New York: Columbia University Press, 1975.

Maschner, Herbert D. G. "The Evolution of Northwest Coast Warfare." In *Troubled Times: Violence and Warfare in the Past*, edited by Debra L. Martin and David W. Frayer, 267–302. Amsterdam: Gordon and Breach, 1997.

Maslow, Abraham. *Toward a Psychology of Being.* Princeton, NJ: Van Nostrand, 1968.

Maslow, Abraham. *The Farther Reaches of Human Nature.* New York: Viking, 1971.

Masters, William, Virginia Johnson, and Robert Levin. *The Pleasure Bond: A New Look at Sexuality and Commitment.* Boston: Little, Brown, 1975.

Maturana, Humberto, and Francisco Varela, *The Tree of Knowledge: The Biological Roots of Human Understanding.* Boston: Shambhala, 1992.

Maturana, Humberto, and Gerda Verden-Zoller. *Origins of Humanness in the Biology of Love.* Durham, NC: Duke University Press, 1998.

Maybury-Lewis, David. *Millennium: Tribal Wisdom and the Modern World.* New York: Viking, 1992.

Mayr, Ernst. "Cause and Effect in Biology." *Science* 134 (1961): 1501–1506. doi: 10.1126/science.134.3489.1501.

Maxwell, Elizabeth. "Self as Phoenix: A Comparison of Assagioli's and Dabrowski's Developmental Theories." *Advanced Development* 4 (1992): 31–48.

McCloskey, Laura, and Riane Eisler. "Family Structure and Family Violence and Nonviolence." In *Encyclopedia of Violence, Peace, and Conflict, Volume 2*, edited by Lester Kurtz et al., 1–11. San Diego, CA: Academic Press, 1999.

McCord, Ethan. "Innocence Lost: Ethan McCord Recounts Aftermath of Iraqi Civilian Massacre, UNPC 7/24/2010." Accessed December 3, 2016. Available online: https://www.youtube.com/watch?v=3ihPGtcHjNk.

McCraty, Rollin, Mike Atkinson, and Raymond Bradley. "Electrophysiological Evidence of Intuition: Part 1, The Surprising Role of the Heart." *Journal of Alternative and Complementary Medicine* 10 (2004): 133–143. doi: 10.1089/107555304322849057.

McCullough, Michael. *Beyond Revenge: The Evolution of the Forgiveness Instinct.* San Francisco: Jossey-Bass, 2008.

McLelland, David. *Power.* New York: Irvington, 1980.

McLeod, Saul. "Bowlby's Attachment Theory." *SimplyPsychology,* 2007. Available online: https://www.simplypsychology.org/bowlby.html.

Mednick, Sarnoff, and Barry Hutchings. "Registered Criminality in Adoptive and Biological Parents of Registered Male Criminal Adoptees." *Proceedings of the Annual Meeting of the American Psychopathological Association* 63 (1975): 105–116.

Meggitt, Mervyn. *Desert People: A Study of the Walbiri Aborigines of Central Australia.* Chicago: University of Chicago Press, 1965.

Mellaart, James. *Çatal Hüyük.* New York: McGraw Hill, 1967.

Menchú, Rigoberta, Elizabeth Burgos-Debray, and Ann Wright. *I, Rogoberta Menchu: An Indian Woman in Guatemala.* New York: Verso, 1987.

Mernissi, Fatima. *Beyond the Veil: Male-Female Dynamics in Modern Muslim Society.* Bloomington: University of Indiana Press, 1987.

Mezzofiore, Gianluca. "The Toronto Suspect Apparently Posted about an 'Incel Rebellion.' Here's What that Means." *CNN.* April 25, 2018. Available online: https://www.cnn.com/2018/04/25/us/incel-rebellion-alek-minassian-toronto-attack-trnd/index.html.

Miklikowska, Marta, and Douglas P. Fry. "Natural Born Nonkillers: A Critique of the Killers-Have-More-Kids Idea." In *Nonkilling Psychology,* edited by Daniel J. Christie and Joám Evans Pim, 43–70. Honolulu: Center for Global Nonkilling, 2012.

Milburn, Michael. Interviewed by Brian Braiker. "See No Evil—A Political Psychologist Explains the Roles Denial, Emotion and Childhood Punishment Play in Politics." *Newsweek.* Last modified May 13, 2004. Accessed March 18, 2018. Available online: http://nospank.net/n-m05r.htm.

Milburn, Michael, and Sheree Conrad. *The Politics of Denial.* Cambridge, MA: MIT Press, 1996.

Milburn, Michael, and Sheree Conrad. *Raised to Rage: The Politics of Anger and the Roots of Authoritarianism.* Cambridge, MA: MIT Press, 2018.

Miles, Margaret. *Carnal Knowing: Female Nakedness and Religious Meaning in the Christian West.* Boston: Beacon Press, 1989.

Milgram, Stanley. "Behavioral Study of Obedience." *Journal of Abnormal and Social Psychology* 67 (1963): 371–378. doi: 10.1037/h0040525.

Miller, Alice. *For Your Own Good: Hidden Cruelty in Child-Rearing and the Roots of Violence.* Translated by Hildegarde Hannum and Hunter Hannum. New York: Farrar, Straus and Giroux, 1990.

Miller, George, Eugene Galanter, and Karl Pribram. *Plans and the Structure of Behavior.* New York: Adams Bannister Cox, 1986.

Miller, Jean, and Irene Stiver. *The Healing Connection: How Women Form Relationships in Therapy and in Life*. Boston: Beacon Press, 1997.

"Millions Face School Violence across Asia." *Australia Broadcasting Corporation (ABC)*, last modified October 8, 2008. Available online: http://www.abc.net.au/ra/programguide/stories/200810/s2385881.htm.

Min, Jiajin, editor. *The Chalice and the Blade in Chinese Culture: Gender Relations and Social Models*. Beijing: China Social Sciences Publishing House.

Minturn, Leigh, Martin Grosse, and Santoah Haider. "Cultural Patterning of Sexual Beliefs and Behavior." *Ethnology* 8 (1969): 301–308. doi: 10.2307/3772759.

Mischel, Nicholas, Ida Llewellyn-Smith, and Patrick Mueller. "Physical (In)Activity-Dependent Structural Plasticity in Bulbospinal Catecholaminergic Neurons of Rat Rostral Ventrolateral Medulla." *Journal of Comparative Neurology* 522, (2014): 499–513. doi: 10.1002/cne.23464.

Moll, Jorge, Frank Krueger, Roland Zahn, Matteo Pardini, Ricardo de Oliveira-Souza, and Jordan Grafman. "Human Fronto–Mesolimbic Networks Guide Decisions about Charitable Donation." *Proceedings of the National Academy of Sciences (PNAS)* 103 (2006): 15623–15628. doi: 10.1073/pnas.0604475103.

Molloy, Barry. "Martial Minoans? War as a Social Process, Practice, and Event in Bronze Age Crete." *Annual of the British School at Athens* 107 (2012): 87–142. doi: 10.1017/S0068245412000044.

Monnet, Jean. *Memoirs*. New York: Doubleday, 1978.

Montagu, Ashley. *Touching*. New York: Columbia University Press, 1971.

Montagu, Ashley, editor. *Learning Non-Aggression: The Experience of Non-Literate Societies*. New York: Oxford University Press, 1978.

Montagu, Ashley. *Growing Young*. New York: McGraw-Hill, 1981.

Moore, John H. "The Reproductive Success of Cheyenne War Chiefs: A Contrary Case to Chagnon's Yanomamö." *Current Anthropology* 31 (1990): 322–330. doi: 10.1086/203846.

Morgan, Barak, Diane Sunar, C. Sue Carter, James F. Leckman, Douglas P. Fry, Eric B. Keverne, Iris-Tatjana Kolassa, Robert Kumsta, and David Olds. "Human Biological Development and Peace: Genes, Brains, Safety, and Justice." In *Pathways to Peace: The Transformative Power of Children and Families*, edited by James F. Leckman, Catherine Panter-Brick, and Rima Salah, 95–128. Cambridge, MA: MIT Press, 2014.

Mosher, Donald, and Silvan Tomkins. "Scripting the Macho Man: Hypermasculine Socialization and Enculturation." *Journal of Sex Research* 25 (1988): 60–84. doi: 10.1080/00224498809551445.

Mubanga, Mwenya, Liisa Byberg, Christoph Nowak, A. Egenvall, P. Magnusson, E. Ingelsson, and T. Fall. "Dog Ownership and the Risk of Cardiovascular Disease and Death—A Nationwide Cohort Study." *Scientific Reports* 7 (2017): 15821. doi: 10.1038/s41598-017-16118-6.

Muller, Martin, Frank Marlowe, Revocatus Bugumba, and Peter Ellison. "Testosterone and Paternal Care in East African Foragers and Pastoralists." *Proceedings of the Royal Society B: Biological Sciences* 276 (2009): 347–354. doi: 10.1098/rspb.2008.1028.

Murdock, George P. "The Current Status of the World's Hunting and Gathering Peoples." In *Man the Hunter*, edited by Richard B. Lee and Irvin DeVore, 13–20. Chicago: Aldine, 1968.

Murdock, George P. "Ethnographic Atlas: A Summary." *Ethnology* 6 (1967): 109–236.

Murdock, George P., and Douglas R. White. "Standard Cross-Cultural Sample." *Ethnology* 8 (1969): 329–369.

Nakao, Hisashi, Kohei Tamura, Yui Arimatsu, Tomomi Nakagawa, Naoko Matsumoto, and Takehiko Matsugi. "Violence in the Prehistoric Period of Japan: The Spatio-Temporal Pattern of Skeletal Evidence for Violence in the Jomon Period." *Biology Letters* 12 (2016): doi: 10.1098/rsbl.2016.0028.

Nakazawa, Donna. *Childhood Disrupted: How Your Biography Becomes Your Biology and How You Can Heal.* New York: Atria Books, 2016.

Narvaez, Darcia. "The 99 Percent—Development and Socialization within an Evolutionary Context: Growing Up to Become 'A Good and Useful Human Being.'" In *War, Peace, and Human Nature: The Convergence of Evolutionary and Cultural Views*, edited by Douglas P. Fry, 341–357. New York: Oxford University Press, 2013.

Narvaez, Darcia. *Neurobiology and the Development of Human Morality: Evolution, Culture, and Wisdom.* New York: Norton, 2014.

Narvaez, Darcia, Kristin Valentino, Agustin Fuentes, James J. McKenna, and Peter Gray, editors. *Ancestral Landscapes in Human Evolution: Culture, Childrearing and Social Wellbeing.* New York: Oxford University Press, 2014.

National Center for Educational Statistics. *National Assessment of Adult Literacy (NAAL).* Available online: https://nces.ed.gov/naal/lit_history.asp.

Nauta, Walle. "The Problem of the Frontal Lobe: A Reinterpretation." *Journal of Psychiatric Research* 8 (1971): 167–187. doi: 10.1016/0022-3956(71)90017-3.

Navai, Ramita. "Broken Lives: Nigeria's Child Brides Who End Up on the Streets." *Times* (November 28, 2008). Available online: http://www.timesonline.co.uk/tol/news/world/africa/article5248224.ece.

Niehoff, Debra. *The Biology of Violence: How Understanding the Brain, Behavior, and Environment Can Break the Vicious Circle of Aggression*. New York: The Free Press, 1999.

Nietzsche, Friedrich. *On the Genealogy of Morality*. Translated by Maudemarie Clark and Alan J. Swensen. New York: Vintage Books, 1967, originally published in 1887.

Nietzche, Friedrich. *Thus Spoke Zarathustra*. Hollywood, FL: Simon and Brown, 2012.

Noble, David. *A World without Women: The Christian Clerical Culture of Western Science*. New York: Knopf, 1992.

No Spank. "Countries Where Spanking Is Prohibited by Law in the Home, at School, Everywhere!" Last modified March 2007. Available online: www.nospank.net/totalban.htm.

Novembre, John. "Human Evolution: Ancient DNA Steps into the Language Debate." *Nature* 522 (2015): 164–165. doi: 10.1038/522164a.

Odling-Smee, F. John, Kevin Laland, and Marcus Feldman. *Niche Construction: The Neglected Process in Evolution*. Princeton, NJ: Monographs in Population Biology, Volume 37, 2003.

O'Brien, Joan. "Nammu, Mami, Eve and Pandora: 'What's in a Name?'" *Classical Journal* 79 (1983): 35–45.

O'Keeffe, Gwenn Schurgin, and Kathleen Clarke-Pearson. "The Impact of Social Media on Children, Adolescents, and Families." *Pediatrics* 127 (2011): 800–804. doi: 10.1542/peds.2011-0054.

Okin, Susan Moller. *Women in Western Political Thought*. Princeton, NJ: Princeton University Press, 1979.

Oliner, Samuel, and Pearl Oliner. *The Altruistic Personality: Rescuers of Jews in Nazi Europe*. New York: The Free Press, 1988.

Olweus, Dan, Åke Mattsson, Daisy Schalling, and Hans Low. "Circulating Testosterone Levels and Aggression in Adolescent Males: A Causal Analysis." *Psychosomatic Medicine* 50 (1988): 261–272.

Olweus, Dan. "Tackling Peer-Victimization with a School-Based Intervention Program." In *Cultural Variation in Conflict Resolution: Alternatives to Violence*, edited by Douglas P. Fry and Kaj Björkqvist, 215–231. Mahwah, NJ: Erlbaum, 1997.

Olweus, Dan. "Cyber Bullying: A Critical Overview." In *Aggression and Violence: A Social Psychological Perspective*, 225–240. New York: Routledge, 2017.

Olweus, Dan, and Jan Helge Kallestad. "The Olweus Bullying Prevention Program: Effects of Classroom Components at Different Grade Levels."

In *Indirect and Direct Aggression*, edited by Karin Österman. Frankfurt am Main: Peter Lang, 2010, 115–131.

O'Manique, John. *The Origins of Justice: The Evolution of Morality, Human Rights, and Law*. Philadelphia: University of Pennsylvania Press, 2003.

O'Nell, Carl. "Hostility Management and the Control of Aggression in a Zapotec Community." *Aggressive Behavior* 7 (1981): 351–366. doi: 10.1002/1098-2337(1981)7:4<351.

O'Nell, Carl. "Some Primary and Secondary Effects of Violence Control among the Nonviolent Zapotec." *Anthropological Quarterly* 59 (1986): 184–190. doi: 10.2307/3317333.

O'Nell, Carl. "The Non-Violent Zapotec." In *Societies at Peace: Anthropological Perspectives*, edited by Signe Howell and Roy Willis, 117–132 (New York: Routledge, 1989).

Ornstein, Robert. *The Psychology of Consciousness*. Oxford: Penguin, 1972.

Österman, Karin, Kaj Björkqvist, and Kristian Wahlbeck. "Twenty-Eight Years after the Complete Ban on the Physical Punishment of Children in Finland: Trends and Psychosocial Concomitants." *Aggressive Behavior* 40 (2014): 568–581. doi: 10.1002/ab.21537.

Otterbein, Keith. "Internal War: A Cross-Cultural Study." *American Anthropologist* 70 (1968): 277–289. doi: 10.1525/aa.1968.70.2.02a00040.

Otterbein, Keith. *The Evolution of War: A Cross-Cultural Study*. New Haven, CT: Human Relations Area Files Press, 1970.

Pagels, Elaine. *The Gnostic Gospels*. New York: Random House, 1979.

Pagels, Elaine. *Adam, Eve, and the Serpent*. New York: Vintage, 1988.

Palmer, Craig, and Randy Thornhill. *A Natural History of Rape: Biological Bases of Sexual Coercion*. Cambridge, MA: MIT Press, 2000.

Palmer, Stuart. "Murder and Suicide in Forty Non-Literate Societies." *Journal of Criminal Law, Criminology, and Police Science* 56 (1965): 320–324. doi: 10.2307/1141241.

Panksepp, Jaak. *Affective Neuroscience: The Foundations of Human and Animal Emotions*. New York: Oxford University Press, 1998.

Panksepp, Jaak, Eric Nelson, and Marni Bekkedal. "Brain Systems for the Mediation of Social Separation-Distress and Social-Reward Evolutionary Antecedents and Neuropeptide Intermediaries." *Annals of the New York Academy of Sciences* 807 (1997): 78–100. doi: 10.1111/j.1749-6632.1997.tb51914.x.

Patai, Raphael. *The Hebrew Goddess*. New York: Avon, 1978.

Patton, Robert, and Lytt Gardner. *Growth Failure in Maternal Deprivation*. Springfield, IL: Charles Thomas, 1963.

"Peaceful Societies: Alternatives to Violence and War." University of Alabama at Birmingham, Department of Anthropology. Accessed March 23, 2018. Available online: https://cas.uab.edu/peacefulsocieties/.

Peirce, Kate. "Socialization of Teenage Girls through Teen-Magazine Fiction: The Making of a New Woman or an Old Lady?" *Sex Roles* 29 (1993): 59–68. doi: 10.1007/BF00289996.

Perry, Bruce. "Childhood Experience and the Expression of Genetic Potential: What Childhood Neglect Tells Us about Nature and Nurture." *Brain and Mind* 3 (2002): 79–100. doi: 10.1023/A:1016557824657.

Perry, Bruce, Ronnie Pollard, Toi Blakley, William Baker, and Domenico Vigilante. "Childhood Trauma, The Neurobiology of Adaptation, and 'Use-Dependent' Development of the Brain: How 'States' Become 'Traits.'" *Infant Mental Health Journal* 16 (1995): 271–291. doi: 10.1002/1097-0355(199524).

Perry, Gina. *Behind the Shock Machine: The Untold Story of the Notorious Milgram Psychology Experiments*. New York: The New Press, 2013.

Perry, Mary Elizabeth. *"Deviant Women and Cultural Transformation."* Paper presented at the panel "Dominator and Partnership Models as Analytical Tools, 20th Anniversary Conference of the Western Association of Women Historians," Asilomar, Pacific Grove, CA, 1989.

Perry, Mary Elizabeth. "The Black Madonna of Montserrat." In *Views of Women's Lives in Western Tradition*, edited by Frances Richardson Keller, 110–128. Lewiston, NY: Edwin Mellen Press, 1990.

Pietila, Hilkka. "Eradicating Poverty by Building a Welfare Society: Finland as a Case Study." *Cooperation South* 2 (2001): 79–96.

Piff, Paul. "Wealth and the Inflated Self: Class, Entitlement, and Narcissism." *Personality and Social Psychology Bulletin* 40 (2014): 34–43. doi: 10.1177/0146167213501699.

Pinker, Steven. *How the Mind Works*. New York: W.W. Norton, 1997.

Pinker, Steven. *The Blank Slate: The Modern Denial of Human Nature*. New York: Viking, 2002.

Pinker, Steven. *Better Angels of Our Nature: Why Violence Has Declined*. New York: Viking, 2011.

Platon, Nikolas. *Crete*. Geneva: Nagel Publishers, 1966.

Plotnik, Joshua, Richard Lair, Wirot Suphachoksahakun, and Frans de Waal. "Elephants Know When They Need a Helping Trunk in a Cooperative Task." *Proceedings of the National Academy of Sciences (PNAS)* 108

(2011): 5116–5121. doi: 10.1073/pnas.1101765108. Available online: http://www.pnas.org/content/108/12/5116.

Post, Robert. "Transduction of Psychosocial Stress into the Neurobiology of Recurrent Affective Disorder." *American Journal of Psychiatry* 149 (1992): 999–1010. doi: 10.1176/ajp.149.8.999.

Pribram, Karl. "The Primate Frontal Cortex—Executive of the Brain." In *Psychophysiology of the Frontal Lobes*, edited by Karl Pribram and Aleksandr Luria, 293–314. New York: Academic Press, 1973.

Price, Douglas, and James Brown. *Prehistoric Hunter-Gatherers: The Emergence of Cultural Complexity*. New York: Academic Press, 1985.

Przybylski, Andrew, and Netta Weinstein. "Can You Connect with Me Now? Showing Interference with Face-to-Face Contacts of Mere Presence of a Cell Phone." *Journal of Social and Personal Relationships* 30 (2012): 237–246. doi: 10.1177/0265407512453827.

Quartz, Steven, and Terrence Sejnowski. *Liars, Lovers, and Heroes: What the New Brain Science Reveals about How We Become Who We Are*. New York: William Morrow, 2002.

Quartz, Steven, and Terrence Sejnowski. *The Neural Basis of Cognitive Development: About How We Become Who We Are*. New York: Harper-Collins, 2002.

Rand, Ayn. *The Virtue of Selfishness*. New York: Signet, 1964.

Rando, Licia. "The Caring and Connected Parenting Guide." Available online: www.centerforpartnership or www.saiv.org.

Ranke-Heinemann, Uta. *Eunuchs for the Kingdom of Heaven: Women, Sexuality, and the Catholic Church*. Translated by Peter Heinegg. New York: Doubleday, 1990.

Read, John, Roar Fosse, Andrew Moskowitz, and Bruce Perry. "The Traumagenic Neurodevelopmental Model of Psychosis Revisited." *Neuropsychiatry* 4 (2014): 1–15. doi: 10.2217/npy.13.89.

Real, Terrence. *I Don't Want to Talk about It: Overcoming the Secret Legacy of Male Depression*. New York: Scribner, 1997.

Reeves, Minou. *Female Warriors of Allah: Women and the Islamic Revolution*. New York: Dutton, 1989.

Repetti, Rena, and Jenifer Wood. "Families Accommodating to Chronic Stress." In *Coping with Chronic Stress*, edited by Benjamin H. Gottlieb, 191–220. Boston: Springer, 1997.

Report on Child Brides under the Mullahs Rule in Iran. National Council of Resistance of Iran (NCRI), Women's Committee 2015. Available online: http://women.ncr-iran.org/images/documents/child-brides-Iran-en.pdf.

Reuther, Rosemary. *Sexism and God Talk: Toward a Feminist Theology.* Boston: Beacon Press, 1993.

Reyna, S. P. "A Mode of Domination Approach to Organized Violence." In *Studying War: Anthropological Perspectives,* edited by S. P. Reyna and R. E. Downs, 29–65. Amsterdam: Gordon and Breach, 1994.

Rideout, Vicky. *The Common Sense Census: Media Use by Tweens and Teens.* San Francisco: Common Sense Media, 2015. Available online: https://www.commonsensemedia.org/sites/default/files/uploads/research/census_researchreport.pdf.

Rilling, James. "Neuroscientific Approaches and Applications within Anthropology." *Yearbook of Physical Anthropology* 51 (2008): 2–32. doi: 10.1002/ajpa.20947.

Rilling, James. "The Neurobiology of Cooperation and Altruism." In *Origins of Altruism and Cooperation,* edited by Robert W. Sussman and C. Robert Cloninger, 295–306. New York: Springer, 2011.

Rilling, James, Andrea Glenn, Meeta Jairam, Giuseppe Pagnoni, David Goldsmith, Hanie Elfenbein, and Scott Lilienfeld. "Neural Correlates of Social Cooperation and Non-Cooperation as a Function of Psychopathy." *Biological Psychiatry* 61 (2007): 1260–1271. doi: 10.1016/j.biopsych.2006.07.021.

Rilling, James, David Gutman, Thorsten Zeh, Giuseppe Pagnoni, Gregory Berns, Clinton Kilts. "A Neural Basis for Social Cooperation." *Neuron* 35 (2002): 395–405. doi: 10.1016/S0896-6273(02)00755-9.

Rilling, James, Alan Sanfey, Jessica Aronson, Leigh Nystrom, and Jonathan Cohen. "Opposing BOLD Responses to Reciprocated and Unreciprocated Altruism in Putative Reward Pathways." *NeuroReport* 15 (2004): 1–5.

Rilling, James, J. Scholz, T. Preuss, M. Glasser, B. Errangi, and T. Behrens. "Differences between Chimpanzees and Bonobos in Neural Systems Supporting Social Cognition." *Social Cognitive and Affective Neuroscience* 7 (2011): 369–379. doi: 10.1093/scan/nsr017.

Rizzolatti, Giacomo, Luciano Fadiga, Vittorio Gallese, and Leonardo Fogassi. "Premotor Cortex and the Recognition of Motor Actions." *Cognitive Brain Research* 3 (1996): 131–141. doi: 10.1016/0926-6410(95)00038-0.

Robarchek, Clayton. "The Image of Nonviolence: World View of the Semai Senoi." *Federated Museums Journal (Malaysia)* 25 (1980): 103–117.

Robarchek, Clayton, and Carole Robarchek. "Waging Peace: The Psychological and Sociocultural Dynamics of Positive Peace." In *Anthropological Contributions to Conflict Resolution,* edited by Alvin W. Wolfe and Honggang Yang, 64–80. Athens: University of Georgia Press, 1996.

Robarchek, Clayton, and Carole Robarchek. *Waorani: The Contexts of Violence and War*. Fort Worth, TX: Harcourt Brace, 1998.

Robotham, Sheila. *Women, Resistance, and Revolution*. New York: Vintage, 1974.

"Romantic Love Is Long-Term Focused Attention." *Toronto Star* (February 14, 2003).

Romm, Cari. "Rethinking One of Psychology's Most Infamous Experiments." *Atlantic*, January 28, 2015. Available online: https://www.theatlantic.com/health/archive/2015/01/rethinking-one-of-psychologys-most-infamous-experiments/384913/.

Roper, Marilyn K. "A Survey of the Evidence for Intrahuman Killing in the Pleistocene." *Current Anthropology* 10 (1969): 427–459. doi: 10.1086/201038.

Roscoe, John. *The Bakitara or Bunyoro*. Cambridge, UK: Cambridge University Press, 1923.

Roseboom, Tessa, Susanne de Rooij, and Rebecca Painter. "The Dutch Famine and Its Long-Term Consequences to Adult Health." *Early Human Development* 82 (2006): 485–491. doi: 10.1016/j.earlhumdev.2006.07.001.

Rosenblum, L., and G. Paully. "The Effects of Varying Environmental Demands on Maternal and Infant Behavior." *Child Development* 55 (1984): 305–314. doi: 10.2307/1129854.

Rosin, Hanna. "A Tough Plan for Raising Children Draws Fire: 'Babywise' Guides Worry Pediatricians and Others." *Washington Post,* last modified February 27, 1999, A01. Available online: https://www.highbeam.com/doc/1P2-571764.html.

Ross, Marc. *The Culture of Conflict: Interpretations and Interests in Comparative Perspective*. New Haven, CT: Yale University Press, 1993.

Rousseau, Jean Jacques. *The Confessions of Jean Jacques Rousseau, 1712-1778, Book I*. New York: The Modern Library, 1945.

Rubel, Arthur, and Carl W. O'Nell. *Susto: A Folk Illness*. Berkeley: University of California Press, 1991.

Rutter, Michael. "Maternal Deprivation, 1972-1978: New Findings, New Concepts, New Approaches." *Child Development* 50 (1979): 283–305. doi: 10.2307/1129404.

Sachs, Jeffrey. *The Price of Civilization*. New York: Random House, 2012.

Sachs, Jeffrey. *To Move the World: JFK's Quest for Peace*. New York: Random House, 2013.

Sadker, Myra, and David Sadker. "Sexism in the Schoolroom of the '80s." *Psychology Today* March (1985): 54–57.

Sagioglou, Christina, and Tobias Greitemeyer. "Facebook's Emotional Consequences: Why Facebook Causes a Decrease in Mood and Why People Still Use It." *Computers in Human Behavior* 35 (2014): 359–363. doi: 10.1016/j.chb.2014.03.003.

Sahlins, Marshall. *The Western Illusion of Human Nature.* Chicago: Prickly Paradigm Press, 2008.

Samborn, Hope Viner. "Media Bias against Women: Stuck in a Bygone Era." *Perspectives* 19 (2011): 1–4.

Sanday, Peggy. *Female Power and Male Dominance: On the Origins of Sexual Inequality.* Cambridge, UK: Cambridge University Press, 1981.

Sanday, Peggy. *Women at the Center.* Ithaca, NY: Cornell University Press, 2002.

Sapolsky, Robert M. *The Trouble with Testosterone and Other Essays on the Biology of the Human Predicament.* New York: Touchstone, 1998.

Sapolsky, Robert M. "Rousseau with a Tail: Maintaining a Tradition of Peace among Baboons." In *War, Peace, and Human Nature: Convergence of Evolutionary and Cultural Views,* edited by Douglas P. Fry, 421–438. New York: Oxford University Press, 2013.

Sapolsky, Robert M. *Behave: The Biology of Humans at Our Best and Worst.* New York: Penguin, 2017.

Sapolsky Robert M., and Lisa Share. "A Pacific Culture among Wild Baboons: Its Emergence and Transmission." *Public Library of Science Biology* 2 (2004): e106. doi: 10.1371/journal.pbio.0020106.

Savage-Rumbaugh, Sue, and R. Lewin. *Kanzi: The Ape on the Brink of the Human Mind.* New York: Wiley, 1994.

Save the Children: Annual Report 2001, 70th Anniversary Issue. Westport, CT: Save the Children, 2001.

Schachter, Stanley, and Jerome Singer. "Cognitive, Social and Psychological Determinants of Emotional State." *Psychological Review* 69 (1962): 379–399. doi: 10.1037/h0046234.

Schaffer, H. Rudolph, and Peggy Emerson. *The Development of Social Attachments in Infancy.* Lafayette, IN: Purdue University Press, 1964.

Scheck, Raffael. "Childhood in German Autobiographical Writings, 1740-1820." *Journal of Psychohistory* 15 (1987): 391–422.

Schiess, Ueli, and Jacqueline Schön-Bühlmann. *Satellitenkonto Haushaltsproduktion Pilotversuch für die Schweiz.* Neuchâtel, Switzerland: Statistik der Schweiz, 2004.

Schiff, Michel, Michel Duyme, Annick Dumaret, Stanislaw Tomkiewicz. "How Much Could We Boost Scholastic Achievement and IQ Scores? A Direct

Answer from a French Adoption Study." *Cognition* 12 (1982): 165–196. doi: 10.1016/0010-0277(82)90011-7.

Schlegel, Alice. "Contentious but Not Violent: The Hopi of Northern Arizona." In *Keeping the Peace: Conflict Resolution and Peaceful Societies around the World*, edited by Graham Kemp and Douglas P. Fry, 19–33. New York: Routledge, 2004.

Schlegel, Stuart. *Tiruray Justice: Traditional Tiruray Law and Morality*. Berkeley: University of California Press, 1970.

Schlegel, Stuart. *Wisdom from a Rainforest*. Athens: University of Georgia Press, 1998.

Schneider, Karen. "Living with the Enemy." *People,* June 1, 1992. Available online: http://people.com/archive/living-with-the-enemy-vol-37-no-21/.

Schradin, Carsten, DeeAnn Reeder, Sally Mendoza, and Gustl Anzenberger. "Prolactin and Paternal Care: Comparison of Three Species of Monogamous New World Monkeys." *Journal of Comparative Psychology* 117 (2003): 166–175. doi: 10.1037/0735-7036.117.2.166.

Schrauf, Cornelia, Josep Call, Koki Fuwa, and Satoshi Hirata. "Do Chimpanzees Use Weight to Select Hammer Tools?" *PLoS ONE* 7 (2012): e41044. doi:10.1371/journal.pone.0041044.

Segardahl, Pär, William Fields, and Sue Savage-Rumbaugh. *Kanzi's Primal Language: The Cultural Initiation of Primates into Language.* New York: Palgrave Macmillan, 2005.

Service, Elman R. *Profiles in Ethnology*. New York: Harper and Row, 1971, revised edition.

Sherman, Paul. "Nepotism and the Evolution of Alarm Calls." *Science* 197 (1977): 1246–1253. doi: 10.1126/science.197.4310.1246.

Shifferd, Kent, Patrick Hiller, and David Swanson. *A Global Security System: An Alternative to War*. Charlottesville, VA: World Beyond War, 2017.

Shih, Chuan-kang. *Quest for Harmony: The Moso Traditions of Sexual Union and Family Life*. Palo Alto, CA: Stanford University Press, 2009.

Shih, Chuan-kang, and Mark Jenike. "A Cultural–Historical Perspective on the Depressed Fertility among the Matrilineal Moso in Southwest China." *Human Ecology* 30 (2002): 21–47. doi: 10.1023/A:1014579404548.

Shirer, William. *The Rise and Fall of the Third Reich*. New York: Simon and Schuster, 1960.

Singer, Emily. "Mistreatment during Childhood and Low Enzyme Activity May Make Men More Violent." *Los Angeles Times*, August 2, 2002. Available online: http://www.latimes.com/news/nationworld/nation/la-sci-abuse2aug02.stor.

Slocum, Sally. "Woman the Gatherer: Male Bias in Anthropology." In *Toward an Anthropology of Women*, edited by Reina Reciter, 36–50. New York: Monthly Review Press, 1975.

Smith, David Livingstone. *The Most Dangerous Animal: Human Nature and the Origins of War*. New York: St. Martin's Griffin, 2007.

Smuts, Barbara. *Sex and Friendship in Baboons*. New York: Aldine du Gruyter, 1985.

Snow, Dean. "Sexual Dimorphism in European Upper Paleolithic Cave Art." *American Antiquity* 78 (2013): 746–761. doi: 10.7183/0002-7316.78.4.746.

Snow, Dean. "Were the First Artists Mostly Women?" *National Geographic*, October 8, 2013. Available online: http://news.nationalgeographic.com/news/2013/10/131008-women-handprints-oldest-neolithic-cave-art/.

Snowden, Charles, and T. Zeigler. "Growing Up Cooperatively: Family Processes and Infant Development in Marmosets and Tamarins." *Journal of Developmental Processes* 2 (2007): 40–66. Available online: http://citeseerx.ist.psu.edu/viewdoc/download?doi=10.1.1.325.8840&rep=rep1&type=pdf.

Söderberg, Patrik, and Douglas P. Fry. "Anthropological Aspects of Ostracism." In *Ostracism, Exclusion, and Rejection*, edited by Kipling D. Williams and Steve A. Nida, 258–272. New York: Routledge, 2017.

Souillac, Geneviève. *A Study in Transborder Ethics: Justice, Citizenship, and Civility*. Brussels: Peter Lang, 2012.

Souillac, Geneviève, and Douglas P. Fry. "Indigenous Lessons for Conflict Resolution." In *The Handbook of Conflict Resolution Theory and Practice*, edited by Peter T. Coleman, Morton Deutsch, and Eric C. Marcus, 604–622. San Francisco: Jossey-Bass, 2014.

Souillac, Geneviève, and Douglas P. Fry. "Anthropology: Implications for Peace." In *The Palgrave Handbook of Disciplinary and Regional Approaches to Peace*, edited by Oliver P. Richmond, Sandra Pogodda, and Jasmine Ramovic, 69–81. London: Palgrave, 2016.

Spangler, Todd. "Hooked on Hardware? Tech Giants Face Tough Questions over Device Addiction." *Variety*, accessed March 19, 2018. Available online: http://variety.com/2018/digital/features/smartphone-addiction-apps-apple-facebook-google-1202724489/.

"Speak Truth to Power: Telling Stories to Effect Change." *Public Broadcasting Service*. Available online: http://www.pbs.org/speaktruthtopower/rana.html.

Speier, Jackie. "Rapes of Women in Military 'a National Disgrace,'" *SF Gate*, last modified April 16, 2011. Available online: https://www.sfgate.com/opinion/article/Rapes-of-women-in-military-a-national-disgrace-2374845.php.

Spiritual Alliance to Stop Intimate Violence (SAIV). Accessed May 7, 2018. Available online: www.saiv.org.

Sprenger, Jakob. *The Malleus Maleficarum of Heinrich Kramer and James Sprenger*. New York: Dover, 1971.

Stanton, Emily. "Study: At Least 100,000 Children Being Used in U.S. Sex Trade." *U.S. News*, last modified July 8, 2013. Available online: https://www.usnews.com/news/blogs/washington-whispers/2013/07/08/study-at-least-100000-children-being-used-in-us-sex-trade.

Statista. "Pay Gap between CEOs and Average Workers in 2014, by Country." Accessed March 13, 2018. Available online: https://www.statista.com/statistics/424159/pay-gap-between-ceos-and-average-workers-in-world-by-country/.

Straub, Ervin. *The Psychology of Good and Evil: Why Children, Adults, and Groups Help and Harm Others*. Cambridge, UK: Cambridge University Press, 2003.

Straub, Ervin. *The Roots of Goodness and Resistance to Evil*. New York: Oxford University Press, 2015.

Straus, Murray, and Anita Mathur. "Social Change and Trends in Approval of Corporal Punishment by Parents from 1968 to 1994." In *Family Violence against Children: A Challenge for Society*, edited by Detlev Frehsee, Wiebke Horn, and Kai-D. Bussmann, 91–105. New York: De Gruyter, 1996.

Stellar, Jennifer, Vida M. Manzo, Michael Kraus, and Dacher Keltner. "Class and Compassion: Socioeconomic Factors Predict Responses to Suffering." *Emotion* 12 (2012): 449–459. doi: 10.1037/a0026508.

Steward, Julian. "Causal Factors and Processes in the Evolution of Pre-Farming Societies." In *Man the Hunter*, edited by Richard B. Lee and Irven DeVore, 312–334. Chicago: Aldine, 1968.

Stewart, Alexander, and Joshua Plotkin. "From Extortion to Generosity, Evolution in the Iterated Prisoner's Dilemma." *Proceedings of the National Academy of Sciences (PNAS)* 110 (2013): 15348–15353. doi: 10.1073/pnas.1306246110.

Stinson, Carol, Barry Bogin, and Dennis O'Rourke. *Human Biology: An Evolutionary and Biocultural Perspective*. New York: John Wiley and Sons, 2012.

Stothart, Cary, Ainsley Mitchum, and Courtney Yehnert. "The Attentional Cost of Receiving a Cell Phone Notification." *Journal of Experimental Psychology* 41 (2015): 893–897. doi: 10.1037/xhp0000100.

Strayer, Joseph. *The Albigensian Crusades*. Ann Arbor: University of Michigan Press, 1992.

Strier, Karen. "Social Plasticity and Demographic Variation in Primates." In *Origins of Altruism and Cooperation*, edited by Robert W. Sussman and C. Robert Cloninger, 179–192. New York: Springer, 2011.

Super, Charles M., and Sara Harkness. "The Developmental Niche: A Conceptualization at the Interface of Child and Culture." *International Journal of Behavioral Development* 9 (1986): 545–569. doi: 10.1177/016502548600900409.

Sussman, Robert W. "Why the Legend of the Killer Ape Never Dies: The Enduring Power of Cultural Beliefs to Distort Our View of Human Nature." In *War, Peace, and Human Nature: Convergence of Evolutionary and Cultural Views*, edited by Douglas P. Fry, 97–111. New York: Oxford University Press, 2013.

Talle, Aud. "Maasai." In *Encyclopedia of Sex and Gender, Volume 2*, edited by Carol R. Ember and Melvin Ember, 608–616. New York: Kluwar Academic/Plenum Publishers, 2004.

Tandoc, Edson, Patrick Ferrucci, and Margaret Duff. "Facebook Use, Envy, and Depression among College Students: Is Facebooking Depressing?" *Computers in Human Behavior* 43 (2015): 139–146. doi: 10.1016/j.chb.2014.10.053.

Tanner, Nancy. *On Becoming Human*. Cambridge, UK: Cambridge University Press, 1981.

Tanner, Nancy, and Adrienne Zihlman. "Women in Evolution. Part I: Innovation and Selection in Human Origins." *Signs: Journal of Women in Culture and Society* 1 (1976): 585–608. doi: 10.1086/493245.

Taylor, J. Rattray. *Sex in History*. New York: Ballantine Books, 1954.

Taylor, Shelley. *The Tending Instinct: How Nurturing Is Essential to Who We Are and How We Live*. New York: Henry Holt, 2002.

Tienari, Pekka, Layman Wynne, Juha Moring, Ilpo Lahti, M. Naarala, A. Sorri, K. Wahlberg, O. Saarento, M. Seitamaa, and M. Kaleva. "The Finnish Adoptive Family Study of Schizophrenia: Implications for Family Research." *British Journal of Psychiatry,* 164 (Supplement 23, 1994): 20–26.

Textor, Robert B. *A Cross Cultural Summary*. New Haven, CT: Human Relations Area Files, 1967.

Thomas, Elizabeth M. "Management of Violence among the Ju/wasi of Nyae Nyae: The Old Way and a New Way." In *Studying War: Anthropological Perspectives*, edited by S. P. Reyna and R. E. Downs, 69–84. Amsterdam: Gordon and Breach, 1994.

Thompson, Paul, Jay Giedd, Roger Woods, David MacDonald, Alan Evans, and Arthur Toga. "Growth Patterns in the Developing Brain Detected by

Using Continuum Mechanical Tensor Maps." *Nature* 404 (2002): 190–193. doi: 10.1038/35004593.

Tonkinson, Robert. *The Jigalong Mob: Aboriginal Victors of the Desert Crusade.* Menlo Park, CA: Cummings Publishing Company, 1974.

Tonkinson, Robert. "Resolving Conflict within the Law: The Mardu Aborigines of Australia." In *Keeping the Peace: Conflict Resolution and Peaceful Societies around the World*, edited by Graham Kemp and Douglas P. Fry, 89–104. New York: Routledge, 2004.

Trivers, Robert. *Social Evolution.* San Francisco: Benjamin-Cummings, 1985.

Turner, Angela. "Genetic and Hormonal Influences on Male Violence." In *Male Violence*, edited by John Archer, 233–252. New York: Routledge, 1994.

Twenge, Jean. *iGen: Why Today's Super-Connected Kids Are Growing Up Less Rebellious, More Tolerant, Less Happy—and Completely Unprepared for Adulthood—and What that Means for the Rest of Us.* New York: Atria Books, 2017.

"UN Body Accuses Brazil's Military Police of Killing Kids to 'Clean Streets' for Olympics, World Cup." *teleSUR*, last modified October 13, 2015. Available online: https://www.telesurtv.net/english/news/UN-Brazils-Police-Kill-Kids-to-Clean-Streets-for-Olympics-20151013-0044.html.

Uncapher, Melina, Lin Lin, Larry Rosen, Heather Kirkorian, Naomi Baron, Kira Bailey, Joanne Cantor, David Strayer, Thomas Parsons, and Anthony Wagner. "Media Multitasking and Cognitive, Psychological, Neural, and Learning Differences." *Pediatrics* 140 (2017): S62–S66. doi: 10.1542/peds.2016-1758D.

United Nations. "Convention on the Elimination of All Forms of Discrimination against Women." December 18, 1979. Available online: https://treaties.un.org/doc/Publication/MTDSG/Volume%20I/Chapter%20IV/IV-8.en.pdf.

United Nations. "Declaration on the Elimination of Violence against Women." December 20, 1993. Available online: http://www.un.org/documents/ga/res/48/a48r104.htm.

United Nations, General Assembly. *Universal Declaration of Human Rights.* December 10, 1948. Available online: http://www.un.org/en/universal-declaration-human-rights/.

United Nations, General Assembly. *Promotion and Protections of the Rights of Children.* Report A/61/150 (2006), 13.

United Nations, High Commissioner for Refugees. "Convention on the Rights of the Child." November 20, 1989. Available online: http://www.unhcr.org/en-us/protection/children/50f941fe9/united-nations-convention-rights-child-crc.html.

United Nations, Office on Drugs and Crime. "Global Study on Homicide, 2013: Trends, Context, Data." Accessed on March 23, 2018. Available online: https://www.unodc.org/documents/data-and-analysis/statistics/GSH2013/2014_GLOBAL_HOMICIDE_BOOK_web.pdf.

United Nations, Population Fund (FPA). "State of the World Population, 2005: Report, Child Marriage Fact Sheet." Available online: http://www.unfpa.org/swp/2005/presskit/factsheets/facts_child_marriage.htm.

United Nations Children's Fund (UNICIF). *We the Children*. New York: UNICEF, 2001. Available online: http://www.un.org/en/events/pastevents/pdfs/we_the_children.pdf.

United Nations Children's Fund (UNICEF), UK. *"Commercial Sexual Exploitation Position Statement."* January 28, 2004.

United Nations Development Fund for Women (UNIFEM), Donors Working Group. "Platform for Action towards the Abandonment of Female Genital Mutilation/Cutting (FGM/C)." Available online: http://www.who.int/reproductivehealth/publications/fgm/platform_for_action_fgm/en/.

United Nations Development Program. "Human Development Reports—Table 3: Inequality-adjusted Human Development Index." Accessed April 28, 2018. Available online: http://hdr.undp.org/en/composite/IHDI.

United Nations Educational, Scientific and Cultural Organization (UNESCO). *School Violence and Bullying: Global Status Report*. Paris: UNESCO, 2017. Available online: http://unesdoc.unesco.org/images/0024/002469/246970e.pdf.

United Nations News. *"Annan Welcomes Study on Violence against Children that Calls for Urgent Global Action,"* last modified October 11, 2006. Available online: www.un.org/apps/news/story.asp?NewsID=20225&Cr=child&Cr1.

United States Census Bureau. *Selected Highlights from 65+ in the United States: 2005, Appendix*. Washington, DC: US Census Bureau.

United States Department of Health and Human Services. *A Profile of Older Americans: 2014*. Available online: https://www.acl.gov/sites/default/files/Aging%20and%20Disability%20in%20America/2014-Profile.pdf.

United States Department of Labor. *List of Products Produced by Forced or Indentured Child Labor*. Available online: https://www.dol.gov/ilab/reports/child-labor/list-of-products/.

United States Department of State. *Major Forms of Trafficking in Persons: Trafficking in Persons, 2009*. Available online: http://www.state.gov/g/tip/rls/tiprpt/2009/123126.htm.

Uvnäs-Moberg, Kerstin. "Oxytocin May Mediate the Benefits of Positive Social Interactions and Emotions." *Psychoneuroendoctrinology* 23 (1998): 819–835, doi: https://doi.org/10.1016/S0306-4530(98)00056-0.

Uvnas-Moberg, Kerstin, and Maria Petersson. "Oxytocin, a Mediator of Anti-Stress, Well-Being, Social Interaction, Growth and Healing." *Zeitschrift fur Psychosomatische Medizin und Psychotherapie* 51 (2005): 57–80. https://pdfs.semanticscholar.org/0ac8/c14228b62b9c87636f5b6eb536a434fd04de.pdf.

Valentino, Kristin, Michelle Comas, and Amy K. Nuttall. "Child Maltreatment and Early Mother-Child Interactions." In *Ancestral Landscapes in Human Evolution*, edited by Darcia Narvaez, Kristin Valentino, Agustin Fuentes, James J. McKenna, and Peter Gray, 265–281. New York: Oxford University Press, 2014.

Van Cleve, Thomas Curtis. *The Emperor of Frederick II if Hohenstaufen: Immutator Mundi*. Oxford: Oxford University Press, 1972.

van der Kolk, Bessel. *The Body Keeps the Score: Brain, Mind, and Body in the Healing of Trauma*. New York: Penguin, 2015.

Vitale, Alyssa A. *Reproductive Ecology of Black Bears in Maine: Maternal Effect, Philopatry, and Primiparity*. Ph.D. Dissertation, University of Maine (2015). Available online: Alyssa A. Vitale. "Reproductive Ecology of Black Bears in Maine: Maternal Effect, Philopatry, and Primiparity." *Electronic Theses and Dissertations* 2305 (2012), https://digitalcommons.library.umaine.edu/etd/2305.

Walters, David. *Physical and Sexual Abuse of Children: Causes and Treatment*. Bloomington: Indiana University Press, 1975.

Wang, Yanan. "Discovery of Prehistoric Massacre May Point to Origins of Human Warfare." *Washington Post*, Science section, last modified January 21, 2016. Accessed March 6, 2018. Available online: https://www.washingtonpost.com/news/morning-mix/wp/2016/01/21/discovery-of-prehistoric-massacre-may-point-to-origins-of-human-warfare/?utm_term=.906645897504.

Ward, Adrian, Kristen Duke, Ayelet Gneezy, and Maarten W. Bos. "Brain Drain: The Mere Presence of One's Own Smartphone Reduces Available Cognitive Capacity." *Journal of the Association for Consumer Research* 2 (2017): 140–154. doi: 10.1086/691462.

Warneken, Felix, and Michael Tomasello. "Altruistic Helping in Human Infants and Young Chimpanzees." *Science* 311 (2006): 1301–1303. doi: 10.1126/science.1121448.

Warwick, Liz. "More Cuddles, Less Stress." *Bulletin of the Centre of Excellence for Early Childhood* 4 (October 2005), 2. Available at: http://excellence-jeunesenfants.ca/documents/BulletinVol4No2Oct05ANG.pdf.

Watson, John, and Rosalie Rayner. "Conditioned Emotional Reactions." *Journal of Experimental Psychology* 3 (1920): 1–14. doi: 10.1037/h0069608.

Welch, David. *The Third Reich*. New York: Routledge, 1993.

Wertheim, Margaret. *Pythagoras' Trousers: God, Physics, and the Gender Wars*. New York: Norton, 1997.

Wesson, Kenneth. "Memory and the Brain." *Independent Schools* 63 (2002): 89.

"What Animal Has the Longest Pregnancy?" *Live Science*. March 2, 2011. Available online: https://www.livescience.com/33086-what-animal-has-the-longest-pregnancy.html.

Wheeler, Gerald C. *The Tribe, and Intertribal Relations in Australia*. London: John Murray, 1910.

White, Douglas R. "Focused Ethnographic Bibliography: Standard Cross-Cultural Sample." *Behavior Science Research* 23 (1989): 1–145. doi: 10.1177/106939718902300102.

White, Frances, Michel Waller, and Klaree J. Boose. "Evolution of Primate Peace." In *War, Peace, and Human Nature: Convergence of Evolutionary and Cultural Views*, edited by Douglas P. Fry, 389–405. New York: Oxford University Press, 2013.

White, Robert. "Motivation Reconsidered: The Concept of Competence." *Psychological Review* 66 (1959): 297–333. doi: 10.1037/h0040934.

Whitecotton, Joseph. *The Zapotecs: Priests, Princes and Peasants*. Norman: University of Oklahoma Press, 1977.

Widom, Cathy, and Michael Maxfield. "An Update on the 'Cycle of Violence,'" US Department of Justice, last modified February 2001. Available online: https://www.ncjrs.gov/pdffiles1/nij/184894.pdf.

Wiessner, Polly, and Nitze Pupu. "Toward Peace: Foreign Arms and Indigenous Institutions in a Papua New Guinea Society." *Science* 337 (2012): 1651–1654. doi: 10.1126/science.1221685.

Wilkinson, Richard, and Kate Pickett. *The Spirit Level: Why Equality Is Better for Everyone*. London: Penguin, 2009.

Wilson, Edmund. *To the Finland Station: A Study in the Writings and Acting of History*. New York: Doubleday, 1953.

Wilson, Edward O. *Sociobiology: The New Synthesis*. Cambridge, MA: Harvard University Press, 1975.

Wilson, Michael L. "Chimpanzees, Warfare, and the Invention of Peace." In *War, Peace, and Human Nature: Convergence of Evolutionary and Cultural Views*, edited by Douglas P. Fry, 361–388. New York: Oxford University Press, 2013.

Winter, David. *The Power Motive*. New York: The Free Press, 1973.

Wolf, Eric. "Cycles of Violence: The Anthropology of War and Peace." In *Understanding Violence*, edited by David P. Barash, 192–199. Boston: Allyn and Bacon, 2001.

Wood, Julia. "Gendered Media: The Influence of Media on Views of Gender." In *Gendered Lives: Communication, Gender, and Culture*, edited by Julia T. Wood, 231–244. Belmont, CA: Wadsworth Publishing, 1994.

Woodburn, James. "Egalitarian Societies." *Man* 17 (1982): 431–451.

Wooldridge, Mike. "Iran's Grim History of Death by Stoning." *BBC News*, last modified July 9, 2010. Available online: http://www.bbc.com/news/10579121.

World Health Organization. "Genital Mutilation (FGM)." (no date). Available online: http://www.who.int/reproductivehealth/topics/fgm/prevalence/en/.

World Health Organization. *Fact Sheet: Female Genital Mutilation*. (2010). Available online: http://www.who.int/mediacentre/factsheets/fs241/en/.

"The Worldwide War on Baby Girls." *Economist*, March 4, 2010. Available online: http://www.economist.com/research/articlesBySubject/displaystory. cfm?subjectid=348951&story_id=15636231.

Worthman, Carol M. "The Ecology of Human Development: Evolving Models for Cultural Psychology." *Journal of Cross-Cultural Psychology* 41 (2010): 546–562. doi: 10.1177/0022022110362627.

Wrangham, Richard, and Dale Peterson. *Demonic Males: Apes and the Origins of Human Violence*. Boston: Houghton Mifflin, 1999.

Wrangham, Richard, and Luke Glowacki. "Intergroup Aggression in Chimpanzees and War in Nomadic Hunter-Gatherers." *Human Nature* 23 (2012): 5–29. doi: 10.1007/s12110-012-9132-1.

Young, Larry, Miranda Lim, Brenden Gingrich, and Thomas Insel. "Cellular Mechanisms of Social Attachment." *Hormones and Behavior* 40 (2001): 133–138. doi: 10.1006/hbeh.2001.1691.

Zak, Paul, Angela A. Stanton, and Sheila Ahmadi. "Oxytocin Increases Generosity in Humans." *PLoS ONE* 11 (2007): e1128. doi: 10.1371/journal. pone.0001128.

Ziegler, Dave. *Raising Children Who Refuse to Be Raised*. Jaspar Mountain, OR: Jaspar Mountain Press, 2002.

Zihlman, Adrienne. "Women in Evolution, Part II: Subsistence and Social Organization among Early Hominids." *Signs: Journal of Women in Culture and Society* 4 (1978): 4–20. doi: 10.1086/493566.

Zihlman, Adrienne. "Women's Bodies, Women's Lives: An Evolutionary Perspective." In *The Evolving Female: A Life-History Perspective,* edited by Mary Ellen Morbeck, Alison Galloway, and Adrienne L. Zihlman, 185–197. Princeton, NJ: Princeton University Press, 1997.

Zihlman, Adrienne. "The Paleolithic Glass Ceiling: Women in Human Evolution." In *Women in Human Evolution,* edited by Lori D. Hager, 91–113. New York: Routledge, 1997.

Index

in nomadic forager societies, 161–63
normative narratives about, 14–15
in Paleolithic/Old Stone Age, 60
portrayal in children's tales, 191
religious teachings about, 263–64
sexual intimacy and, 202–4
Sheherazade (Persian fable), 191
in Soviet Union, 206
violence against, 245
Women, Men, and the Global Quality of Life
  (Center for Partnership Studies), 287
Women's Bodies, Women's Wisdom
  (Northrup), 272–73

women's rights, 46, 100–1, 271, 274, 286
"women's work," 60, 131, 201, 287,
  290, 291–92, 296*t*
Woodburn, James, 161
workplaces, 108–9, 142*t*, 291–92
A World Without Women
  (Nobel), 264

Zapotec communities, 234–37,
  235–36*b*, 238
Ziegler, Dave, 54
Zihlman, Adrienne, 59, 60
Zoroaster, 203